...Is a Learning Experience!

Other *For Better or For Worse*® Collections

She's Turning Into One of Them!
Never Wink at a Worried Woman
Striking a Chord
Reality Check
With This Ring
Family Business
Graduation: A Time for Change
The Big 5-0
Sunshine and Shadow
Middle Age Spread
Growing Like a Weed
Love Just Screws Everything Up
Starting from Scratch
"There Goes My Baby!"
Things Are Looking Up . . .
What, Me Pregnant?
If This Is a Lecture, How Long Will It Be?
Pushing 40
It's All Downhill from Here
Keep the Home Fries Burning
The Last Straw
Just One More Hug
"It Must Be Nice to Be Little"
Is This "One of Those Days," Daddy?
I've Got the One-More-Washload Blues . . .

Retrospectives

Suddenly Silver: 25 Years of For Better or For Worse®
All About April
The Lives Behind the Lines: 20 Years of For Better or For Worse®
Remembering Farley: A Tribute to the Life of Our Favorite Cartoon Dog
It's the Thought That Counts . . . Fifteenth Anniversary Collection
A Look Inside . . . For Better or For Worse®: The 10th Anniversary Collection*

With Andie Parton

I Love My Grandpa!
So You're Going to Be a Grandma!
Graduation: Just the Beginning!
Leaving Home
Wags and Kisses

Teaching

...Is a Learning Experience!

A *For Better or For Worse*® Collection by Lynn Johnston

**Andrews McMeel
Publishing, LLC**

Kansas City

For Better or For Worse® is distributed by Universal Press Syndicate.

Teaching Is a Learning Experience copyright © 2007 by Lynn Johnston Productions, Inc. All rights reserved. Printed in the United States of America. No part of this book may be used or reproduced in any manner whatsoever without written permission except in the case of reprints in the context of reviews. For permission information, write Andrews McMeel Publishing, LLC, 4520 Main St., Kansas City, Missouri 64111.

07 08 09 10 11 BAM 10 9 8 7 6 5 4 3 2 1

ISBN-13: 978-0-7407-6354-0
ISBN-10: 0-7407-6354-7

Library of Congress Control Number: 2006937280

www.andrewsmcmeel.com

www.FBorFW.com

ATTENTION: SCHOOLS AND BUSINESSES

Andrews McMeel books are available at quantity discounts with bulk purchase for educational, business, or sales promotional use. For information, please write to: Special Sales Department, Andrews McMeel Publishing, LLC, 4520 Main Street, Kansas City, Missouri 64111.

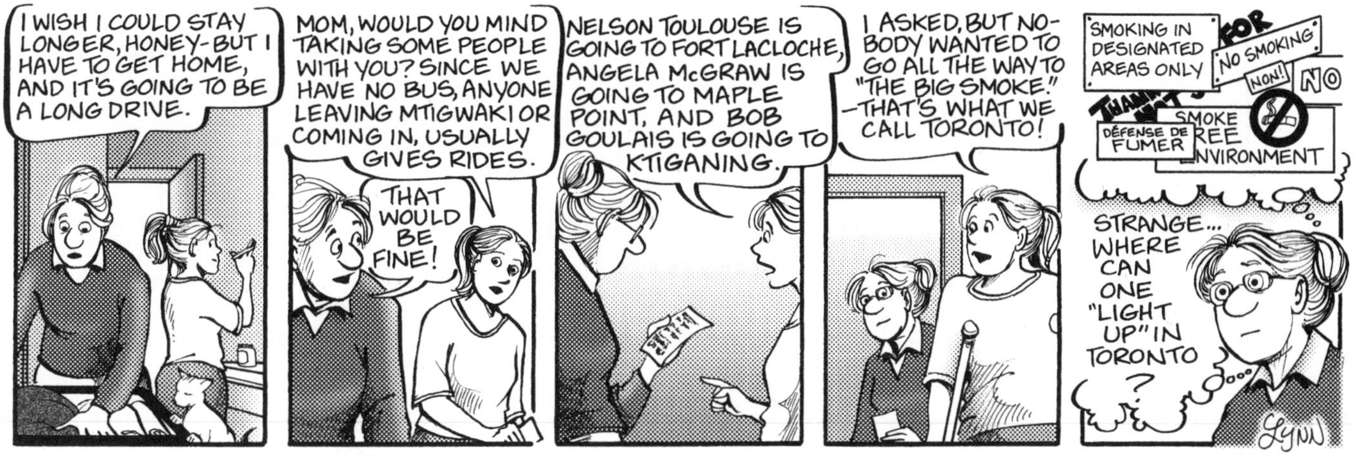
I WISH I COULD STAY LONGER, HONEY- BUT I HAVE TO GET HOME, AND IT'S GOING TO BE A LONG DRIVE.
MOM, WOULD YOU MIND TAKING SOME PEOPLE WITH YOU? SINCE WE HAVE NO BUS, ANYONE LEAVING MTIGWAKI OR COMING IN, USUALLY GIVES RIDES.
THAT WOULD BE FINE!
NELSON TOULOUSE IS GOING TO FORT LACLOCHE, ANGELA McGRAW IS GOING TO MAPLE POINT, AND BOB GOULAIS IS GOING TO KTIGANING.
I ASKED, BUT NO-BODY WANTED TO GO ALL THE WAY TO "THE BIG SMOKE." -THAT'S WHAT WE CALL TORONTO!
SMOKING IN DESIGNATED AREAS ONLY
NO SMOKING
NON!
NO
DÉFENSE DE FUMER
SMOKE
STRANGE... WHERE CAN ONE "LIGHT UP" IN TORONTO ?
LYNN

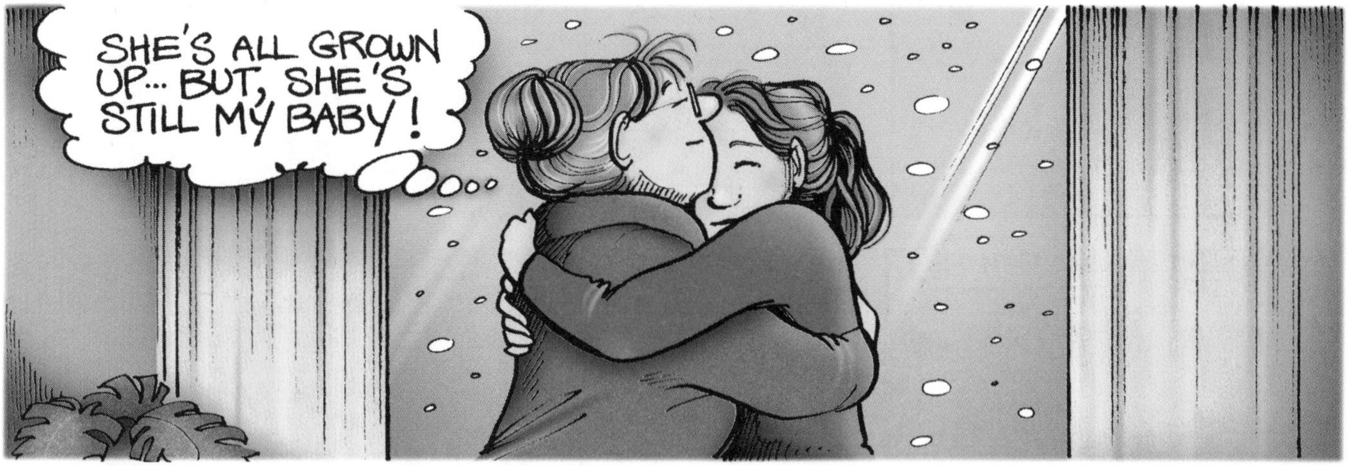
SHE'S ALL GROWN UP... BUT, SHE'S STILL MY BABY!

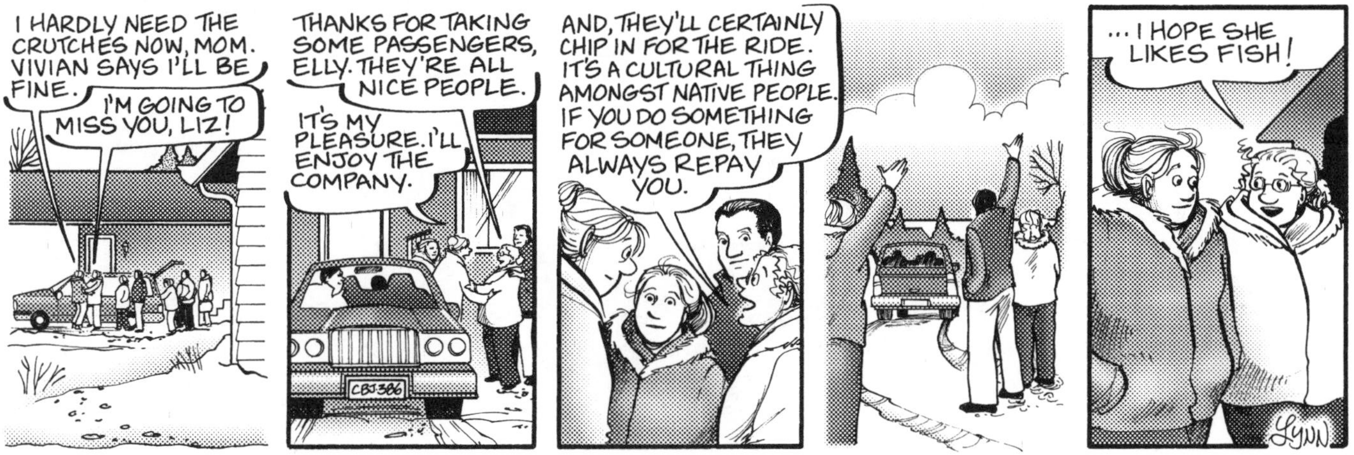
I HARDLY NEED THE CRUTCHES NOW, MOM. VIVIAN SAYS I'LL BE FINE.
I'M GOING TO MISS YOU, LIZ!
THANKS FOR TAKING SOME PASSENGERS, ELLY. THEY'RE ALL NICE PEOPLE.
IT'S MY PLEASURE. I'LL ENJOY THE COMPANY.
CBJ 386
AND, THEY'LL CERTAINLY CHIP IN FOR THE RIDE. IT'S A CULTURAL THING AMONGST NATIVE PEOPLE. IF YOU DO SOMETHING FOR SOMEONE, THEY ALWAYS REPAY YOU.
...I HOPE SHE LIKES FISH!
LYNN

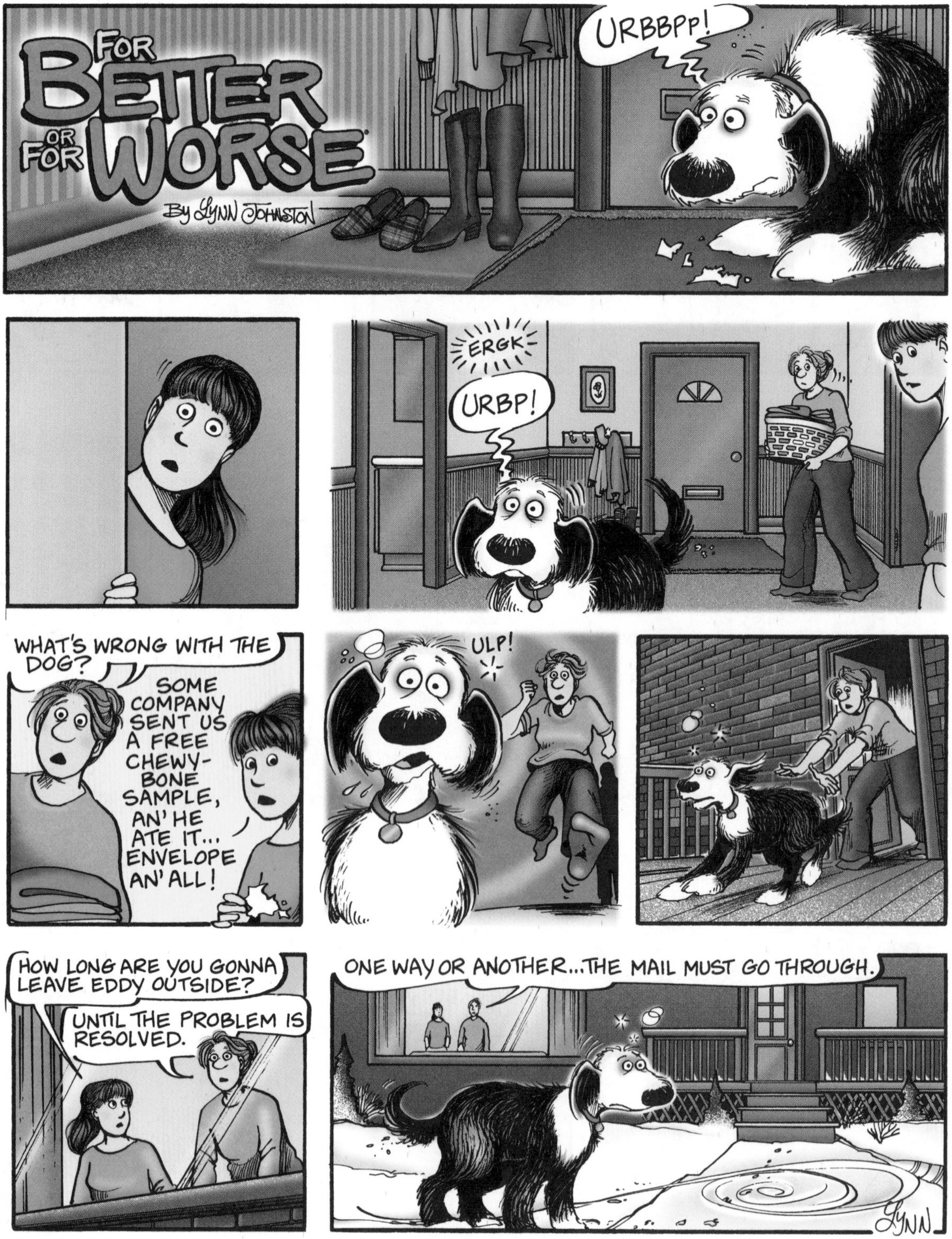
FOR BETTER OR FOR WORSE
BY LYNN JOHNSTON
URBBPP!
ERGK
URBP!
WHAT'S WRONG WITH THE DOG?
SOME COMPANY SENT US A FREE CHEWY-BONE SAMPLE, AN' HE ATE IT... ENVELOPE AN' ALL!
ULP!
HOW LONG ARE YOU GONNA LEAVE EDDY OUTSIDE?
UNTIL THE PROBLEM IS RESOLVED.
ONE WAY OR ANOTHER...THE MAIL MUST GO THROUGH.
LYNN

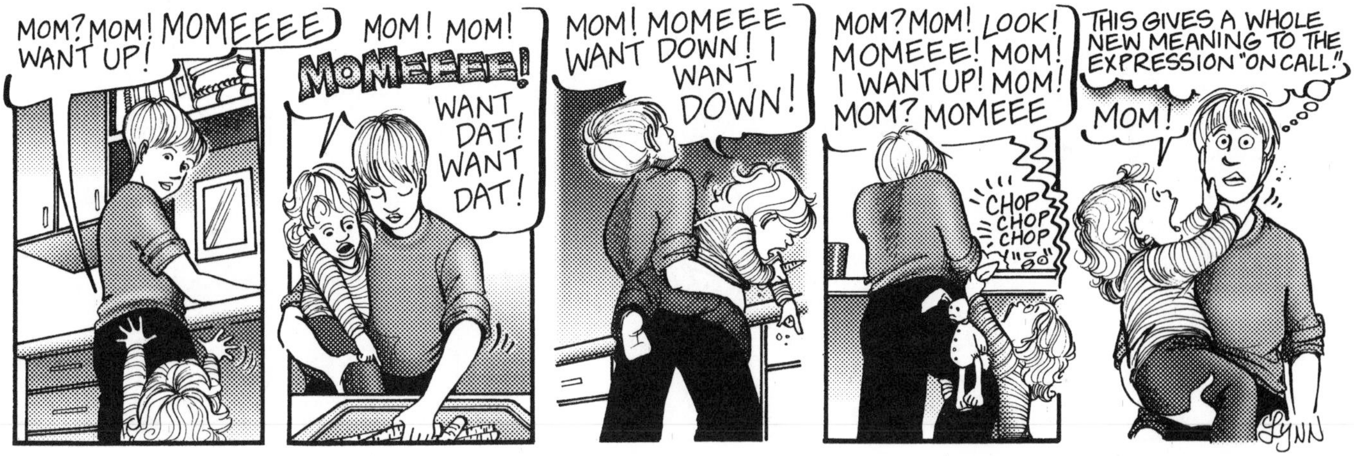
MOM? MOM! MOMEEEE WANT UP!
MOM! MOM! MOMEEEE! WANT DAT! WANT DAT!
MOM! MOMEEE WANT DOWN! I WANT DOWN!
MOM? MOM! LOOK! MOMEEE! MOM! I WANT UP! MOM! MOM? MOMEEE
CHOP CHOP CHOP
THIS GIVES A WHOLE NEW MEANING TO THE EXPRESSION "ON CALL."
MOM!
LYNN

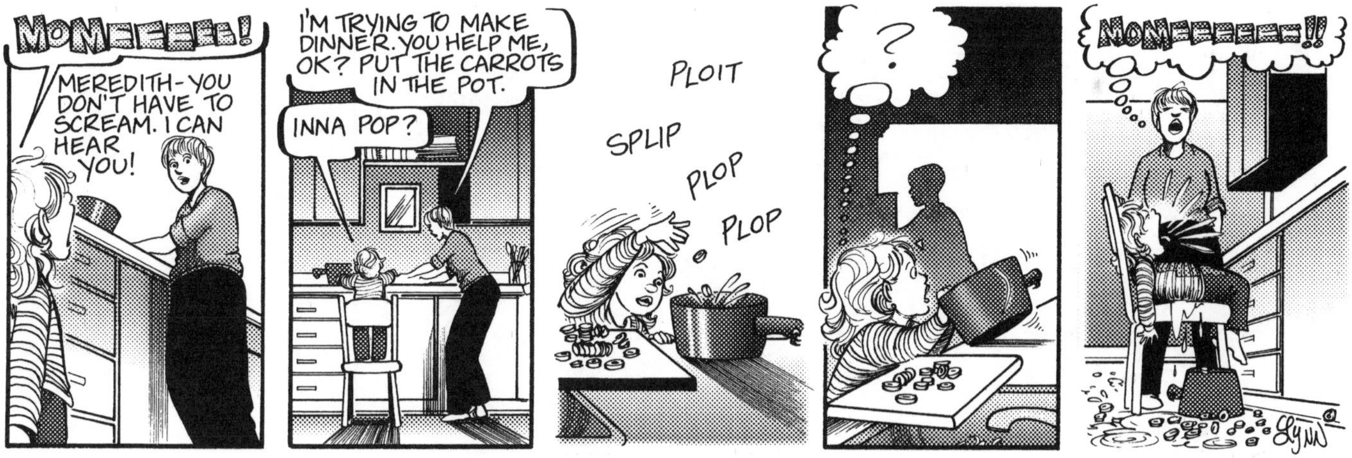
MOMEEEEE!
MEREDITH- YOU DON'T HAVE TO SCREAM. I CAN HEAR YOU!
I'M TRYING TO MAKE DINNER. YOU HELP ME, OK? PUT THE CARROTS IN THE POT.
INNA POP?
PLOIT
SPLIP
PLOP
PLOP
?
MOMEEEEEE!!
LYNN

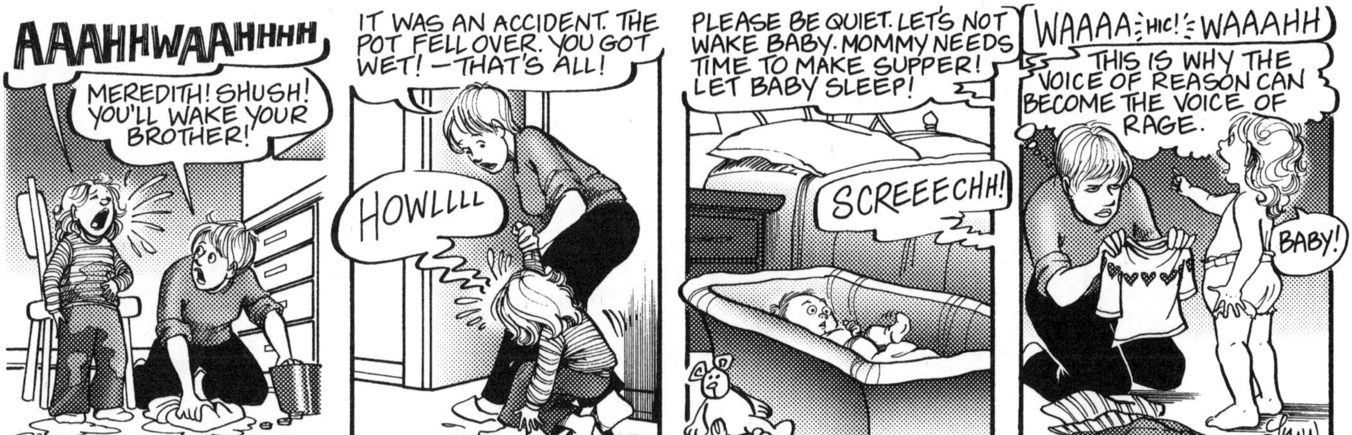
AAAHHWAAHHHH
MEREDITH! SHUSH! YOU'LL WAKE YOUR BROTHER!
IT WAS AN ACCIDENT. THE POT FELL OVER. YOU GOT WET! —THAT'S ALL!
HOWLLLL
PLEASE BE QUIET. LET'S NOT WAKE BABY. MOMMY NEEDS TIME TO MAKE SUPPER! LET BABY SLEEP!
SCREEECHH!
WAAAA HIC! WAAAHH
THIS IS WHY THE VOICE OF REASON CAN BECOME THE VOICE OF RAGE.
BABY!
LYNN

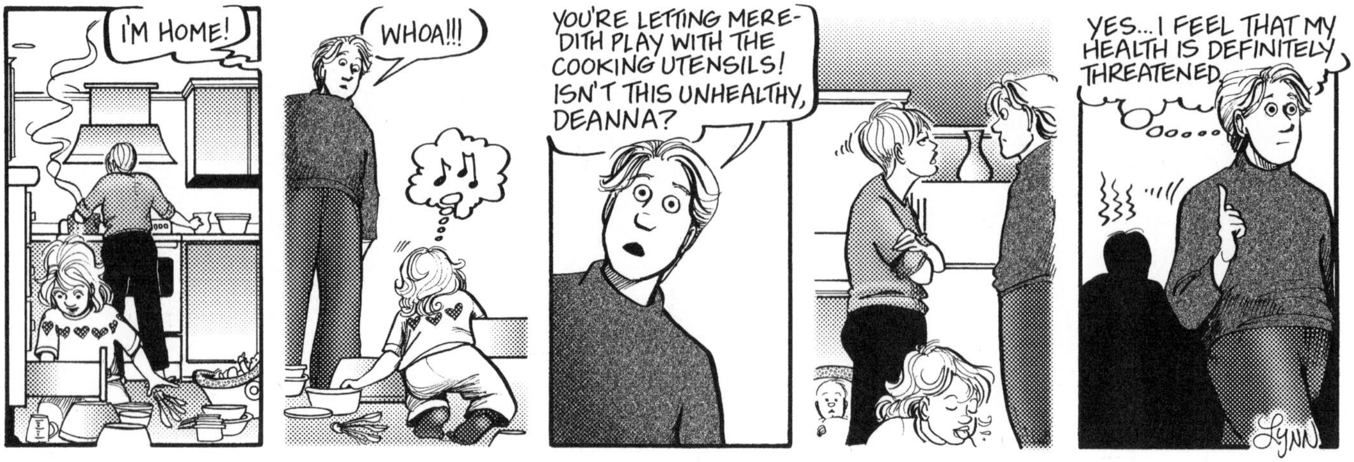
I'M HOME!
WHOA!!!
YOU'RE LETTING MEREDITH PLAY WITH THE COOKING UTENSILS! ISN'T THIS UNHEALTHY, DEANNA?
YES... I FEEL THAT MY HEALTH IS DEFINITELY THREATENED.
LYNN

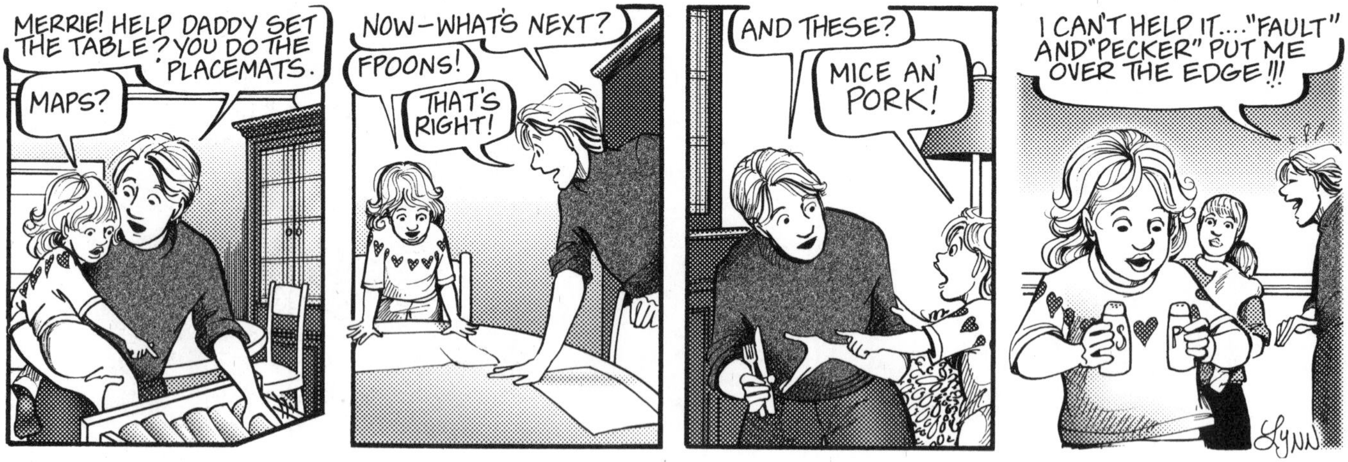
MERRIE! HELP DADDY SET THE TABLE? YOU DO THE PLACEMATS.
MAPS?
NOW–WHAT'S NEXT?
FPOONS!
THAT'S RIGHT!
AND THESE?
MICE AN' PORK!
I CAN'T HELP IT...."FAULT" AND "PECKER" PUT ME OVER THE EDGE!!!
LYNN

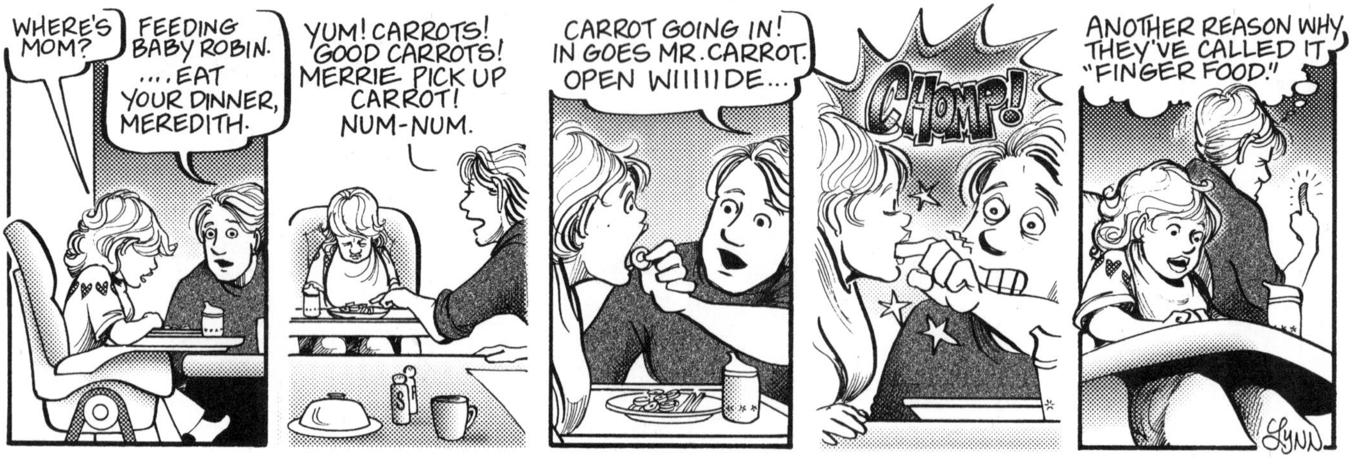
WHERE'S MOM?
FEEDING BABY ROBIN. ....EAT YOUR DINNER, MEREDITH.
YUM! CARROTS! GOOD CARROTS! MERRIE PICK UP CARROT! NUM-NUM.
CARROT GOING IN! IN GOES MR. CARROT. OPEN WIIIIIDE...
CHOMP!
ANOTHER REASON WHY THEY'VE CALLED IT "FINGER FOOD."
LYNN

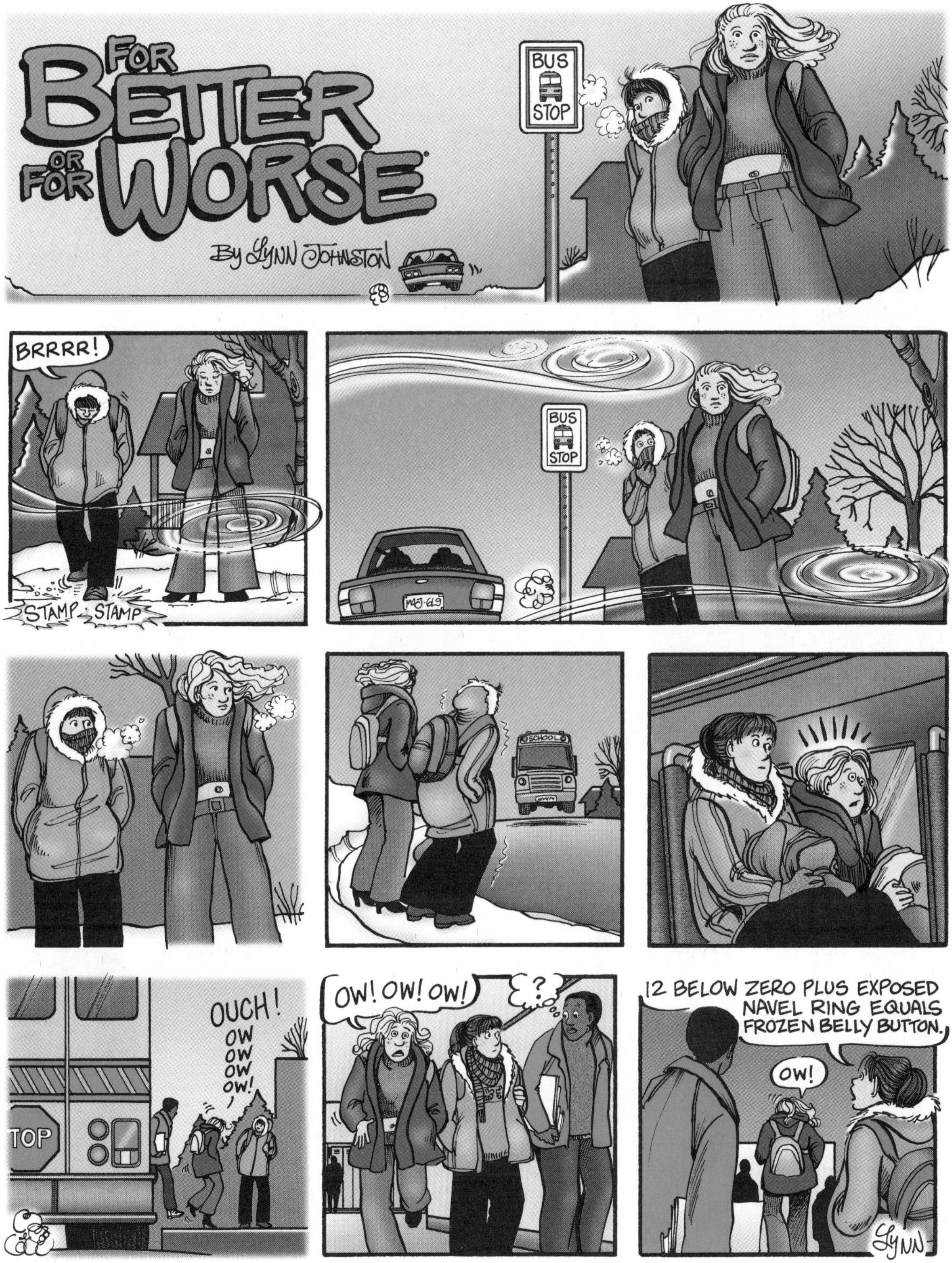
For Better or For Worse
By Lynn Johnston
BUS STOP
BRRRR!
STAMP STAMP
BUS STOP
OUCH! OW OW OW OW!
OW! OW! OW!
?
12 BELOW ZERO PLUS EXPOSED NAVEL RING EQUALS FROZEN BELLY BUTTON.
OW!
Lynn

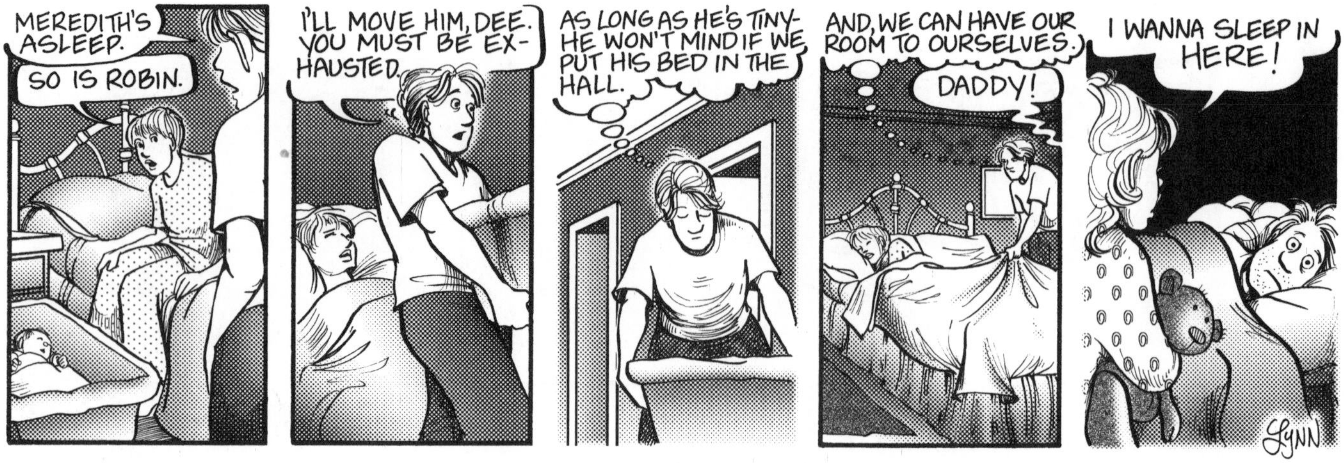
MEREDITH'S ASLEEP.
SO IS ROBIN.
I'LL MOVE HIM, DEE. YOU MUST BE EX-HAUSTED.
AS LONG AS HE'S TINY-HE WON'T MIND IF WE PUT HIS BED IN THE HALL.
AND, WE CAN HAVE OUR ROOM TO OURSELVES.
DADDY!
I WANNA SLEEP IN HERE!
LYNN

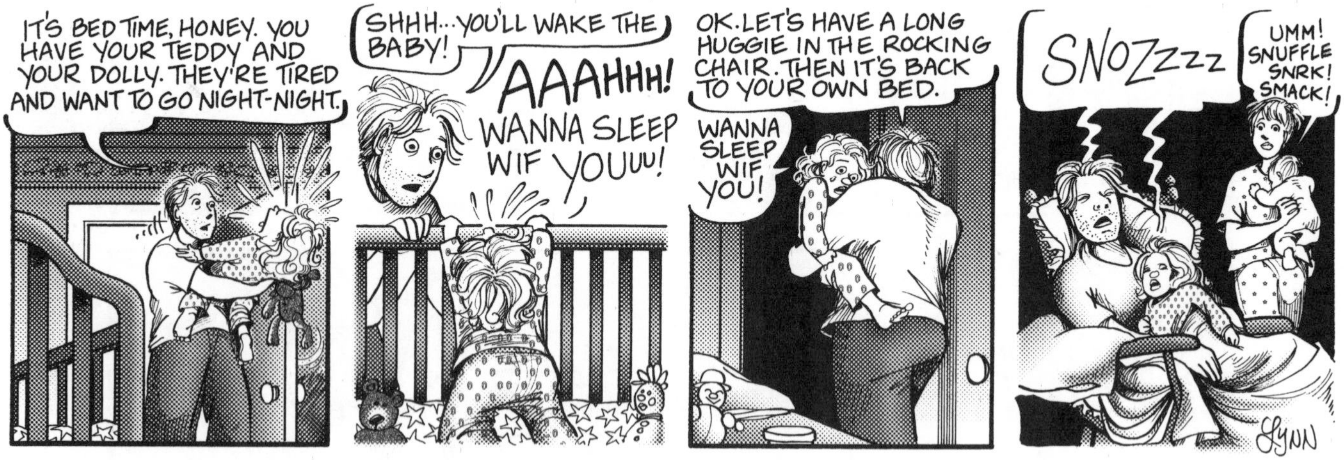
IT'S BED TIME, HONEY. YOU HAVE YOUR TEDDY AND YOUR DOLLY. THEY'RE TIRED AND WANT TO GO NIGHT-NIGHT.
SHHH... YOU'LL WAKE THE BABY!
AAAHHH! WANNA SLEEP WIF YOUUU!
OK. LET'S HAVE A LONG HUGGIE IN THE ROCKING CHAIR. THEN IT'S BACK TO YOUR OWN BED.
WANNA SLEEP WIF YOU!
SNOZzzz
UMM! SNUFFLE SNRK! SMACK!
LYNN

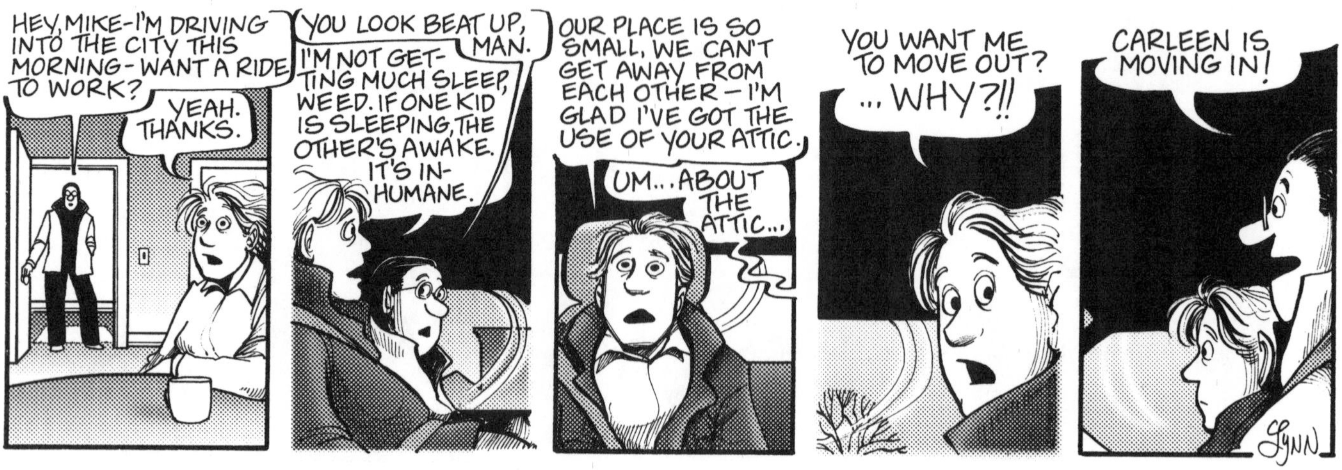
HEY, MIKE-I'M DRIVING INTO THE CITY THIS MORNING-WANT A RIDE TO WORK?
YEAH. THANKS.
YOU LOOK BEAT UP, MAN.
I'M NOT GET-TING MUCH SLEEP, WEED. IF ONE KID IS SLEEPING, THE OTHER'S AWAKE. IT'S IN-HUMANE.
OUR PLACE IS SO SMALL, WE CAN'T GET AWAY FROM EACH OTHER – I'M GLAD I'VE GOT THE USE OF YOUR ATTIC.
UM... ABOUT THE ATTIC...
YOU WANT ME TO MOVE OUT? ... WHY?!!
CARLEEN IS MOVING IN!
LYNN

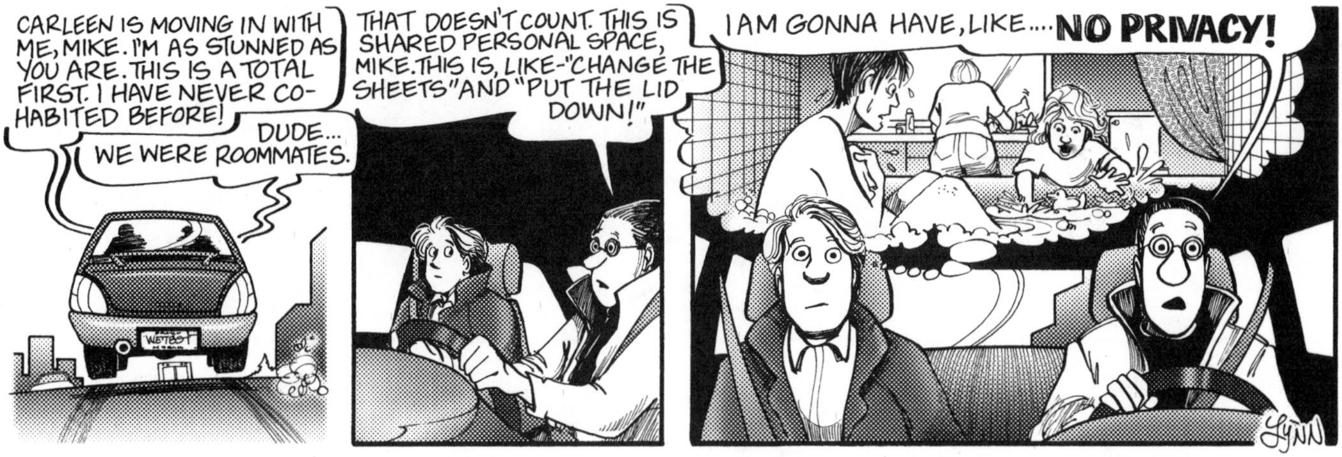
CARLEEN IS MOVING IN WITH ME, MIKE. I'M AS STUNNED AS YOU ARE. THIS IS A TOTAL FIRST. I HAVE NEVER CO-HABITED BEFORE!
DUDE... WE WERE ROOMMATES.
THAT DOESN'T COUNT. THIS IS SHARED PERSONAL SPACE, MIKE. THIS IS, LIKE-"CHANGE THE SHEETS" AND "PUT THE LID DOWN!"
I AM GONNA HAVE, LIKE.... **NO PRIVACY!**
LYNN

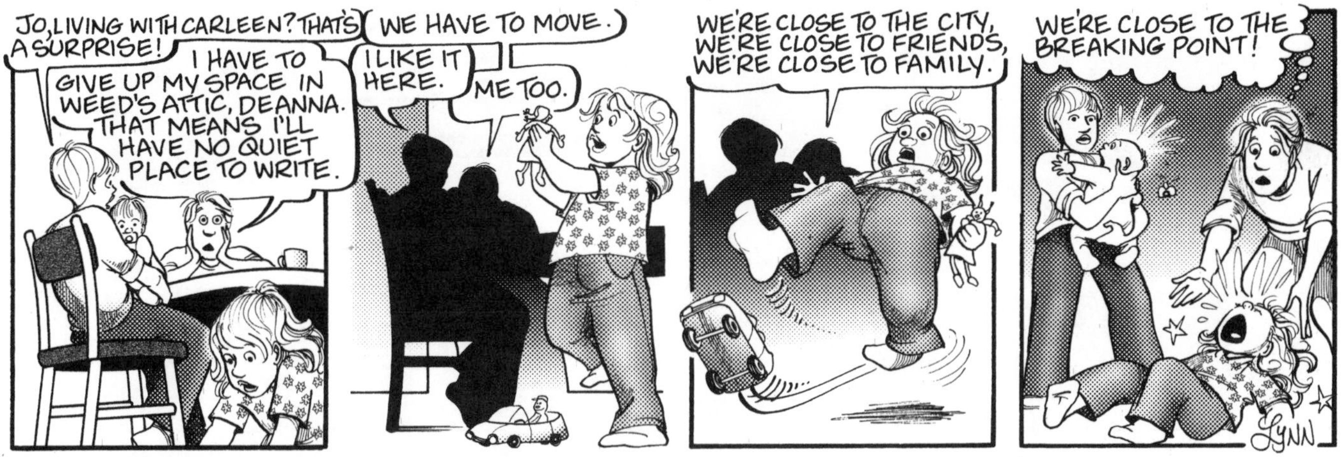
JO, LIVING WITH CARLEEN? THAT'S A SURPRISE!
I HAVE TO GIVE UP MY SPACE IN WEED'S ATTIC, DEANNA. THAT MEANS I'LL HAVE NO QUIET PLACE TO WRITE.
WE HAVE TO MOVE.
I LIKE IT HERE.
ME TOO.
WE'RE CLOSE TO THE CITY, WE'RE CLOSE TO FRIENDS, WE'RE CLOSE TO FAMILY.
WE'RE CLOSE TO THE BREAKING POINT!
LYNN

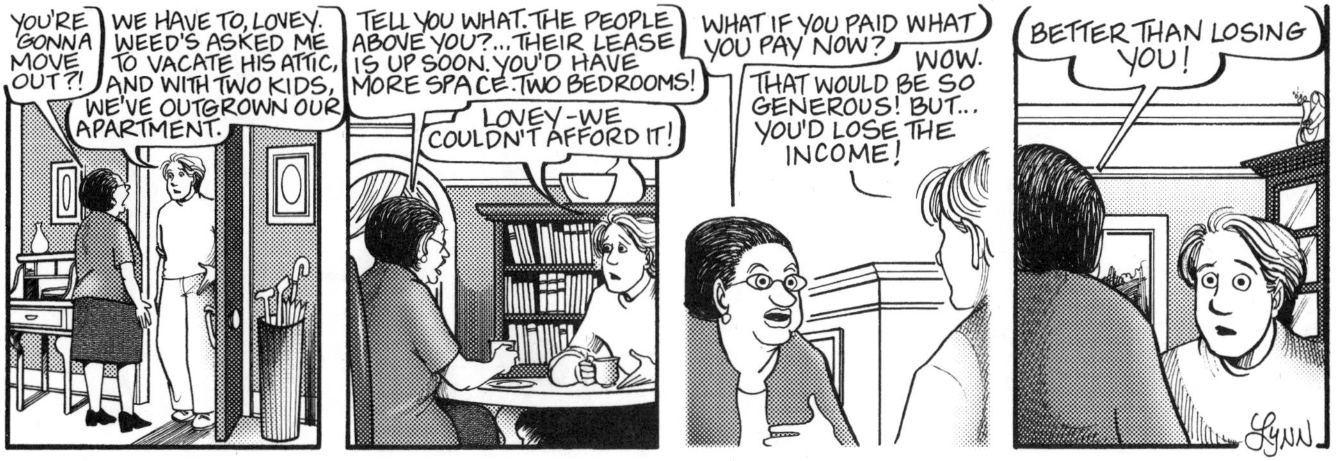
YOU'RE GONNA MOVE OUT?!
WE HAVE TO, LOVEY. WEED'S ASKED ME TO VACATE HIS ATTIC, AND WITH TWO KIDS, WE'VE OUTGROWN OUR APARTMENT.
TELL YOU WHAT. THE PEOPLE ABOVE YOU?... THEIR LEASE IS UP SOON. YOU'D HAVE MORE SPACE. TWO BEDROOMS!
LOVEY-WE COULDN'T AFFORD IT!
WHAT IF YOU PAID WHAT YOU PAY NOW?
WOW. THAT WOULD BE SO GENEROUS! BUT... YOU'D LOSE THE INCOME!
BETTER THAN LOSING YOU!
LYNN

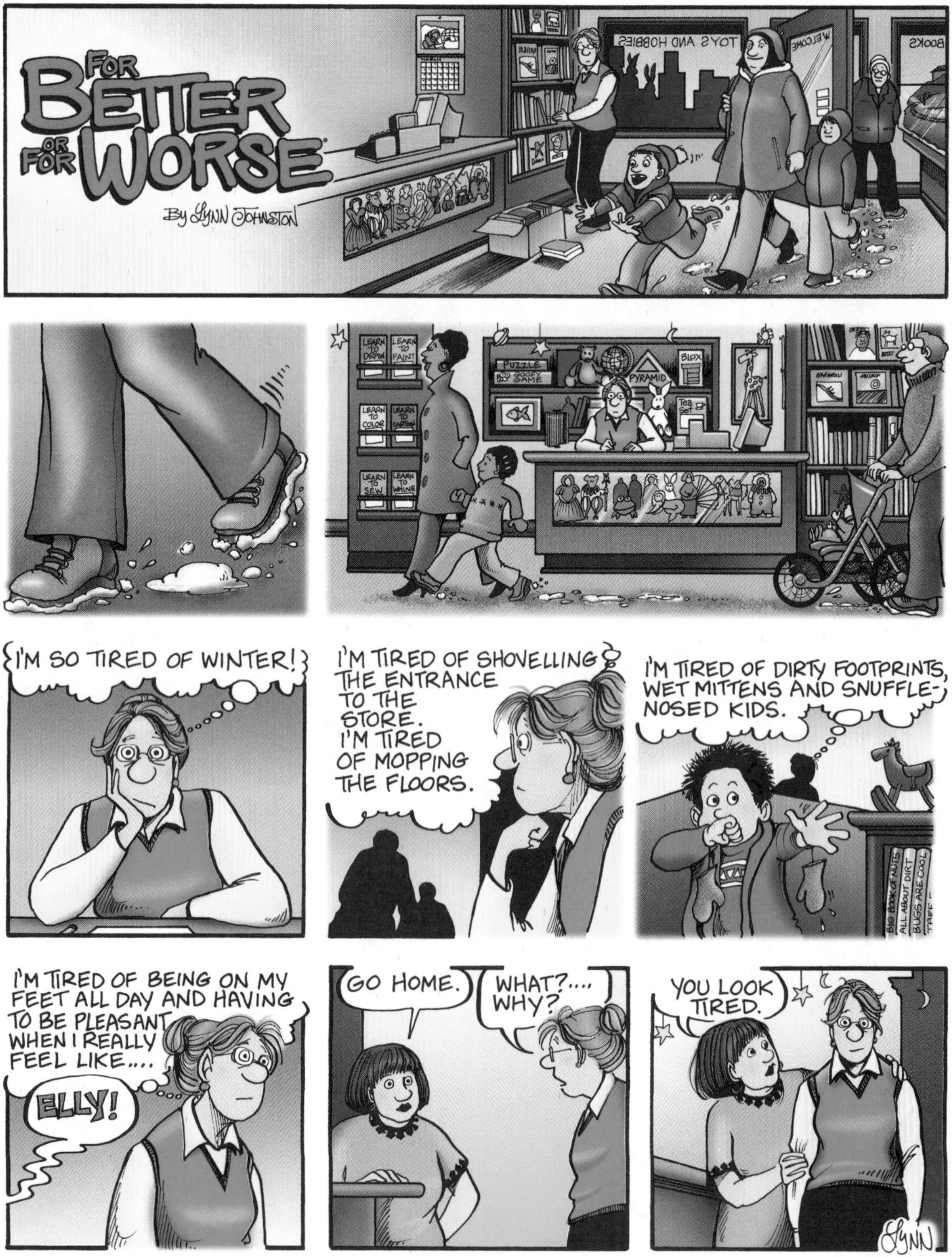

FOR BETTER OR FOR WORSE
BY LYNN JOHNSTON
LEARN TO DRAW
LEARN TO PAINT
LEARN TO COLOR
LEARN TO CARTOON
LEARN TO SEW
LEARN TO WHINE
PUZZLE
GOOFY GAME
PYRAMID
BLOX
TEA SET
I'M SO TIRED OF WINTER!
I'M TIRED OF SHOVELLING THE ENTRANCE TO THE STORE. I'M TIRED OF MOPPING THE FLOORS.
I'M TIRED OF DIRTY FOOTPRINTS, WET MITTENS AND SNUFFLE-NOSED KIDS.
BIG BOOK OF NUTS
ALL ABOUT DIRT
BUGS ARE COOL
I'M TIRED OF BEING ON MY FEET ALL DAY AND HAVING TO BE PLEASANT WHEN I REALLY FEEL LIKE....
ELLY!
GO HOME.
WHAT?.... WHY?
YOU LOOK TIRED.
LYNN

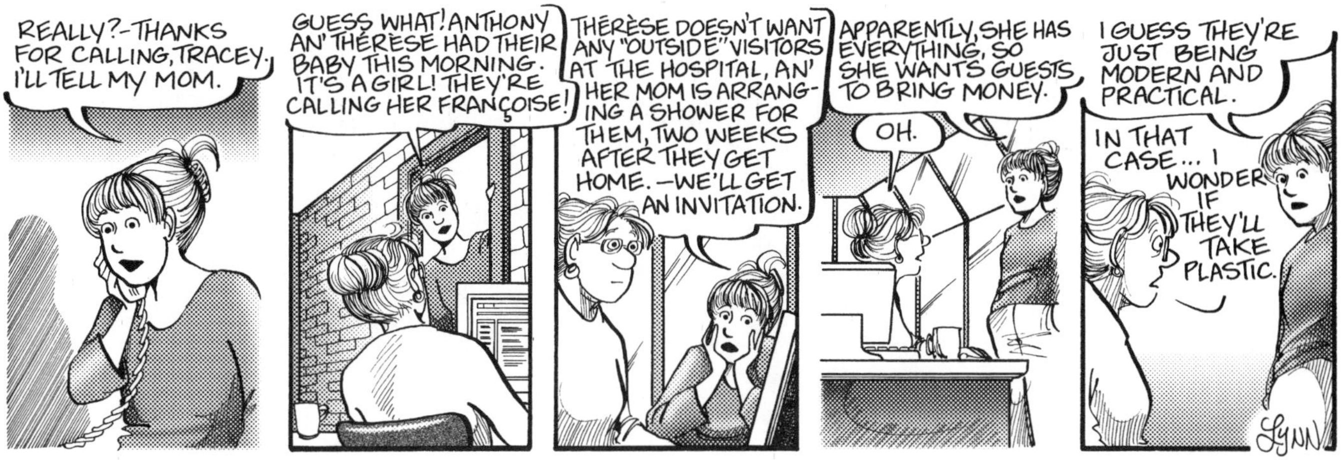
REALLY?-THANKS FOR CALLING, TRACEY. I'LL TELL MY MOM.
GUESS WHAT! ANTHONY AN' THÉRÈSE HAD THEIR BABY THIS MORNING. IT'S A GIRL! THEY'RE CALLING HER FRANÇOISE!
THÉRÈSE DOESN'T WANT ANY "OUTSIDE" VISITORS AT THE HOSPITAL, AN' HER MOM IS ARRANGING A SHOWER FOR THEM, TWO WEEKS AFTER THEY GET HOME. —WE'LL GET AN INVITATION.
APPARENTLY, SHE HAS EVERYTHING, SO SHE WANTS GUESTS TO BRING MONEY.
OH.
I GUESS THEY'RE JUST BEING MODERN AND PRACTICAL.
IN THAT CASE... I WONDER IF THEY'LL TAKE PLASTIC.
LYNN

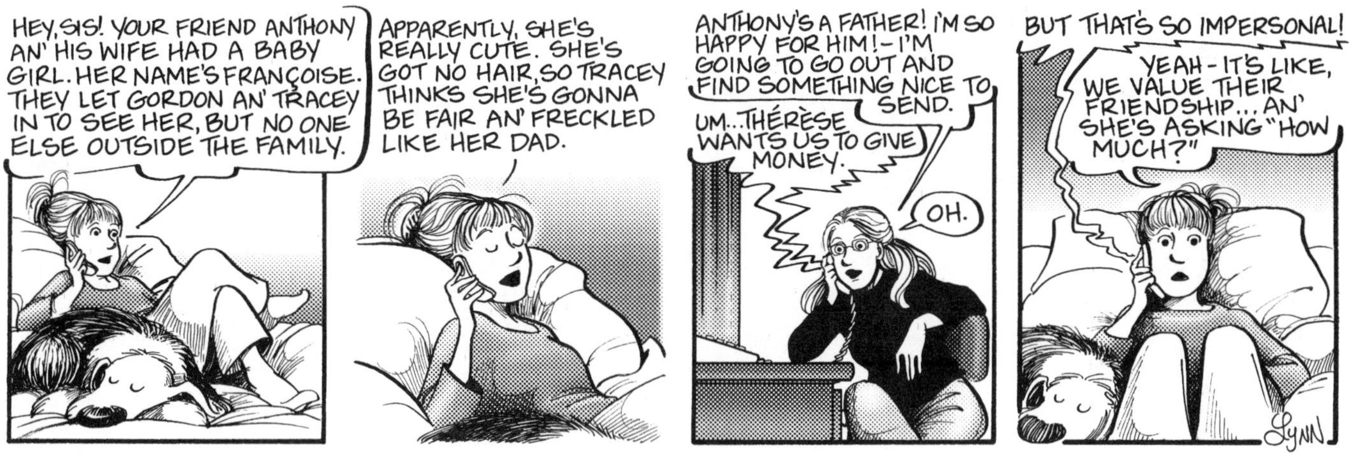
HEY, SIS! YOUR FRIEND ANTHONY AN' HIS WIFE HAD A BABY GIRL. HER NAME'S FRANÇOISE. THEY LET GORDON AN' TRACEY IN TO SEE HER, BUT NO ONE ELSE OUTSIDE THE FAMILY.
APPARENTLY, SHE'S REALLY CUTE. SHE'S GOT NO HAIR, SO TRACEY THINKS SHE'S GONNA BE FAIR AN' FRECKLED LIKE HER DAD.
ANTHONY'S A FATHER! I'M SO HAPPY FOR HIM! —I'M GOING TO GO OUT AND FIND SOMETHING NICE TO SEND.
UM... THÉRÈSE WANTS US TO GIVE MONEY.
OH.
BUT THAT'S SO IMPERSONAL!
YEAH - IT'S LIKE, WE VALUE THEIR FRIENDSHIP... AN' SHE'S ASKING "HOW MUCH?"
LYNN

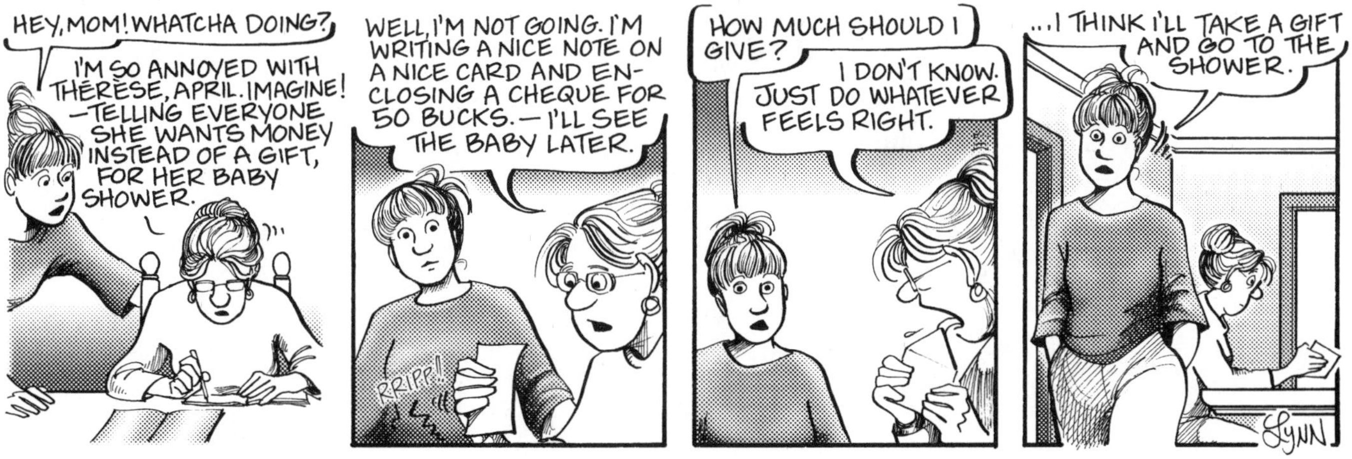
HEY, MOM! WHATCHA DOING?
I'M SO ANNOYED WITH THÉRÈSE, APRIL. IMAGINE! —TELLING EVERYONE SHE WANTS MONEY INSTEAD OF A GIFT, FOR HER BABY SHOWER.
WELL, I'M NOT GOING. I'M WRITING A NICE NOTE ON A NICE CARD AND ENCLOSING A CHEQUE FOR 50 BUCKS. — I'LL SEE THE BABY LATER.
RRIPP!
HOW MUCH SHOULD I GIVE?
I DON'T KNOW. JUST DO WHATEVER FEELS RIGHT.
...I THINK I'LL TAKE A GIFT AND GO TO THE SHOWER.
LYNN

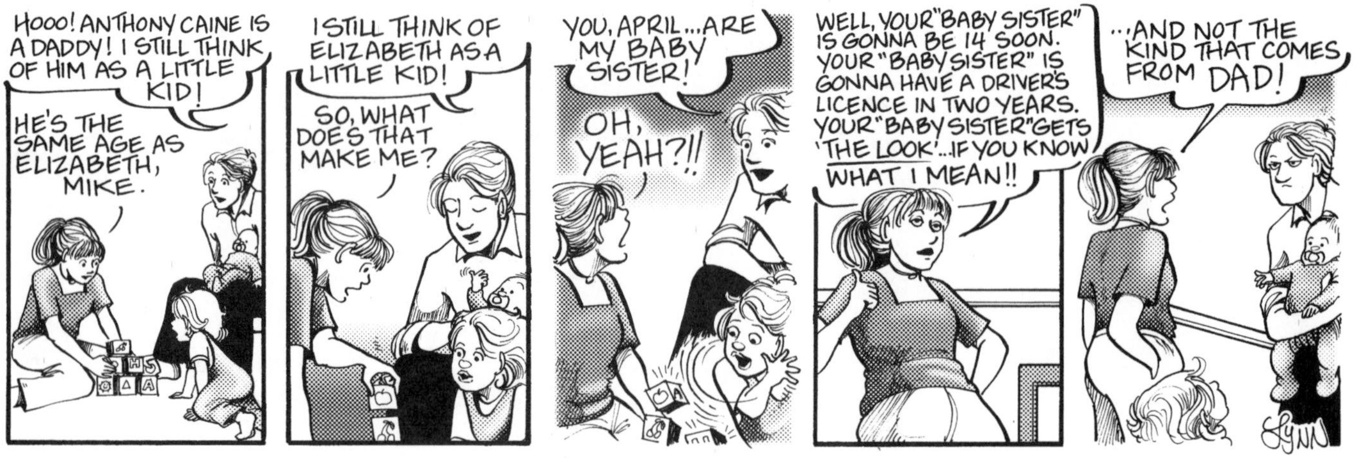
HOOO! ANTHONY CAINE IS A DADDY! I STILL THINK OF HIM AS A LITTLE KID!
HE'S THE SAME AGE AS ELIZABETH, MIKE.
I STILL THINK OF ELIZABETH AS A LITTLE KID!
SO, WHAT DOES THAT MAKE ME?
YOU, APRIL...ARE MY BABY SISTER!
OH, YEAH?!!
WELL, YOUR "BABY SISTER" IS GONNA BE 14 SOON. YOUR "BABY SISTER" IS GONNA HAVE A DRIVER'S LICENCE IN TWO YEARS. YOUR "BABY SISTER" GETS 'THE LOOK'...IF YOU KNOW WHAT I MEAN!!
...AND NOT THE KIND THAT COMES FROM DAD!
LYNN

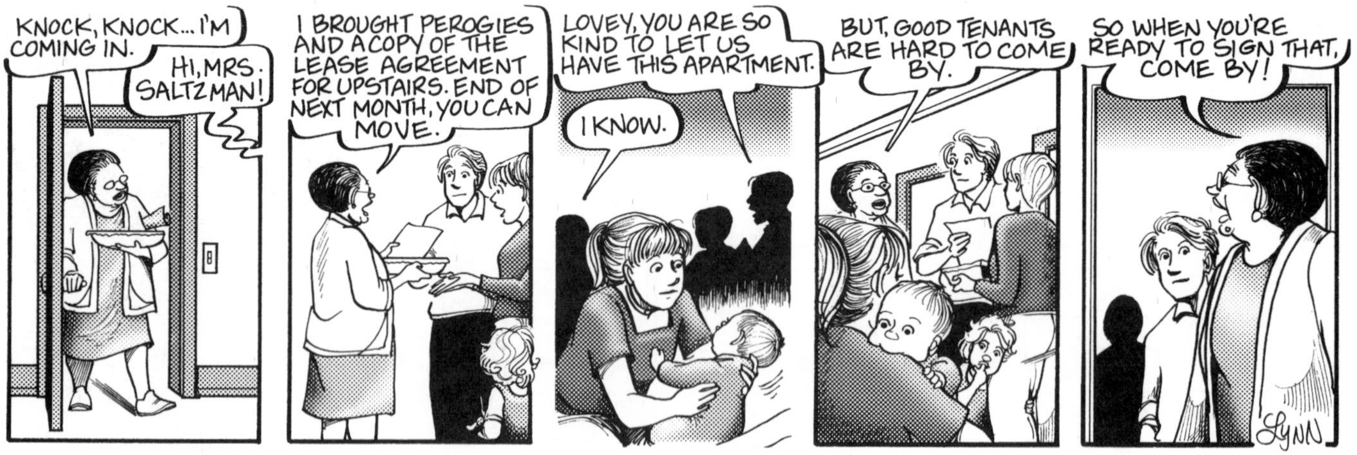
KNOCK, KNOCK...I'M COMING IN.
HI, MRS. SALTZMAN!
I BROUGHT PEROGIES AND A COPY OF THE LEASE AGREEMENT FOR UPSTAIRS. END OF NEXT MONTH, YOU CAN MOVE.
LOVEY, YOU ARE SO KIND TO LET US HAVE THIS APARTMENT.
I KNOW.
BUT, GOOD TENANTS ARE HARD TO COME BY.
SO WHEN YOU'RE READY TO SIGN THAT, COME BY!
LYNN

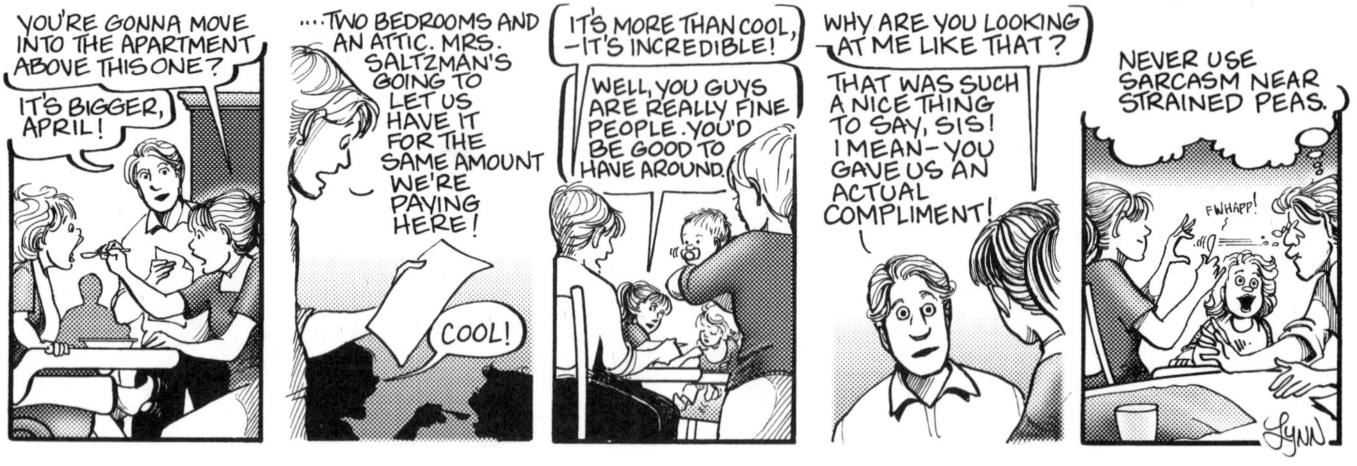
YOU'RE GONNA MOVE INTO THE APARTMENT ABOVE THIS ONE?
IT'S BIGGER, APRIL!
...TWO BEDROOMS AND AN ATTIC. MRS. SALTZMAN'S GOING TO LET US HAVE IT FOR THE SAME AMOUNT WE'RE PAYING HERE!
COOL!
IT'S MORE THAN COOL, -IT'S INCREDIBLE!
WELL, YOU GUYS ARE REALLY FINE PEOPLE. YOU'D BE GOOD TO HAVE AROUND.
WHY ARE YOU LOOKING AT ME LIKE THAT?
THAT WAS SUCH A NICE THING TO SAY, SIS! I MEAN-YOU GAVE US AN ACTUAL COMPLIMENT!
NEVER USE SARCASM NEAR STRAINED PEAS.
FWHAPP!
LYNN

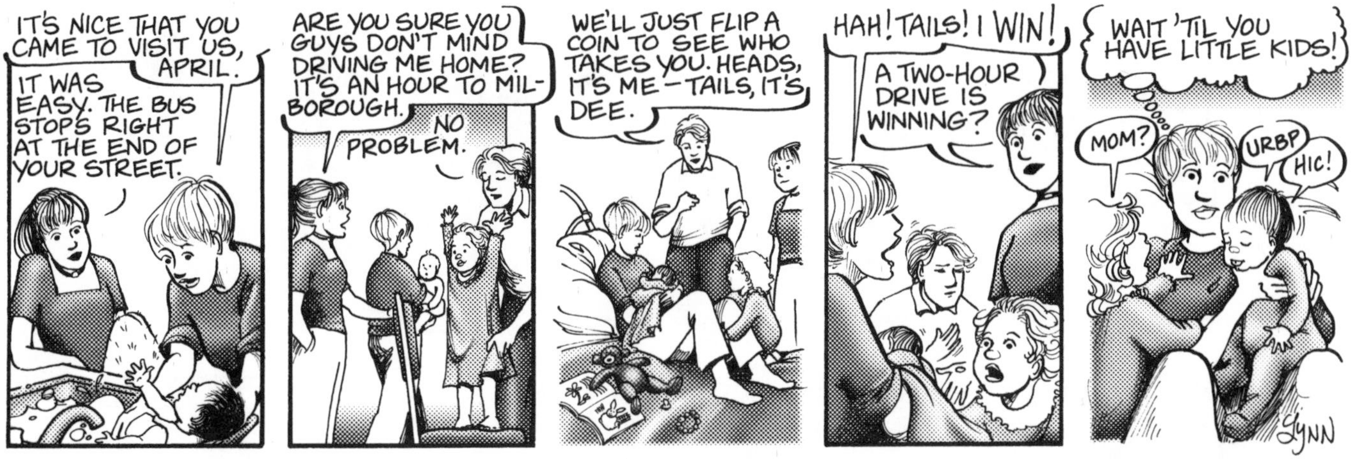
IT'S NICE THAT YOU CAME TO VISIT US, APRIL.
IT WAS EASY. THE BUS STOPS RIGHT AT THE END OF YOUR STREET.
ARE YOU SURE YOU GUYS DON'T MIND DRIVING ME HOME? IT'S AN HOUR TO MILBOROUGH.
NO PROBLEM.
WE'LL JUST FLIP A COIN TO SEE WHO TAKES YOU. HEADS, IT'S ME – TAILS, IT'S DEE.
HAH! TAILS! I WIN!
A TWO-HOUR DRIVE IS WINNING?
WAIT 'TIL YOU HAVE LITTLE KIDS!
MOM?
URBP
HIC!
LYNN

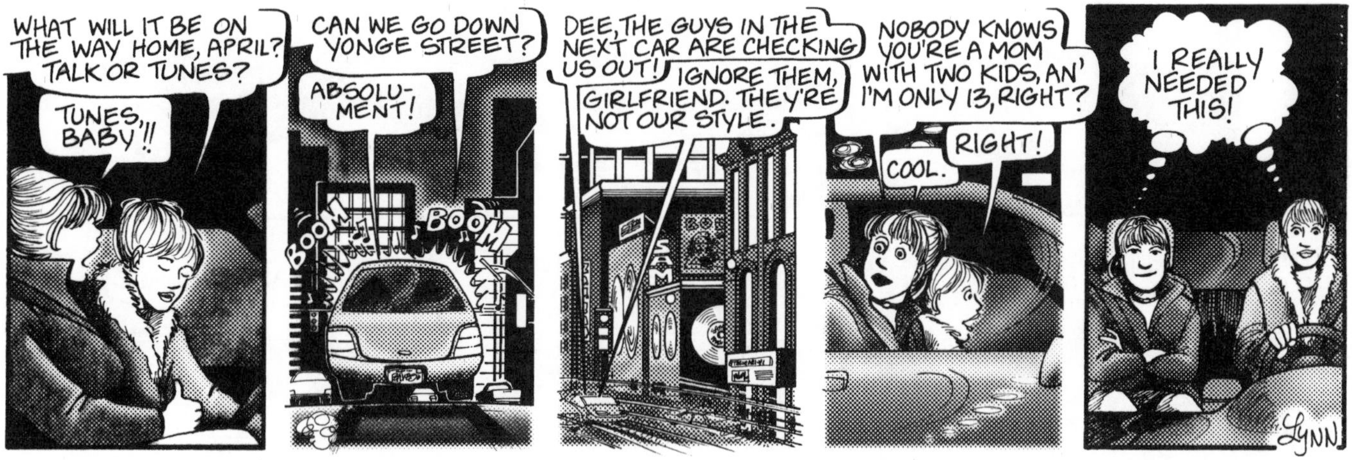
WHAT WILL IT BE ON THE WAY HOME, APRIL? TALK OR TUNES?
TUNES, BABY!!
CAN WE GO DOWN YONGE STREET?
ABSOLU-MENT!
BOOM
BOOM
DEE, THE GUYS IN THE NEXT CAR ARE CHECKING US OUT!
IGNORE THEM, GIRLFRIEND. THEY'RE NOT OUR STYLE.
NOBODY KNOWS YOU'RE A MOM WITH TWO KIDS, AN' I'M ONLY 13, RIGHT?
COOL.
RIGHT!
I REALLY NEEDED THIS!
LYNN

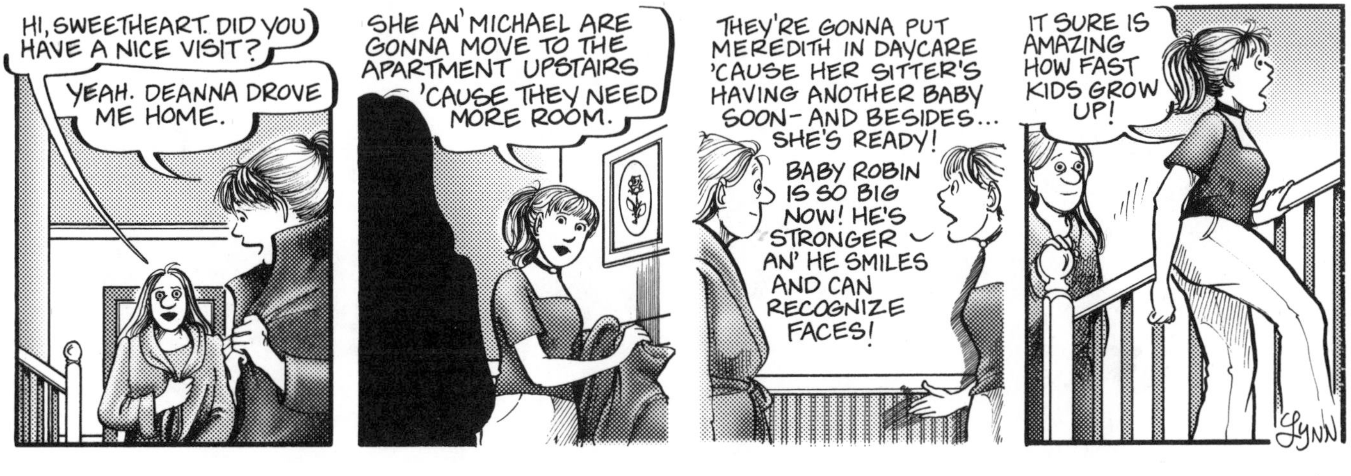
HI, SWEETHEART. DID YOU HAVE A NICE VISIT?
YEAH. DEANNA DROVE ME HOME.
SHE AN' MICHAEL ARE GONNA MOVE TO THE APARTMENT UPSTAIRS 'CAUSE THEY NEED MORE ROOM.
THEY'RE GONNA PUT MEREDITH IN DAYCARE 'CAUSE HER SITTER'S HAVING ANOTHER BABY SOON – AND BESIDES... SHE'S READY!
BABY ROBIN IS SO BIG NOW! HE'S STRONGER AN' HE SMILES AND CAN RECOGNIZE FACES!
IT SURE IS AMAZING HOW FAST KIDS GROW UP!
LYNN

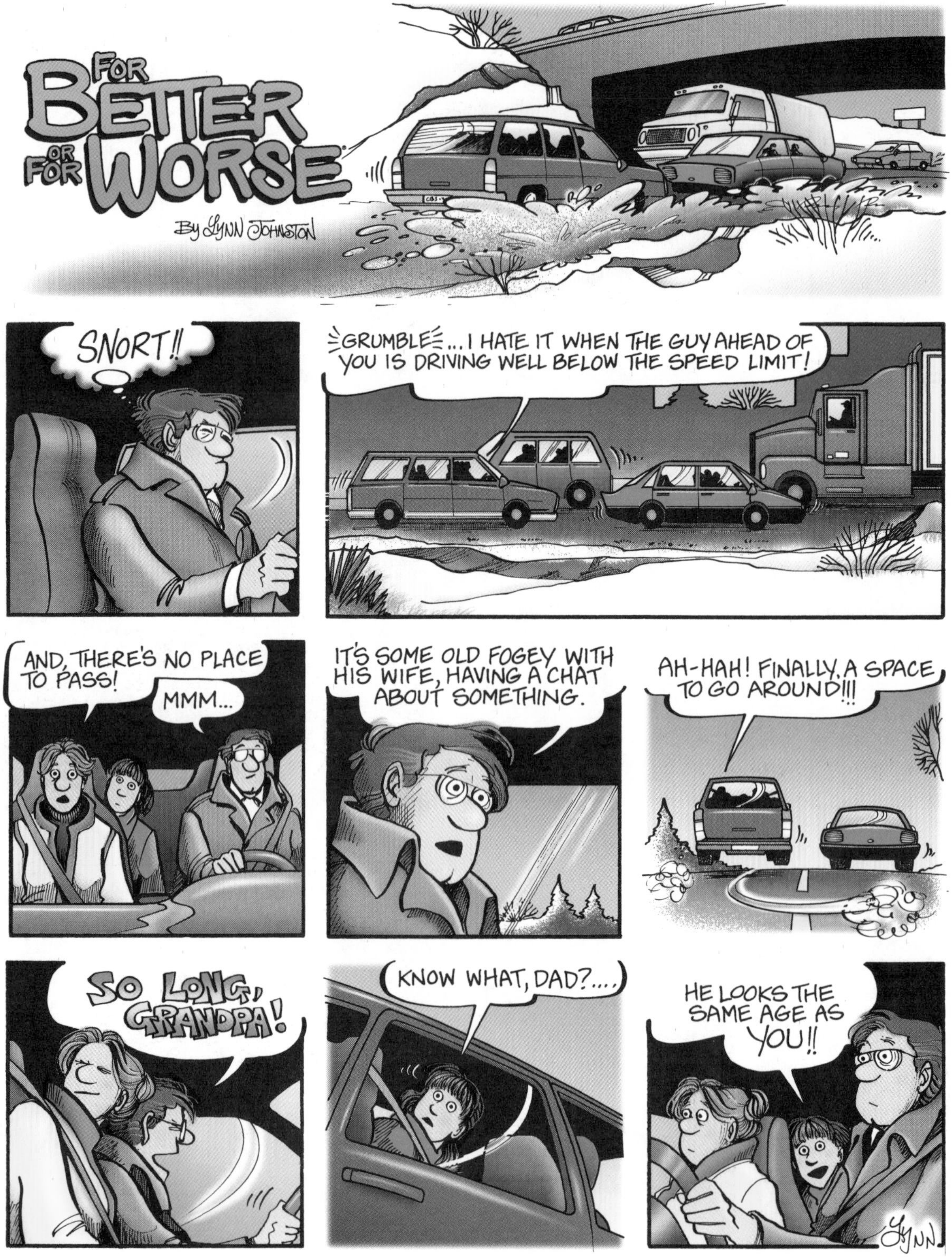
FOR BETTER OR FOR WORSE
By Lynn Johnston
SNORT!!
GRUMBLE... I HATE IT WHEN THE GUY AHEAD OF YOU IS DRIVING WELL BELOW THE SPEED LIMIT!
AND, THERE'S NO PLACE TO PASS!
MMM...
IT'S SOME OLD FOGEY WITH HIS WIFE, HAVING A CHAT ABOUT SOMETHING.
AH-HAH! FINALLY, A SPACE TO GO AROUND!!!
SO LONG, GRANDPA!
KNOW WHAT, DAD?....
HE LOOKS THE SAME AGE AS YOU!!
Lynn

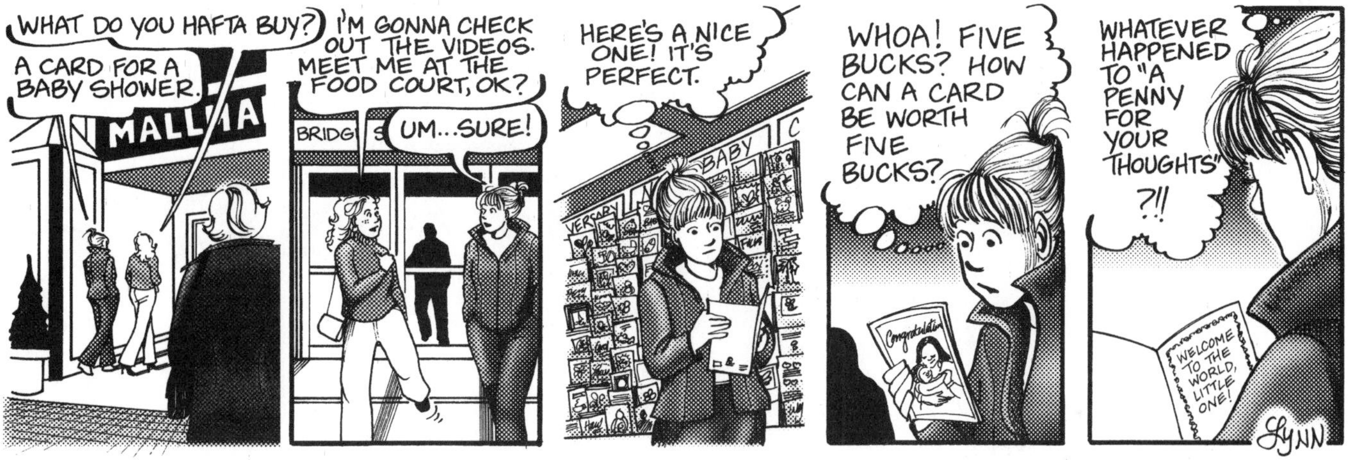
WHAT DO YOU HAFTA BUY?
A CARD FOR A BABY SHOWER.
MALLMA
I'M GONNA CHECK OUT THE VIDEOS. MEET ME AT THE FOOD COURT, OK?
UM...SURE!
HERE'S A NICE ONE! IT'S PERFECT.
BABY
WHOA! FIVE BUCKS? HOW CAN A CARD BE WORTH FIVE BUCKS?
Congratulations
WHATEVER HAPPENED TO "A PENNY FOR YOUR THOUGHTS"
?!!
WELCOME TO THE WORLD, LITTLE ONE!
LYNN

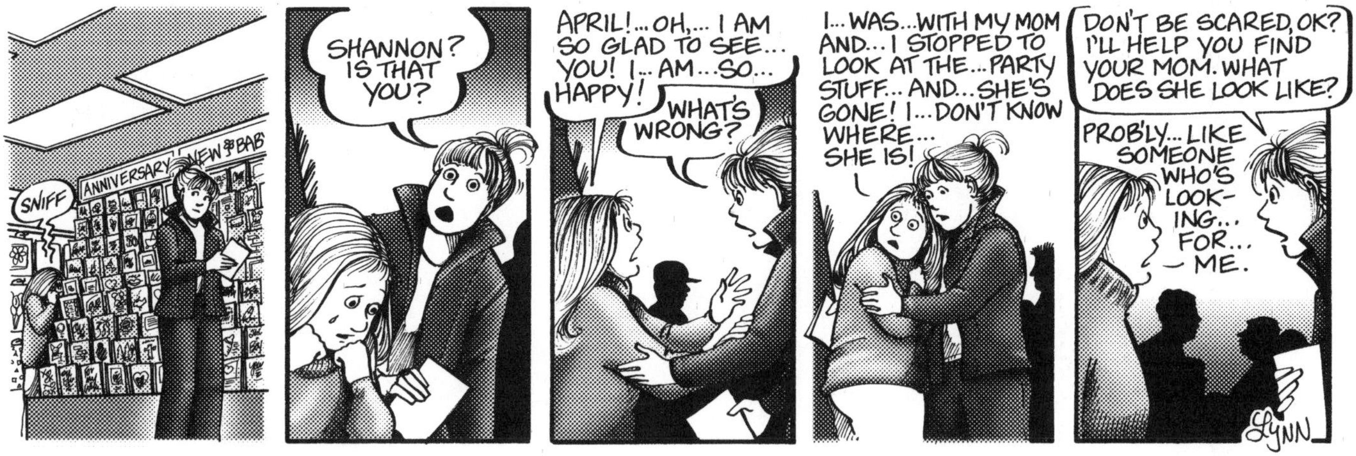
ANNIVERSARY
NEW BAB
SNIFF
SHANNON? IS THAT YOU?
APRIL!...OH,... I AM SO GLAD TO SEE... YOU! I... AM... SO... HAPPY!
WHAT'S WRONG?
I...WAS...WITH MY MOM AND... I STOPPED TO LOOK AT THE...PARTY STUFF... AND...SHE'S GONE! I... DON'T KNOW WHERE... SHE IS!
DON'T BE SCARED, OK? I'LL HELP YOU FIND YOUR MOM. WHAT DOES SHE LOOK LIKE?
PROB'LY... LIKE SOMEONE WHO'S LOOK-ING... FOR... ME.
LYNN

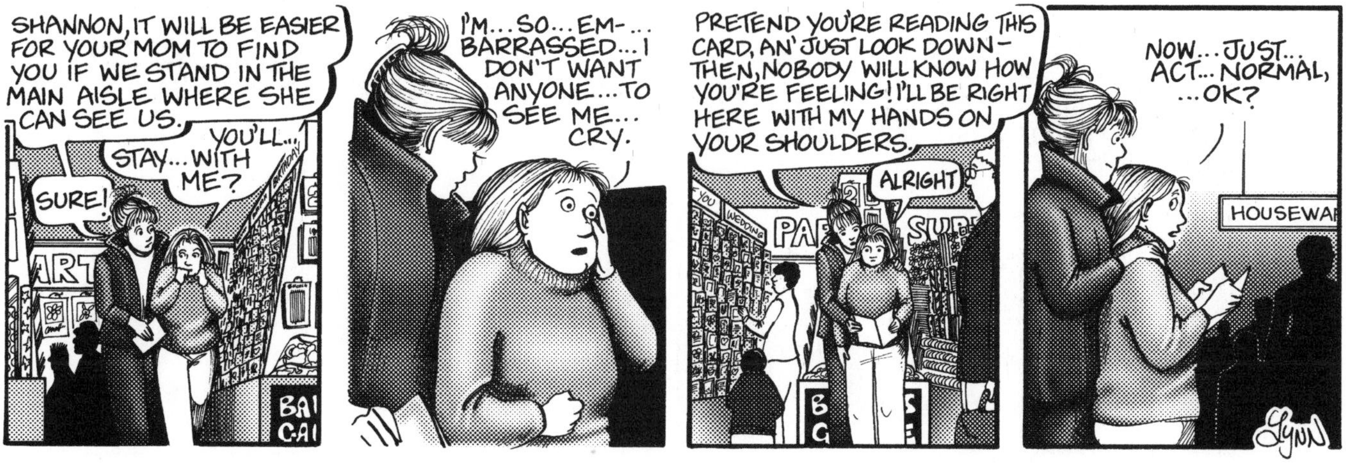
SHANNON, IT WILL BE EASIER FOR YOUR MOM TO FIND YOU IF WE STAND IN THE MAIN AISLE WHERE SHE CAN SEE US.
YOU'LL... STAY... WITH ME?
SURE!
I'M... SO... EM-... BARRASSED... I DON'T WANT ANYONE... TO SEE ME... CRY.
PRETEND YOU'RE READING THIS CARD, AN' JUST LOOK DOWN—THEN, NOBODY WILL KNOW HOW YOU'RE FEELING! I'LL BE RIGHT HERE WITH MY HANDS ON YOUR SHOULDERS.
ALRIGHT
NOW... JUST... ACT... NORMAL, ...OK?
HOUSEWA
LYNN

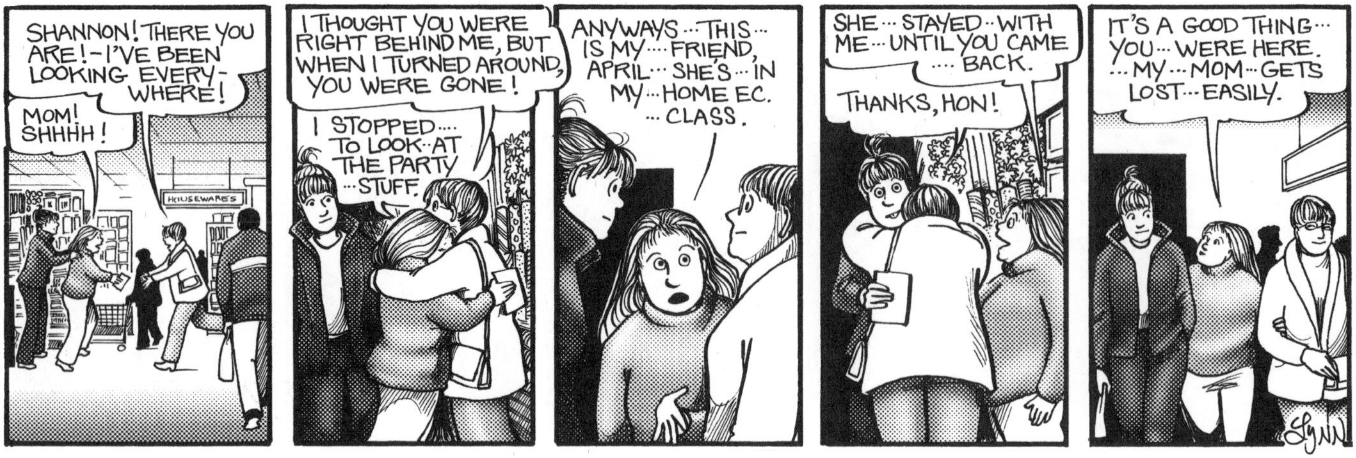
SHANNON! THERE YOU ARE! – I'VE BEEN LOOKING EVERY-WHERE!
MOM! SHHHH!
HOUSEWARES
I THOUGHT YOU WERE RIGHT BEHIND ME, BUT WHEN I TURNED AROUND, YOU WERE GONE!
I STOPPED.... TO LOOK··AT THE PARTY ···STUFF.
ANYWAYS···THIS···IS MY····FRIEND, APRIL···SHE'S···IN MY···HOME EC. ···CLASS.
SHE···STAYED··WITH ME···UNTIL YOU CAME ····BACK.
THANKS, HON!
IT'S A GOOD THING···YOU···WERE HERE. ···MY···MOM···GETS LOST···EASILY.
LYNN

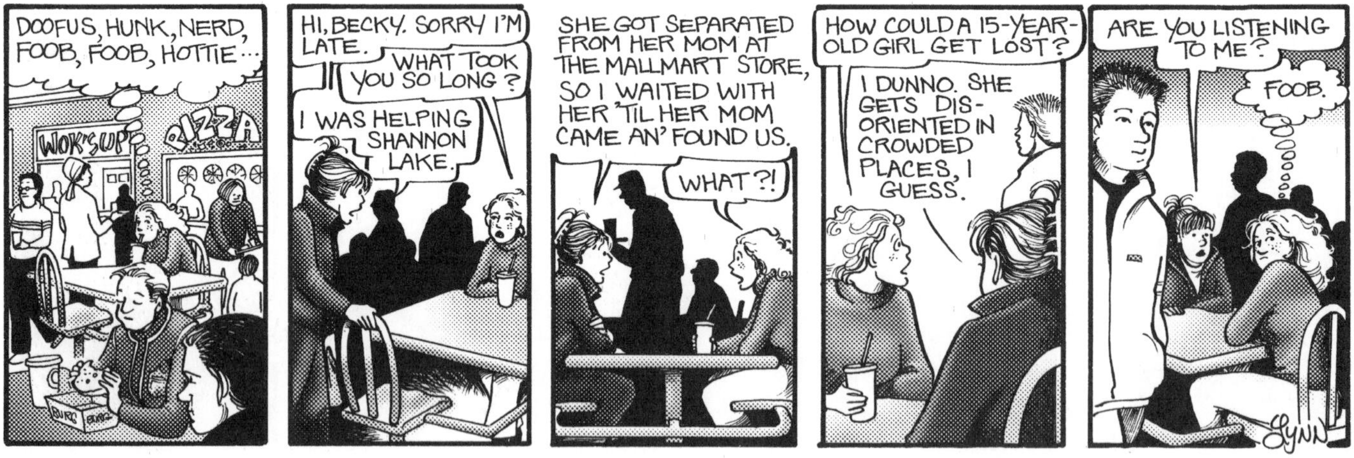
DOOFUS, HUNK, NERD, FOOB, FOOB, HOTTIE···
WOK'SUP
PIZZA
HI, BECKY. SORRY I'M LATE.
WHAT TOOK YOU SO LONG?
I WAS HELPING SHANNON LAKE.
SHE GOT SEPARATED FROM HER MOM AT THE MALLMART STORE, SO I WAITED WITH HER 'TIL HER MOM CAME AN' FOUND US.
WHAT?!
HOW COULD A 15-YEAR-OLD GIRL GET LOST?
I DUNNO. SHE GETS DIS-ORIENTED IN CROWDED PLACES, I GUESS.
ARE YOU LISTENING TO ME?
FOOB.
LYNN

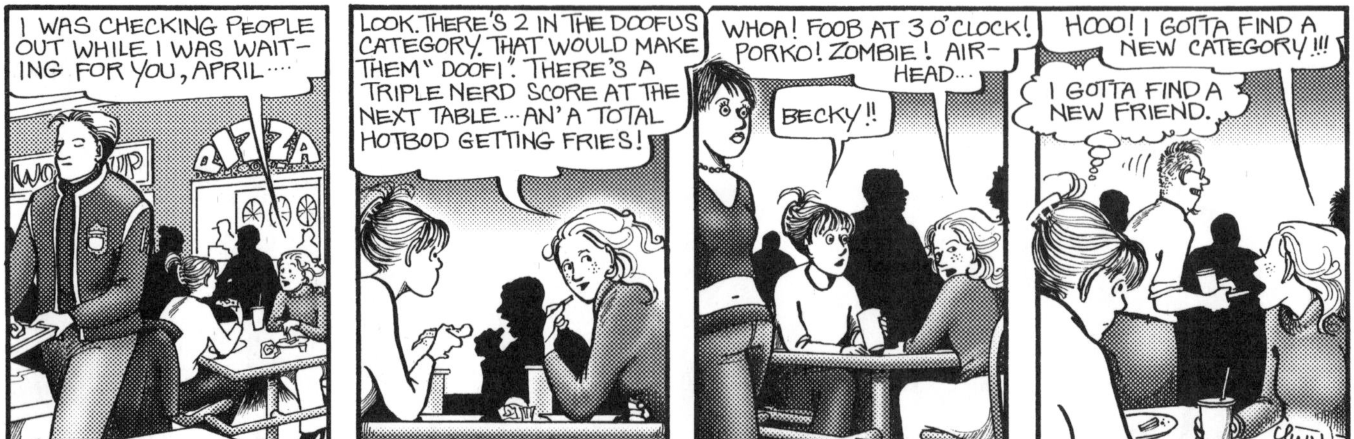
I WAS CHECKING PEOPLE OUT WHILE I WAS WAIT-ING FOR YOU, APRIL····
PIZZA
LOOK. THERE'S 2 IN THE DOOFUS CATEGORY. THAT WOULD MAKE THEM "DOOFI". THERE'S A TRIPLE NERD SCORE AT THE NEXT TABLE···AN' A TOTAL HOTBOD GETTING FRIES!
WHOA! FOOB AT 3 O'CLOCK! PORKO! ZOMBIE! AIR-HEAD···
BECKY!!
HOOO! I GOTTA FIND A NEW CATEGORY!!!
I GOTTA FIND A NEW FRIEND.
LYNN

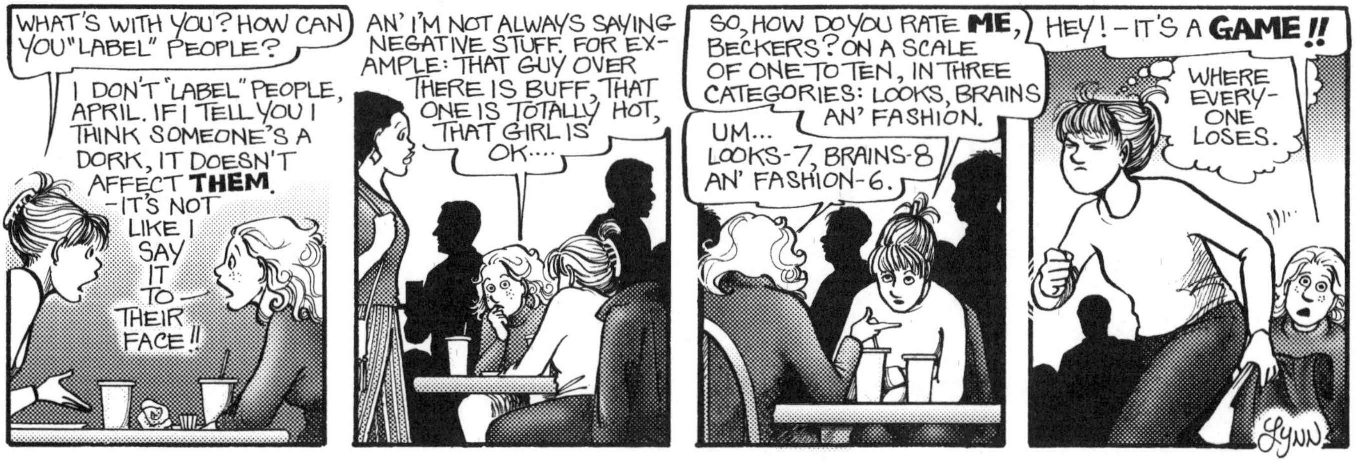
WHAT'S WITH YOU? HOW CAN YOU "LABEL" PEOPLE?
I DON'T "LABEL" PEOPLE, APRIL. IF I TELL YOU I THINK SOMEONE'S A DORK, IT DOESN'T AFFECT **THEM**. -IT'S NOT LIKE I SAY IT TO THEIR FACE!!
AN' I'M NOT ALWAYS SAYING NEGATIVE STUFF. FOR EXAMPLE: THAT GUY OVER THERE IS BUFF, THAT ONE IS TOTALLY HOT, THAT GIRL IS OK....
SO, HOW DO YOU RATE **ME**, BECKERS? ON A SCALE OF ONE TO TEN, IN THREE CATEGORIES: LOOKS, BRAINS AN' FASHION.
UM... LOOKS-7, BRAINS-8 AN' FASHION-6.
HEY! - IT'S A **GAME!!**
WHERE EVERY-ONE LOSES.
LYNN

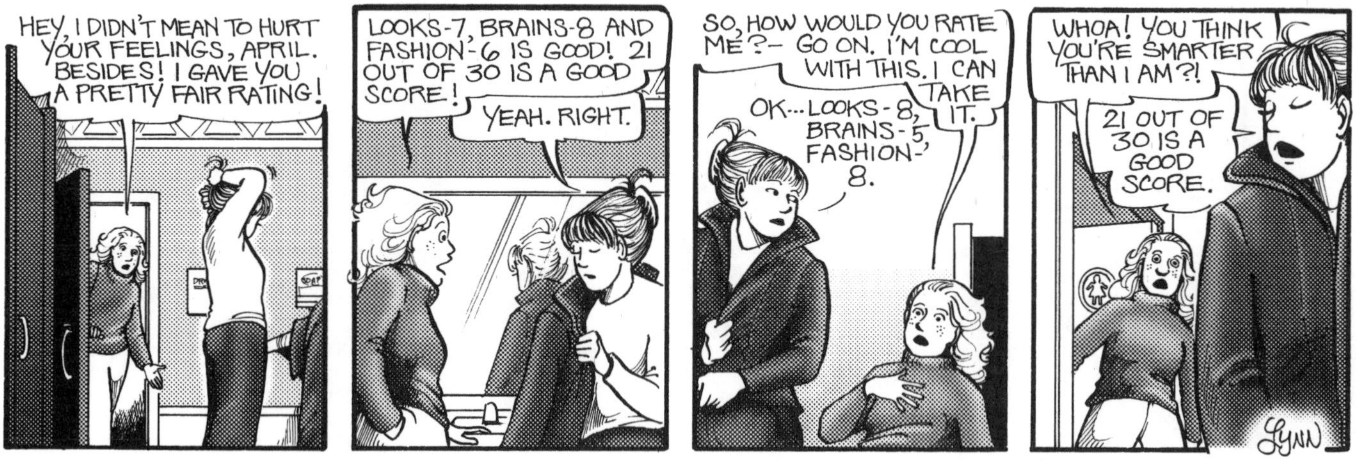
HEY, I DIDN'T MEAN TO HURT YOUR FEELINGS, APRIL. BESIDES! I GAVE YOU A PRETTY FAIR RATING!
LOOKS-7, BRAINS-8 AND FASHION-6 IS GOOD! 21 OUT OF 30 IS A GOOD SCORE!
YEAH. RIGHT.
SO, HOW WOULD YOU RATE ME?- GO ON. I'M COOL WITH THIS. I CAN TAKE IT.
OK... LOOKS-8, BRAINS-5, FASHION-8.
WHOA! YOU THINK YOU'RE SMARTER THAN I AM?!
21 OUT OF 30 IS A GOOD SCORE.
LYNN

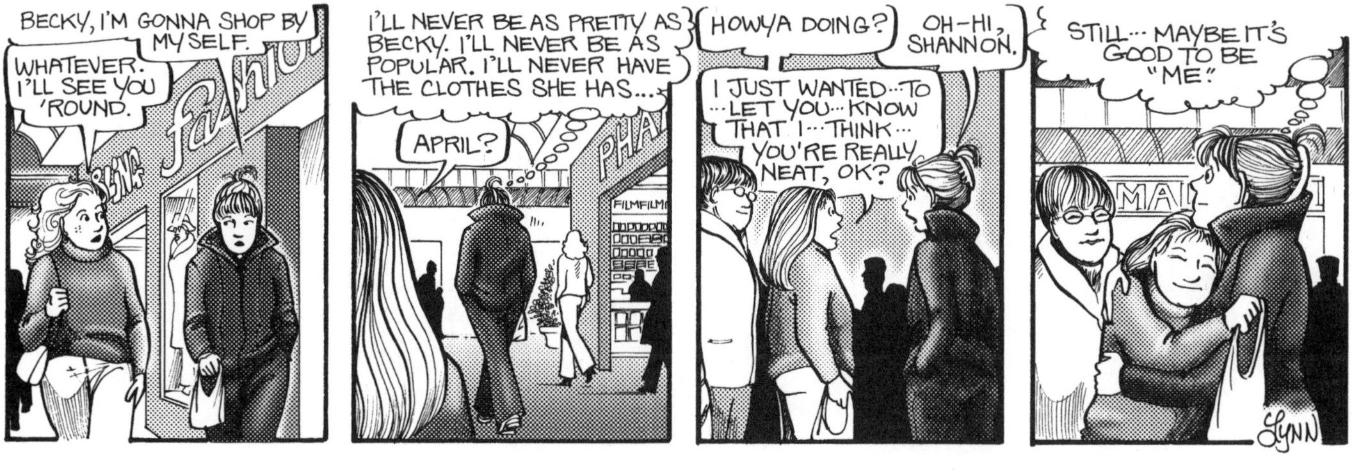
BECKY, I'M GONNA SHOP BY MYSELF.
WHATEVER. I'LL SEE YOU 'ROUND.
I'LL NEVER BE AS PRETTY AS BECKY. I'LL NEVER BE AS POPULAR. I'LL NEVER HAVE THE CLOTHES SHE HAS...
APRIL?
HOW'YA DOING?
OH-HI, SHANNON.
I JUST WANTED...TO ...LET YOU...KNOW THAT I...THINK... YOU'RE REALLY NEAT, OK?
STILL... MAYBE IT'S GOOD TO BE "ME."
LYNN

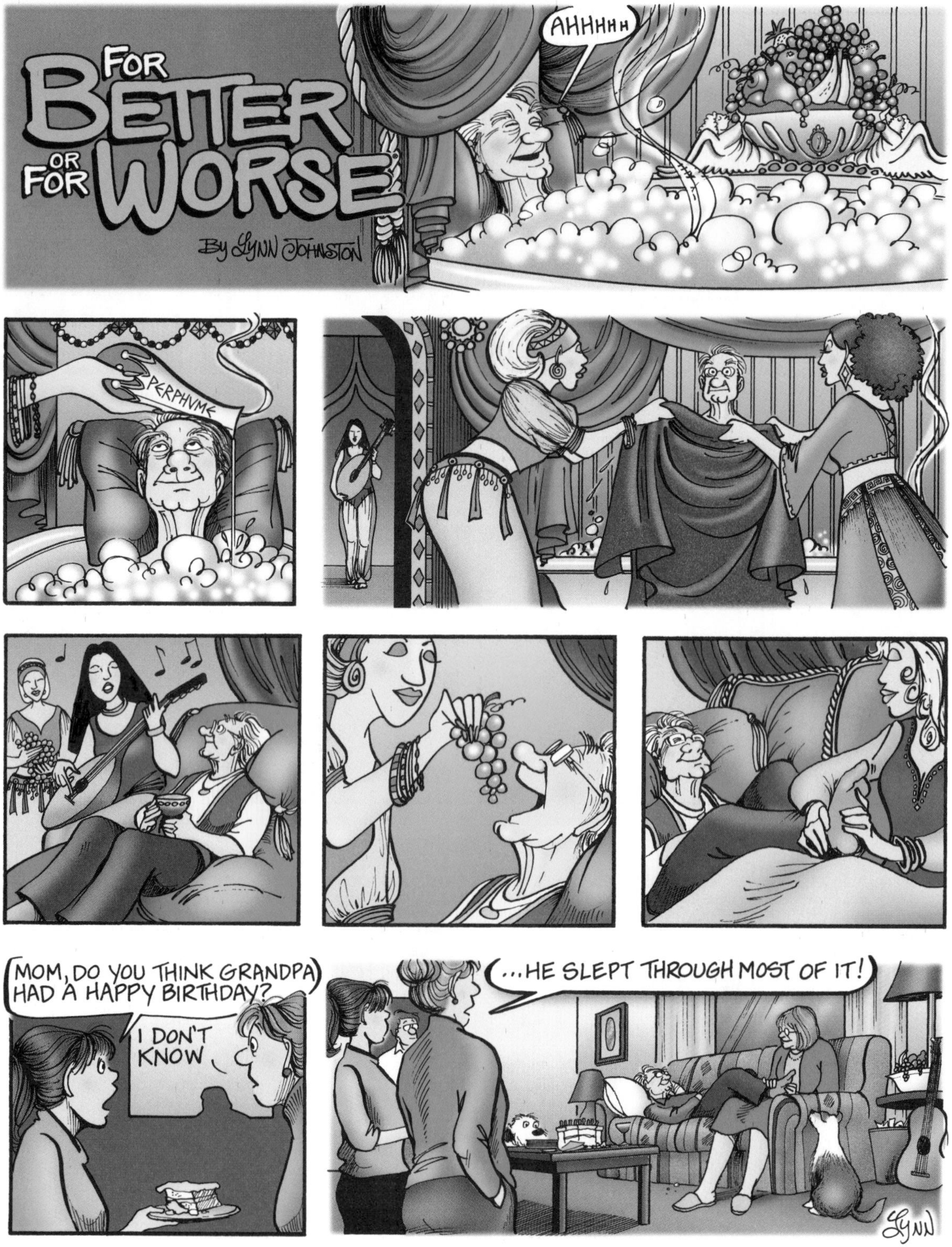
FOR BETTER OR FOR WORSE
BY LYNN JOHNSTON
AHHHHH
PERPHVME
MOM, DO YOU THINK GRANDPA HAD A HAPPY BIRTHDAY?
I DON'T KNOW
...HE SLEPT THROUGH MOST OF IT!
LYNN

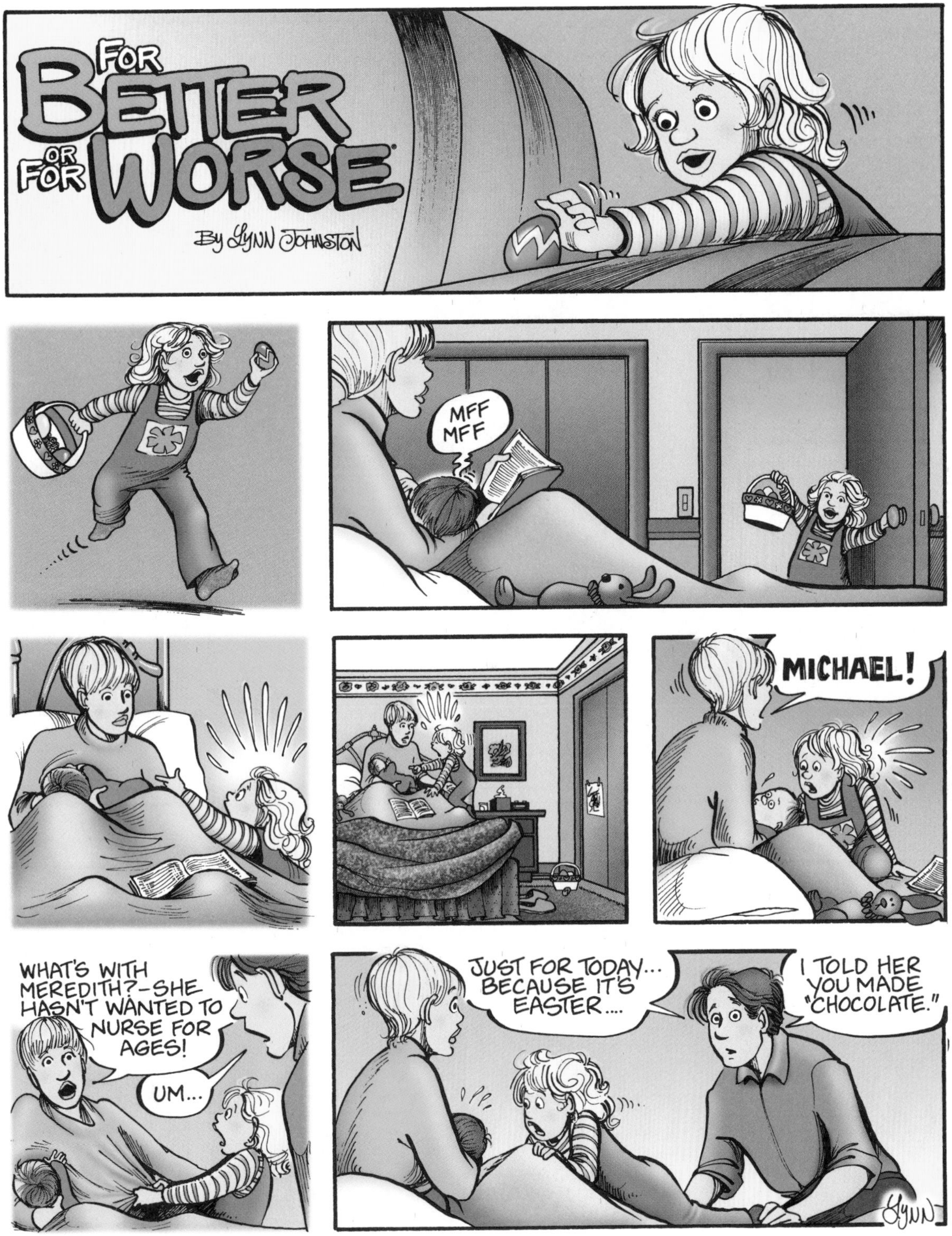
FOR BETTER OR FOR WORSE
BY LYNN JOHNSTON
MFF MFF
MICHAEL!
WHAT'S WITH MEREDITH?-SHE HASN'T WANTED TO NURSE FOR AGES!
UM...
JUST FOR TODAY... BECAUSE IT'S EASTER....
I TOLD HER YOU MADE "CHOCOLATE."
LYNN

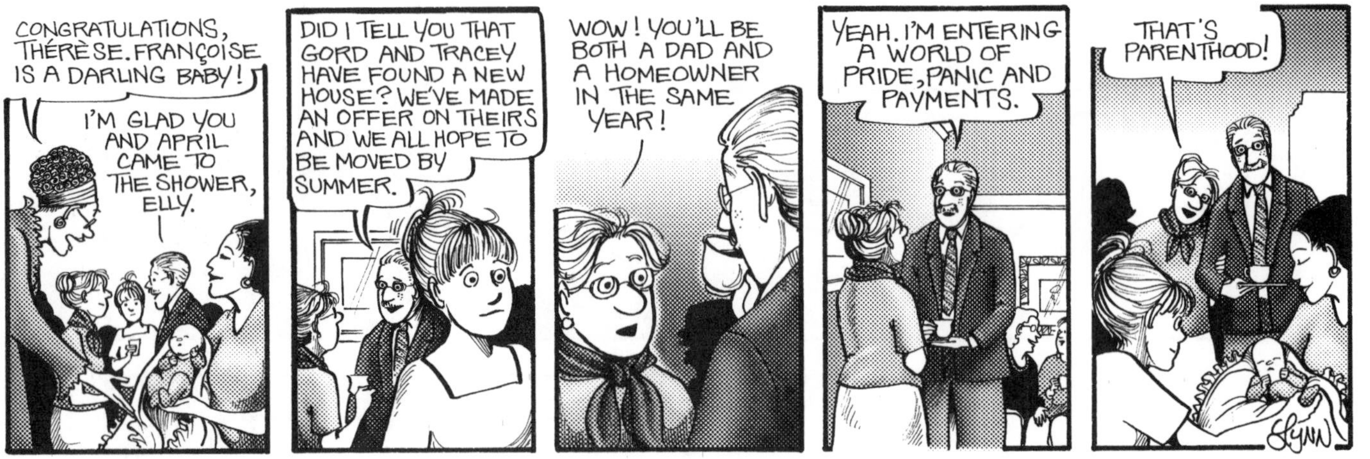
CONGRATULATIONS, THÉRÈSE. FRANÇOISE IS A DARLING BABY!
I'M GLAD YOU AND APRIL CAME TO THE SHOWER, ELLY.
DID I TELL YOU THAT GORD AND TRACEY HAVE FOUND A NEW HOUSE? WE'VE MADE AN OFFER ON THEIRS AND WE ALL HOPE TO BE MOVED BY SUMMER.
WOW! YOU'LL BE BOTH A DAD AND A HOMEOWNER IN THE SAME YEAR!
YEAH. I'M ENTERING A WORLD OF PRIDE, PANIC AND PAYMENTS.
THAT'S PARENTHOOD!
LYNN

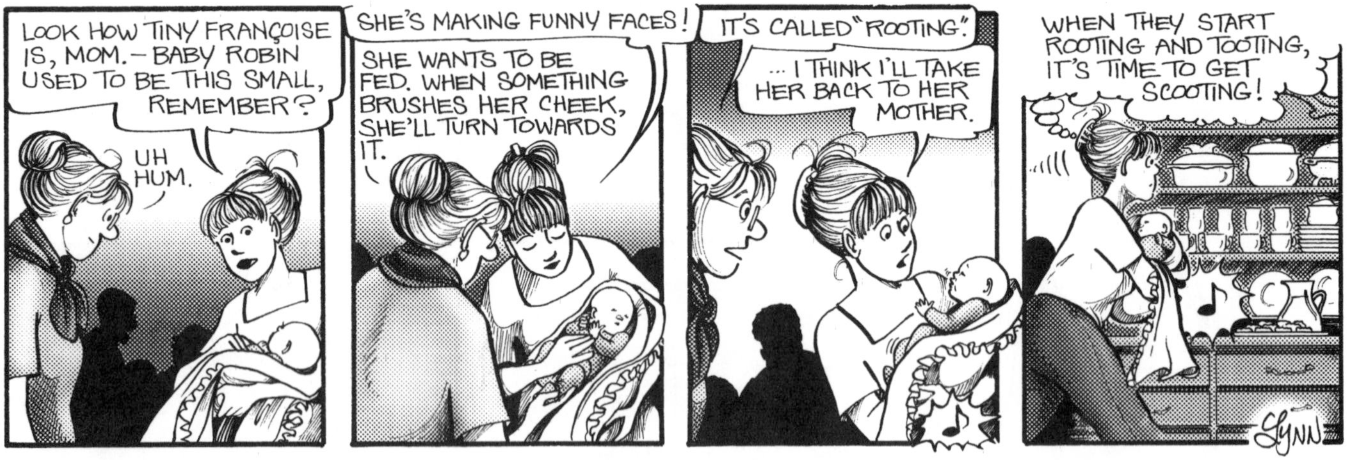
LOOK HOW TINY FRANÇOISE IS, MOM. – BABY ROBIN USED TO BE THIS SMALL, REMEMBER?
UH HUM.
SHE'S MAKING FUNNY FACES!
SHE WANTS TO BE FED. WHEN SOMETHING BRUSHES HER CHEEK, SHE'LL TURN TOWARDS IT.
IT'S CALLED "ROOTING."
... I THINK I'LL TAKE HER BACK TO HER MOTHER.
WHEN THEY START ROOTING AND TOOTING, IT'S TIME TO GET SCOOTING!
LYNN

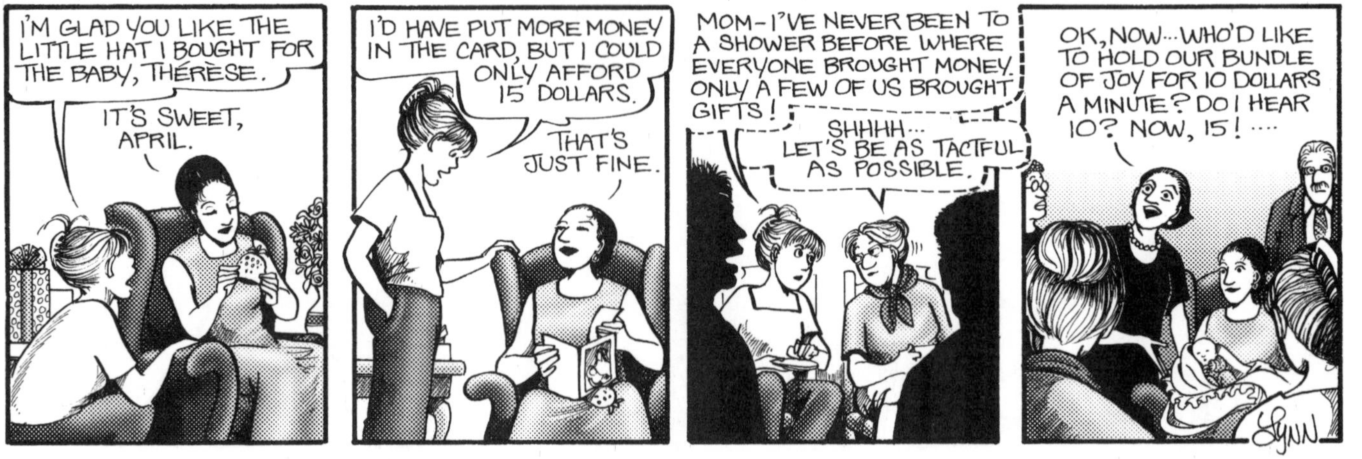
I'M GLAD YOU LIKE THE LITTLE HAT I BOUGHT FOR THE BABY, THÉRÈSE.
IT'S SWEET, APRIL.
I'D HAVE PUT MORE MONEY IN THE CARD, BUT I COULD ONLY AFFORD 15 DOLLARS.
THAT'S JUST FINE.
MOM – I'VE NEVER BEEN TO A SHOWER BEFORE WHERE EVERYONE BROUGHT MONEY. ONLY A FEW OF US BROUGHT GIFTS!
SHHHH... LET'S BE AS TACTFUL AS POSSIBLE.
OK, NOW... WHO'D LIKE TO HOLD OUR BUNDLE OF JOY FOR 10 DOLLARS A MINUTE? DO I HEAR 10? NOW, 15! ....
LYNN

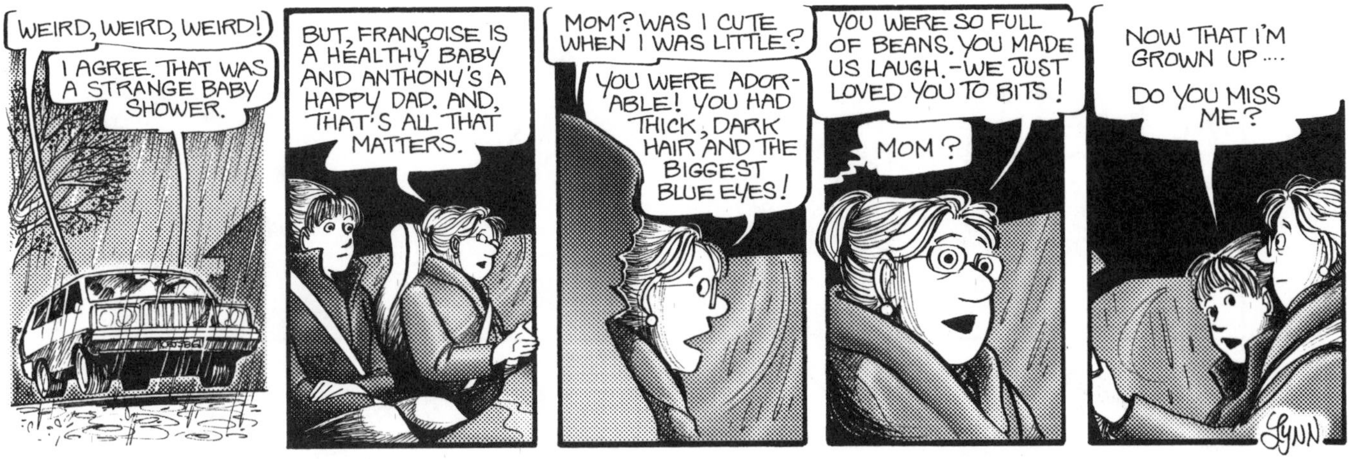
WEIRD, WEIRD, WEIRD!
I AGREE. THAT WAS A STRANGE BABY SHOWER.
BUT, FRANÇOISE IS A HEALTHY BABY AND ANTHONY'S A HAPPY DAD. AND, THAT'S ALL THAT MATTERS.
MOM? WAS I CUTE WHEN I WAS LITTLE?
YOU WERE ADORABLE! YOU HAD THICK, DARK HAIR AND THE BIGGEST BLUE EYES!
YOU WERE SO FULL OF BEANS. YOU MADE US LAUGH. -WE JUST LOVED YOU TO BITS!
MOM?
NOW THAT I'M GROWN UP....
DO YOU MISS ME?
LYNN

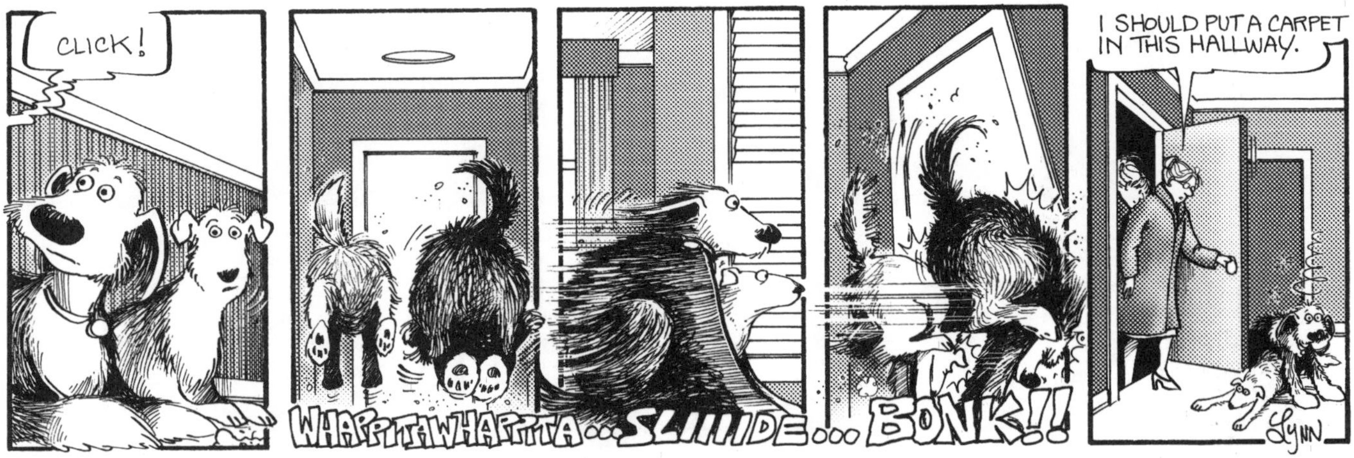
CLICK!
WHAPPITAWHAPPITA...
SLIIIIDE...
BONK!!
I SHOULD PUT A CARPET IN THIS HALLWAY.
LYNN

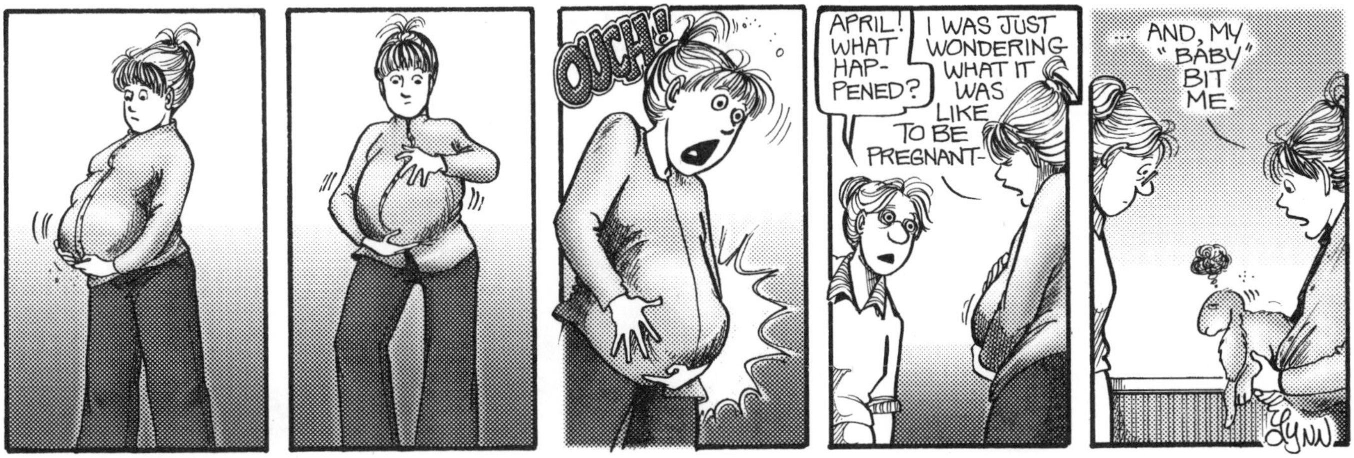
OUCH!
APRIL! WHAT HAPPENED?
I WAS JUST WONDERING WHAT IT WAS LIKE TO BE PREGNANT-
... AND, MY "BABY" BIT ME.
LYNN

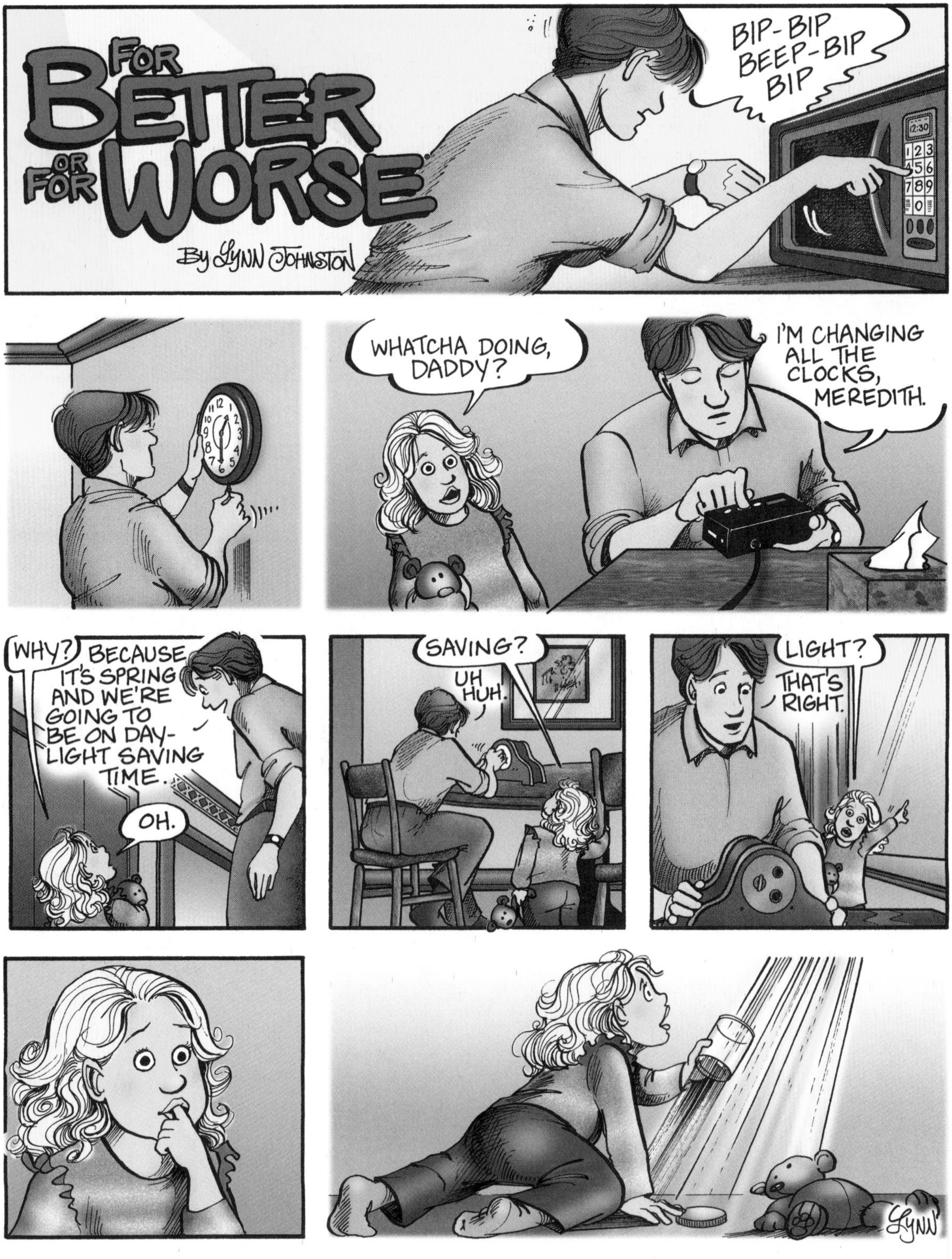
FOR BETTER OR FOR WORSE
BY LYNN JOHNSTON
BIP-BIP BEEP-BIP BIP
WHATCHA DOING, DADDY?
I'M CHANGING ALL THE CLOCKS, MEREDITH.
WHY?
BECAUSE IT'S SPRING AND WE'RE GOING TO BE ON DAY-LIGHT SAVING TIME.
OH.
SAVING?
UH HUH.
LIGHT?
THAT'S RIGHT.
LYNN

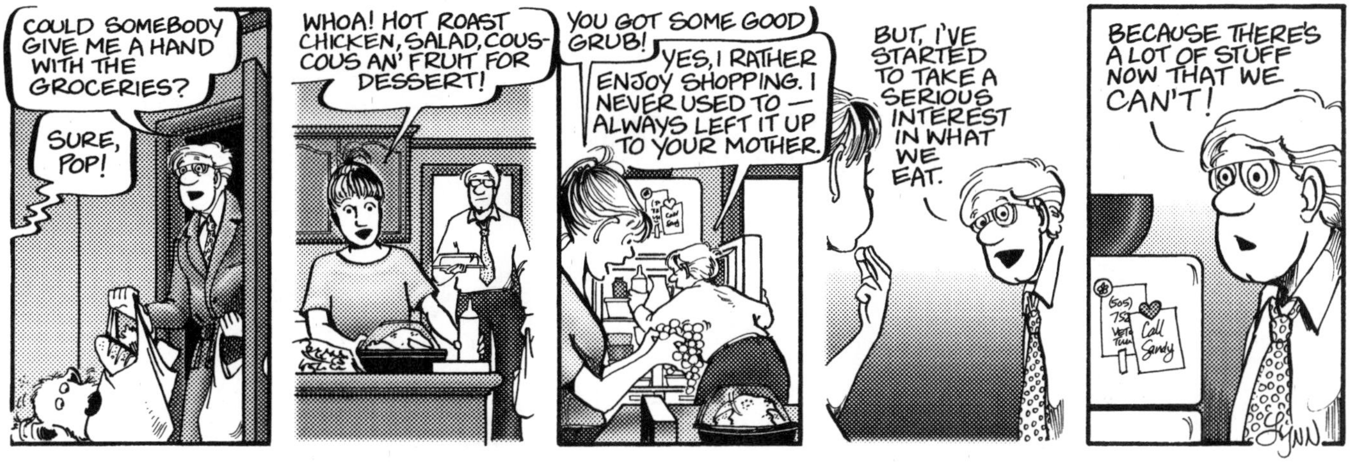
COULD SOMEBODY GIVE ME A HAND WITH THE GROCERIES?
SURE, POP!
WHOA! HOT ROAST CHICKEN, SALAD, COUS-COUS AN' FRUIT FOR DESSERT!
YOU GOT SOME GOOD GRUB!
YES, I RATHER ENJOY SHOPPING. I NEVER USED TO — ALWAYS LEFT IT UP TO YOUR MOTHER.
BUT, I'VE STARTED TO TAKE A SERIOUS INTEREST IN WHAT WE EAT.
BECAUSE THERE'S A LOT OF STUFF NOW THAT WE CAN'T!
Call Sandy
LYNN

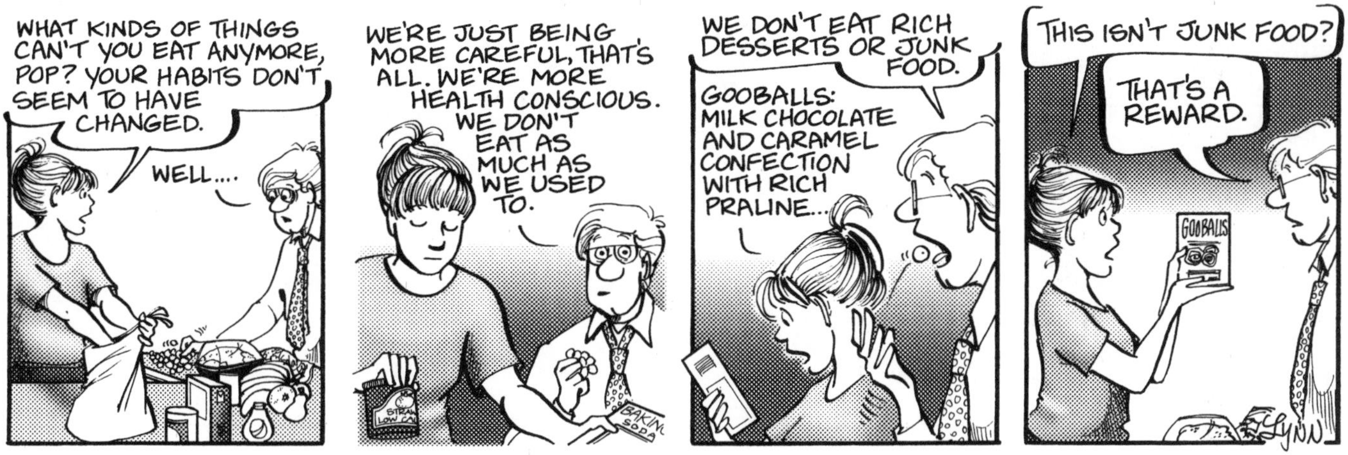
WHAT KINDS OF THINGS CAN'T YOU EAT ANYMORE, POP? YOUR HABITS DON'T SEEM TO HAVE CHANGED.
WELL....
WE'RE JUST BEING MORE CAREFUL, THAT'S ALL. WE'RE MORE HEALTH CONSCIOUS. WE DON'T EAT AS MUCH AS WE USED TO.
BAKING SODA
WE DON'T EAT RICH DESSERTS OR JUNK FOOD.
GOOBALLS: MILK CHOCOLATE AND CARAMEL CONFECTION WITH RICH PRALINE...
THIS ISN'T JUNK FOOD?
THAT'S A REWARD.
GOOBALLS
LYNN

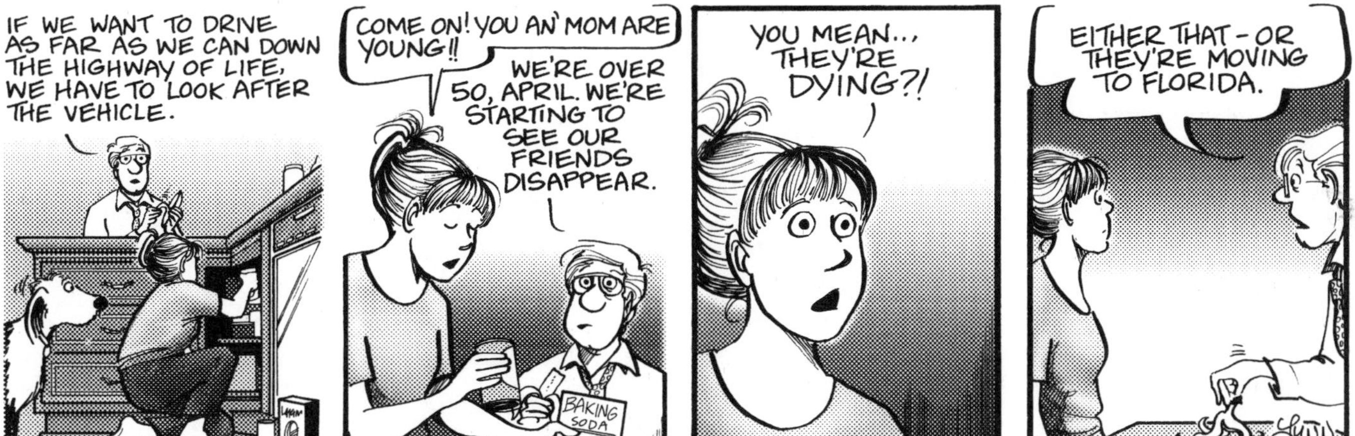
IF WE WANT TO DRIVE AS FAR AS WE CAN DOWN THE HIGHWAY OF LIFE, WE HAVE TO LOOK AFTER THE VEHICLE.
COME ON! YOU AN' MOM ARE YOUNG!!
WE'RE OVER 50, APRIL. WE'RE STARTING TO SEE OUR FRIENDS DISAPPEAR.
BAKING SODA
YOU MEAN..., THEY'RE DYING?!
EITHER THAT - OR THEY'RE MOVING TO FLORIDA.
LYNN

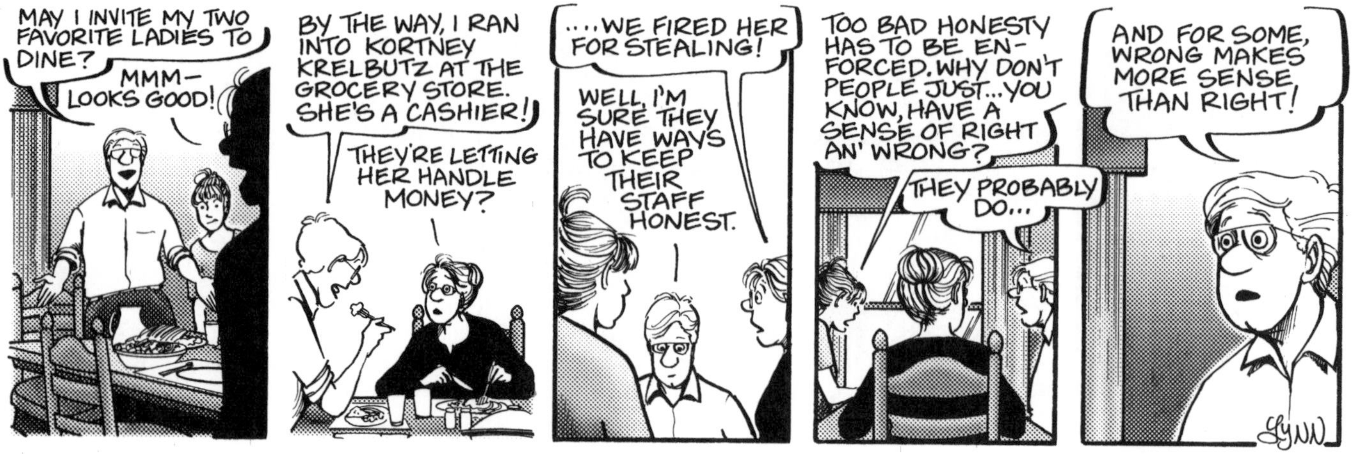
MAY I INVITE MY TWO FAVORITE LADIES TO DINE?
MMM— LOOKS GOOD!
BY THE WAY, I RAN INTO KORTNEY KRELBUTZ AT THE GROCERY STORE. SHE'S A CASHIER!
THEY'RE LETTING HER HANDLE MONEY?
...WE FIRED HER FOR STEALING!
WELL, I'M SURE THEY HAVE WAYS TO KEEP THEIR STAFF HONEST.
TOO BAD HONESTY HAS TO BE ENFORCED. WHY DON'T PEOPLE JUST...YOU KNOW, HAVE A SENSE OF RIGHT AN' WRONG?
THEY PROBABLY DO...
AND FOR SOME, WRONG MAKES MORE SENSE THAN RIGHT!
LYNN

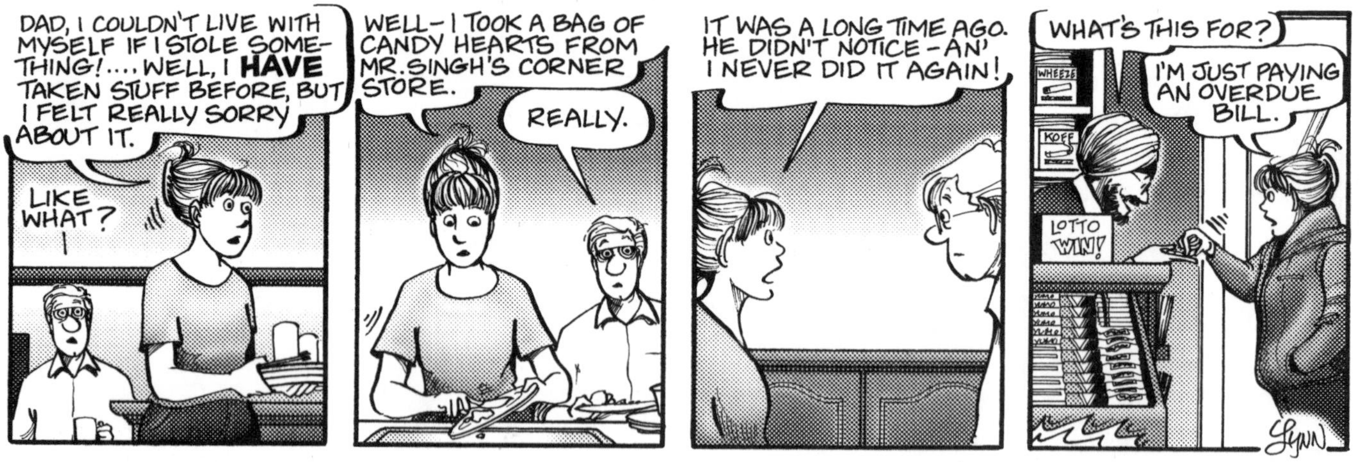
DAD, I COULDN'T LIVE WITH MYSELF IF I STOLE SOMETHING!.... WELL, I **HAVE** TAKEN STUFF BEFORE, BUT I FELT REALLY SORRY ABOUT IT.
LIKE WHAT?
WELL– I TOOK A BAG OF CANDY HEARTS FROM MR. SINGH'S CORNER STORE.
REALLY.
IT WAS A LONG TIME AGO. HE DIDN'T NOTICE – AN' I NEVER DID IT AGAIN!
WHAT'S THIS FOR?
I'M JUST PAYING AN OVERDUE BILL.
WHEEZE
KOFF
LOTTO WIN!
LYNN

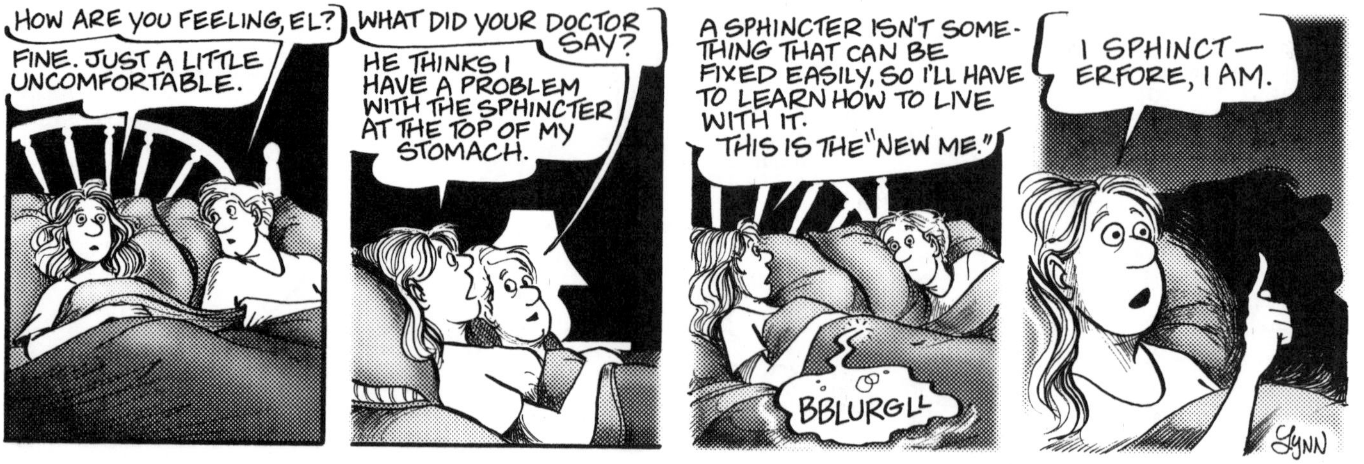
HOW ARE YOU FEELING, EL?
FINE. JUST A LITTLE UNCOMFORTABLE.
WHAT DID YOUR DOCTOR SAY?
HE THINKS I HAVE A PROBLEM WITH THE SPHINCTER AT THE TOP OF MY STOMACH.
A SPHINCTER ISN'T SOMETHING THAT CAN BE FIXED EASILY, SO I'LL HAVE TO LEARN HOW TO LIVE WITH IT.
THIS IS THE "NEW ME."
BBLURGLL
I SPHINCT— ERFORE, I AM.
LYNN

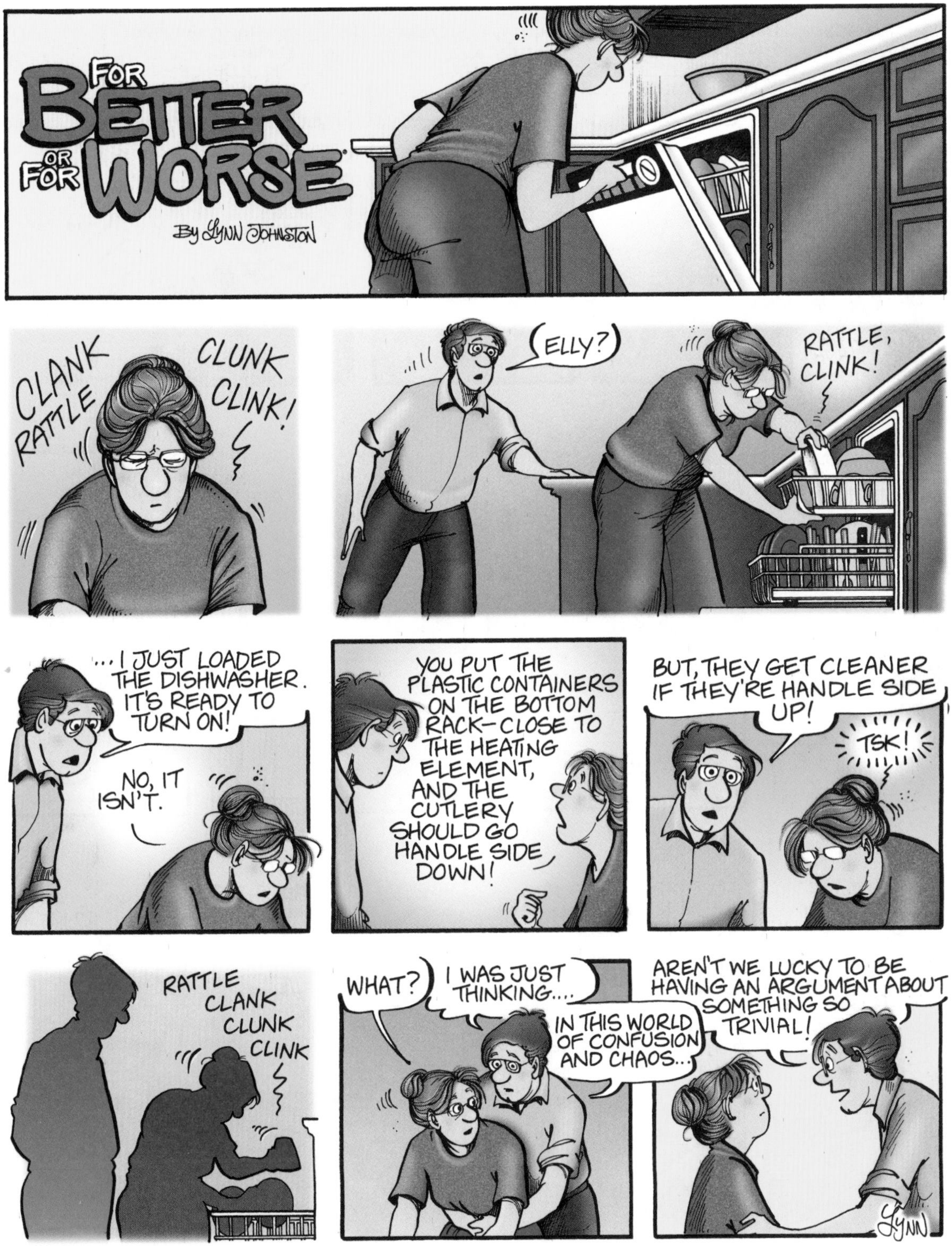
FOR BETTER OR FOR WORSE
BY LYNN JOHNSTON
CLANK RATTLE
CLUNK CLINK!
ELLY?
RATTLE, CLINK!
...I JUST LOADED THE DISHWASHER. IT'S READY TO TURN ON!
NO, IT ISN'T.
YOU PUT THE PLASTIC CONTAINERS ON THE BOTTOM RACK—CLOSE TO THE HEATING ELEMENT, AND THE CUTLERY SHOULD GO HANDLE SIDE DOWN!
BUT, THEY GET CLEANER IF THEY'RE HANDLE SIDE UP!
TSK!
RATTLE CLANK CLUNK CLINK
WHAT?
I WAS JUST THINKING....
IN THIS WORLD OF CONFUSION AND CHAOS...
AREN'T WE LUCKY TO BE HAVING AN ARGUMENT ABOUT SOMETHING SO TRIVIAL!
LYNN

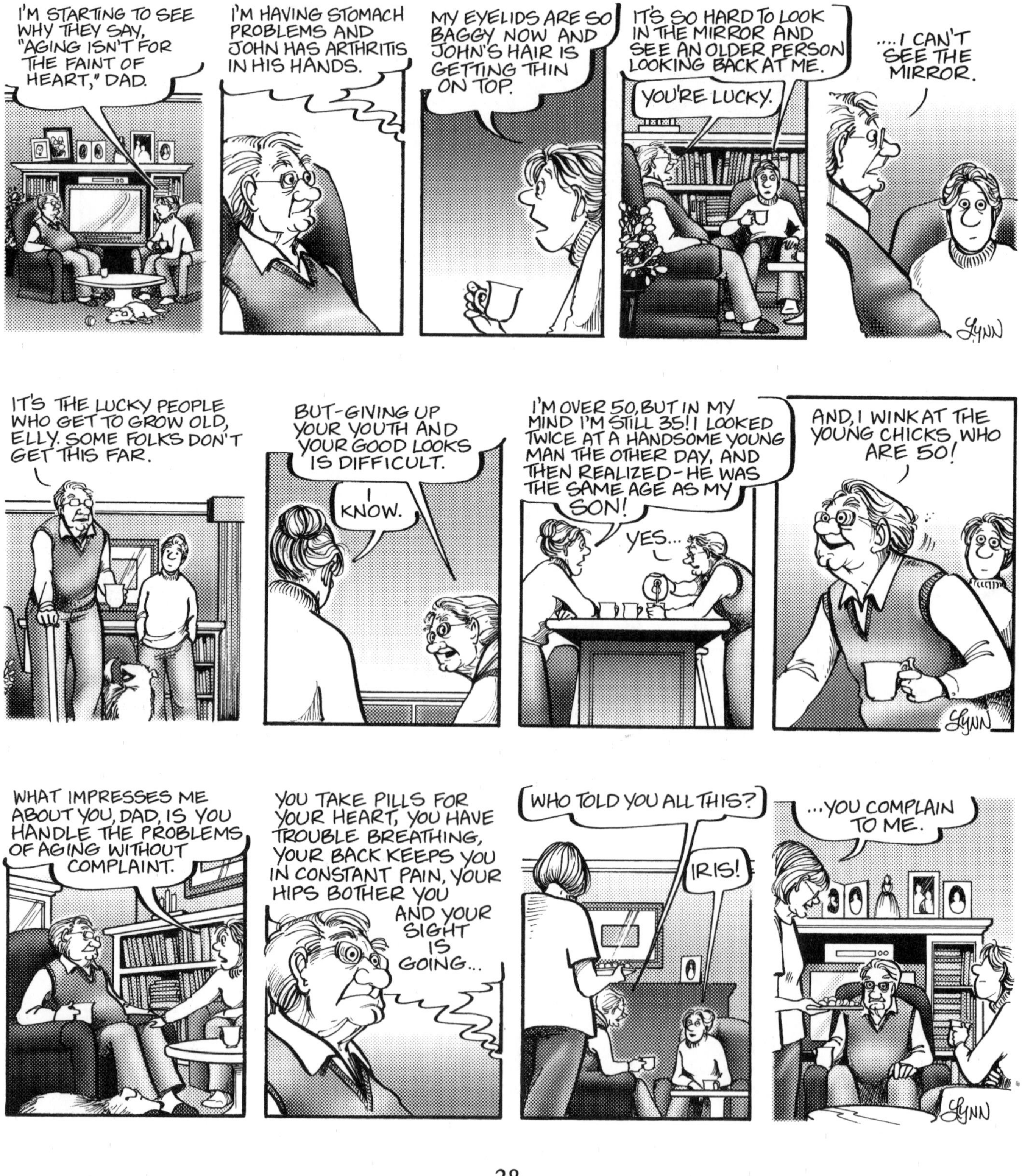
I'M STARTING TO SEE WHY THEY SAY, "AGING ISN'T FOR THE FAINT OF HEART," DAD.
I'M HAVING STOMACH PROBLEMS AND JOHN HAS ARTHRITIS IN HIS HANDS.
MY EYELIDS ARE SO BAGGY NOW AND JOHN'S HAIR IS GETTING THIN ON TOP.
IT'S SO HARD TO LOOK IN THE MIRROR AND SEE AN OLDER PERSON LOOKING BACK AT ME.
YOU'RE LUCKY.
....I CAN'T SEE THE MIRROR.
LYNN
IT'S THE LUCKY PEOPLE WHO GET TO GROW OLD, ELLY. SOME FOLKS DON'T GET THIS FAR.
BUT-GIVING UP YOUR YOUTH AND YOUR GOOD LOOKS IS DIFFICULT.
I KNOW.
I'M OVER 50, BUT IN MY MIND I'M STILL 35! I LOOKED TWICE AT A HANDSOME YOUNG MAN THE OTHER DAY, AND THEN REALIZED-HE WAS THE SAME AGE AS MY SON!
YES...
AND, I WINK AT THE YOUNG CHICKS, WHO ARE 50!
LYNN
WHAT IMPRESSES ME ABOUT YOU, DAD, IS YOU HANDLE THE PROBLEMS OF AGING WITHOUT COMPLAINT.
YOU TAKE PILLS FOR YOUR HEART, YOU HAVE TROUBLE BREATHING, YOUR BACK KEEPS YOU IN CONSTANT PAIN, YOUR HIPS BOTHER YOU
AND YOUR SIGHT IS GOING...
WHO TOLD YOU ALL THIS?
IRIS!
...YOU COMPLAIN TO ME.
LYNN

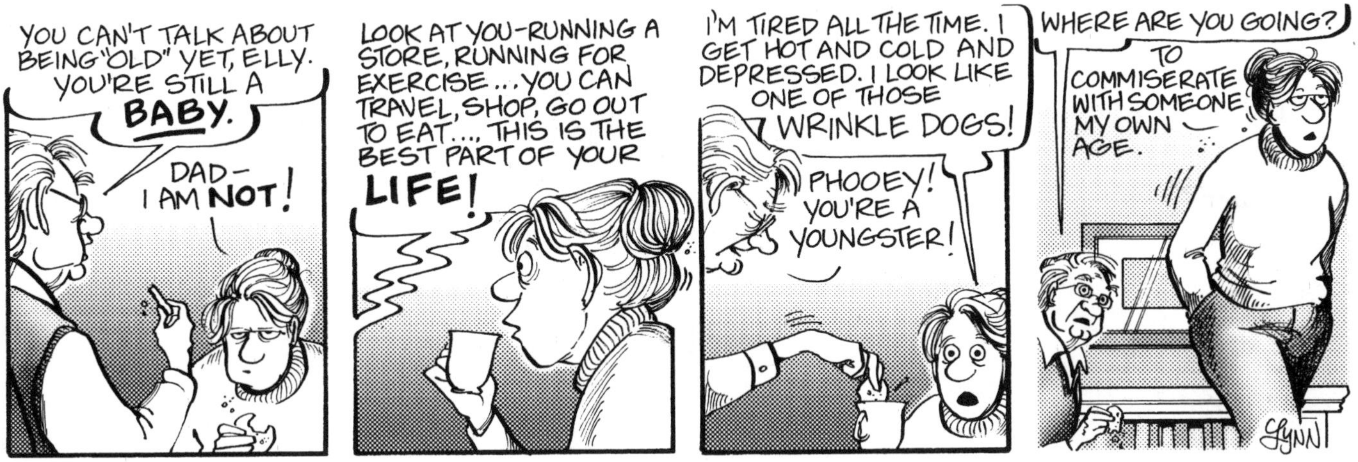
YOU CAN'T TALK ABOUT BEING "OLD" YET, ELLY. YOU'RE STILL A BABY.
DAD— I AM NOT!
LOOK AT YOU—RUNNING A STORE, RUNNING FOR EXERCISE...YOU CAN TRAVEL, SHOP, GO OUT TO EAT..., THIS IS THE BEST PART OF YOUR LIFE!
I'M TIRED ALL THE TIME. I GET HOT AND COLD AND DEPRESSED. I LOOK LIKE ONE OF THOSE WRINKLE DOGS!
PHOOEY! YOU'RE A YOUNGSTER!
WHERE ARE YOU GOING?
TO COMMISERATE WITH SOMEONE MY OWN AGE.
LYNN

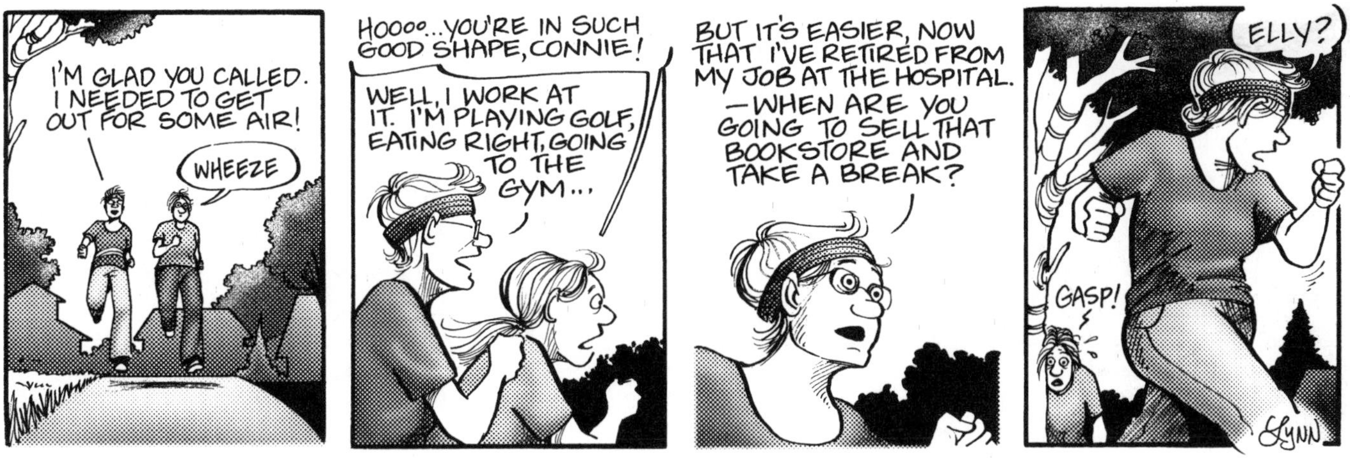
I'M GLAD YOU CALLED. I NEEDED TO GET OUT FOR SOME AIR!
WHEEZE
HOOOO...YOU'RE IN SUCH GOOD SHAPE, CONNIE!
WELL, I WORK AT IT. I'M PLAYING GOLF, EATING RIGHT, GOING TO THE GYM...
BUT IT'S EASIER, NOW THAT I'VE RETIRED FROM MY JOB AT THE HOSPITAL. —WHEN ARE YOU GOING TO SELL THAT BOOKSTORE AND TAKE A BREAK?
ELLY?
GASP!
LYNN

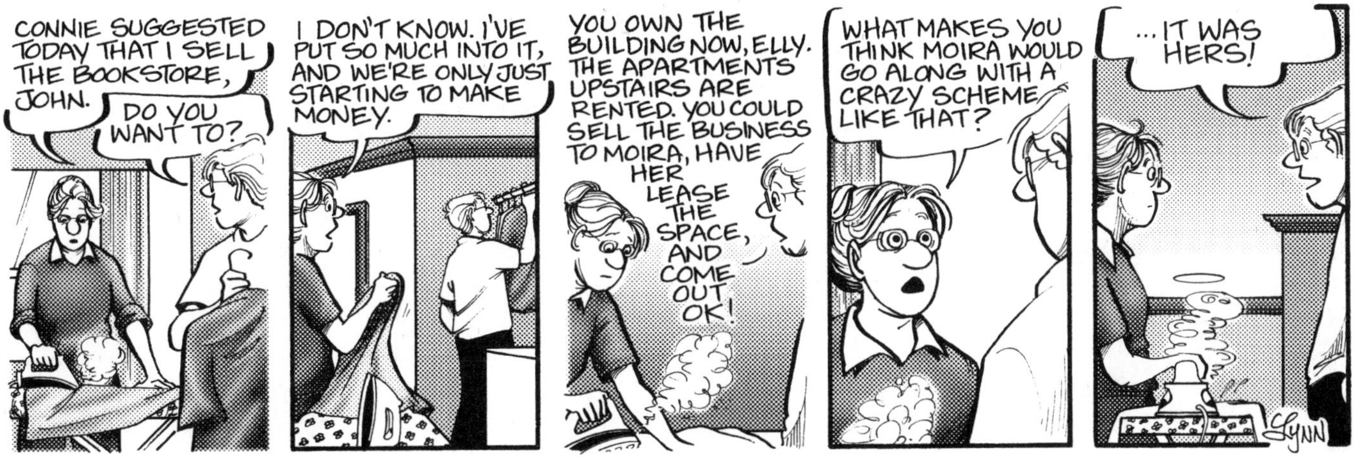
CONNIE SUGGESTED TODAY THAT I SELL THE BOOKSTORE, JOHN.
DO YOU WANT TO?
I DON'T KNOW. I'VE PUT SO MUCH INTO IT, AND WE'RE ONLY JUST STARTING TO MAKE MONEY.
YOU OWN THE BUILDING NOW, ELLY. THE APARTMENTS UPSTAIRS ARE RENTED. YOU COULD SELL THE BUSINESS TO MOIRA, HAVE HER LEASE THE SPACE, AND COME OUT OK!
WHAT MAKES YOU THINK MOIRA WOULD GO ALONG WITH A CRAZY SCHEME LIKE THAT?
...IT WAS HERS!
LYNN

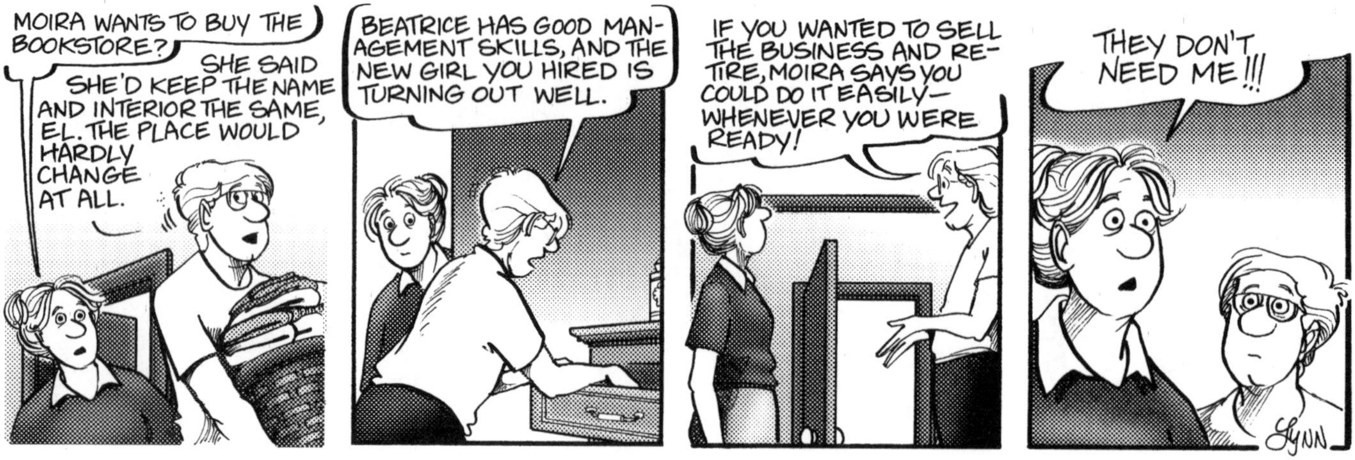
MOIRA WANTS TO BUY THE BOOKSTORE?
SHE SAID SHE'D KEEP THE NAME AND INTERIOR THE SAME, EL. THE PLACE WOULD HARDLY CHANGE AT ALL.
BEATRICE HAS GOOD MANAGEMENT SKILLS, AND THE NEW GIRL YOU HIRED IS TURNING OUT WELL.
IF YOU WANTED TO SELL THE BUSINESS AND RETIRE, MOIRA SAYS YOU COULD DO IT EASILY— WHENEVER YOU WERE READY!
THEY DON'T NEED ME!!!
LYNN

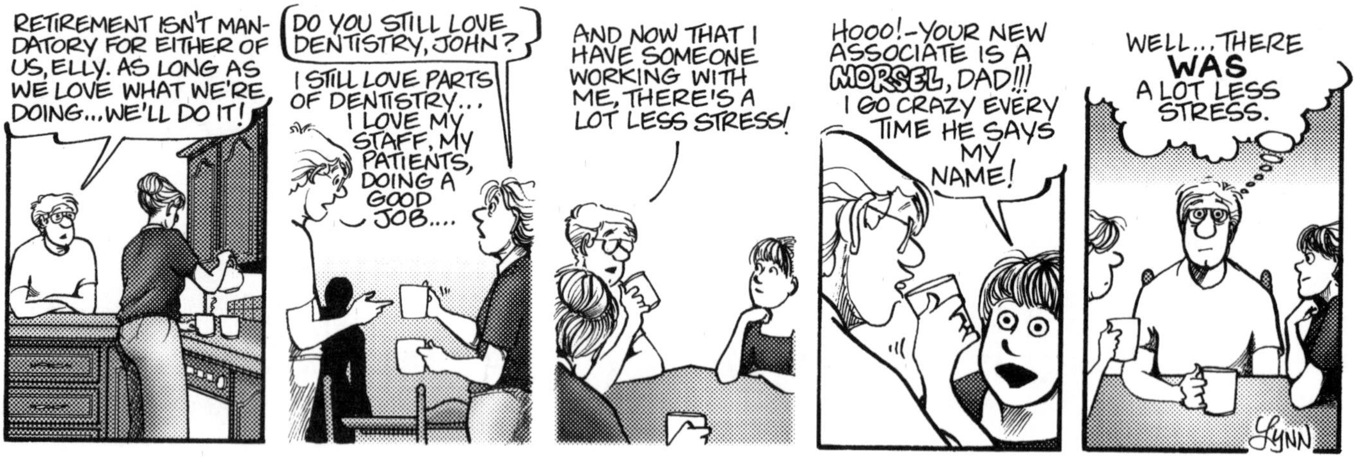
RETIREMENT ISN'T MANDATORY FOR EITHER OF US, ELLY. AS LONG AS WE LOVE WHAT WE'RE DOING... WE'LL DO IT!
DO YOU STILL LOVE DENTISTRY, JOHN?
I STILL LOVE PARTS OF DENTISTRY... I LOVE MY STAFF, MY PATIENTS, DOING A GOOD JOB....
AND NOW THAT I HAVE SOMEONE WORKING WITH ME, THERE'S A LOT LESS STRESS!
HOOO!–YOUR NEW ASSOCIATE IS A MORSEL, DAD!!!
I GO CRAZY EVERY TIME HE SAYS MY NAME!
WELL... THERE WAS A LOT LESS STRESS.
LYNN

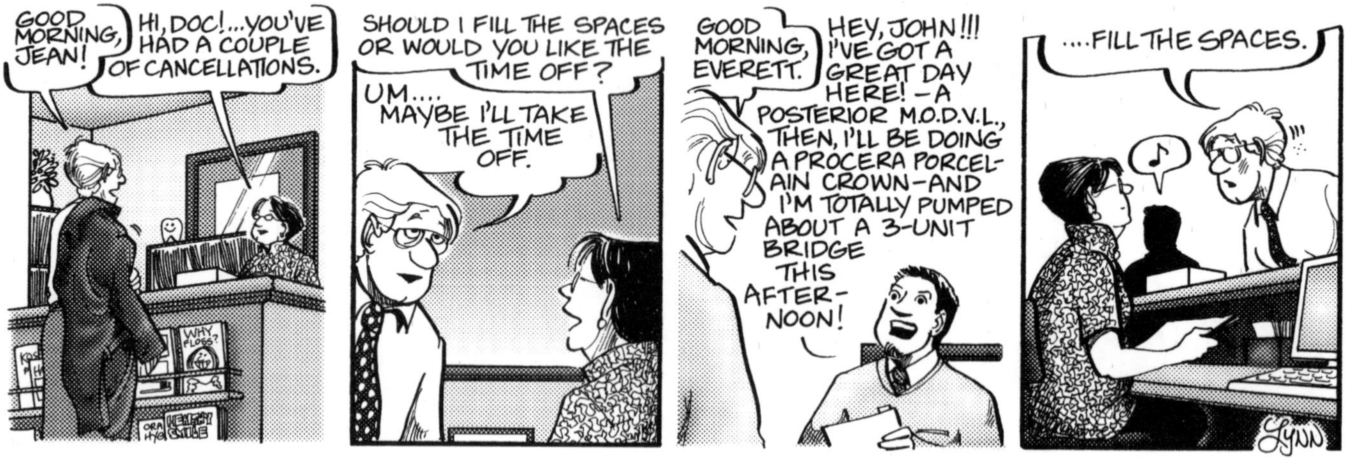
GOOD MORNING, JEAN!
HI, DOC!...YOU'VE HAD A COUPLE OF CANCELLATIONS.
WHY FLOSS?
SHOULD I FILL THE SPACES OR WOULD YOU LIKE THE TIME OFF?
UM.... MAYBE I'LL TAKE THE TIME OFF.
GOOD MORNING, EVERETT.
HEY, JOHN!!! I'VE GOT A GREAT DAY HERE! –A POSTERIOR M.O.D.V.L., THEN, I'LL BE DOING A PROCERA PORCELAIN CROWN–AND I'M TOTALLY PUMPED ABOUT A 3-UNIT BRIDGE THIS AFTERNOON!
....FILL THE SPACES.
LYNN

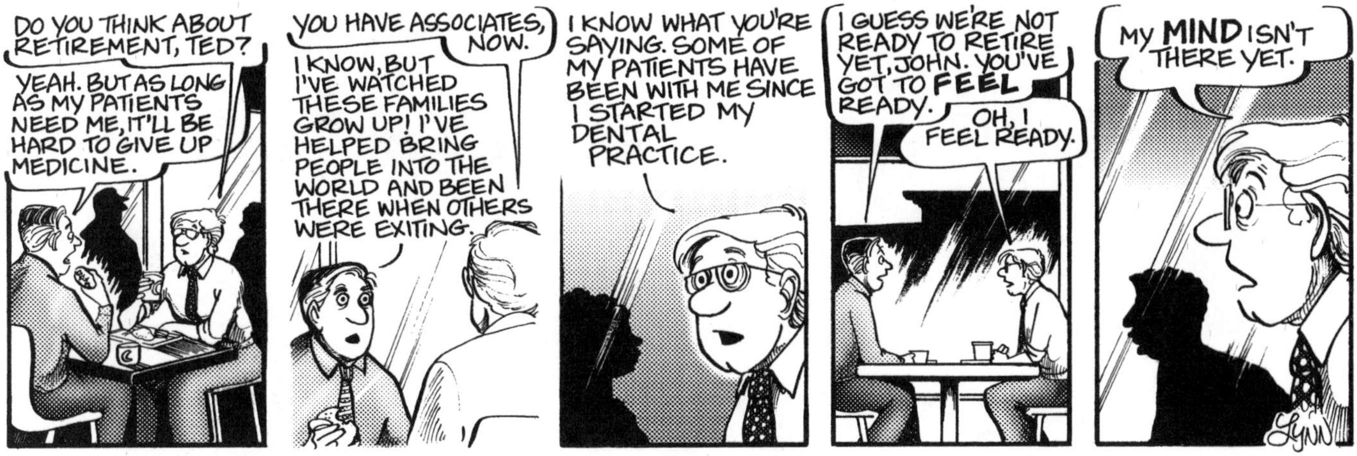
DO YOU THINK ABOUT RETIREMENT, TED?
YEAH. BUT AS LONG AS MY PATIENTS NEED ME, IT'LL BE HARD TO GIVE UP MEDICINE.
YOU HAVE ASSOCIATES, NOW.
I KNOW, BUT I'VE WATCHED THESE FAMILIES GROW UP! I'VE HELPED BRING PEOPLE INTO THE WORLD AND BEEN THERE WHEN OTHERS WERE EXITING.
I KNOW WHAT YOU'RE SAYING. SOME OF MY PATIENTS HAVE BEEN WITH ME SINCE I STARTED MY DENTAL PRACTICE.
I GUESS WE'RE NOT READY TO RETIRE YET, JOHN. YOU'VE GOT TO **FEEL** READY.
OH, I FEEL READY.
MY **MIND** ISN'T THERE YET.
LYNN

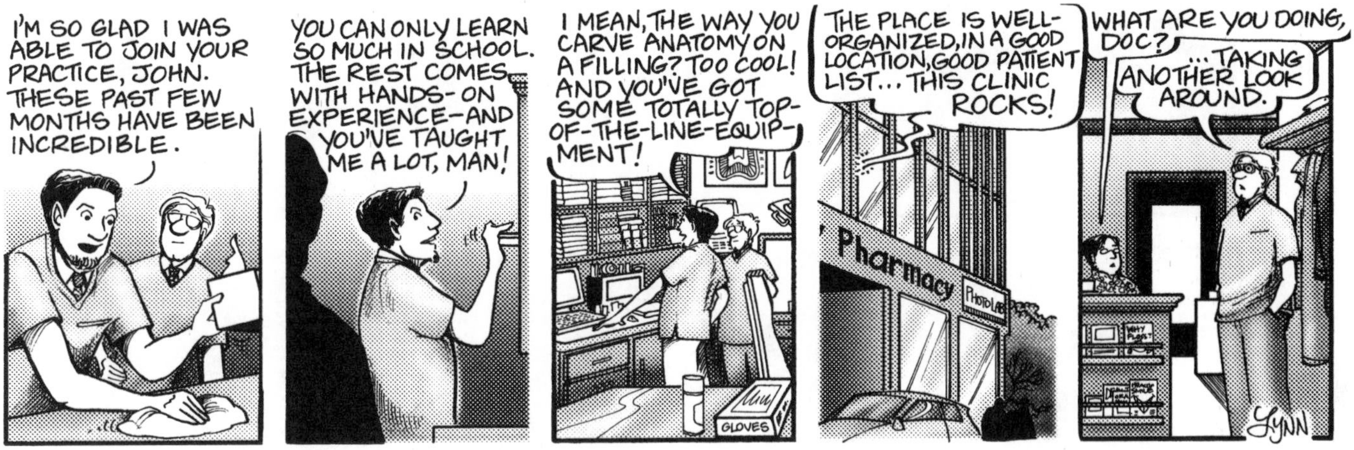
I'M SO GLAD I WAS ABLE TO JOIN YOUR PRACTICE, JOHN. THESE PAST FEW MONTHS HAVE BEEN INCREDIBLE.
YOU CAN ONLY LEARN SO MUCH IN SCHOOL. THE REST COMES WITH HANDS-ON EXPERIENCE—AND YOU'VE TAUGHT ME A LOT, MAN!
I MEAN, THE WAY YOU CARVE ANATOMY ON A FILLING? TOO COOL! AND YOU'VE GOT SOME TOTALLY TOP-OF-THE-LINE-EQUIPMENT!
GLOVES
THE PLACE IS WELL-ORGANIZED, IN A GOOD LOCATION, GOOD PATIENT LIST... THIS CLINIC ROCKS!
Pharmacy
PHOTO LAB
WHAT ARE YOU DOING, DOC?
...TAKING ANOTHER LOOK AROUND.
LYNN

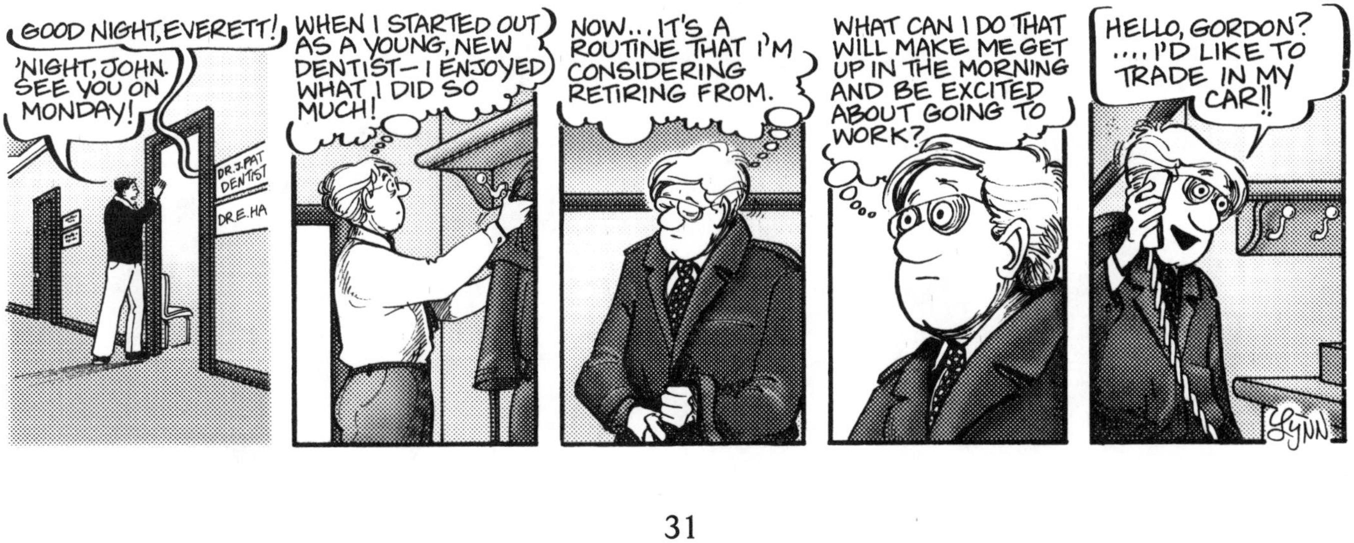
GOOD NIGHT, EVERETT!
'NIGHT, JOHN. SEE YOU ON MONDAY!
DR. J. PAT DENTIST
DR. E. HA
WHEN I STARTED OUT AS A YOUNG, NEW DENTIST— I ENJOYED WHAT I DID SO MUCH!
NOW... IT'S A ROUTINE THAT I'M CONSIDERING RETIRING FROM.
WHAT CAN I DO THAT WILL MAKE ME GET UP IN THE MORNING AND BE EXCITED ABOUT GOING TO WORK?
HELLO, GORDON? ..., I'D LIKE TO TRADE IN MY CAR!!
LYNN

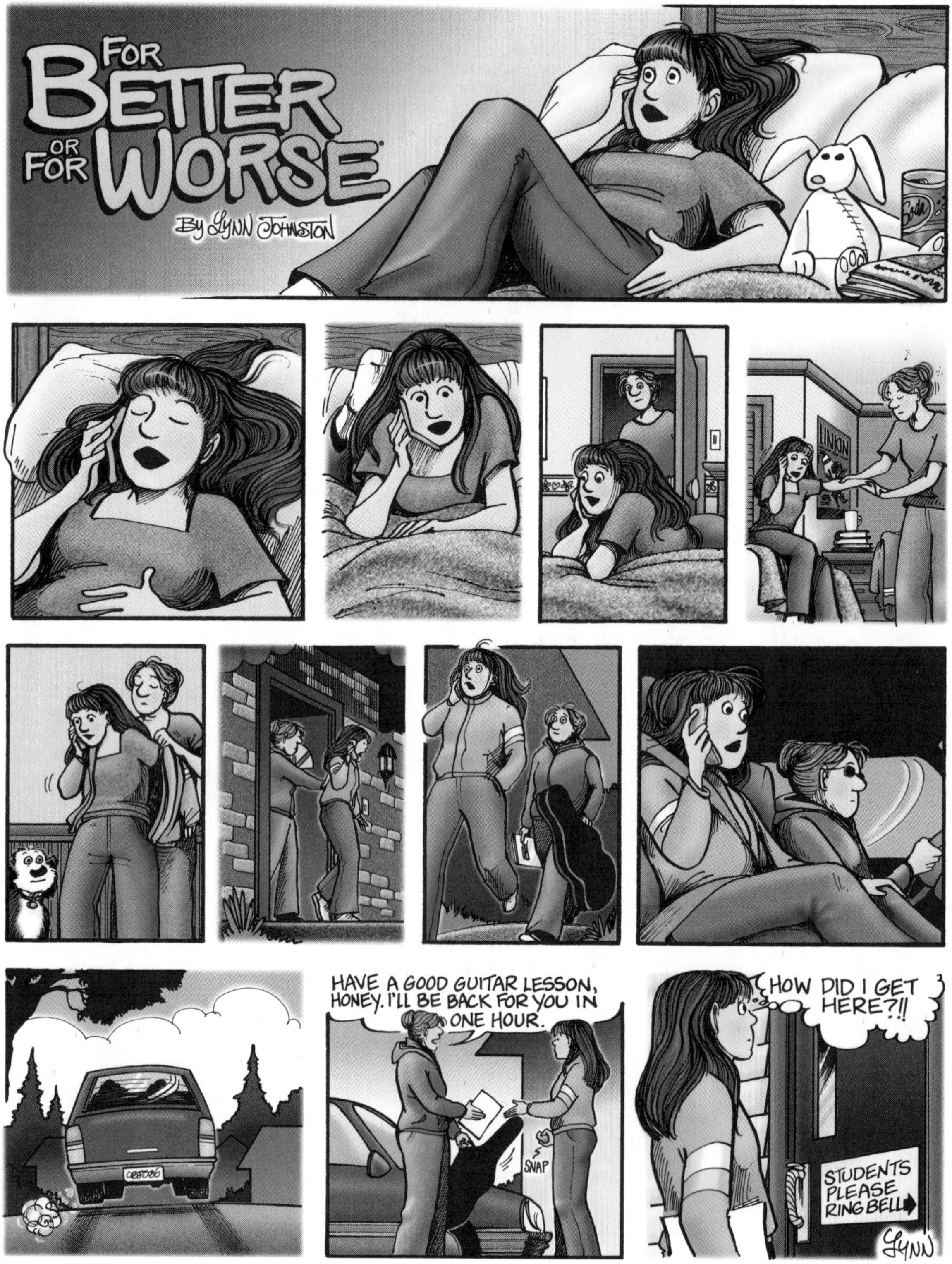
FOR BETTER OR FOR WORSE
BY LYNN JOHNSTON
LINKIN
HAVE A GOOD GUITAR LESSON, HONEY. I'LL BE BACK FOR YOU IN ONE HOUR.
SNAP
HOW DID I GET HERE?!!
STUDENTS PLEASE RING BELL
LYNN

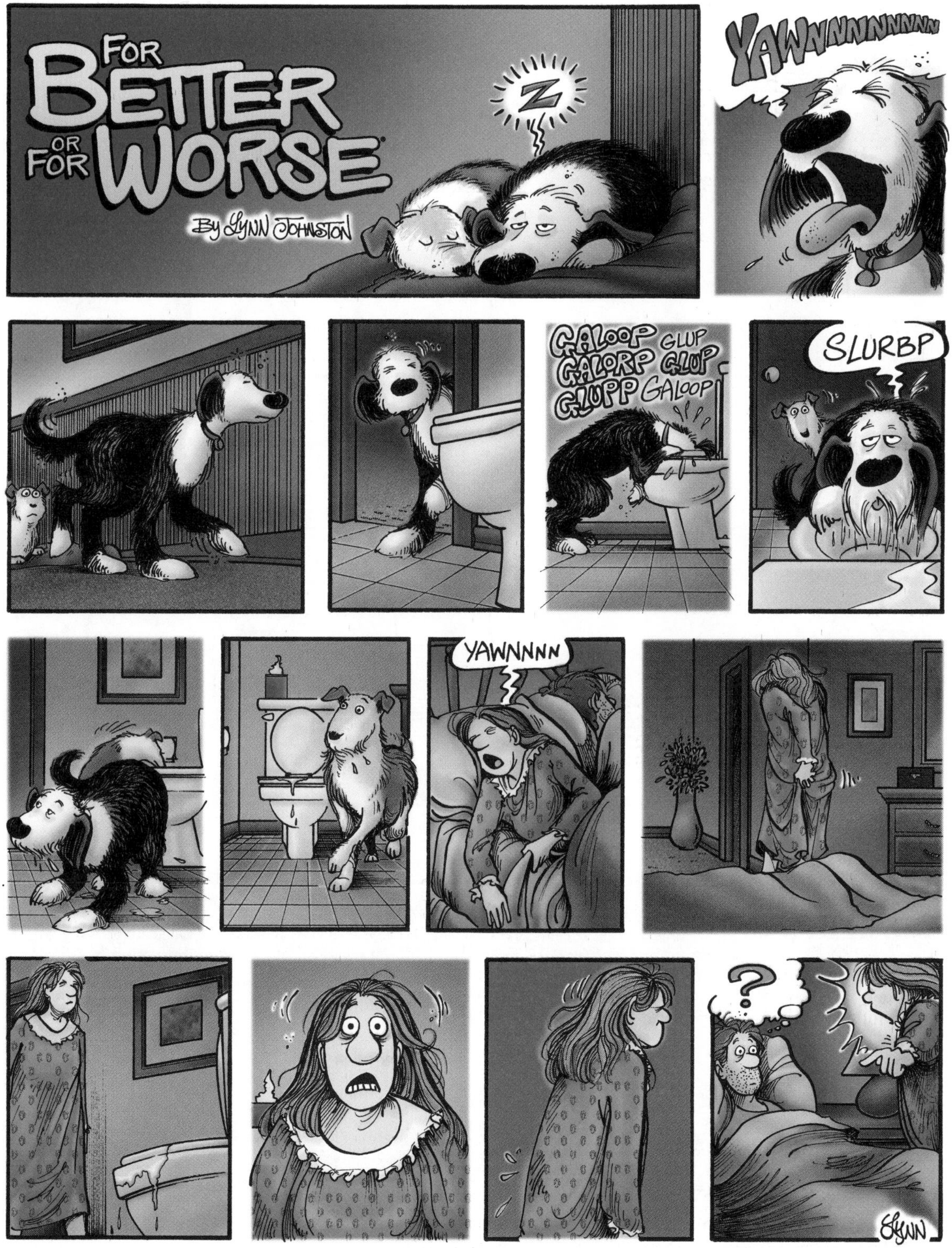
FOR BETTER OR FOR WORSE
BY LYNN JOHNSTON
Z
YAWNNNNNNNN
GALOOP GLUP
GALORP GLUP
GLUPP GALOOP
SLURBP
YAWNNNN
?
LYNN

YOU WANT TO TRADE IN YOUR CAR?!

YEAH.... I WAS THINKING ABOUT IT.

BUT, YOU LOVE THAT CAR! YOU SAID YOU'D ALWAYS WANTED A BUSHWHACKER CONVERTIBLE.

WELL.... UM...

IT'S NEVER BEEN TOO PRACTICAL FOR WINTER.

SO, WHAT DO YOU WANT TO GET?

A PAVO XS50 A.W.D.!!!

INTRODUCING THE PAVO 2005
LET'S TALK TURKEY!

YOU WANT TO BUY A PAVO XS50? .... JOHN, THIS CAR IS LESS PRACTICAL THAN YOUR BUSH-WHACKER!

ELLY, GORDON'S GOING TO GIVE ME SUCH A GOOD DEAL — I CAN HARDLY TURN IT DOWN!

BUT, YOU'RE RIGHT. TRADING IN THE CAR I HAVE ON A PAVO PROBABLY ISN'T THE BEST IDEA.

I'LL JUST BUY IT OUTRIGHT!

BIP BIP BIP

ANOTHER CAR? WE DON'T NEED 3 CARS!!

SURE WE DO. ELIZABETH WILL BE HOME SOON — AND, YOU DON'T WANT HER DRIVING A MOTOR-CYCLE AGAIN.

WE OWNED 3 CARS, REMEMBER? THE LITTLE BLUE ONE WE BOUGHT FOR THE KIDS TO DRIVE WAS ALWAYS PARKED SOMEWHERE. AFTER THEY MOVED OUT, IT WAS HARDLY DRIVEN AT ALL!

WE EVENTUALLY SOLD IT FOR NEXT TO NOTHING!

ELLY, A CAR IS A MEANS OF TRANSPORTATION. IT'S NEVER AN INVESTMENT. YOU EXPECT TO LOSE MONEY WHEN YOU SELL A CAR!

.... WHICH MEANS, YOU LOSE MONEY WHEN YOU BUY ONE.

INTRODUCING THE PAVO 2005
LET'S TALK TURKEY!

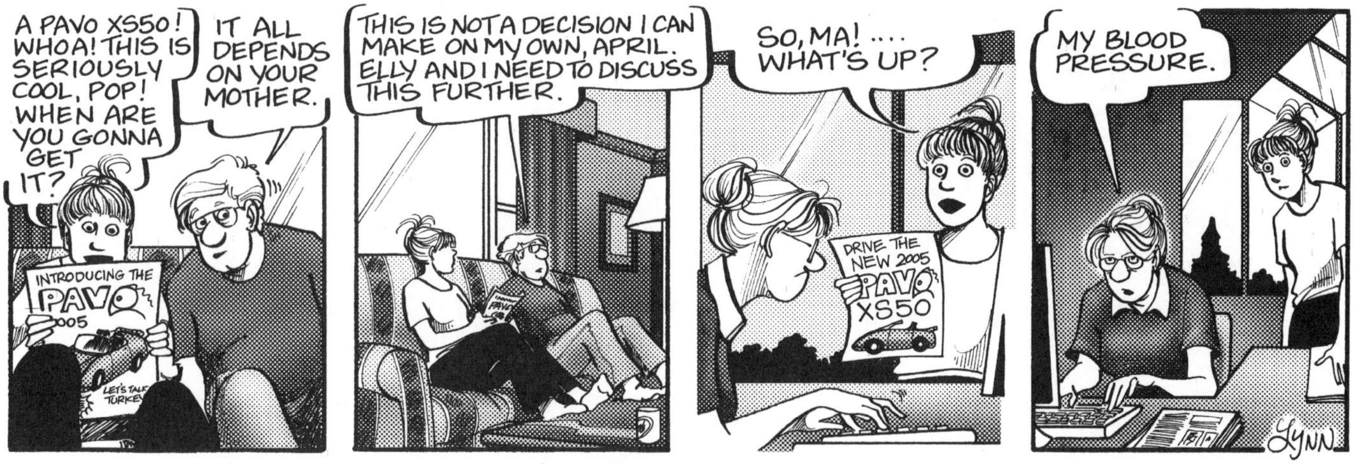
A PAVO XS50! WHOA! THIS IS SERIOUSLY COOL, POP! WHEN ARE YOU GONNA GET IT?
IT ALL DEPENDS ON YOUR MOTHER.
INTRODUCING THE PAVO 2005
THIS IS NOT A DECISION I CAN MAKE ON MY OWN, APRIL. ELLY AND I NEED TO DISCUSS THIS FURTHER.
SO, MA! .... WHAT'S UP?
DRIVE THE NEW 2005 PAVO XS50
MY BLOOD PRESSURE.
LYNN

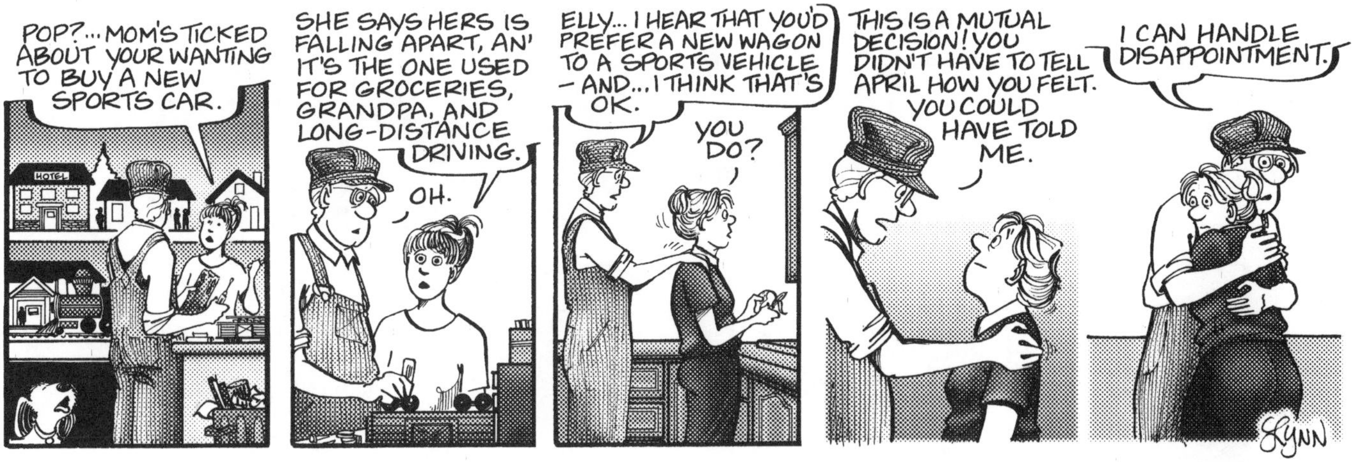
POP?... MOM'S TICKED ABOUT YOUR WANTING TO BUY A NEW SPORTS CAR.
HOTEL
SHE SAYS HERS IS FALLING APART, AN' IT'S THE ONE USED FOR GROCERIES, GRANDPA, AND LONG-DISTANCE DRIVING.
OH.
ELLY... I HEAR THAT YOU'D PREFER A NEW WAGON TO A SPORTS VEHICLE – AND... I THINK THAT'S OK.
YOU DO?
THIS IS A MUTUAL DECISION! YOU DIDN'T HAVE TO TELL APRIL HOW YOU FELT. YOU COULD HAVE TOLD ME.
I CAN HANDLE DISAPPOINTMENT.
LYNN

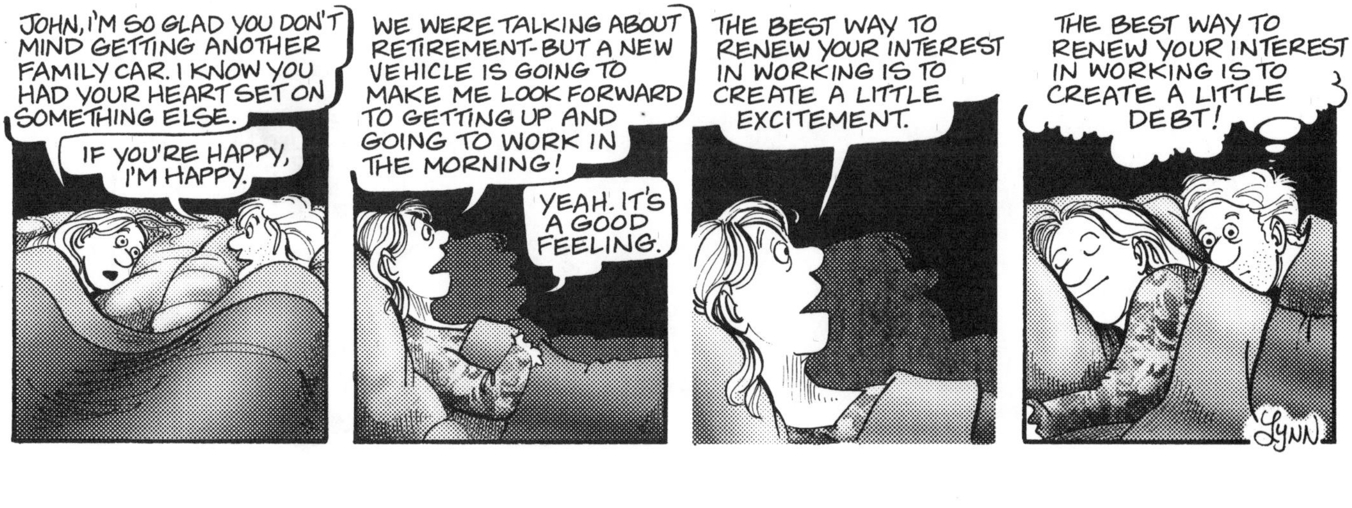
JOHN, I'M SO GLAD YOU DON'T MIND GETTING ANOTHER FAMILY CAR. I KNOW YOU HAD YOUR HEART SET ON SOMETHING ELSE.
IF YOU'RE HAPPY, I'M HAPPY.
WE WERE TALKING ABOUT RETIREMENT- BUT A NEW VEHICLE IS GOING TO MAKE ME LOOK FORWARD TO GETTING UP AND GOING TO WORK IN THE MORNING!
YEAH. IT'S A GOOD FEELING.
THE BEST WAY TO RENEW YOUR INTEREST IN WORKING IS TO CREATE A LITTLE EXCITEMENT.
THE BEST WAY TO RENEW YOUR INTEREST IN WORKING IS TO CREATE A LITTLE DEBT!
LYNN

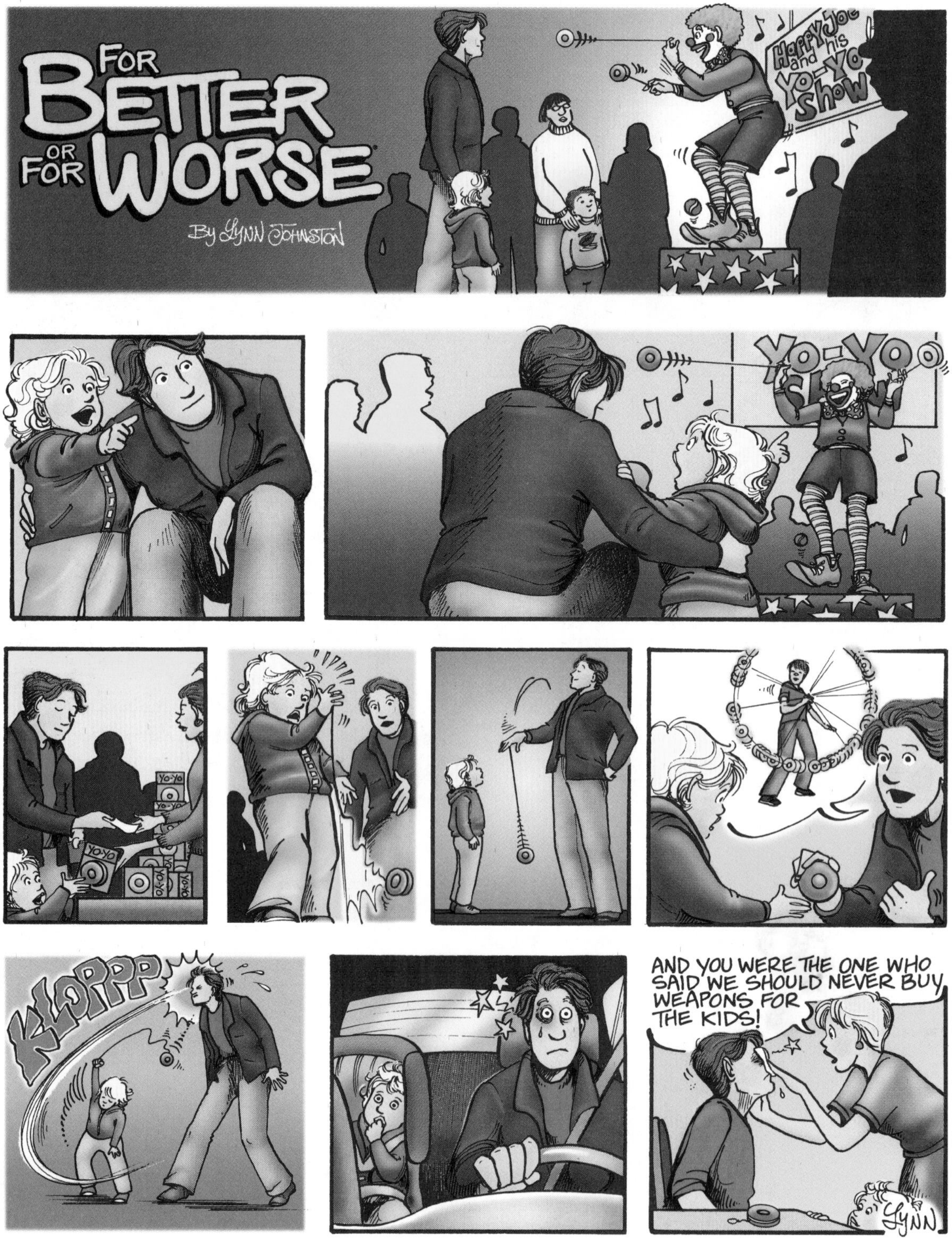
FOR BETTER OR FOR WORSE
By Lynn Johnston
Happy Joe and his Yo-Yo Show
YO-YO
YO-YO
KLOPPP
AND YOU WERE THE ONE WHO SAID WE SHOULD NEVER BUY WEAPONS FOR THE KIDS!
Lynn

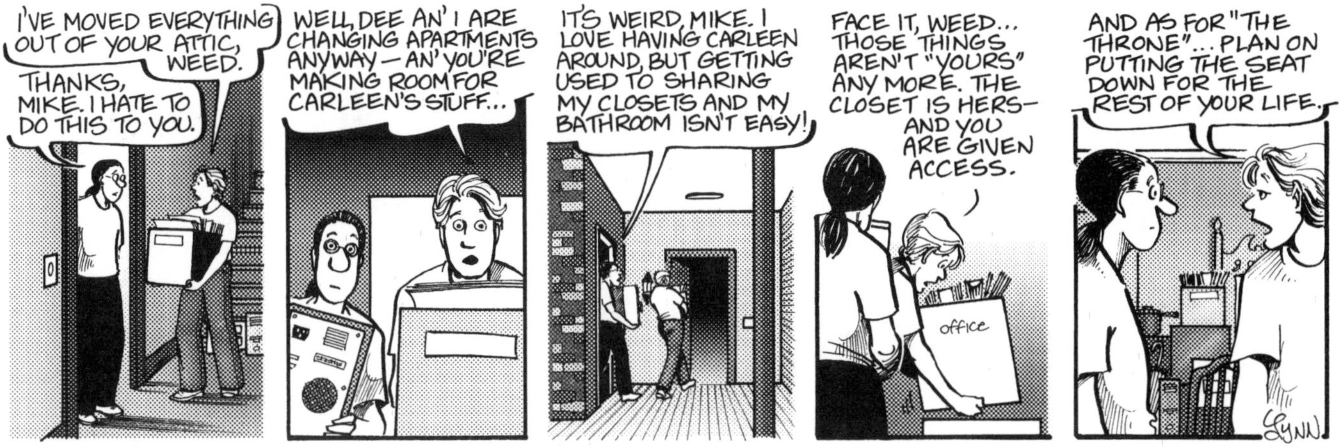
I'VE MOVED EVERYTHING OUT OF YOUR ATTIC, WEED.
THANKS, MIKE. I HATE TO DO THIS TO YOU.
WELL, DEE AN' I ARE CHANGING APARTMENTS ANYWAY — AN' YOU'RE MAKING ROOM FOR CARLEEN'S STUFF...
IT'S WEIRD, MIKE. I LOVE HAVING CARLEEN AROUND, BUT GETTING USED TO SHARING MY CLOSETS AND MY BATHROOM ISN'T EASY!
FACE IT, WEED... THOSE THINGS AREN'T "YOURS" ANY MORE. THE CLOSET IS HERS— AND YOU ARE GIVEN ACCESS.
office
AND AS FOR "THE THRONE"... PLAN ON PUTTING THE SEAT DOWN FOR THE REST OF YOUR LIFE.
LYNN

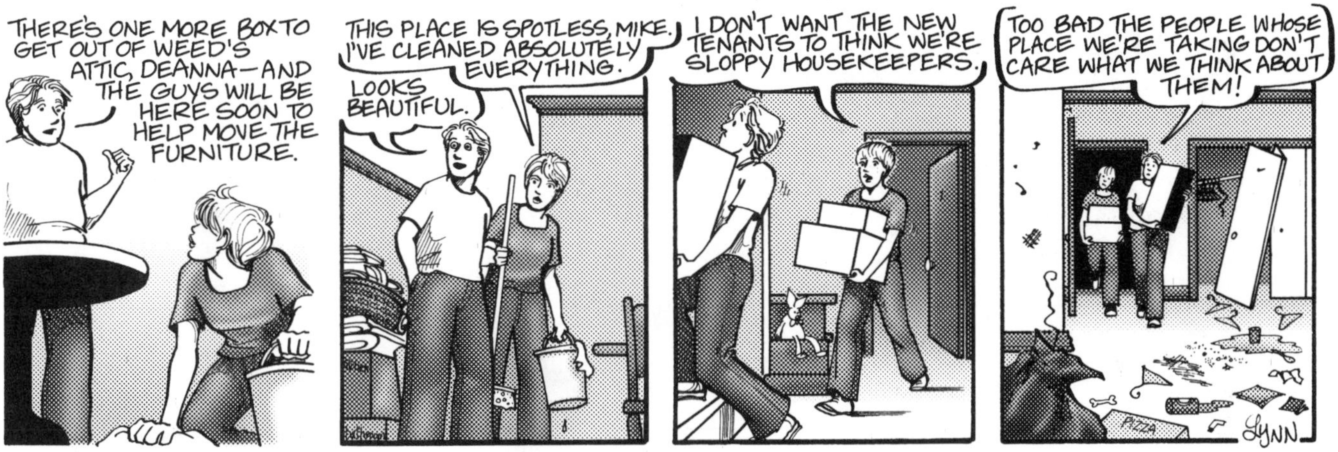
THERE'S ONE MORE BOX TO GET OUT OF WEED'S ATTIC, DEANNA—AND THE GUYS WILL BE HERE SOON TO HELP MOVE THE FURNITURE.
THIS PLACE IS SPOTLESS, MIKE. I'VE CLEANED ABSOLUTELY EVERYTHING.
LOOKS BEAUTIFUL.
I DON'T WANT THE NEW TENANTS TO THINK WE'RE SLOPPY HOUSEKEEPERS.
TOO BAD THE PEOPLE WHOSE PLACE WE'RE TAKING DON'T CARE WHAT WE THINK ABOUT THEM!
PIZZA
LYNN

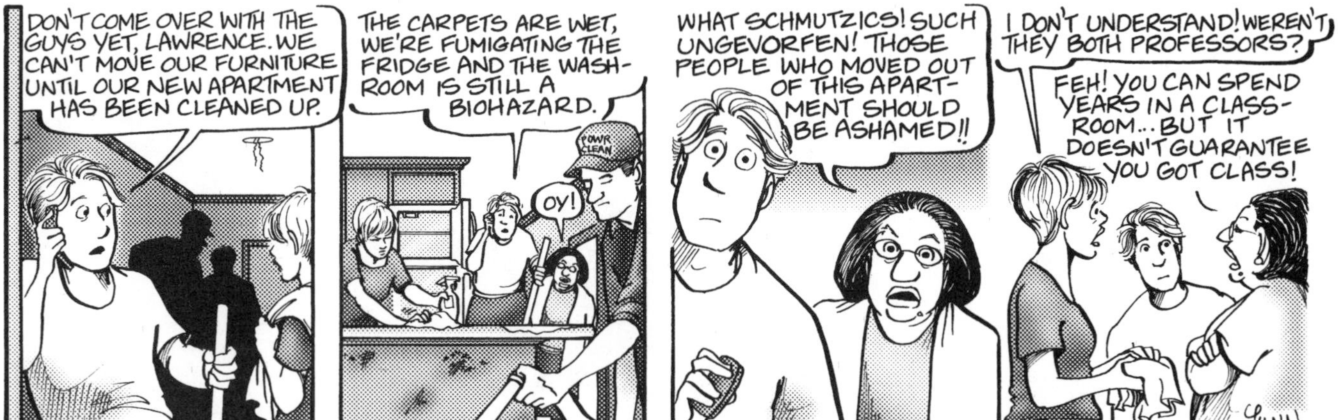
DON'T COME OVER WITH THE GUYS YET, LAWRENCE. WE CAN'T MOVE OUR FURNITURE UNTIL OUR NEW APARTMENT HAS BEEN CLEANED UP.
THE CARPETS ARE WET, WE'RE FUMIGATING THE FRIDGE AND THE WASH-ROOM IS STILL A BIOHAZARD.
POWR CLEAN
OY!
WHAT SCHMUTZICS! SUCH UNGEVORFEN! THOSE PEOPLE WHO MOVED OUT OF THIS APART-MENT SHOULD BE ASHAMED!!
I DON'T UNDERSTAND! WEREN'T THEY BOTH PROFESSORS?
FEH! YOU CAN SPEND YEARS IN A CLASS-ROOM... BUT IT DOESN'T GUARANTEE YOU GOT CLASS!
LYNN

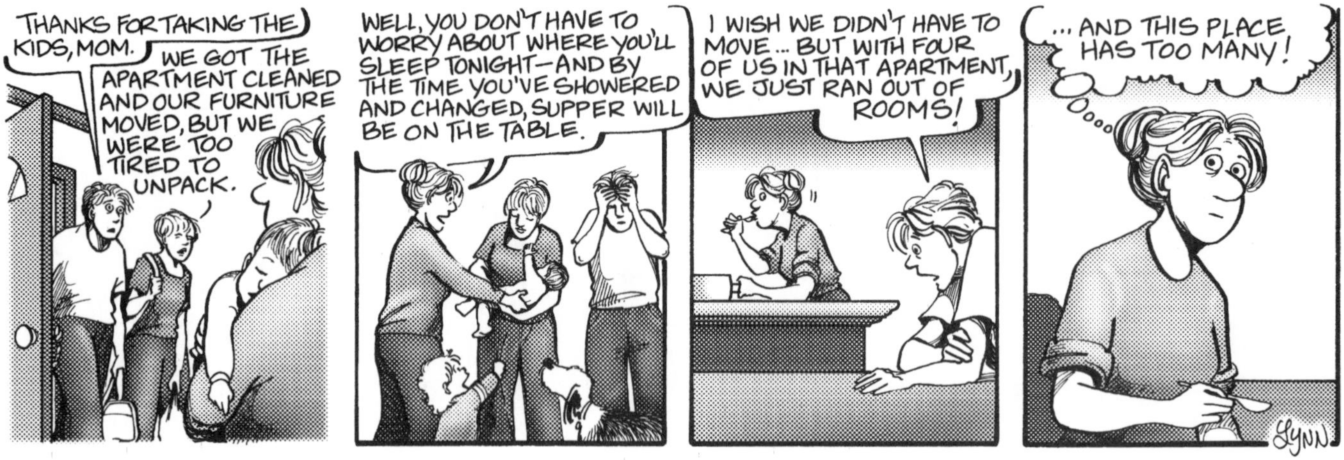
THANKS FOR TAKING THE KIDS, MOM.
WE GOT THE APARTMENT CLEANED AND OUR FURNITURE MOVED, BUT WE WERE TOO TIRED TO UNPACK.
WELL, YOU DON'T HAVE TO WORRY ABOUT WHERE YOU'LL SLEEP TONIGHT—AND BY THE TIME YOU'VE SHOWERED AND CHANGED, SUPPER WILL BE ON THE TABLE.
I WISH WE DIDN'T HAVE TO MOVE... BUT WITH FOUR OF US IN THAT APARTMENT, WE JUST RAN OUT OF ROOMS!
... AND THIS PLACE HAS TOO MANY!
LYNN

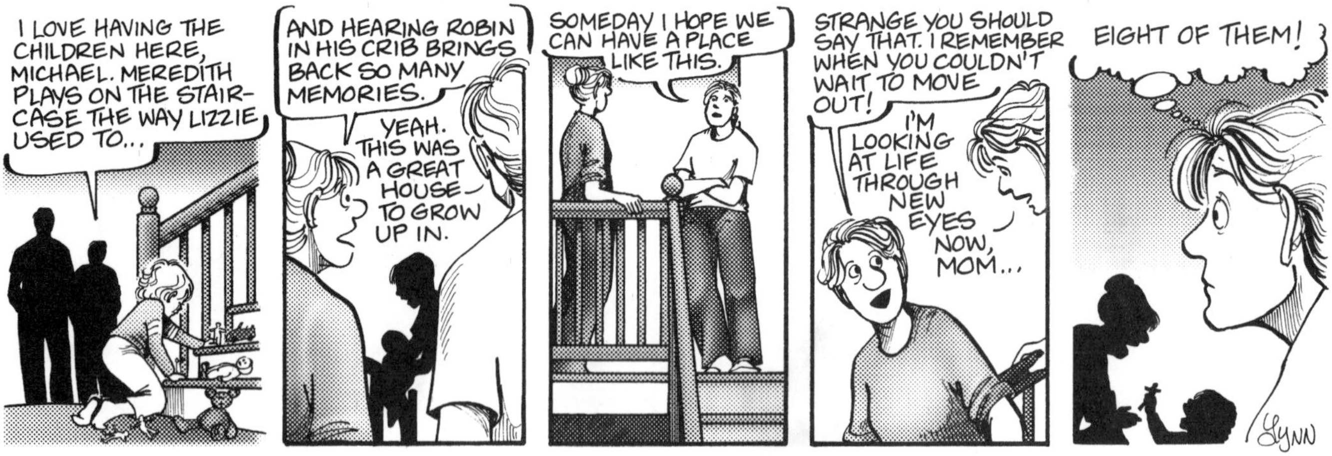
I LOVE HAVING THE CHILDREN HERE, MICHAEL. MEREDITH PLAYS ON THE STAIRCASE THE WAY LIZZIE USED TO...
AND HEARING ROBIN IN HIS CRIB BRINGS BACK SO MANY MEMORIES.
YEAH. THIS WAS A GREAT HOUSE TO GROW UP IN.
SOMEDAY I HOPE WE CAN HAVE A PLACE LIKE THIS.
STRANGE YOU SHOULD SAY THAT. I REMEMBER WHEN YOU COULDN'T WAIT TO MOVE OUT!
I'M LOOKING AT LIFE THROUGH NEW EYES NOW, MOM...
EIGHT OF THEM!
LYNN

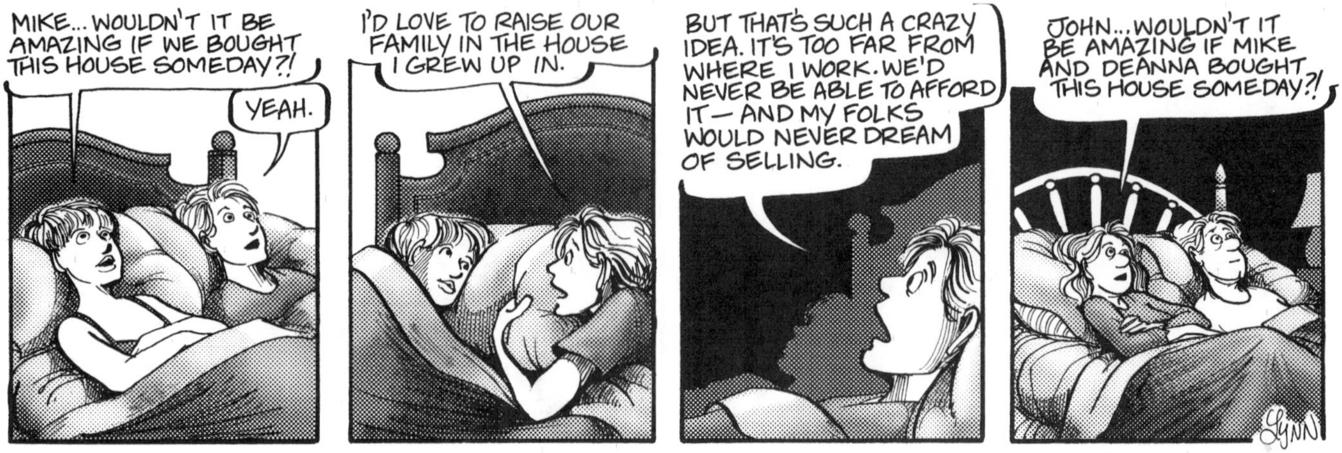
MIKE... WOULDN'T IT BE AMAZING IF WE BOUGHT THIS HOUSE SOMEDAY?!
YEAH.
I'D LOVE TO RAISE OUR FAMILY IN THE HOUSE I GREW UP IN.
BUT THAT'S SUCH A CRAZY IDEA. IT'S TOO FAR FROM WHERE I WORK. WE'D NEVER BE ABLE TO AFFORD IT—AND MY FOLKS WOULD NEVER DREAM OF SELLING.
JOHN... WOULDN'T IT BE AMAZING IF MIKE AND DEANNA BOUGHT THIS HOUSE SOMEDAY?!
LYNN

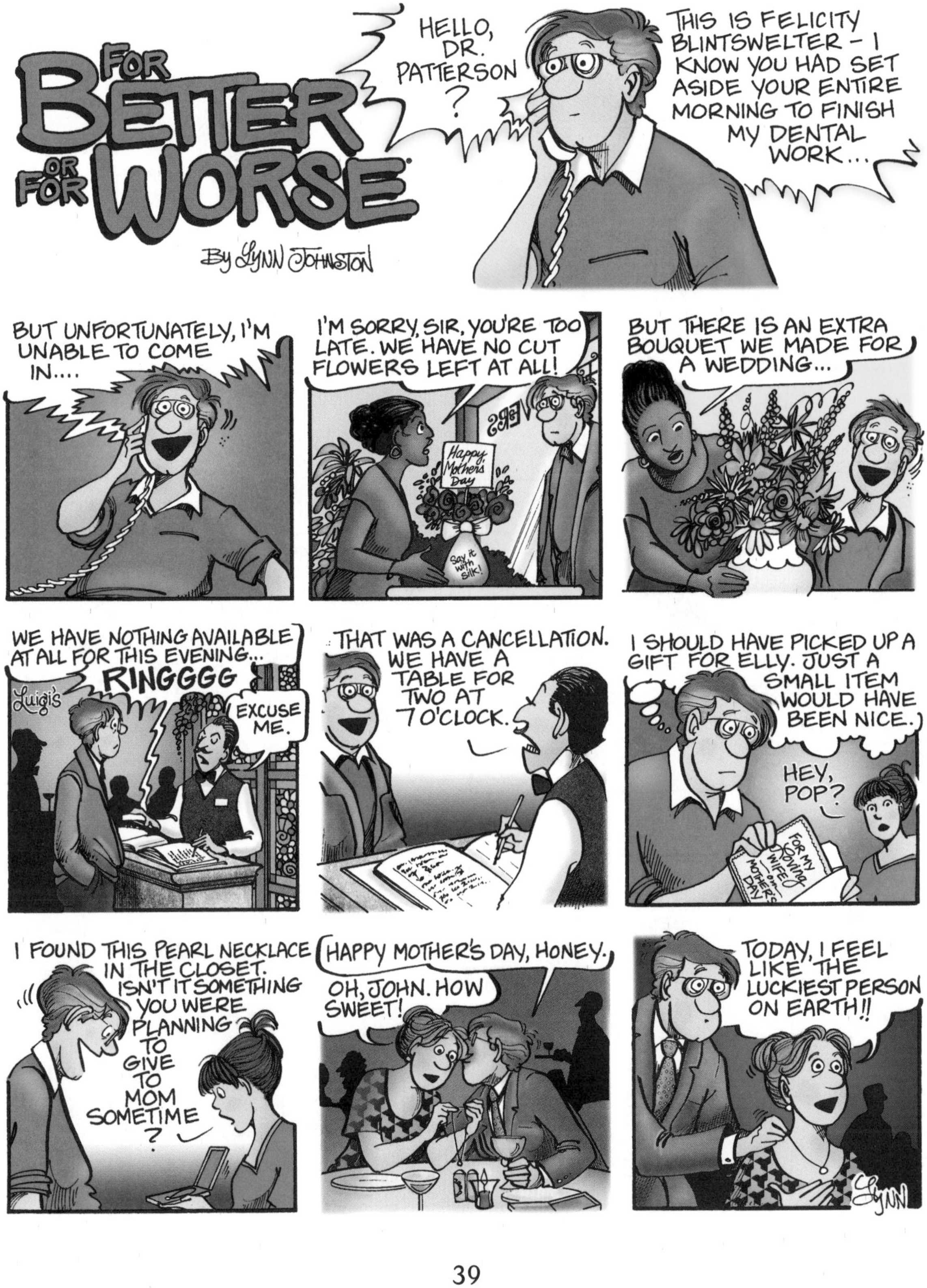
FOR BETTER OR FOR WORSE
BY LYNN JOHNSTON
HELLO, DR. PATTERSON?
THIS IS FELICITY BLINTSWELTER - I KNOW YOU HAD SET ASIDE YOUR ENTIRE MORNING TO FINISH MY DENTAL WORK...
BUT UNFORTUNATELY, I'M UNABLE TO COME IN....
I'M SORRY, SIR, YOU'RE TOO LATE. WE HAVE NO CUT FLOWERS LEFT AT ALL!
Happy Mother's Day
Say it with Silk!
BUT THERE IS AN EXTRA BOUQUET WE MADE FOR A WEDDING...
WE HAVE NOTHING AVAILABLE AT ALL FOR THIS EVENING...
Luigi's
RINGGGG
EXCUSE ME.
THAT WAS A CANCELLATION. WE HAVE A TABLE FOR TWO AT 7 O'CLOCK.
I SHOULD HAVE PICKED UP A GIFT FOR ELLY. JUST A SMALL ITEM WOULD HAVE BEEN NICE.
HEY, POP?
FOR MY Loving WIFE on MOTHER'S DAY
I FOUND THIS PEARL NECKLACE IN THE CLOSET. ISN'T IT SOMETHING YOU WERE PLANNING TO GIVE TO MOM SOMETIME?
HAPPY MOTHER'S DAY, HONEY.
OH, JOHN. HOW SWEET!
TODAY, I FEEL LIKE THE LUCKIEST PERSON ON EARTH!!
Lynn

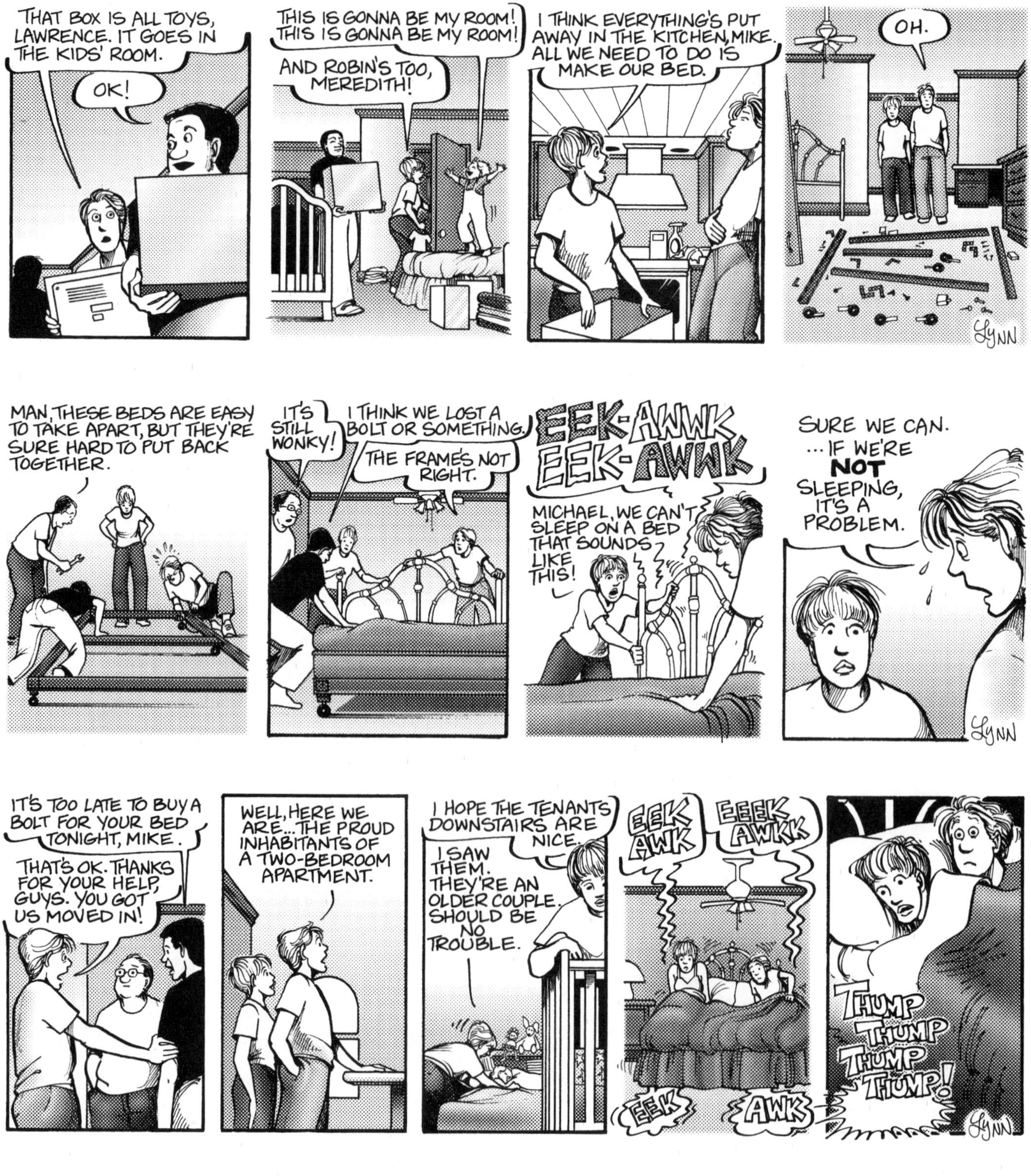
THAT BOX IS ALL TOYS, LAWRENCE. IT GOES IN THE KIDS' ROOM.
OK!
THIS IS GONNA BE MY ROOM! THIS IS GONNA BE MY ROOM!
AND ROBIN'S TOO, MEREDITH!
I THINK EVERYTHING'S PUT AWAY IN THE KITCHEN, MIKE. ALL WE NEED TO DO IS MAKE OUR BED.
OH.
LYNN
MAN, THESE BEDS ARE EASY TO TAKE APART, BUT THEY'RE SURE HARD TO PUT BACK TOGETHER.
IT'S STILL WONKY!
I THINK WE LOST A BOLT OR SOMETHING.
THE FRAME'S NOT RIGHT.
EEK-AWWK EEK-AWWK
MICHAEL, WE CAN'T SLEEP ON A BED THAT SOUNDS LIKE THIS!
SURE WE CAN. ...IF WE'RE NOT SLEEPING, IT'S A PROBLEM.
LYNN
IT'S TOO LATE TO BUY A BOLT FOR YOUR BED TONIGHT, MIKE.
THAT'S OK. THANKS FOR YOUR HELP, GUYS. YOU GOT US MOVED IN!
WELL, HERE WE ARE... THE PROUD INHABITANTS OF A TWO-BEDROOM APARTMENT.
I HOPE THE TENANTS DOWNSTAIRS ARE NICE.
I SAW THEM. THEY'RE AN OLDER COUPLE. SHOULD BE NO TROUBLE.
EEK AWK
EEEK AWKK
EEK
AWK
THUMP THUMP THUMP THUMP!
LYNN

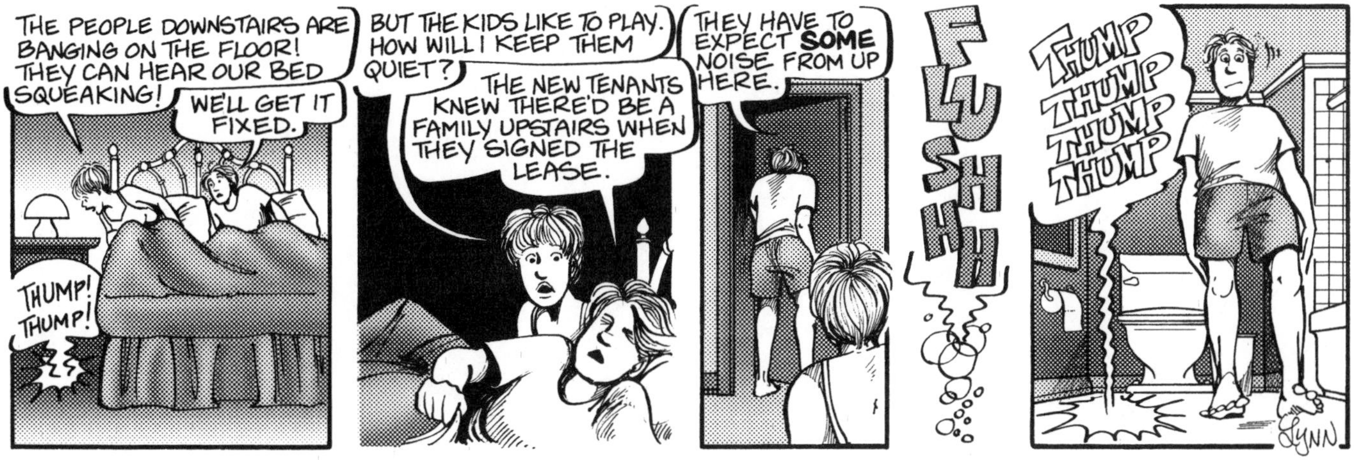
THE PEOPLE DOWNSTAIRS ARE BANGING ON THE FLOOR! THEY CAN HEAR OUR BED SQUEAKING!
WE'LL GET IT FIXED.
THUMP! THUMP!
BUT THE KIDS LIKE TO PLAY. HOW WILL I KEEP THEM QUIET?
THE NEW TENANTS KNEW THERE'D BE A FAMILY UPSTAIRS WHEN THEY SIGNED THE LEASE.
THEY HAVE TO EXPECT **SOME** NOISE FROM UP HERE.
FLUSHHH
THUMP THUMP THUMP THUMP
LYNN

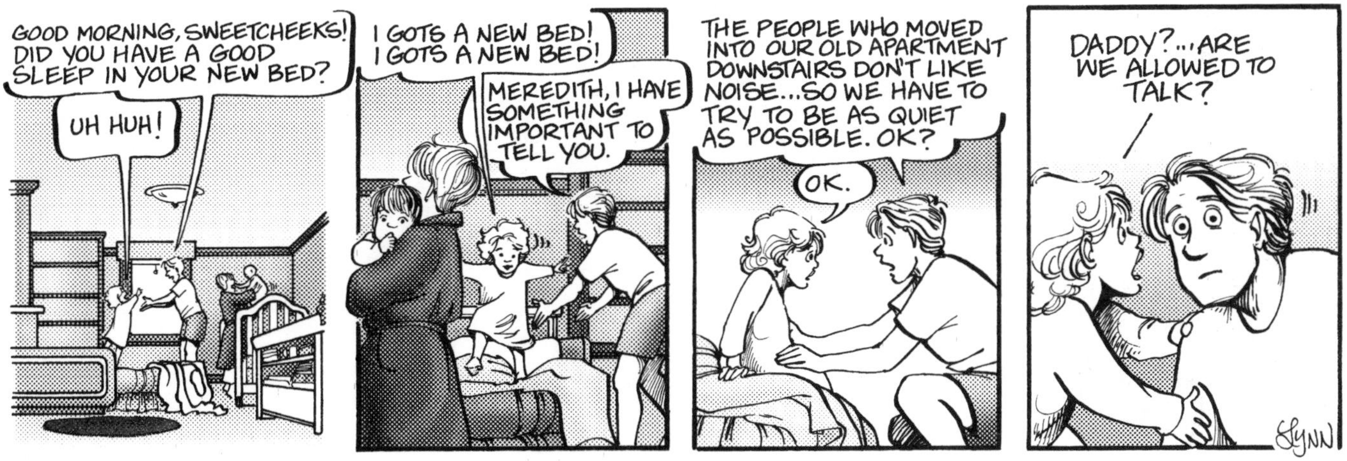
GOOD MORNING, SWEETCHEEKS! DID YOU HAVE A GOOD SLEEP IN YOUR NEW BED?
UH HUH!
I GOTS A NEW BED! I GOTS A NEW BED!
MEREDITH, I HAVE SOMETHING IMPORTANT TO TELL YOU.
THE PEOPLE WHO MOVED INTO OUR OLD APARTMENT DOWNSTAIRS DON'T LIKE NOISE...SO WE HAVE TO TRY TO BE AS QUIET AS POSSIBLE. OK?
OK.
DADDY?...ARE WE ALLOWED TO TALK?
LYNN

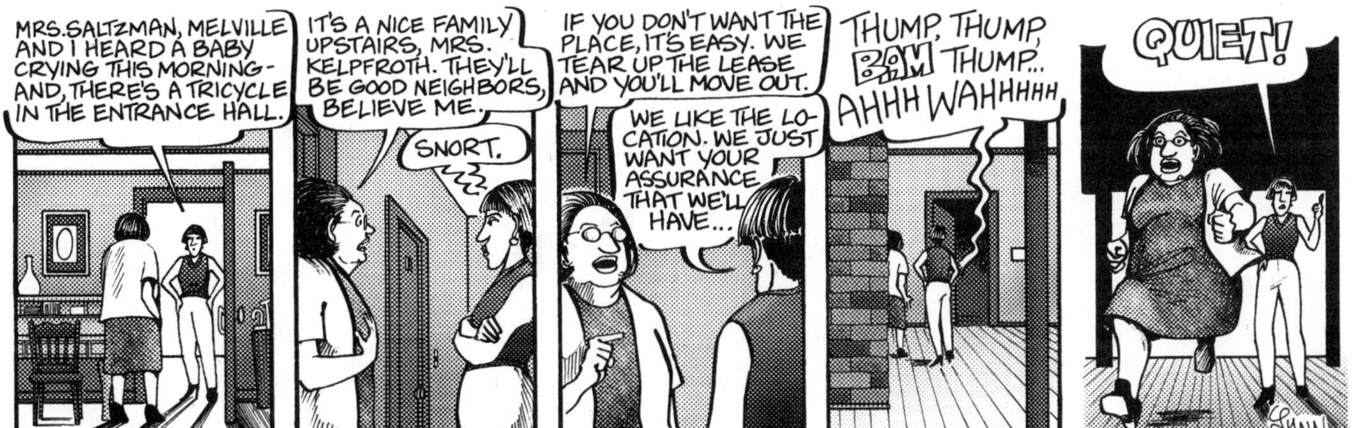
MRS. SALTZMAN, MELVILLE AND I HEARD A BABY CRYING THIS MORNING - AND, THERE'S A TRICYCLE IN THE ENTRANCE HALL.
IT'S A NICE FAMILY UPSTAIRS, MRS. KELPFROTH. THEY'LL BE GOOD NEIGHBORS, BELIEVE ME.
SNORT.
IF YOU DON'T WANT THE PLACE, IT'S EASY. WE TEAR UP THE LEASE AND YOU'LL MOVE OUT.
WE LIKE THE LOCATION. WE JUST WANT YOUR ASSURANCE THAT WE'LL HAVE...
THUMP, THUMP, BAM THUMP... AHHH WAHHHHH
QUIET!
LYNN

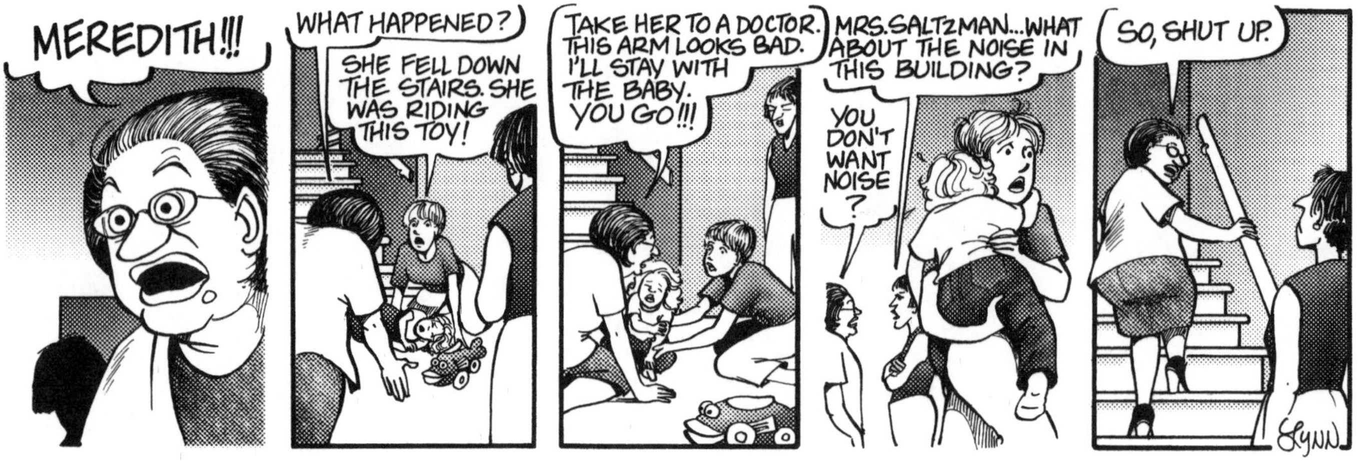
MEREDITH!!!
WHAT HAPPENED?
SHE FELL DOWN THE STAIRS. SHE WAS RIDING THIS TOY!
TAKE HER TO A DOCTOR. THIS ARM LOOKS BAD. I'LL STAY WITH THE BABY. YOU GO!!!
MRS. SALTZMAN...WHAT ABOUT THE NOISE IN THIS BUILDING?
YOU DON'T WANT NOISE?
SO, SHUT UP.
LYNN

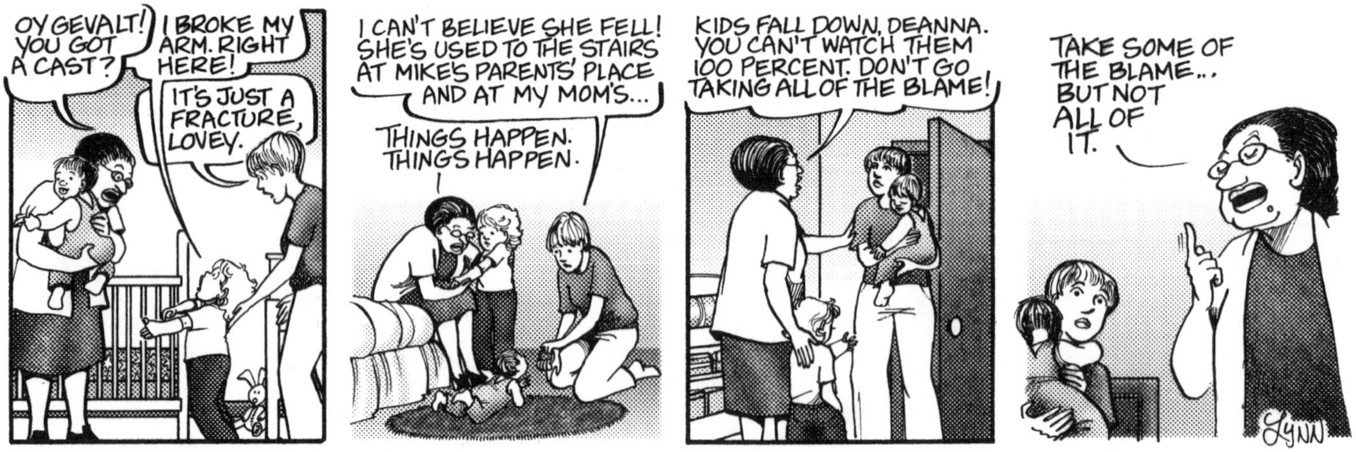
OY GEVALT! YOU GOT A CAST?
I BROKE MY ARM. RIGHT HERE!
IT'S JUST A FRACTURE, LOVEY.
I CAN'T BELIEVE SHE FELL! SHE'S USED TO THE STAIRS AT MIKE'S PARENTS' PLACE AND AT MY MOM'S...
THINGS HAPPEN. THINGS HAPPEN.
KIDS FALL DOWN, DEANNA. YOU CAN'T WATCH THEM 100 PERCENT. DON'T GO TAKING ALL OF THE BLAME!
TAKE SOME OF THE BLAME... BUT NOT ALL OF IT.
LYNN

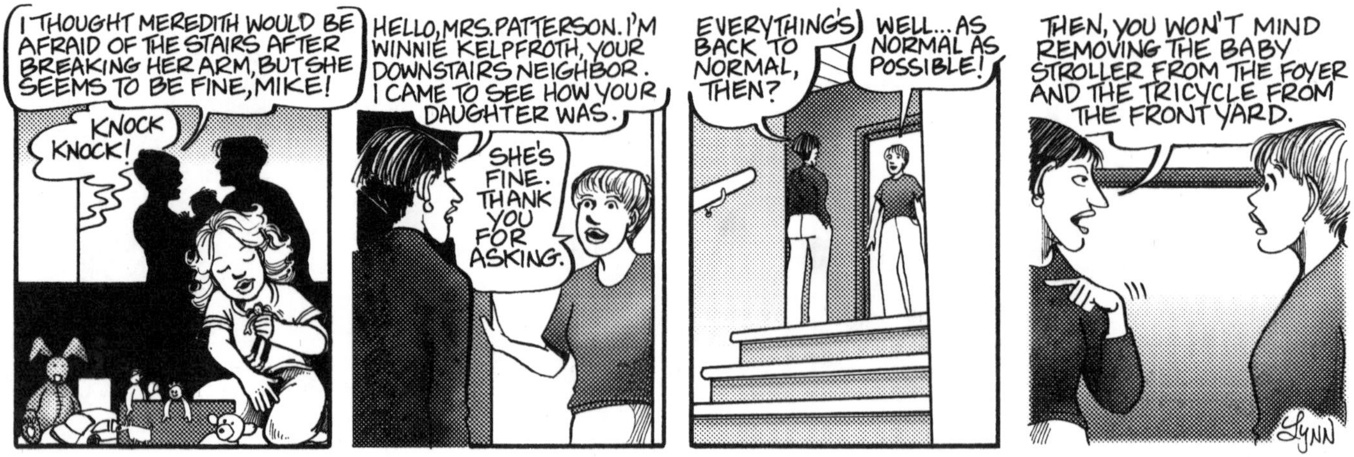
I THOUGHT MEREDITH WOULD BE AFRAID OF THE STAIRS AFTER BREAKING HER ARM, BUT SHE SEEMS TO BE FINE, MIKE!
KNOCK KNOCK!
HELLO, MRS. PATTERSON. I'M WINNIE KELPFROTH, YOUR DOWNSTAIRS NEIGHBOR. I CAME TO SEE HOW YOUR DAUGHTER WAS.
SHE'S FINE. THANK YOU FOR ASKING.
EVERYTHING'S BACK TO NORMAL, THEN?
WELL... AS NORMAL AS POSSIBLE!
THEN, YOU WON'T MIND REMOVING THE BABY STROLLER FROM THE FOYER AND THE TRICYCLE FROM THE FRONT YARD.
LYNN

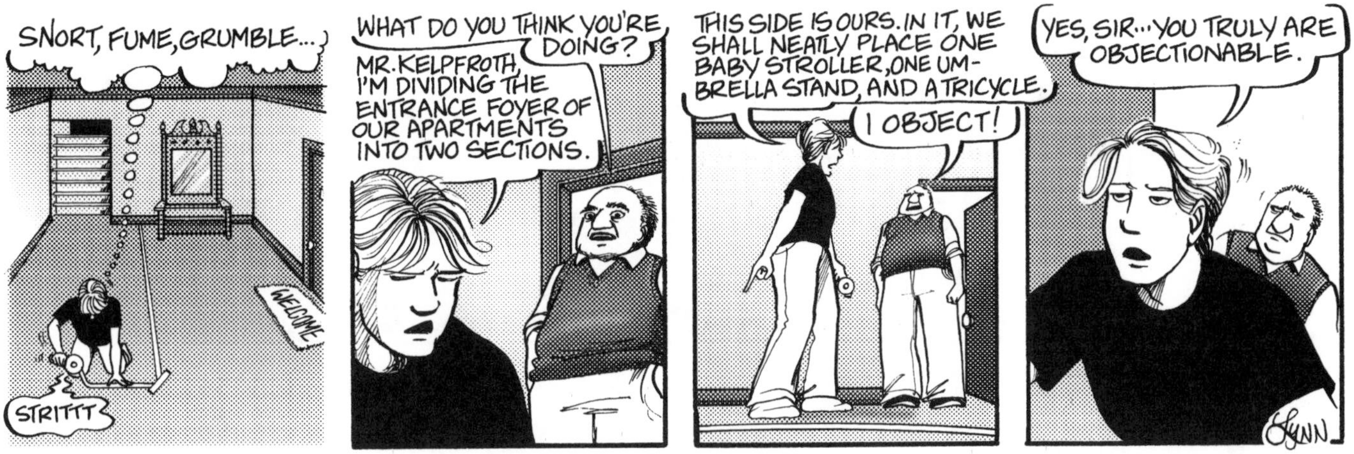
SNORT, FUME, GRUMBLE...
STRITTT
WELCOME
WHAT DO YOU THINK YOU'RE DOING?
MR. KELPFROTH, I'M DIVIDING THE ENTRANCE FOYER OF OUR APARTMENTS INTO TWO SECTIONS.
THIS SIDE IS OURS. IN IT, WE SHALL NEATLY PLACE ONE BABY STROLLER, ONE UMBRELLA STAND, AND A TRICYCLE.
I OBJECT!
YES, SIR... YOU TRULY ARE OBJECTIONABLE.
LYNN

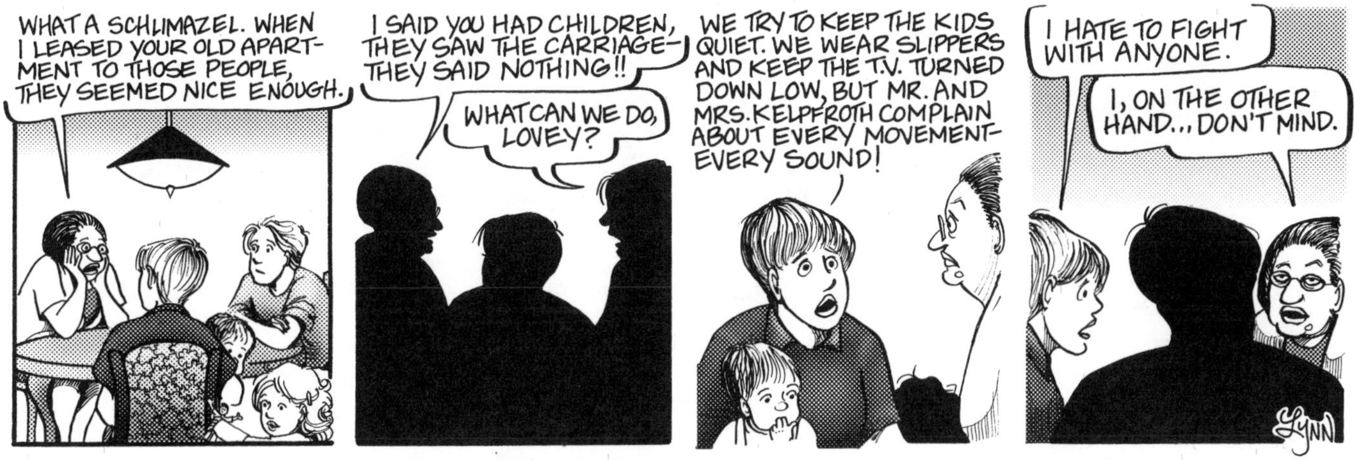
WHAT A SCHLIMAZEL. WHEN I LEASED YOUR OLD APARTMENT TO THOSE PEOPLE, THEY SEEMED NICE ENOUGH.
I SAID YOU HAD CHILDREN, THEY SAW THE CARRIAGE- THEY SAID NOTHING!!
WHAT CAN WE DO, LOVEY?
WE TRY TO KEEP THE KIDS QUIET. WE WEAR SLIPPERS AND KEEP THE T.V. TURNED DOWN LOW, BUT MR. AND MRS. KELPFROTH COMPLAIN ABOUT EVERY MOVEMENT- EVERY SOUND!
I HATE TO FIGHT WITH ANYONE.
I, ON THE OTHER HAND... DON'T MIND.
LYNN

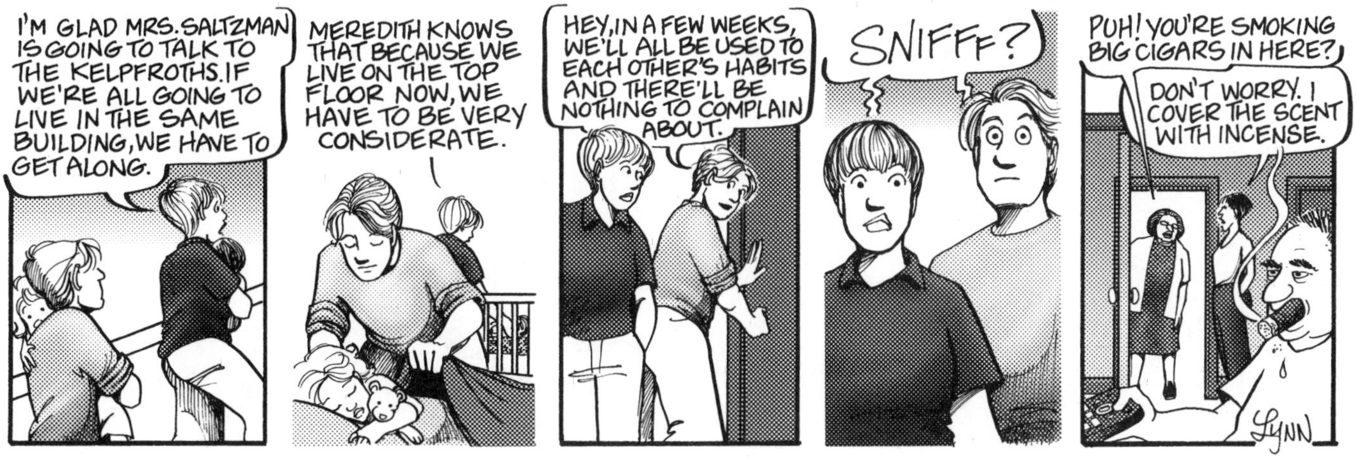
I'M GLAD MRS. SALTZMAN IS GOING TO TALK TO THE KELPFROTHS. IF WE'RE ALL GOING TO LIVE IN THE SAME BUILDING, WE HAVE TO GET ALONG.
MEREDITH KNOWS THAT BECAUSE WE LIVE ON THE TOP FLOOR NOW, WE HAVE TO BE VERY CONSIDERATE.
HEY, IN A FEW WEEKS, WE'LL ALL BE USED TO EACH OTHER'S HABITS AND THERE'LL BE NOTHING TO COMPLAIN ABOUT.
SNIFFF?
PUH! YOU'RE SMOKING BIG CIGARS IN HERE?
DON'T WORRY. I COVER THE SCENT WITH INCENSE.
LYNN

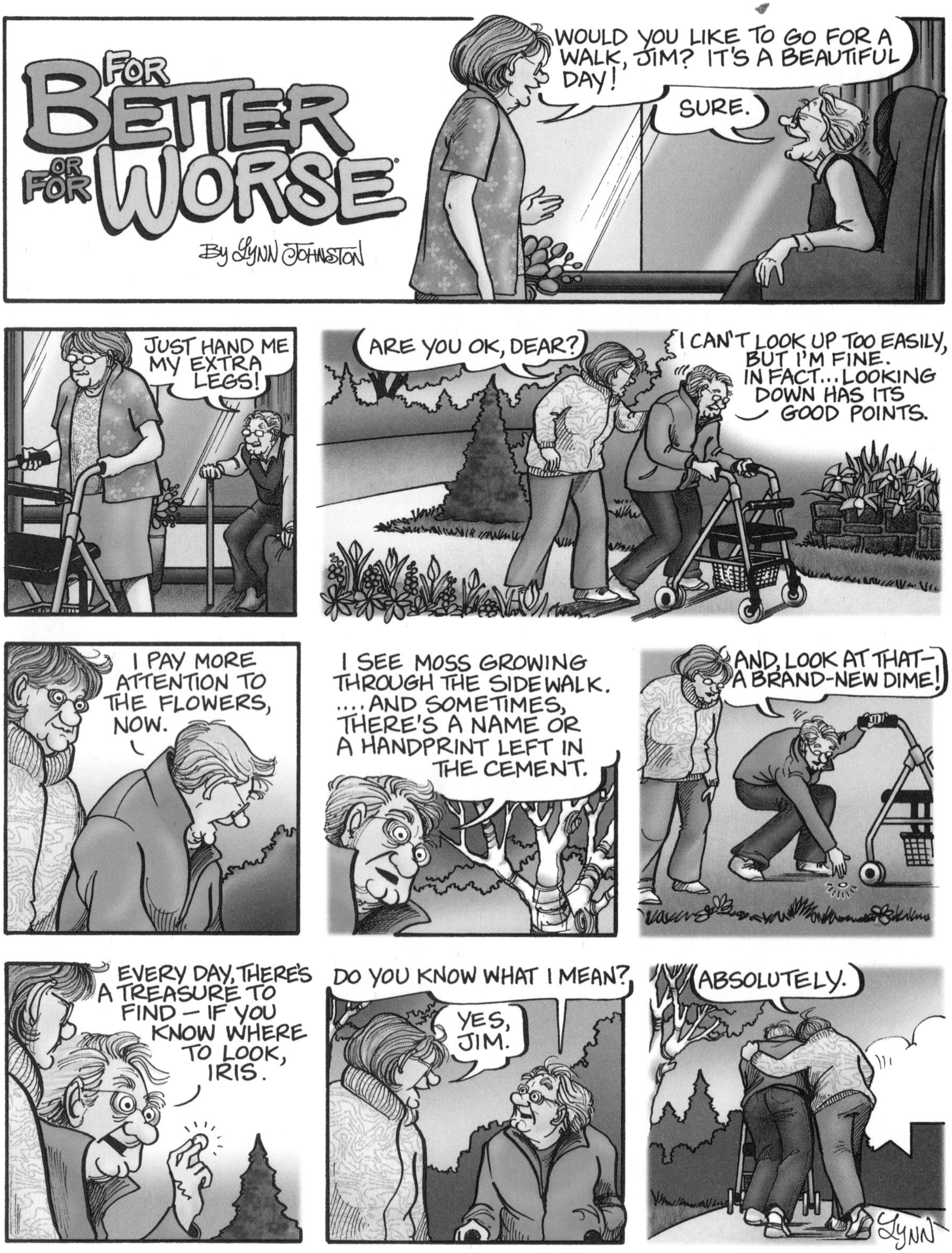
FOR BETTER OR FOR WORSE
BY LYNN JOHNSTON
WOULD YOU LIKE TO GO FOR A WALK, JIM? IT'S A BEAUTIFUL DAY!
SURE.
JUST HAND ME MY EXTRA LEGS!
ARE YOU OK, DEAR?
I CAN'T LOOK UP TOO EASILY, BUT I'M FINE. IN FACT... LOOKING DOWN HAS ITS GOOD POINTS.
I PAY MORE ATTENTION TO THE FLOWERS, NOW.
I SEE MOSS GROWING THROUGH THE SIDEWALK. ....AND SOMETIMES, THERE'S A NAME OR A HANDPRINT LEFT IN THE CEMENT.
AND, LOOK AT THAT– A BRAND-NEW DIME!
EVERY DAY, THERE'S A TREASURE TO FIND – IF YOU KNOW WHERE TO LOOK, IRIS.
DO YOU KNOW WHAT I MEAN?
YES, JIM.
ABSOLUTELY.
LYNN

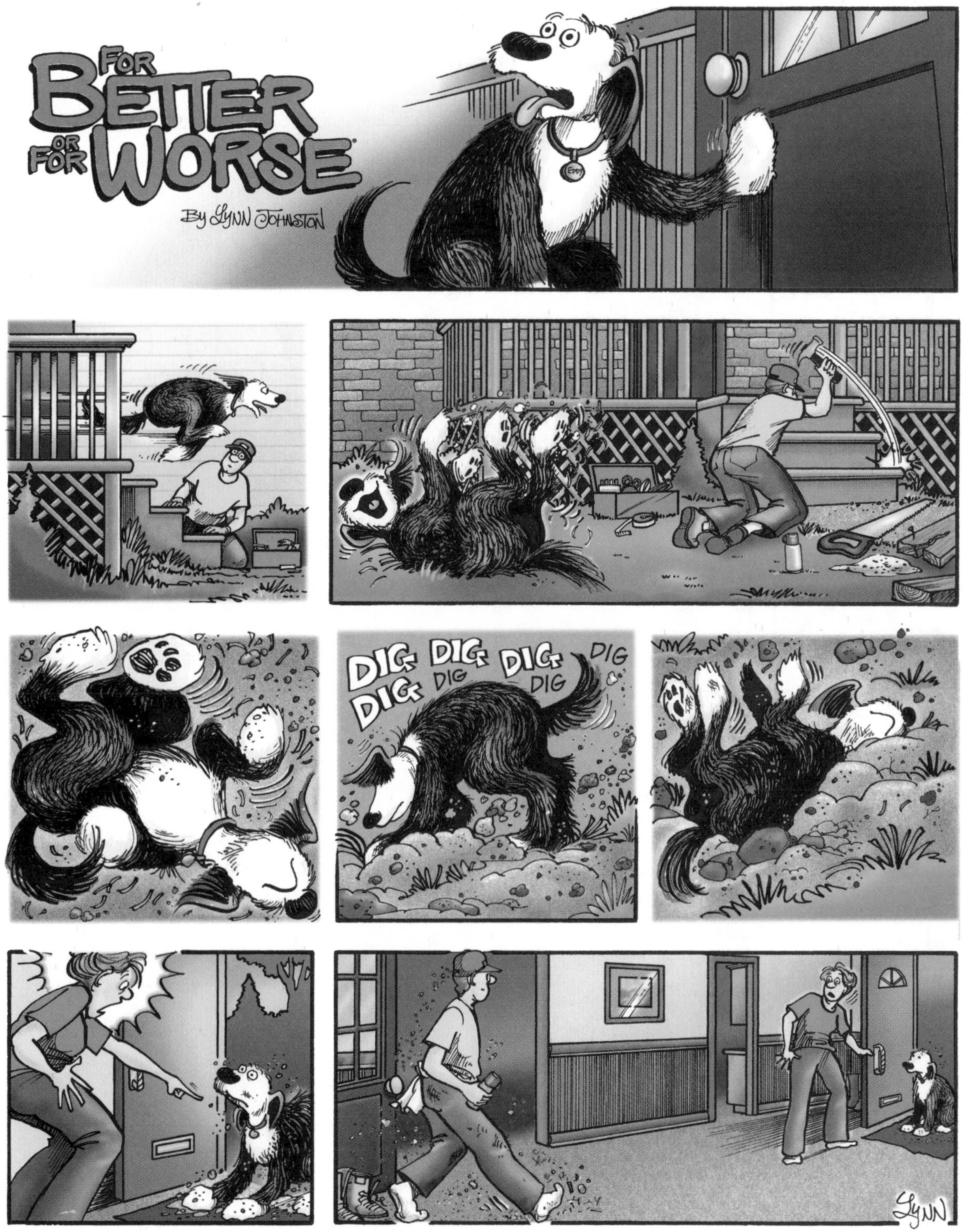

FOR BETTER OR FOR WORSE
By Lynn Johnston
EDDY
DIG DIG DIG DIG
DIG DIG DIG DIG
LYNN

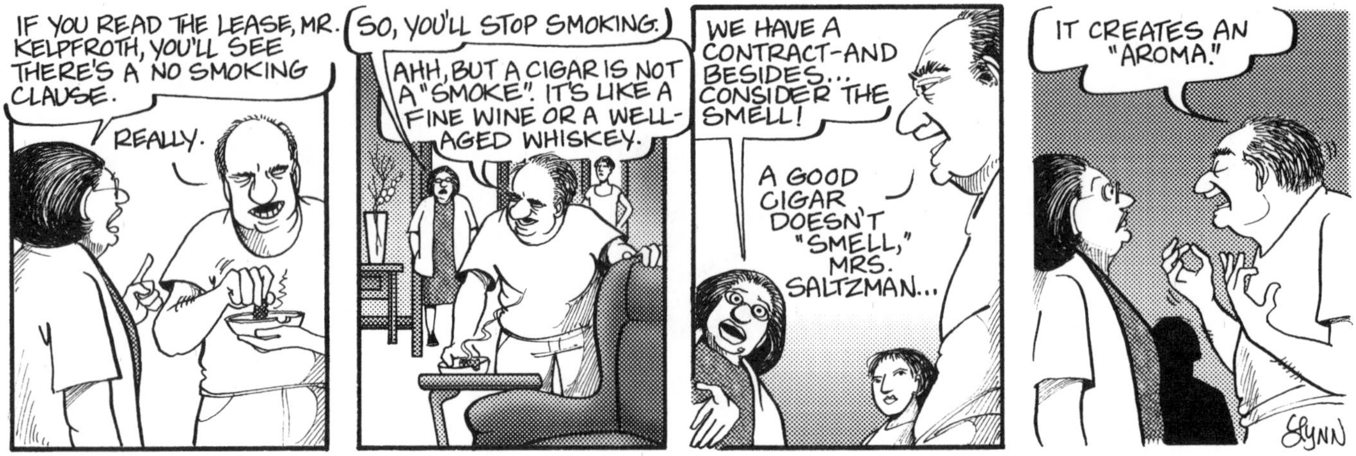
IF YOU READ THE LEASE, MR. KELPFROTH, YOU'LL SEE THERE'S A NO SMOKING CLAUSE.
REALLY.
SO, YOU'LL STOP SMOKING.
AHH, BUT A CIGAR IS NOT A "SMOKE". IT'S LIKE A FINE WINE OR A WELL-AGED WHISKEY.
WE HAVE A CONTRACT-AND BESIDES... CONSIDER THE SMELL!
A GOOD CIGAR DOESN'T "SMELL," MRS. SALTZMAN...
IT CREATES AN "AROMA."
LYNN

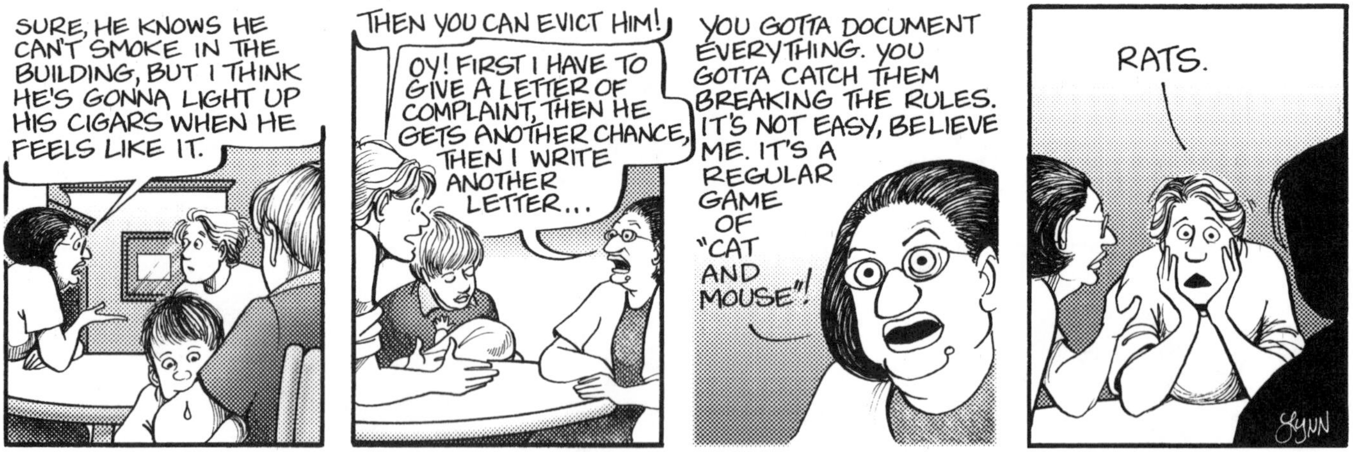
SURE, HE KNOWS HE CAN'T SMOKE IN THE BUILDING, BUT I THINK HE'S GONNA LIGHT UP HIS CIGARS WHEN HE FEELS LIKE IT.
THEN YOU CAN EVICT HIM!
OY! FIRST I HAVE TO GIVE A LETTER OF COMPLAINT, THEN HE GETS ANOTHER CHANCE, THEN I WRITE ANOTHER LETTER...
YOU GOTTA DOCUMENT EVERYTHING. YOU GOTTA CATCH THEM BREAKING THE RULES. IT'S NOT EASY, BELIEVE ME. IT'S A REGULAR GAME OF "CAT AND MOUSE"!
RATS.
LYNN

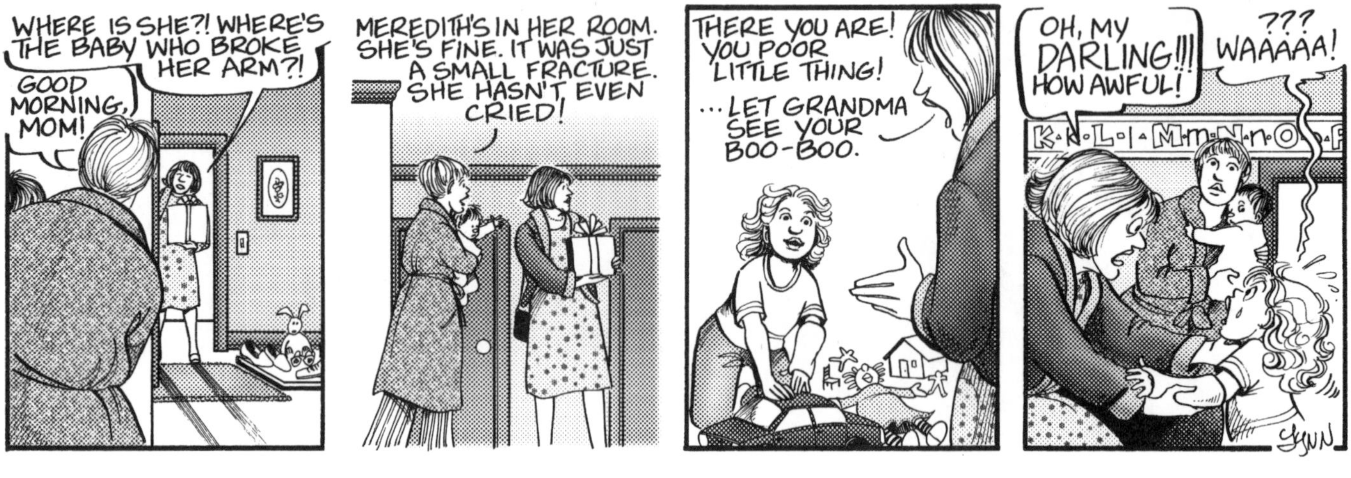
WHERE IS SHE?! WHERE'S THE BABY WHO BROKE HER ARM?!
GOOD MORNING, MOM!
MEREDITH'S IN HER ROOM. SHE'S FINE. IT WAS JUST A SMALL FRACTURE. SHE HASN'T EVEN CRIED!
THERE YOU ARE! YOU POOR LITTLE THING!
...LET GRANDMA SEE YOUR BOO-BOO.
OH, MY DARLING!!! HOW AWFUL!
??? WAAAAAA!
LYNN

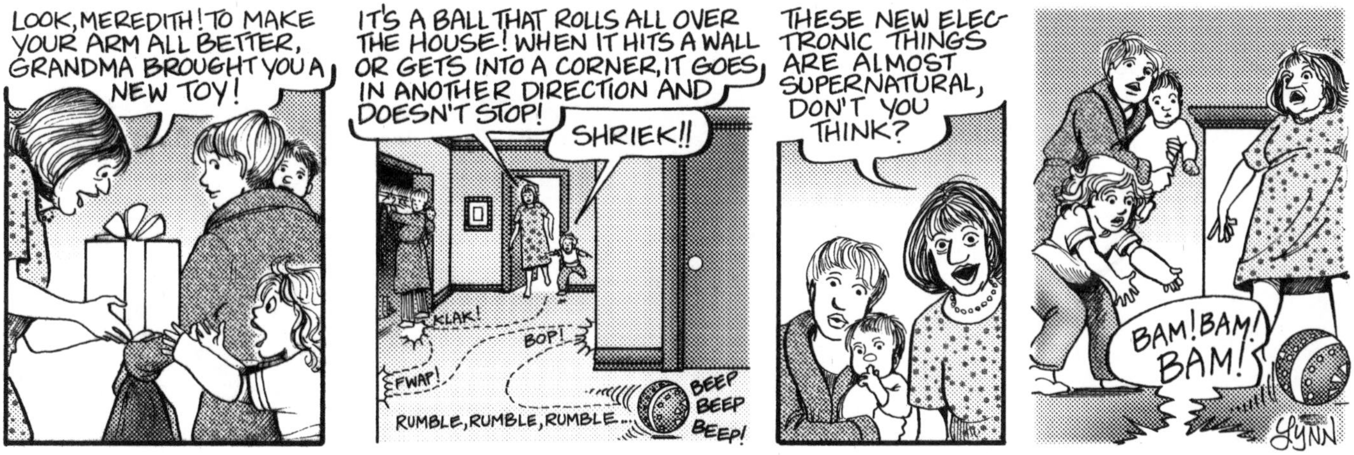
LOOK, MEREDITH! TO MAKE YOUR ARM ALL BETTER, GRANDMA BROUGHT YOU A NEW TOY!
IT'S A BALL THAT ROLLS ALL OVER THE HOUSE! WHEN IT HITS A WALL OR GETS INTO A CORNER, IT GOES IN ANOTHER DIRECTION AND DOESN'T STOP!
SHRIEK!!
KLAK!
BOP!
FWAP!
RUMBLE, RUMBLE, RUMBLE...
BEEP BEEP BEEP!
THESE NEW ELECTRONIC THINGS ARE ALMOST SUPERNATURAL, DON'T YOU THINK?
BAM! BAM! BAM!
LYNN

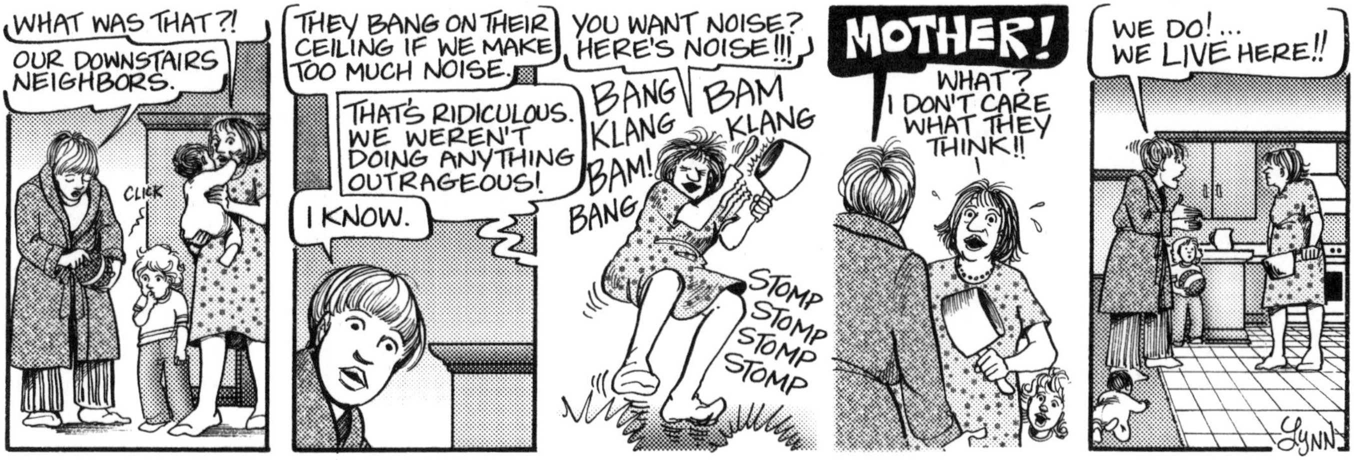
WHAT WAS THAT?!
OUR DOWNSTAIRS NEIGHBORS.
CLICK
THEY BANG ON THEIR CEILING IF WE MAKE TOO MUCH NOISE.
THAT'S RIDICULOUS. WE WEREN'T DOING ANYTHING OUTRAGEOUS!
I KNOW.
YOU WANT NOISE? HERE'S NOISE!!!
BANG KLANG BAM! BANG
BAM KLANG
STOMP STOMP STOMP STOMP
MOTHER!
WHAT? I DON'T CARE WHAT THEY THINK!!
WE DO!... WE LIVE HERE!!
LYNN

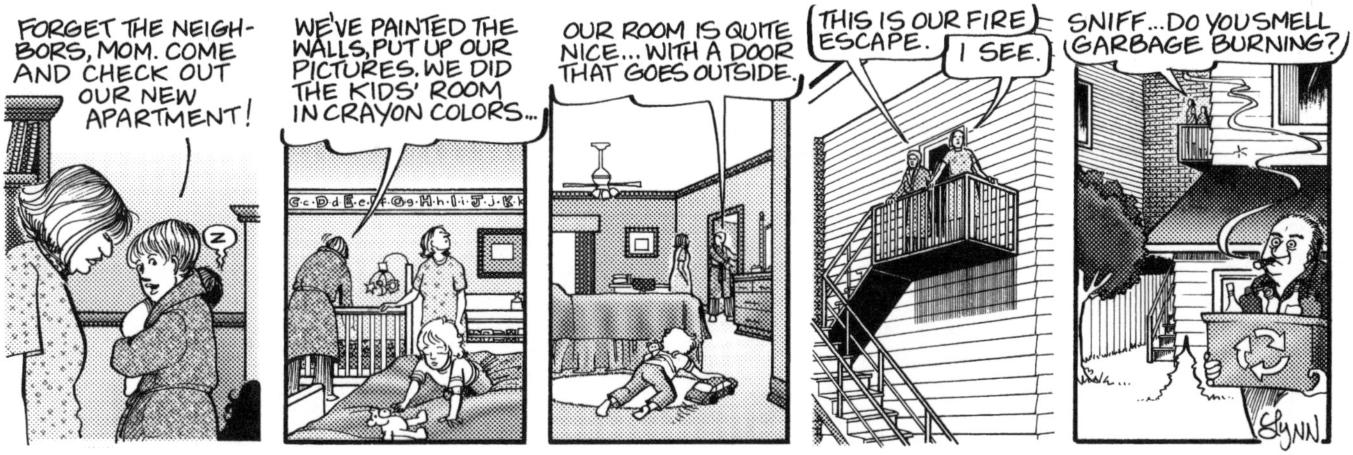
FORGET THE NEIGHBORS, MOM. COME AND CHECK OUT OUR NEW APARTMENT!
WE'VE PAINTED THE WALLS, PUT UP OUR PICTURES. WE DID THE KIDS' ROOM IN CRAYON COLORS...
OUR ROOM IS QUITE NICE... WITH A DOOR THAT GOES OUTSIDE.
THIS IS OUR FIRE ESCAPE.
I SEE.
SNIFF... DO YOU SMELL GARBAGE BURNING?
LYNN

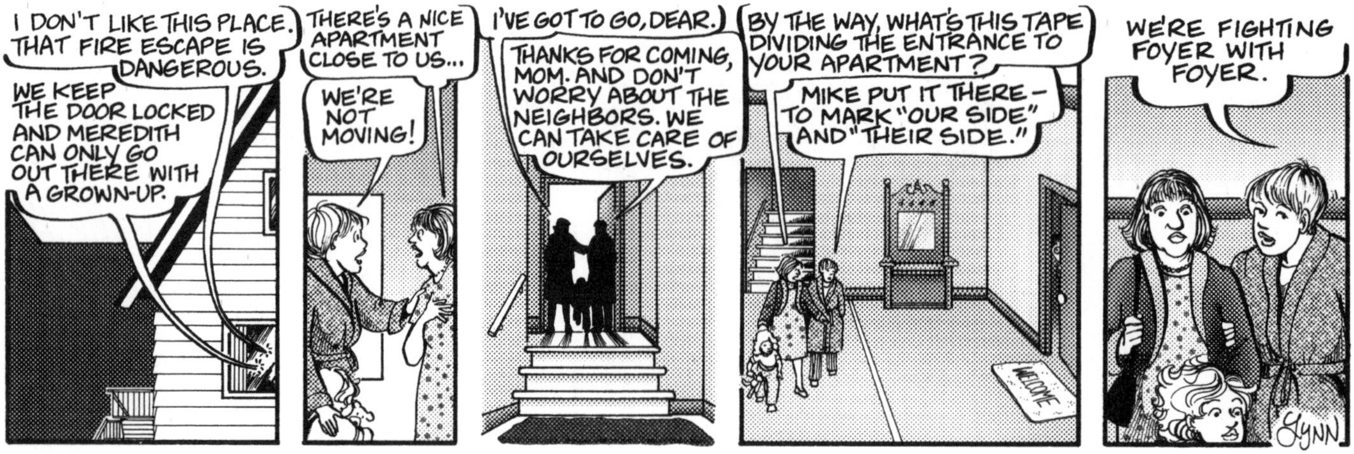
I DON'T LIKE THIS PLACE. THAT FIRE ESCAPE IS DANGEROUS.
WE KEEP THE DOOR LOCKED AND MEREDITH CAN ONLY GO OUT THERE WITH A GROWN-UP.
THERE'S A NICE APARTMENT CLOSE TO US...
WE'RE NOT MOVING!
I'VE GOT TO GO, DEAR.
THANKS FOR COMING, MOM. AND DON'T WORRY ABOUT THE NEIGHBORS. WE CAN TAKE CARE OF OURSELVES.
BY THE WAY, WHAT'S THIS TAPE DIVIDING THE ENTRANCE TO YOUR APARTMENT?
MIKE PUT IT THERE – TO MARK "OUR SIDE" AND "THEIR SIDE."
WELCOME
WE'RE FIGHTING FOYER WITH FOYER.
LYNN

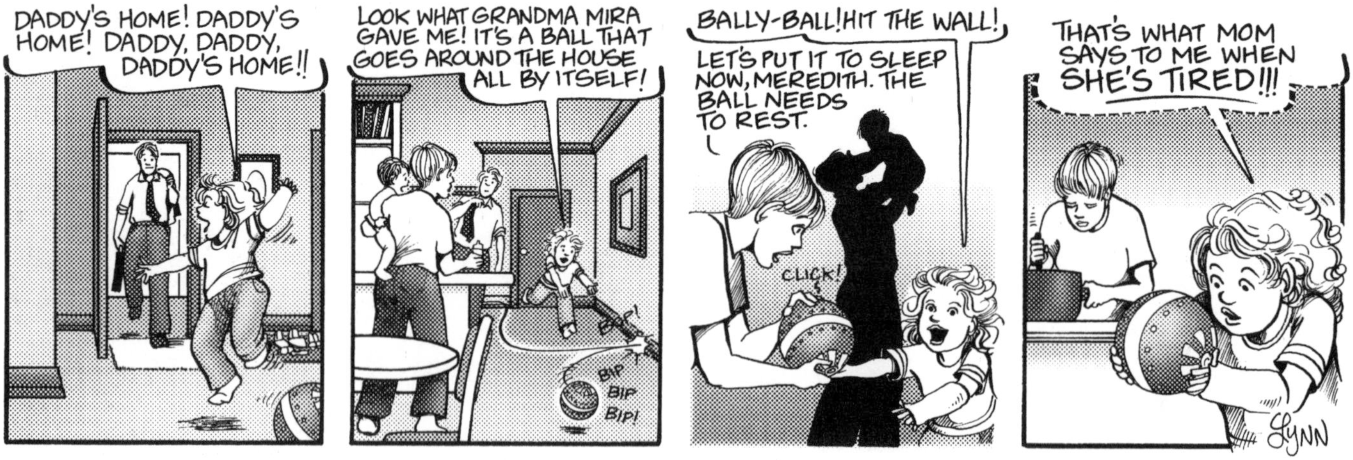
DADDY'S HOME! DADDY'S HOME! DADDY, DADDY, DADDY'S HOME!!
LOOK WHAT GRANDMA MIRA GAVE ME! IT'S A BALL THAT GOES AROUND THE HOUSE ALL BY ITSELF!
BIP BIP BIP!
BALLY-BALL! HIT THE WALL!
LET'S PUT IT TO SLEEP NOW, MEREDITH. THE BALL NEEDS TO REST.
CLICK!
THAT'S WHAT MOM SAYS TO ME WHEN SHE'S TIRED!!!
LYNN

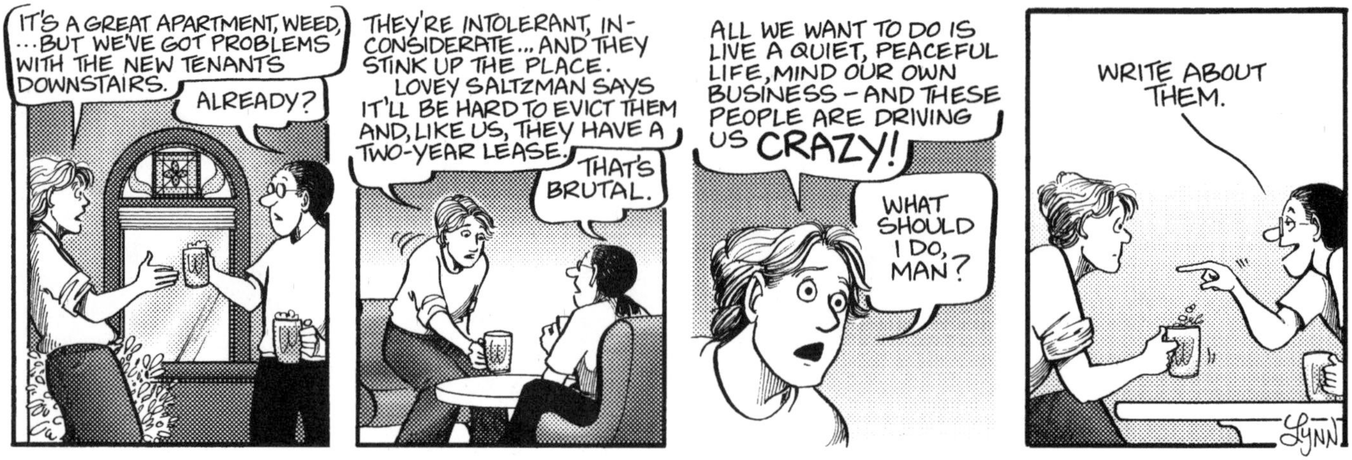
IT'S A GREAT APARTMENT, WEED, ...BUT WE'VE GOT PROBLEMS WITH THE NEW TENANTS DOWNSTAIRS.
ALREADY?
THEY'RE INTOLERANT, INCONSIDERATE... AND THEY STINK UP THE PLACE. LOVEY SALTZMAN SAYS IT'LL BE HARD TO EVICT THEM AND, LIKE US, THEY HAVE A TWO-YEAR LEASE.
THAT'S BRUTAL.
ALL WE WANT TO DO IS LIVE A QUIET, PEACEFUL LIFE, MIND OUR OWN BUSINESS – AND THESE PEOPLE ARE DRIVING US CRAZY!
WHAT SHOULD I DO, MAN?
WRITE ABOUT THEM.
LYNN

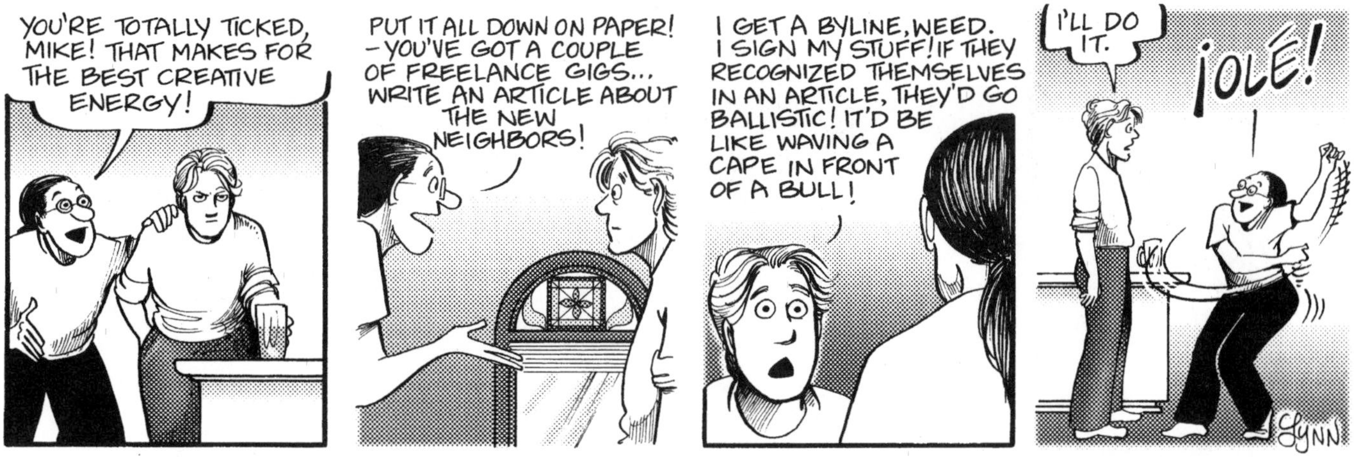
YOU'RE TOTALLY TICKED, MIKE! THAT MAKES FOR THE BEST CREATIVE ENERGY!
PUT IT ALL DOWN ON PAPER! - YOU'VE GOT A COUPLE OF FREELANCE GIGS... WRITE AN ARTICLE ABOUT THE NEW NEIGHBORS!
I GET A BYLINE, WEED. I SIGN MY STUFF! IF THEY RECOGNIZED THEMSELVES IN AN ARTICLE, THEY'D GO BALLISTIC! IT'D BE LIKE WAVING A CAPE IN FRONT OF A BULL!
I'LL DO IT.
¡OLÉ!
LYNN

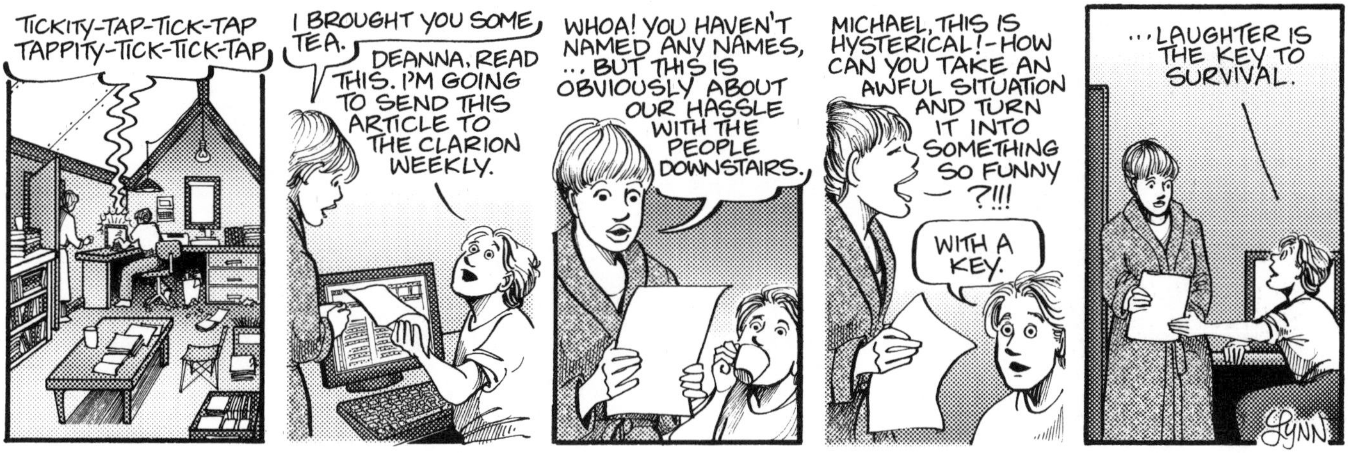
TICKITY-TAP-TICK-TAP TAPPITY-TICK-TICK-TAP
I BROUGHT YOU SOME TEA.
DEANNA, READ THIS. I'M GOING TO SEND THIS ARTICLE TO THE CLARION WEEKLY.
WHOA! YOU HAVEN'T NAMED ANY NAMES, ... BUT THIS IS OBVIOUSLY ABOUT OUR HASSLE WITH THE PEOPLE DOWNSTAIRS.
MICHAEL, THIS IS HYSTERICAL! - HOW CAN YOU TAKE AN AWFUL SITUATION AND TURN IT INTO SOMETHING SO FUNNY ?!!!
WITH A KEY.
... LAUGHTER IS THE KEY TO SURVIVAL.
LYNN

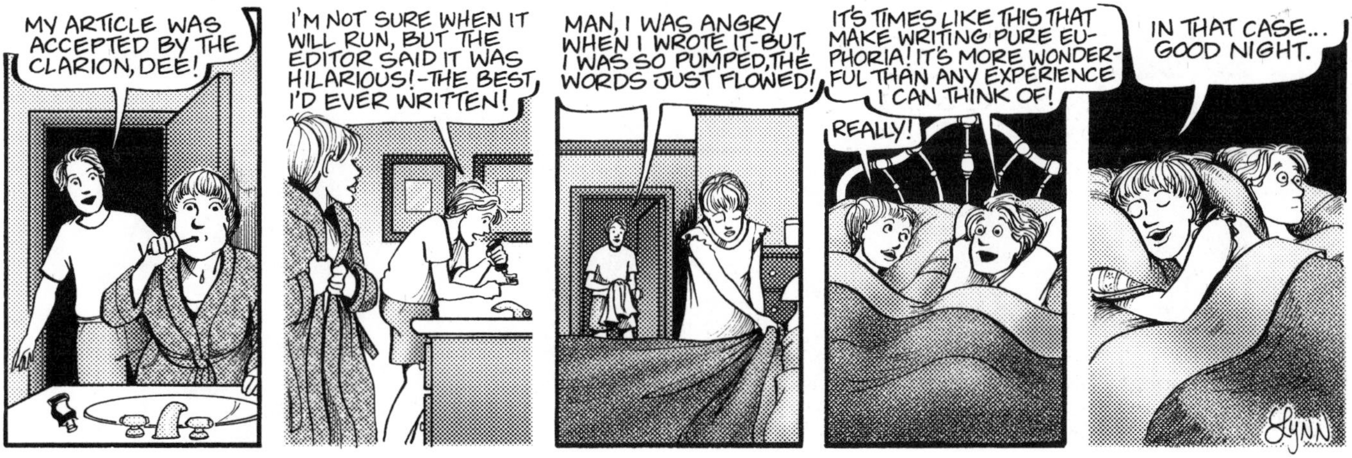
MY ARTICLE WAS ACCEPTED BY THE CLARION, DEE!
I'M NOT SURE WHEN IT WILL RUN, BUT THE EDITOR SAID IT WAS HILARIOUS! - THE BEST I'D EVER WRITTEN!
MAN, I WAS ANGRY WHEN I WROTE IT - BUT, I WAS SO PUMPED, THE WORDS JUST FLOWED!
IT'S TIMES LIKE THIS THAT MAKE WRITING PURE EUPHORIA! IT'S MORE WONDERFUL THAN ANY EXPERIENCE I CAN THINK OF!
REALLY!
IN THAT CASE... GOOD NIGHT.
LYNN

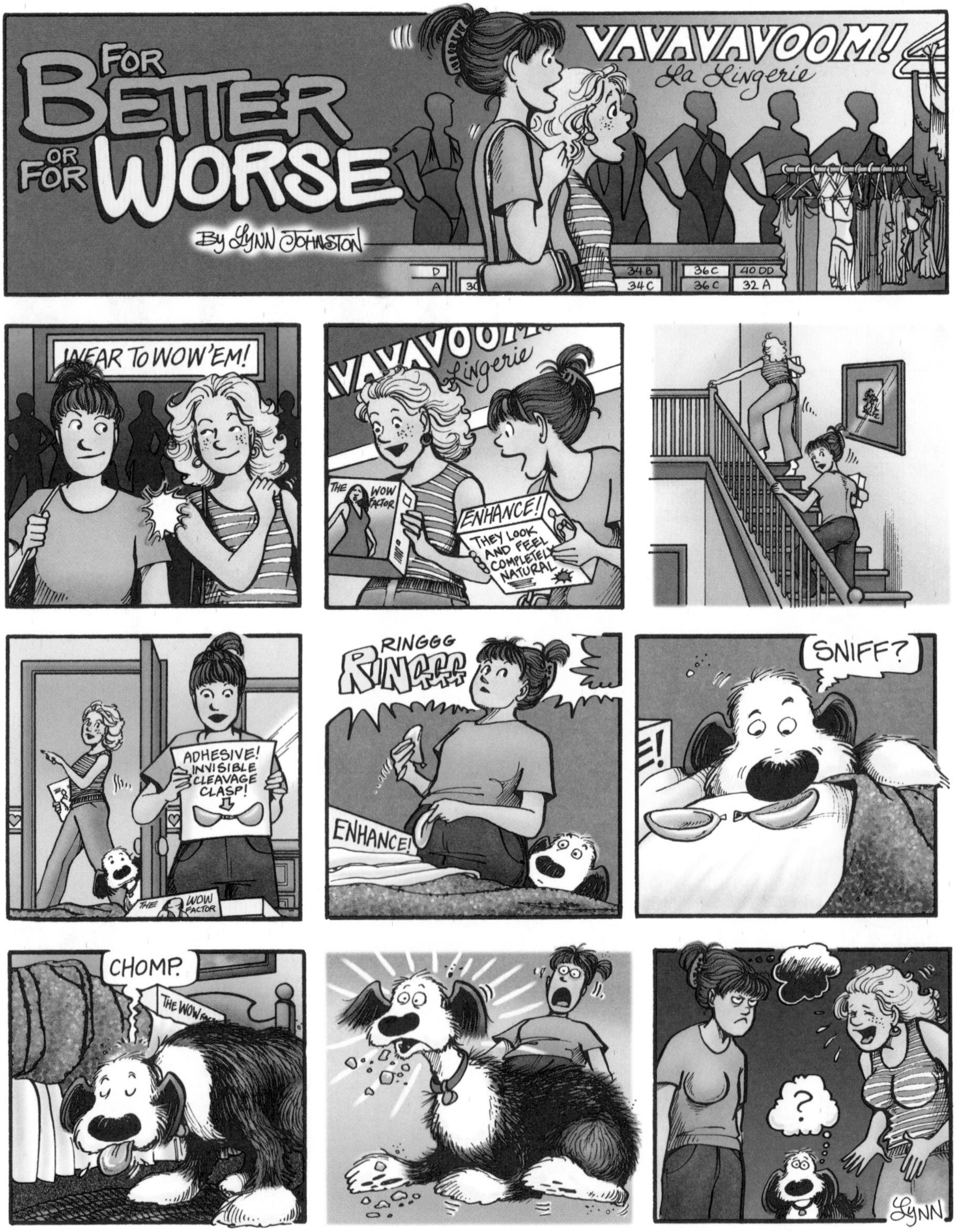
For Better or For Worse
By Lynn Johnston
VAVAVAVOOM!
La Lingerie
WEAR TO WOW'EM!
THE WOW FACTOR
ENHANCE!
THEY LOOK AND FEEL COMPLETELY NATURAL
ADHESIVE! INVISIBLE CLEAVAGE CLASP!
RINGGG
RINGGG
ENHANCE!
SNIFF?
CHOMP.
THE WOW FACTOR
?
LYNN

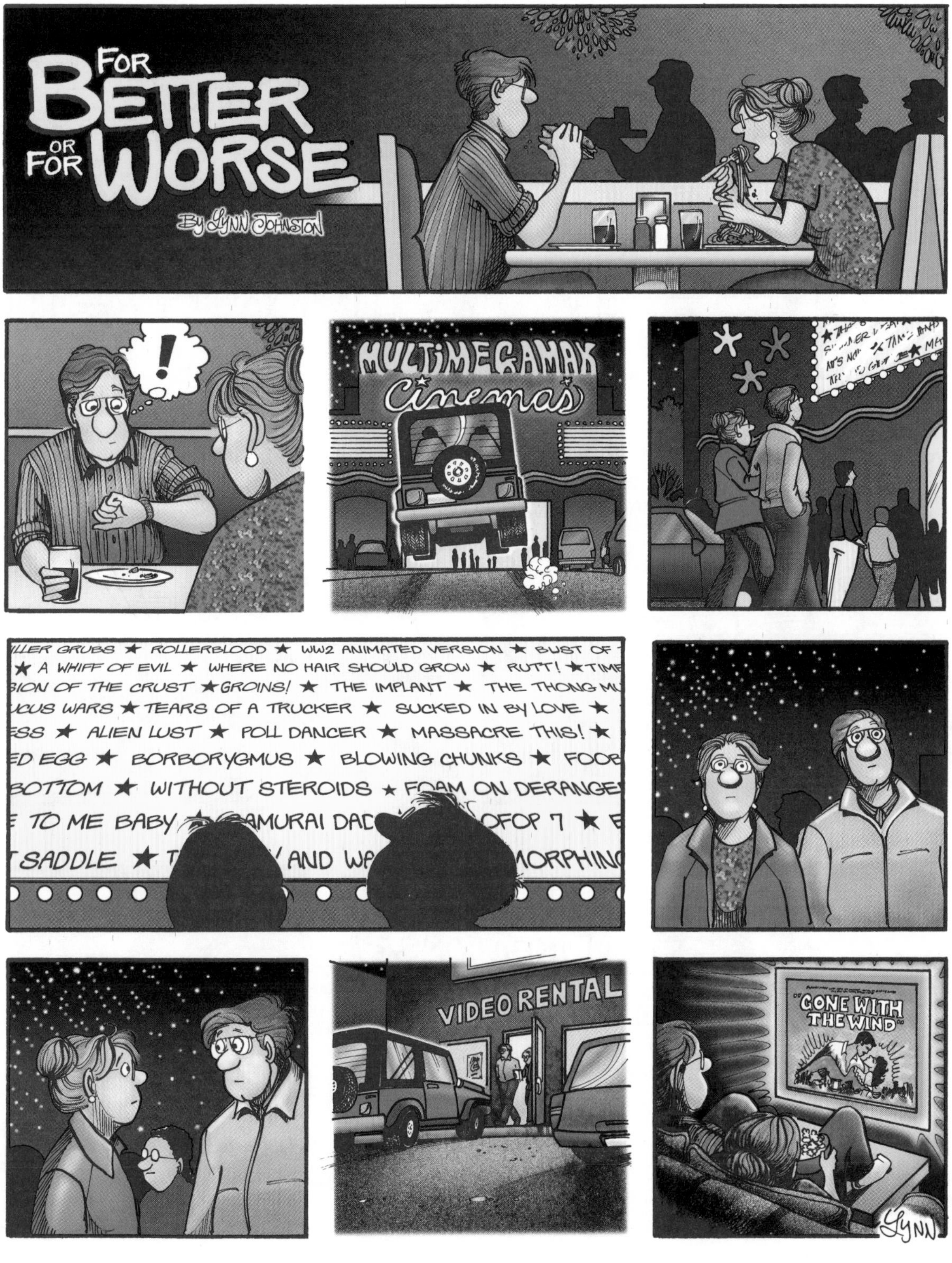

FOR BETTER OR FOR WORSE
BY LYNN JOHNSTON
!
MULTIMEGAMAX
Cinemas
ROLLERBLOOD ★ WW2 ANIMATED VERSION
A WHIFF OF EVIL ★ WHERE NO HAIR SHOULD GROW ★ RUTT!
OF THE CRUST ★ GROINS! ★ THE IMPLANT ★ THE THONG
WARS ★ TEARS OF A TRUCKER ★ SUCKED IN BY LOVE
ALIEN LUST ★ POLL DANCER ★ MASSACRE THIS!
EGG ★ BORBORYGMUS ★ BLOWING CHUNKS
BOTTOM ★ WITHOUT STEROIDS ★ FOAM ON
TO ME BABY
SADDLE
AND
VIDEO RENTAL
GONE WITH THE WIND
LYNN

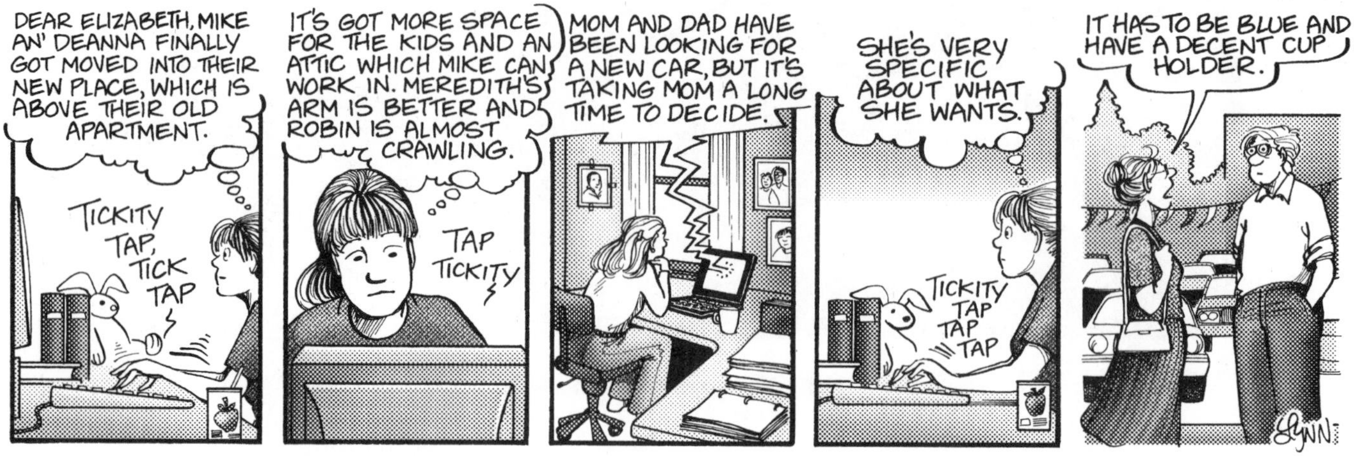
DEAR ELIZABETH, MIKE AN' DEANNA FINALLY GOT MOVED INTO THEIR NEW PLACE, WHICH IS ABOVE THEIR OLD APARTMENT.
TICKITY TAP, TICK TAP
IT'S GOT MORE SPACE FOR THE KIDS AND AN ATTIC WHICH MIKE CAN WORK IN. MEREDITH'S ARM IS BETTER AND ROBIN IS ALMOST CRAWLING.
TAP TICKITY
MOM AND DAD HAVE BEEN LOOKING FOR A NEW CAR, BUT IT'S TAKING MOM A LONG TIME TO DECIDE.
SHE'S VERY SPECIFIC ABOUT WHAT SHE WANTS.
TICKITY TAP TAP TAP
IT HAS TO BE BLUE AND HAVE A DECENT CUP HOLDER.
LYNN

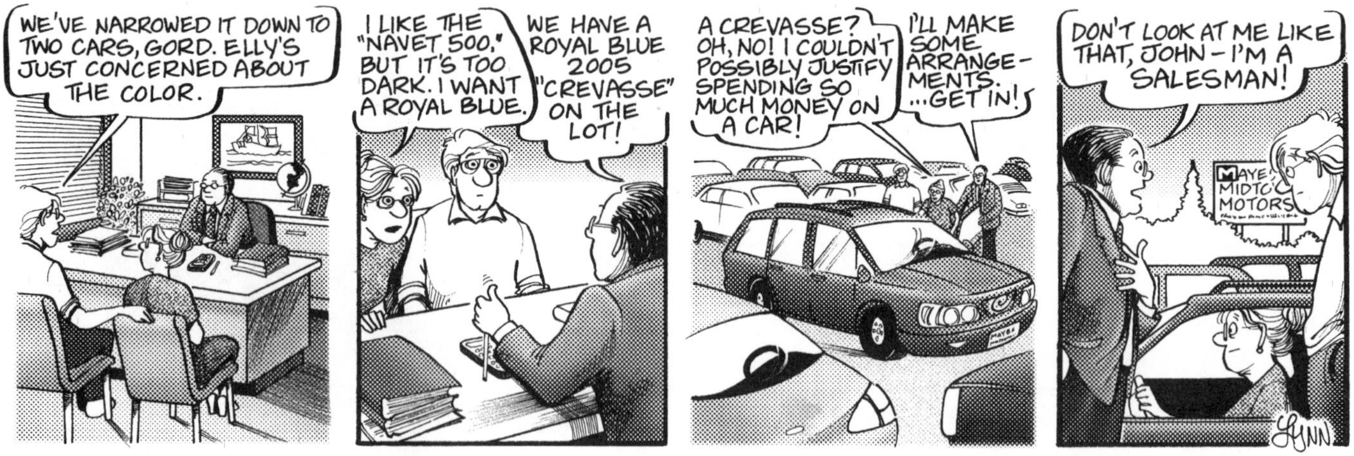
WE'VE NARROWED IT DOWN TO TWO CARS, GORD. ELLY'S JUST CONCERNED ABOUT THE COLOR.
I LIKE THE "NAVET 500," BUT IT'S TOO DARK. I WANT A ROYAL BLUE.
WE HAVE A ROYAL BLUE 2005 "CREVASSE" ON THE LOT!
A CREVASSE? OH, NO! I COULDN'T POSSIBLY JUSTIFY SPENDING SO MUCH MONEY ON A CAR!
I'LL MAKE SOME ARRANGE-MENTS. ...GET IN!
DON'T LOOK AT ME LIKE THAT, JOHN – I'M A SALESMAN!
MIDTO MOTORS
LYNN

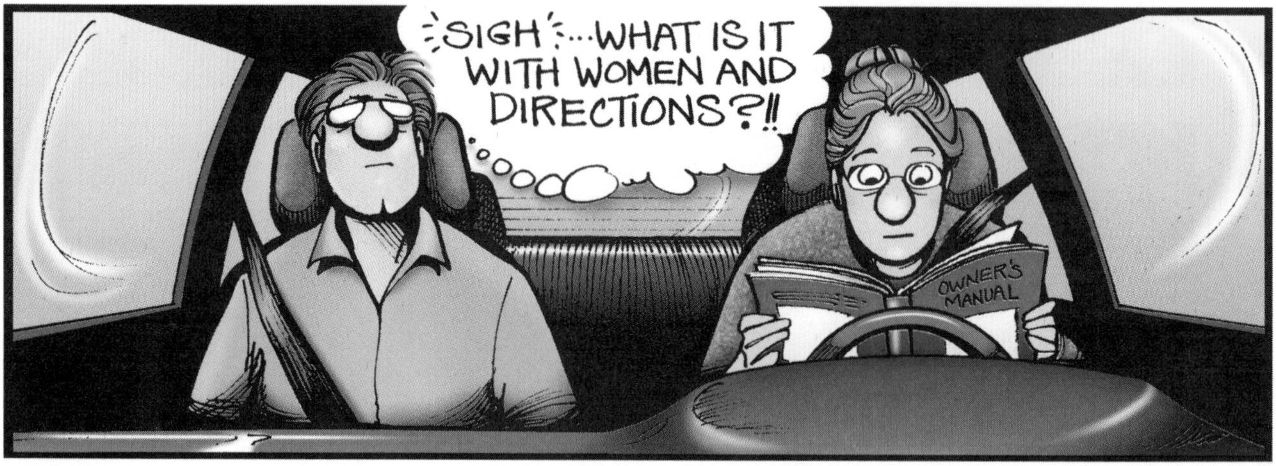
SIGH ...WHAT IS IT WITH WOMEN AND DIRECTIONS?!!
OWNER'S MANUAL

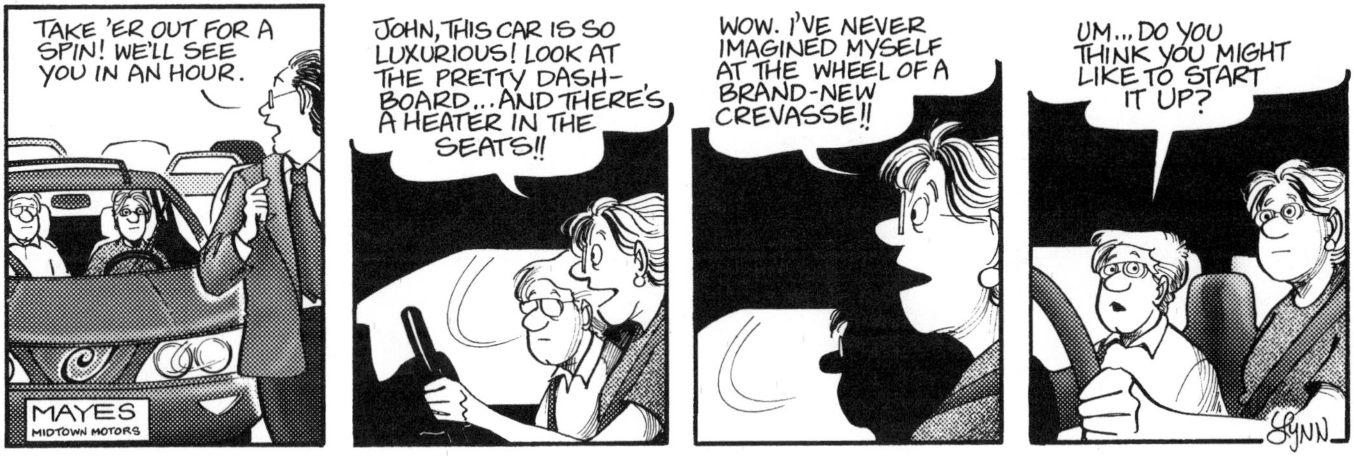
TAKE 'ER OUT FOR A SPIN! WE'LL SEE YOU IN AN HOUR.
MAYES
MIDTOWN MOTORS
JOHN, THIS CAR IS SO LUXURIOUS! LOOK AT THE PRETTY DASH-BOARD... AND THERE'S A HEATER IN THE SEATS!!
WOW. I'VE NEVER IMAGINED MYSELF AT THE WHEEL OF A BRAND-NEW CREVASSE!!
UM... DO YOU THINK YOU MIGHT LIKE TO START IT UP?
LYNN

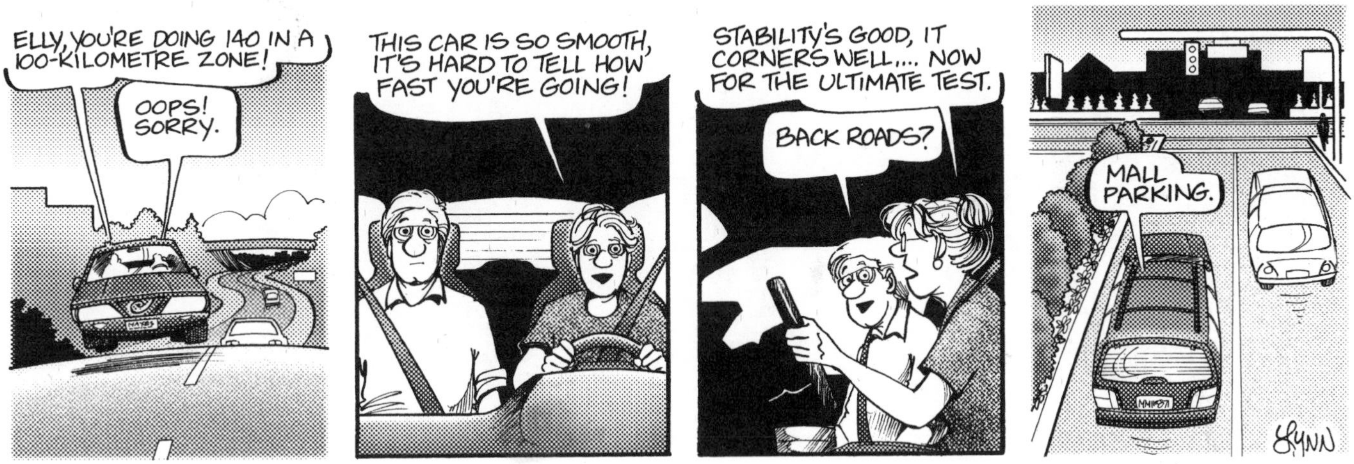
ELLY, YOU'RE DOING 140 IN A 100-KILOMETRE ZONE!
OOPS! SORRY.
THIS CAR IS SO SMOOTH, IT'S HARD TO TELL HOW FAST YOU'RE GOING!
STABILITY'S GOOD, IT CORNERS WELL,... NOW FOR THE ULTIMATE TEST.
BACK ROADS?
MALL PARKING.
LYNN

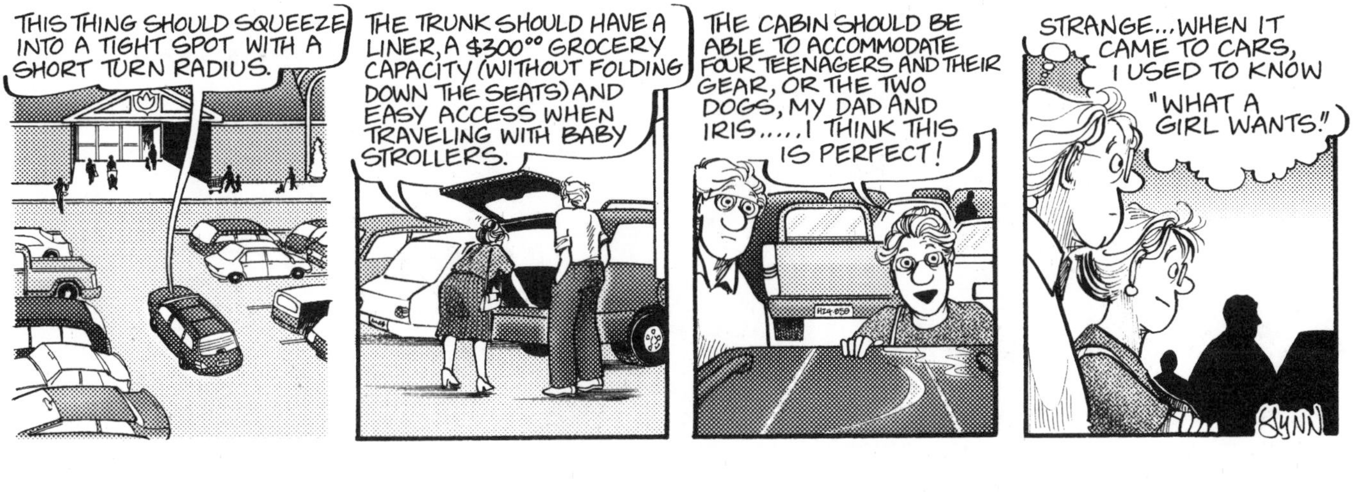
THIS THING SHOULD SQUEEZE INTO A TIGHT SPOT WITH A SHORT TURN RADIUS.
THE TRUNK SHOULD HAVE A LINER, A $300°° GROCERY CAPACITY (WITHOUT FOLDING DOWN THE SEATS) AND EASY ACCESS WHEN TRAVELING WITH BABY STROLLERS.
THE CABIN SHOULD BE ABLE TO ACCOMMODATE FOUR TEENAGERS AND THEIR GEAR, OR THE TWO DOGS, MY DAD AND IRIS..... I THINK THIS IS PERFECT!
STRANGE... WHEN IT CAME TO CARS, I USED TO KNOW "WHAT A GIRL WANTS."
LYNN

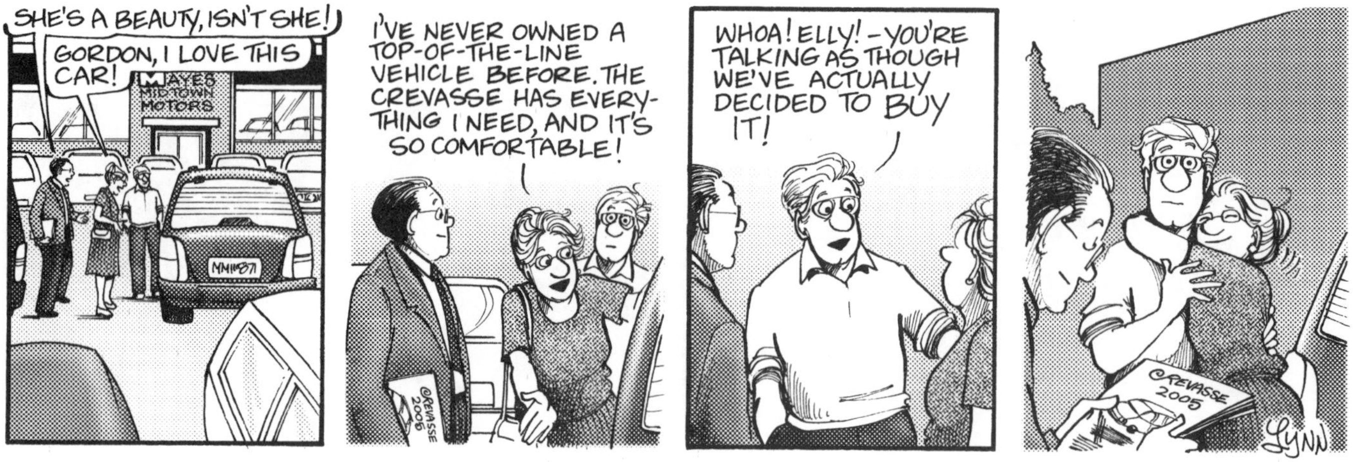
SHE'S A BEAUTY, ISN'T SHE!
GORDON, I LOVE THIS CAR!
MAYES MIDTOWN MOTORS
I'VE NEVER OWNED A TOP-OF-THE-LINE VEHICLE BEFORE. THE CREVASSE HAS EVERY-THING I NEED, AND IT'S SO COMFORTABLE!
WHOA! ELLY! - YOU'RE TALKING AS THOUGH WE'VE ACTUALLY DECIDED TO BUY IT!
CREVASSE 2005
LYNN

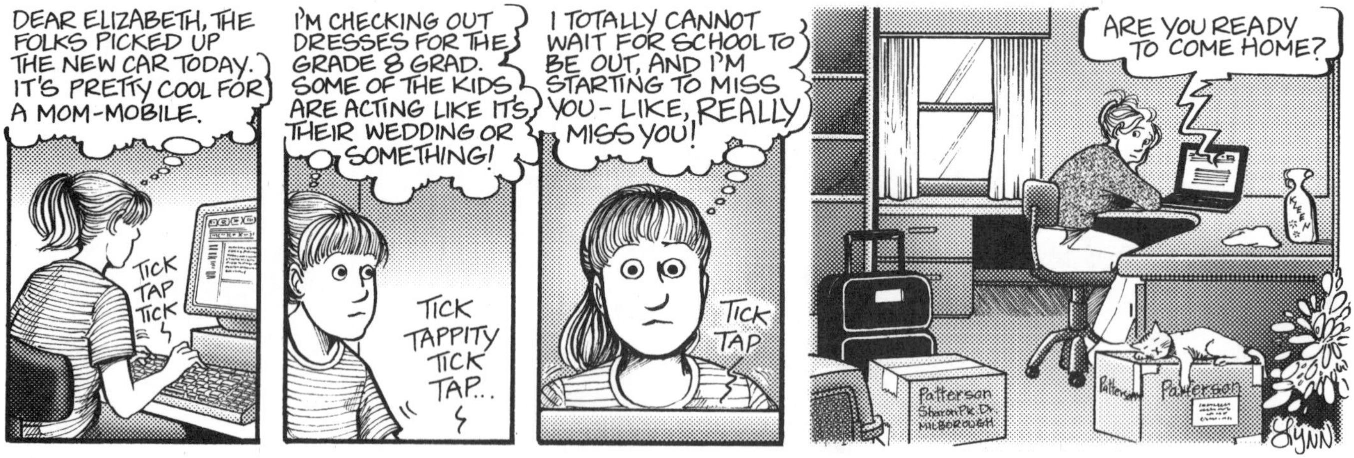
DEAR ELIZABETH, THE FOLKS PICKED UP THE NEW CAR TODAY. IT'S PRETTY COOL FOR A MOM-MOBILE.
TICK TAP TICK
I'M CHECKING OUT DRESSES FOR THE GRADE 8 GRAD. SOME OF THE KIDS ARE ACTING LIKE IT'S THEIR WEDDING OR SOMETHING!
TICK TAPPITY TICK TAP...
I TOTALLY CANNOT WAIT FOR SCHOOL TO BE OUT, AND I'M STARTING TO MISS YOU - LIKE, REALLY MISS YOU!
TICK TAP
ARE YOU READY TO COME HOME?
Patterson
Patterson
LYNN

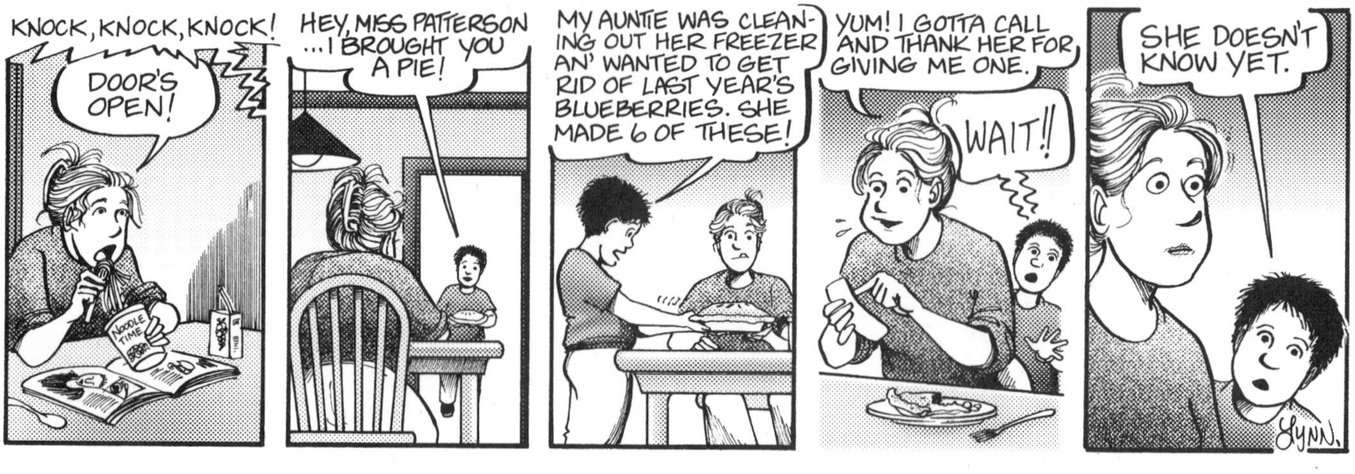
KNOCK, KNOCK, KNOCK!
DOOR'S OPEN!
HEY, MISS PATTERSON ...I BROUGHT YOU A PIE!
MY AUNTIE WAS CLEAN-ING OUT HER FREEZER AN' WANTED TO GET RID OF LAST YEAR'S BLUEBERRIES. SHE MADE 6 OF THESE!
YUM! I GOTTA CALL AND THANK HER FOR GIVING ME ONE.
WAIT!!
SHE DOESN'T KNOW YET.
LYNN

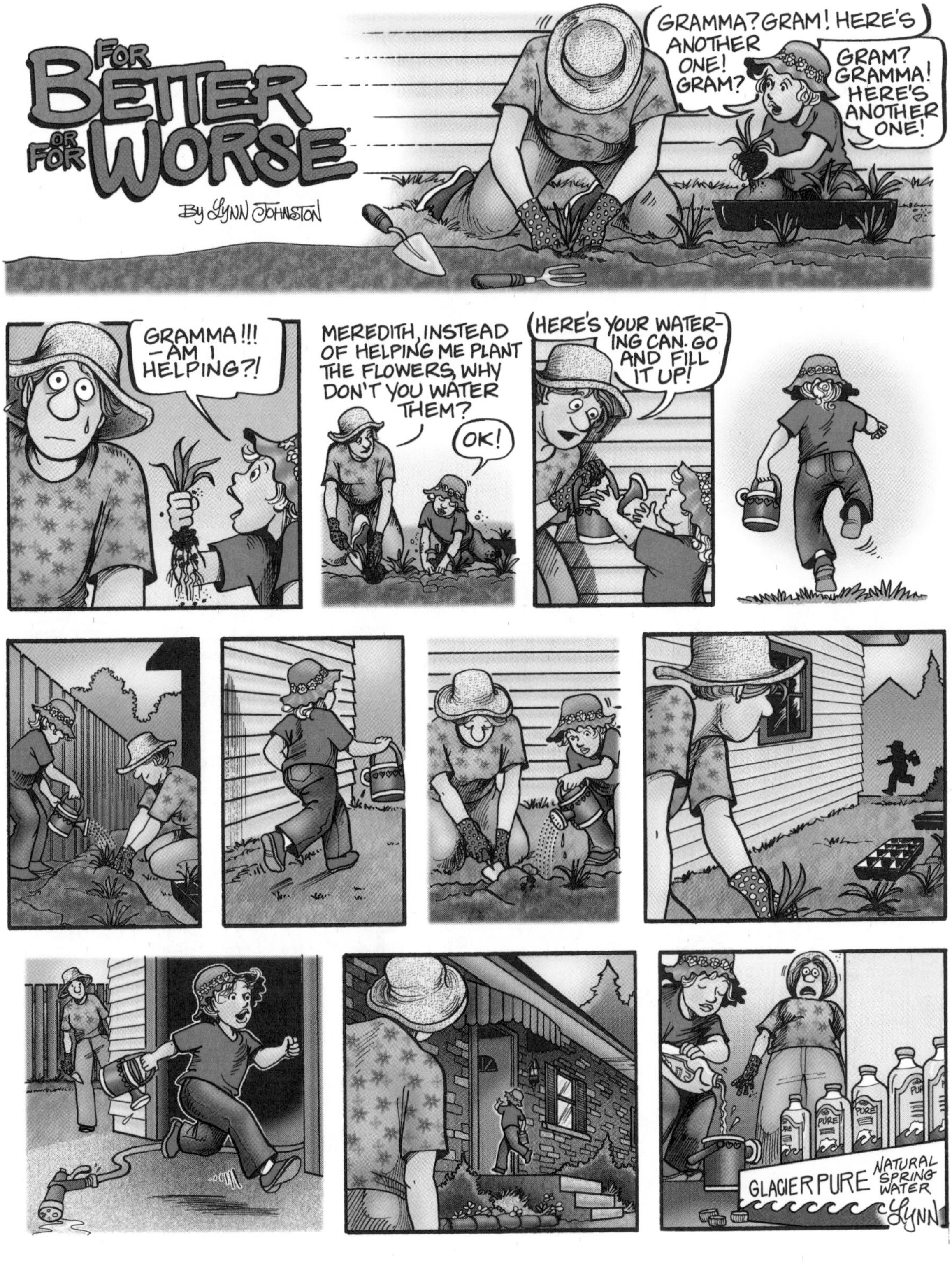
FOR BETTER OR FOR WORSE
BY LYNN JOHNSTON
GRAMMA? GRAM! HERE'S ANOTHER ONE! GRAM?
GRAM? GRAMMA! HERE'S ANOTHER ONE!
GRAMMA!!! —AM I HELPING?!
MEREDITH, INSTEAD OF HELPING ME PLANT THE FLOWERS, WHY DON'T YOU WATER THEM?
OK!
HERE'S YOUR WATERING CAN. GO AND FILL IT UP!
GLACIER PURE NATURAL SPRING WATER
LYNN

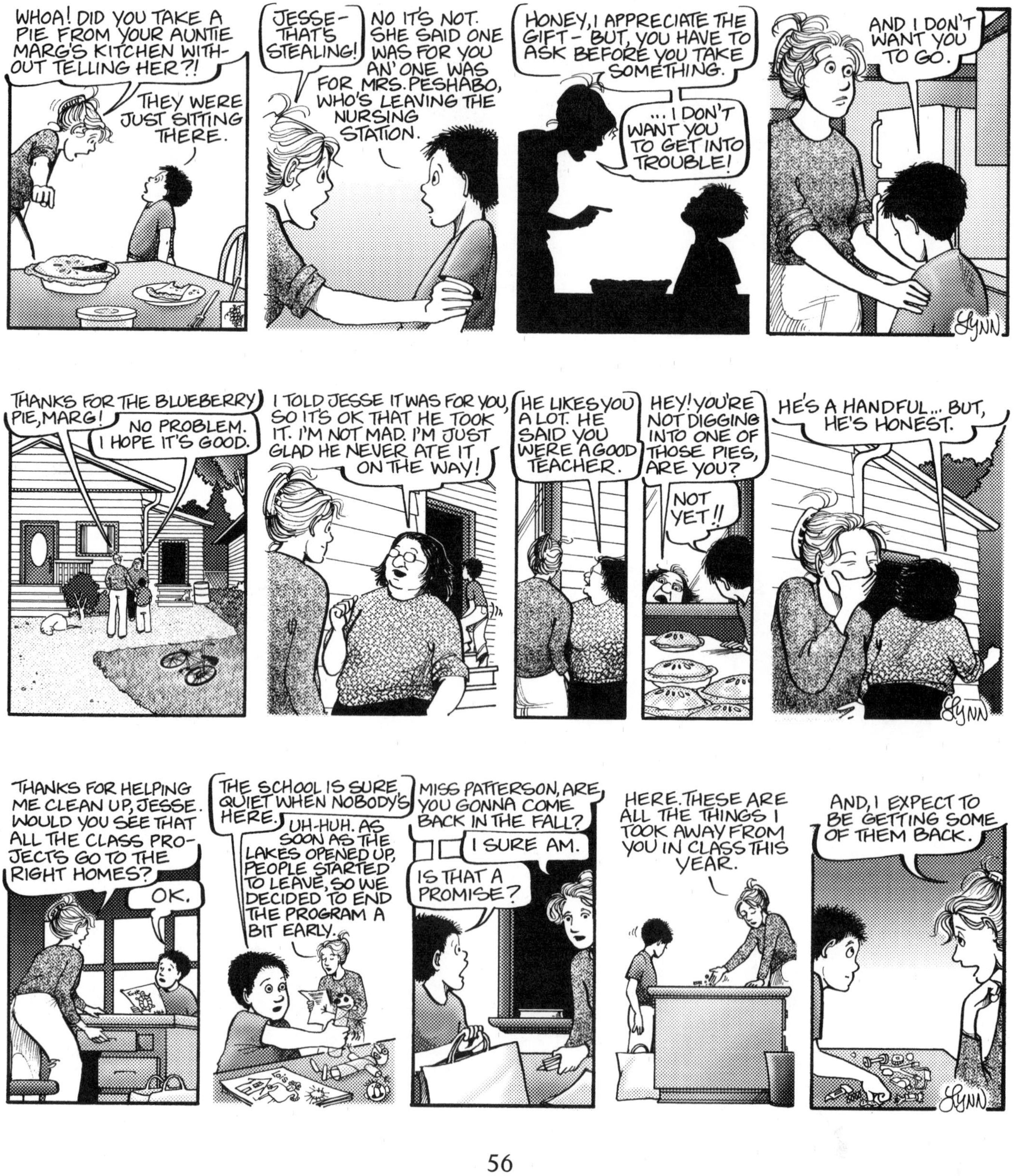
WHOA! DID YOU TAKE A PIE FROM YOUR AUNTIE MARG'S KITCHEN WITHOUT TELLING HER?!
THEY WERE JUST SITTING THERE.
JESSE-THAT'S STEALING!
NO IT'S NOT. SHE SAID ONE WAS FOR YOU AN' ONE WAS FOR MRS. PESHABO, WHO'S LEAVING THE NURSING STATION.
HONEY, I APPRECIATE THE GIFT- BUT, YOU HAVE TO ASK BEFORE YOU TAKE SOMETHING.
... I DON'T WANT YOU TO GET INTO TROUBLE!
AND I DON'T WANT YOU TO GO.
LYNN
THANKS FOR THE BLUEBERRY PIE, MARG!
NO PROBLEM. I HOPE IT'S GOOD.
I TOLD JESSE IT WAS FOR YOU, SO IT'S OK THAT HE TOOK IT. I'M NOT MAD. I'M JUST GLAD HE NEVER ATE IT ON THE WAY!
HE LIKES YOU A LOT. HE SAID YOU WERE A GOOD TEACHER.
HEY! YOU'RE NOT DIGGING INTO ONE OF THOSE PIES, ARE YOU?
NOT YET!!
HE'S A HANDFUL... BUT, HE'S HONEST.
LYNN
THANKS FOR HELPING ME CLEAN UP, JESSE. WOULD YOU SEE THAT ALL THE CLASS PROJECTS GO TO THE RIGHT HOMES?
OK.
THE SCHOOL IS SURE QUIET WHEN NOBODY'S HERE.
UH-HUH. AS SOON AS THE LAKES OPENED UP, PEOPLE STARTED TO LEAVE, SO WE DECIDED TO END THE PROGRAM A BIT EARLY.
MISS PATTERSON, ARE YOU GONNA COME BACK IN THE FALL?
I SURE AM.
IS THAT A PROMISE?
HERE. THESE ARE ALL THE THINGS I TOOK AWAY FROM YOU IN CLASS THIS YEAR.
AND, I EXPECT TO BE GETTING SOME OF THEM BACK.
LYNN

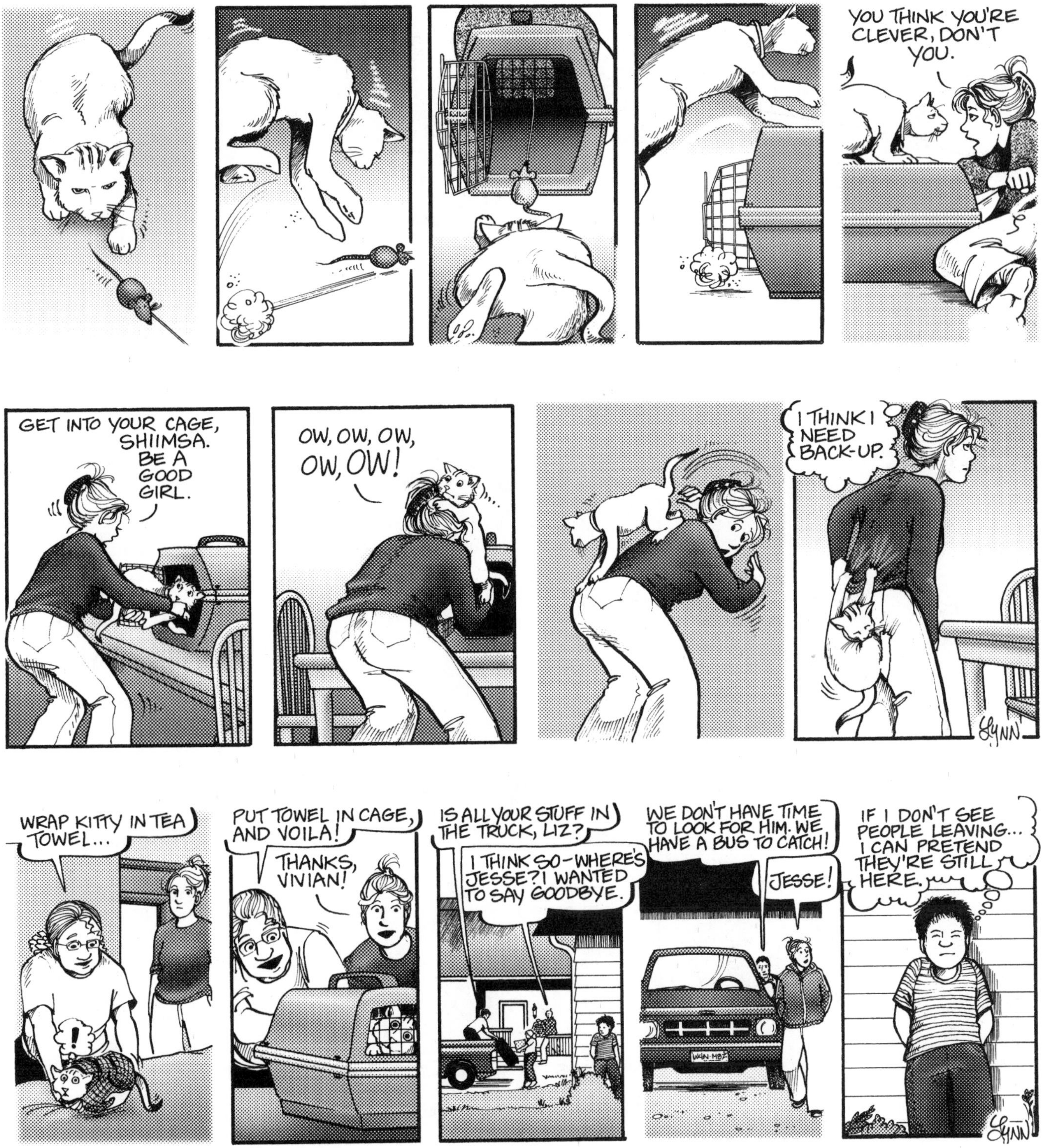
YOU THINK YOU'RE CLEVER, DON'T YOU.
GET INTO YOUR CAGE, SHIIMSA. BE A GOOD GIRL.
OW, OW, OW, OW, OW!
I THINK I NEED BACK-UP.
LYNN
WRAP KITTY IN TEA TOWEL...
!
PUT TOWEL IN CAGE, AND VOILA!
THANKS, VIVIAN!
IS ALL YOUR STUFF IN THE TRUCK, LIZ?
I THINK SO-WHERE'S JESSE? I WANTED TO SAY GOODBYE.
WE DON'T HAVE TIME TO LOOK FOR HIM. WE HAVE A BUS TO CATCH!
JESSE!
IF I DON'T SEE PEOPLE LEAVING... I CAN PRETEND THEY'RE STILL HERE.
LYNN

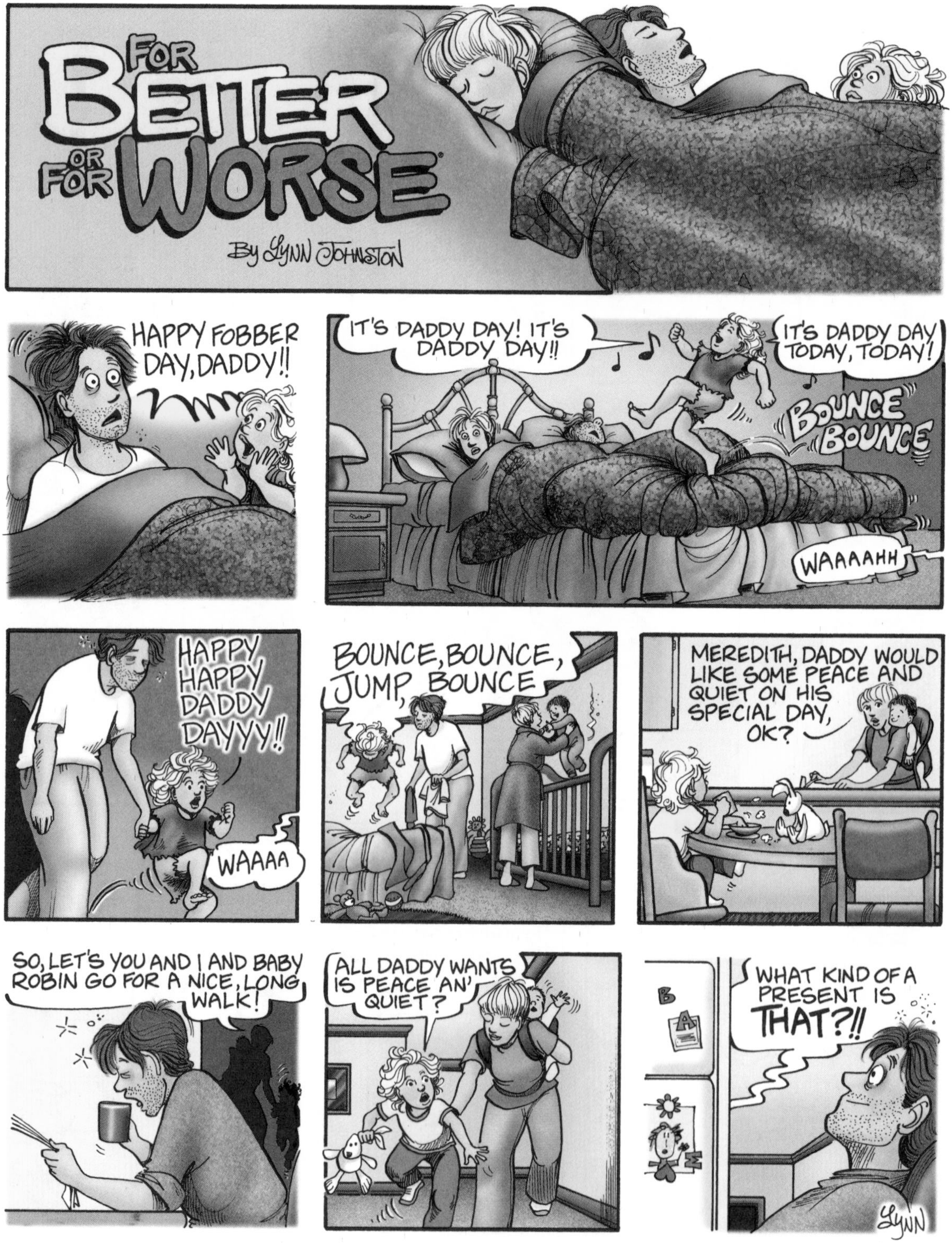
FOR BETTER OR FOR WORSE
By Lynn Johnston
HAPPY FOBBER DAY, DADDY!!
IT'S DADDY DAY! IT'S DADDY DAY!!
IT'S DADDY DAY TODAY, TODAY!
BOUNCE BOUNCE
WAAAAHH
HAPPY HAPPY DADDY DAYYY!!
WAAAA
BOUNCE, BOUNCE, JUMP, BOUNCE
MEREDITH, DADDY WOULD LIKE SOME PEACE AND QUIET ON HIS SPECIAL DAY, OK?
SO, LET'S YOU AND I AND BABY ROBIN GO FOR A NICE, LONG WALK!
ALL DADDY WANTS IS PEACE AN' QUIET?
WHAT KIND OF A PRESENT IS THAT?!!
LYNN

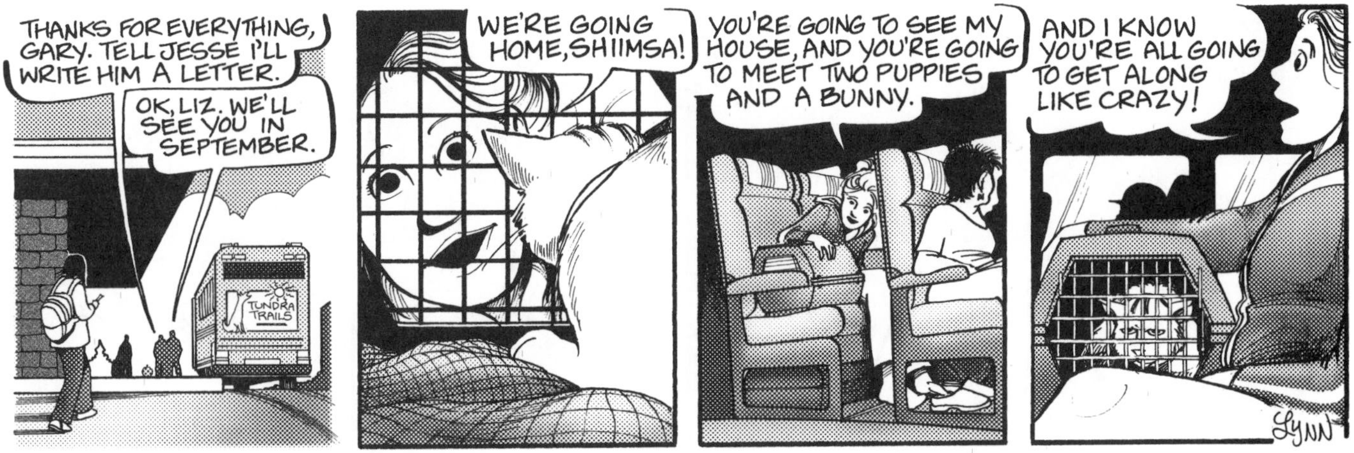
THANKS FOR EVERYTHING, GARY. TELL JESSE I'LL WRITE HIM A LETTER.
OK, LIZ. WE'LL SEE YOU IN SEPTEMBER.
TUNDRA TRAILS
WE'RE GOING HOME, SHIIMSA!
YOU'RE GOING TO SEE MY HOUSE, AND YOU'RE GOING TO MEET TWO PUPPIES AND A BUNNY.
AND I KNOW YOU'RE ALL GOING TO GET ALONG LIKE CRAZY!
LYNN

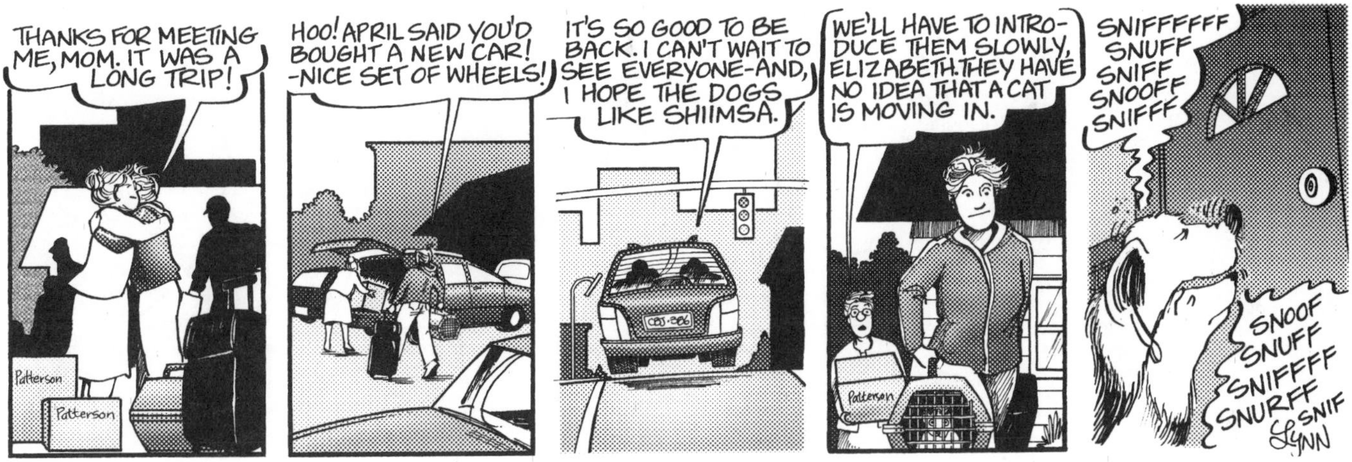
THANKS FOR MEETING ME, MOM. IT WAS A LONG TRIP!
Patterson
Patterson
HOO! APRIL SAID YOU'D BOUGHT A NEW CAR! -NICE SET OF WHEELS!
IT'S SO GOOD TO BE BACK. I CAN'T WAIT TO SEE EVERYONE-AND, I HOPE THE DOGS LIKE SHIIMSA.
WE'LL HAVE TO INTRODUCE THEM SLOWLY, ELIZABETH. THEY HAVE NO IDEA THAT A CAT IS MOVING IN.
Patterson
SNIFFFFFF
SNUFF
SNIFF
SNOOFF
SNIFFF
SNOOF
SNUFF
SNIFFFF
SNURFF
SNIF
LYNN

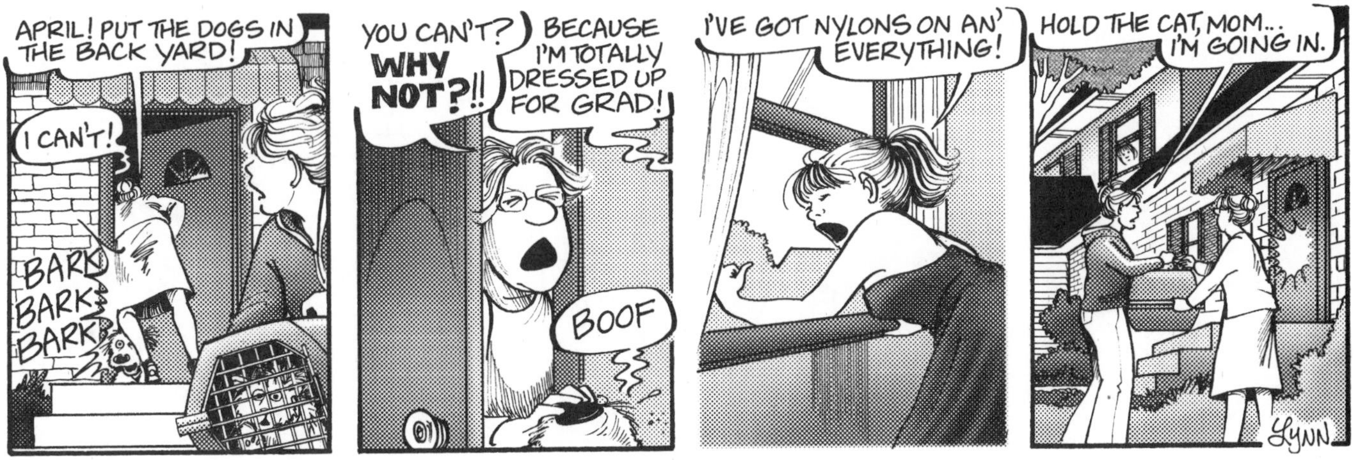
APRIL! PUT THE DOGS IN THE BACK YARD!
I CAN'T!
BARK
BARK
BARK
YOU CAN'T? WHY NOT?!!
BECAUSE I'M TOTALLY DRESSED UP FOR GRAD!
BOOF
I'VE GOT NYLONS ON AN' EVERYTHING!
HOLD THE CAT, MOM... I'M GOING IN.
LYNN

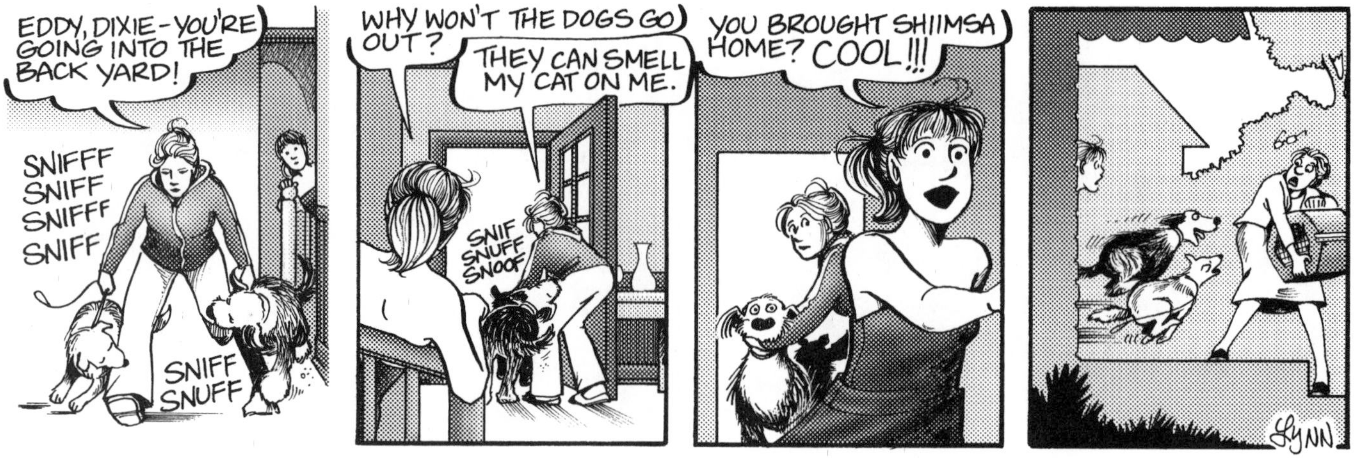
EDDY, DIXIE - YOU'RE GOING INTO THE BACK YARD!
SNIFFF SNIFF SNIFFF SNIFF
SNIFF SNUFF
WHY WON'T THE DOGS GO OUT?
THEY CAN SMELL MY CAT ON ME.
SNIF SNUFF SNOOF
YOU BROUGHT SHIIMSA HOME? COOL!!!
LYNN

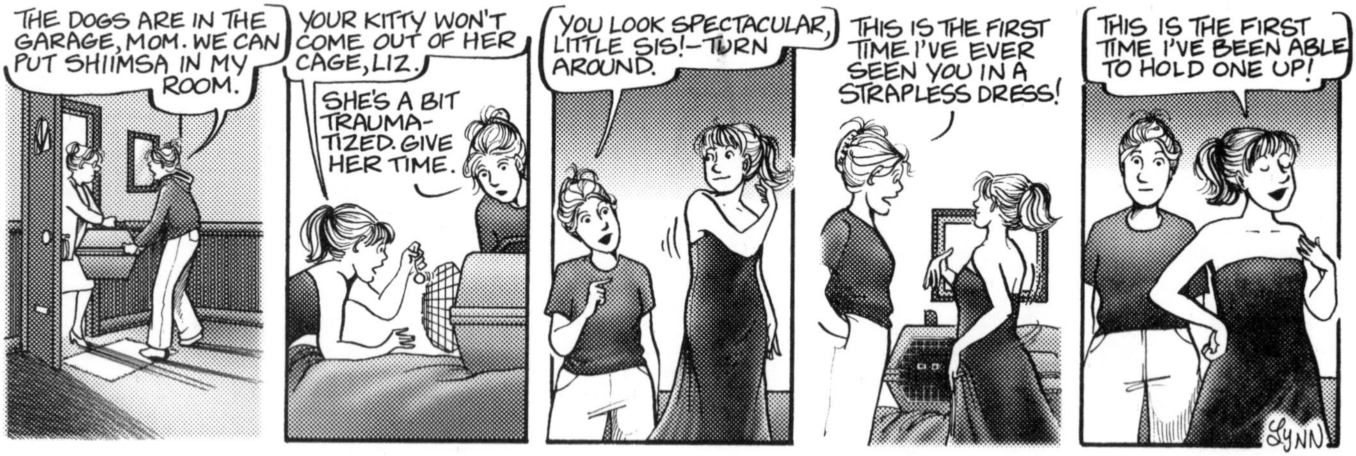
THE DOGS ARE IN THE GARAGE, MOM. WE CAN PUT SHIIMSA IN MY ROOM.
YOUR KITTY WON'T COME OUT OF HER CAGE, LIZ.
SHE'S A BIT TRAUMATIZED. GIVE HER TIME.
YOU LOOK SPECTACULAR, LITTLE SIS!—TURN AROUND.
THIS IS THE FIRST TIME I'VE EVER SEEN YOU IN A STRAPLESS DRESS!
THIS IS THE FIRST TIME I'VE BEEN ABLE TO HOLD ONE UP!
LYNN

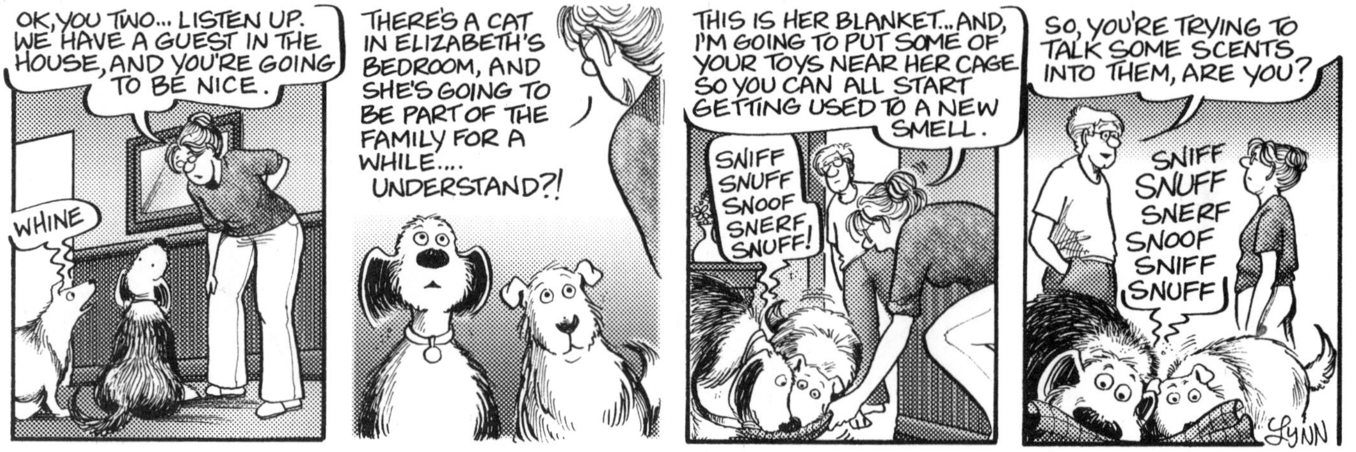
OK, YOU TWO... LISTEN UP. WE HAVE A GUEST IN THE HOUSE, AND YOU'RE GOING TO BE NICE.
WHINE
THERE'S A CAT IN ELIZABETH'S BEDROOM, AND SHE'S GOING TO BE PART OF THE FAMILY FOR A WHILE.... UNDERSTAND?!
THIS IS HER BLANKET... AND, I'M GOING TO PUT SOME OF YOUR TOYS NEAR HER CAGE SO YOU CAN ALL START GETTING USED TO A NEW SMELL.
SNIFF SNUFF SNOOF SNERF SNUFF!
SO, YOU'RE TRYING TO TALK SOME SCENTS INTO THEM, ARE YOU?
SNIFF SNUFF SNERF SNOOF SNIFF SNUFF
LYNN

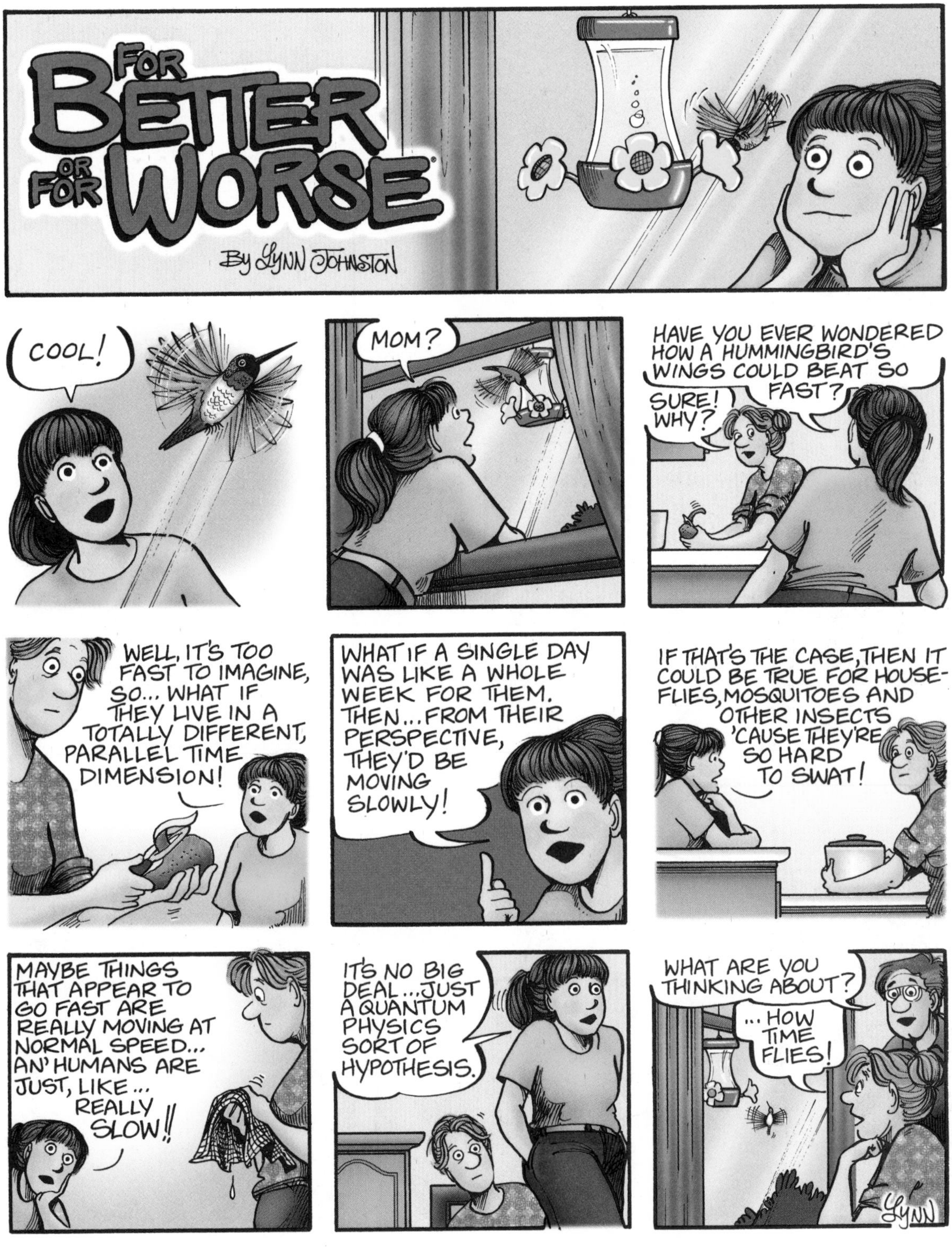
FOR BETTER OR FOR WORSE
BY LYNN JOHNSTON
COOL!
MOM?
HAVE YOU EVER WONDERED HOW A HUMMINGBIRD'S WINGS COULD BEAT SO FAST?
SURE! WHY?
WELL, IT'S TOO FAST TO IMAGINE, SO... WHAT IF THEY LIVE IN A TOTALLY DIFFERENT, PARALLEL TIME DIMENSION!
WHAT IF A SINGLE DAY WAS LIKE A WHOLE WEEK FOR THEM. THEN... FROM THEIR PERSPECTIVE, THEY'D BE MOVING SLOWLY!
IF THAT'S THE CASE, THEN IT COULD BE TRUE FOR HOUSE-FLIES, MOSQUITOES AND OTHER INSECTS 'CAUSE THEY'RE SO HARD TO SWAT!
MAYBE THINGS THAT APPEAR TO GO FAST ARE REALLY MOVING AT NORMAL SPEED... AN' HUMANS ARE JUST, LIKE... REALLY SLOW!!
IT'S NO BIG DEAL... JUST A QUANTUM PHYSICS SORT OF HYPOTHESIS.
WHAT ARE YOU THINKING ABOUT?
...HOW TIME FLIES!
LYNN

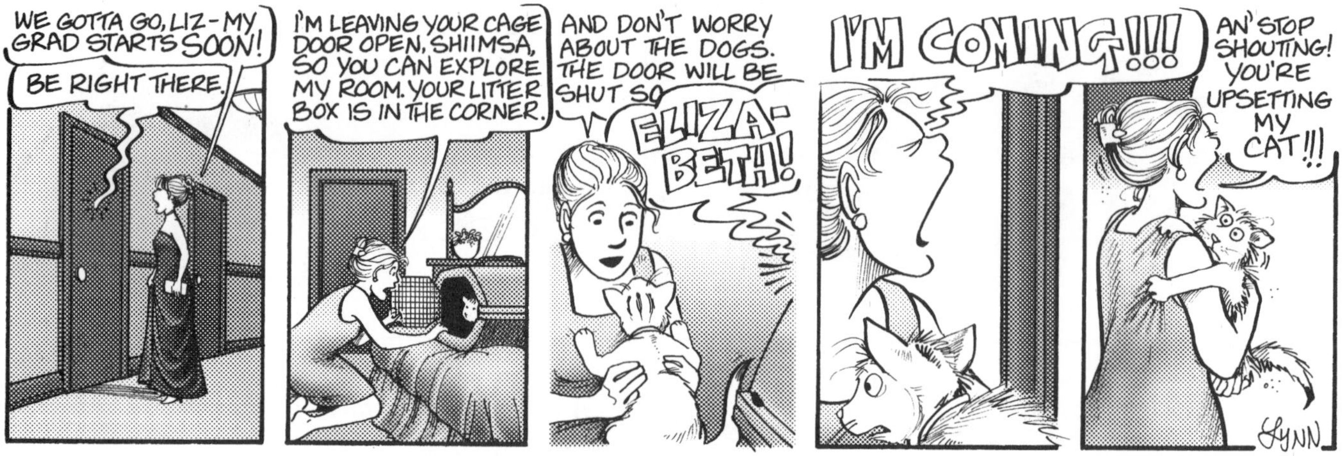
WE GOTTA GO, LIZ- MY GRAD STARTS SOON!
BE RIGHT THERE.
I'M LEAVING YOUR CAGE DOOR OPEN, SHIIMSA, SO YOU CAN EXPLORE MY ROOM. YOUR LITTER BOX IS IN THE CORNER.
AND DON'T WORRY ABOUT THE DOGS. THE DOOR WILL BE SHUT SO
ELIZA-BETH!
I'M COMING!!!
AN' STOP SHOUTING! YOU'RE UPSETTING MY CAT!!!
LYNN

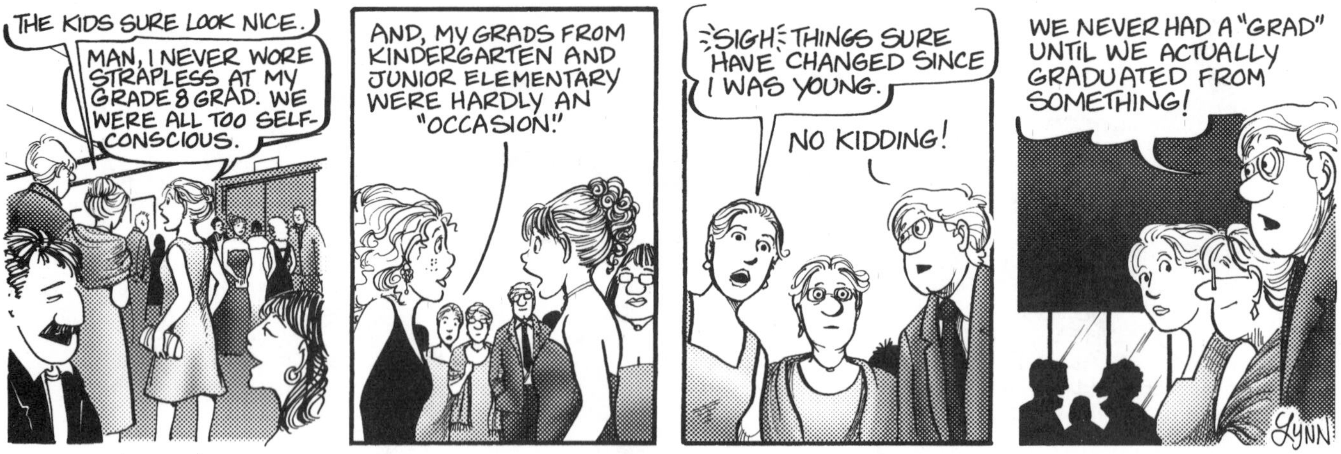
THE KIDS SURE LOOK NICE.
MAN, I NEVER WORE STRAPLESS AT MY GRADE 8 GRAD. WE WERE ALL TOO SELF-CONSCIOUS.
AND, MY GRADS FROM KINDERGARTEN AND JUNIOR ELEMENTARY WERE HARDLY AN "OCCASION."
SIGH THINGS SURE HAVE CHANGED SINCE I WAS YOUNG.
NO KIDDING!
WE NEVER HAD A "GRAD" UNTIL WE ACTUALLY GRADUATED FROM SOMETHING!
LYNN

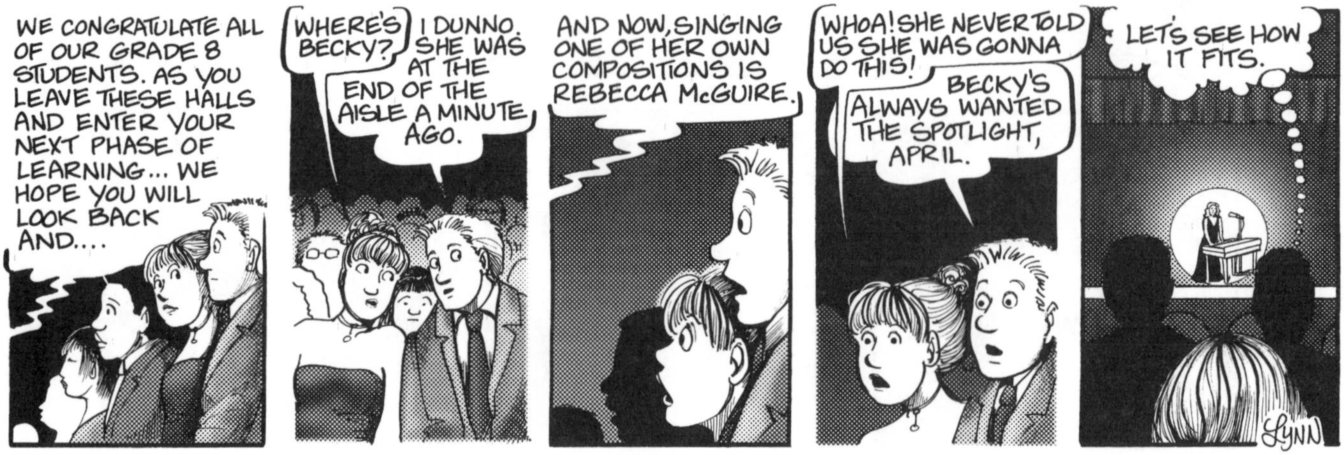
WE CONGRATULATE ALL OF OUR GRADE 8 STUDENTS. AS YOU LEAVE THESE HALLS AND ENTER YOUR NEXT PHASE OF LEARNING... WE HOPE YOU WILL LOOK BACK AND....
WHERE'S BECKY?
I DUNNO. SHE WAS AT THE END OF THE AISLE A MINUTE AGO.
AND NOW, SINGING ONE OF HER OWN COMPOSITIONS IS REBECCA McGUIRE.
WHOA! SHE NEVER TOLD US SHE WAS GONNA DO THIS!
BECKY'S ALWAYS WANTED THE SPOTLIGHT, APRIL.
LET'S SEE HOW IT FITS.
LYNN

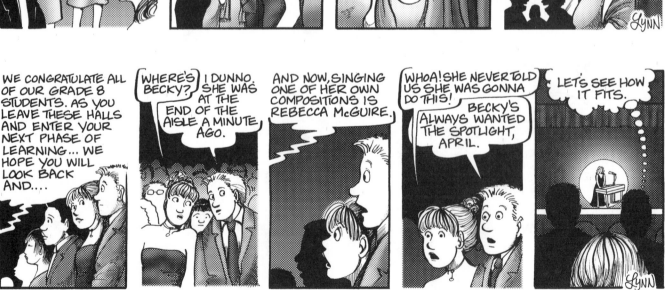

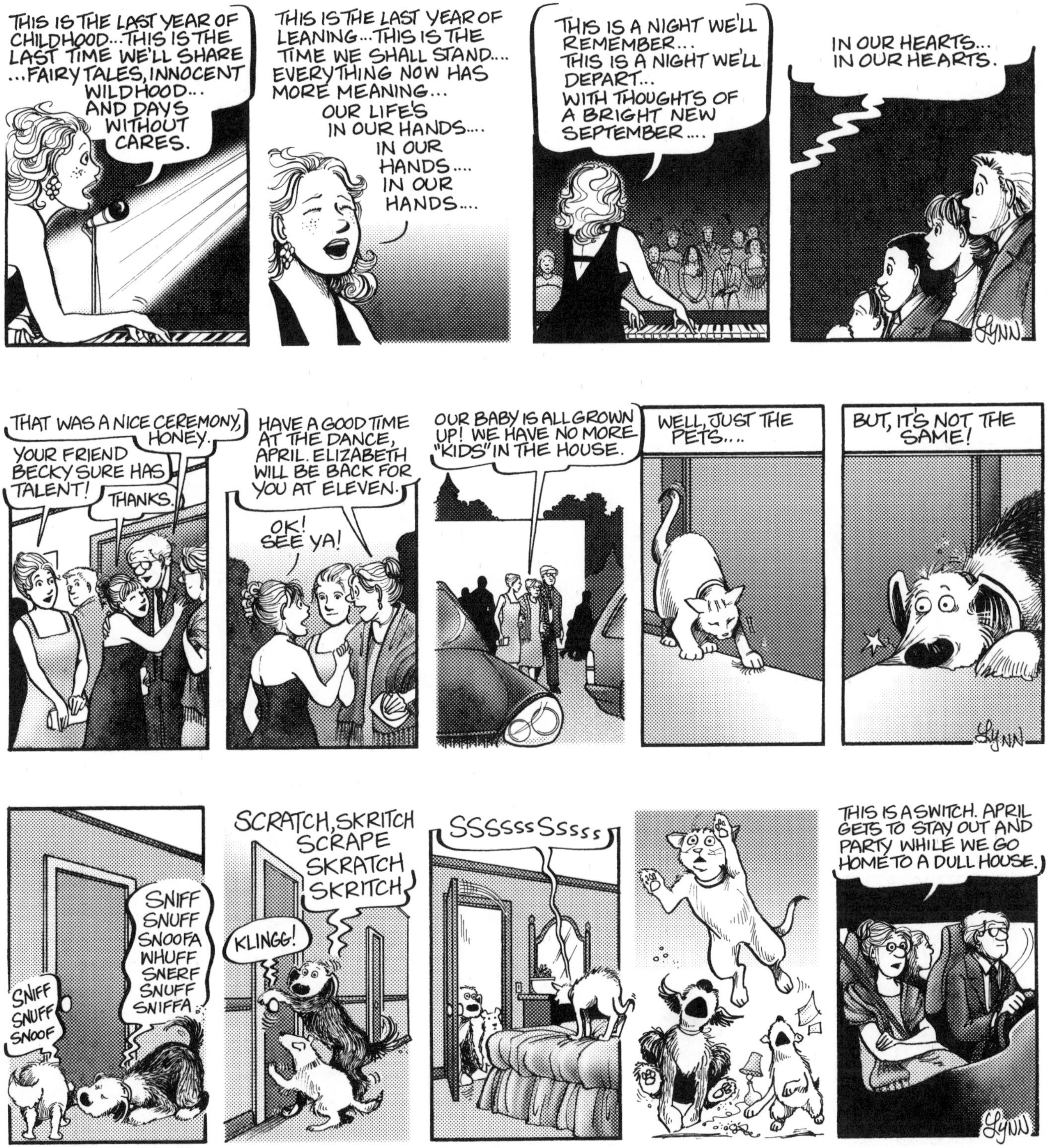
THIS IS THE LAST YEAR OF CHILDHOOD...THIS IS THE LAST TIME WE'LL SHARE ...FAIRY TALES, INNOCENT WILDHOOD... AND DAYS WITHOUT CARES.
THIS IS THE LAST YEAR OF LEANING...THIS IS THE TIME WE SHALL STAND.... EVERYTHING NOW HAS MORE MEANING... OUR LIFE'S IN OUR HANDS.... IN OUR HANDS.... IN OUR HANDS....
THIS IS A NIGHT WE'LL REMEMBER... THIS IS A NIGHT WE'LL DEPART... WITH THOUGHTS OF A BRIGHT NEW SEPTEMBER....
IN OUR HEARTS... IN OUR HEARTS.
LYNN
THAT WAS A NICE CEREMONY, HONEY.
YOUR FRIEND BECKY SURE HAS TALENT!
THANKS.
HAVE A GOOD TIME AT THE DANCE, APRIL. ELIZABETH WILL BE BACK FOR YOU AT ELEVEN.
OK! SEE YA!
OUR BABY IS ALL GROWN UP! WE HAVE NO MORE "KIDS" IN THE HOUSE.
WELL, JUST THE PETS....
BUT, IT'S NOT THE SAME!
LYNN
SNIFF SNUFF SNOOFA WHUFF SNERF SNUFF SNIFFA
SNIFF SNUFF SNOOF
SCRATCH, SKRITCH SCRAPE SKRATCH SKRITCH
KLINGG!
SSSSSSSSSSS
THIS IS A SWITCH. APRIL GETS TO STAY OUT AND PARTY WHILE WE GO HOME TO A DULL HOUSE.
LYNN

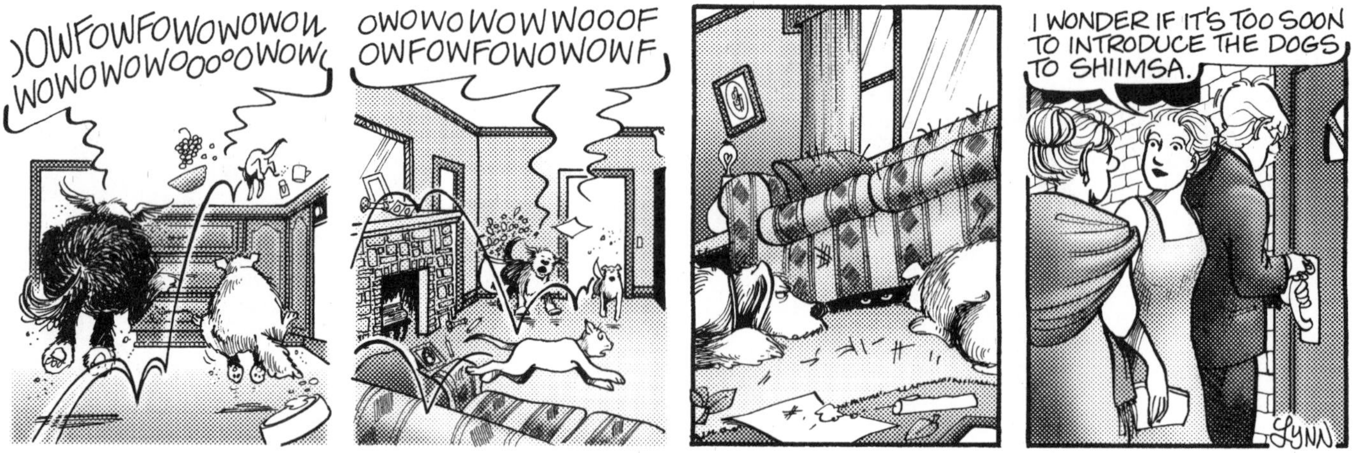
OWFOWFOWOWOWOW WOWOWOWOOooOWOW
OWOWOWOWWOOOF OWFOWFOWOWOWF
I WONDER IF IT'S TOO SOON TO INTRODUCE THE DOGS TO SHIIMSA.
LYNN

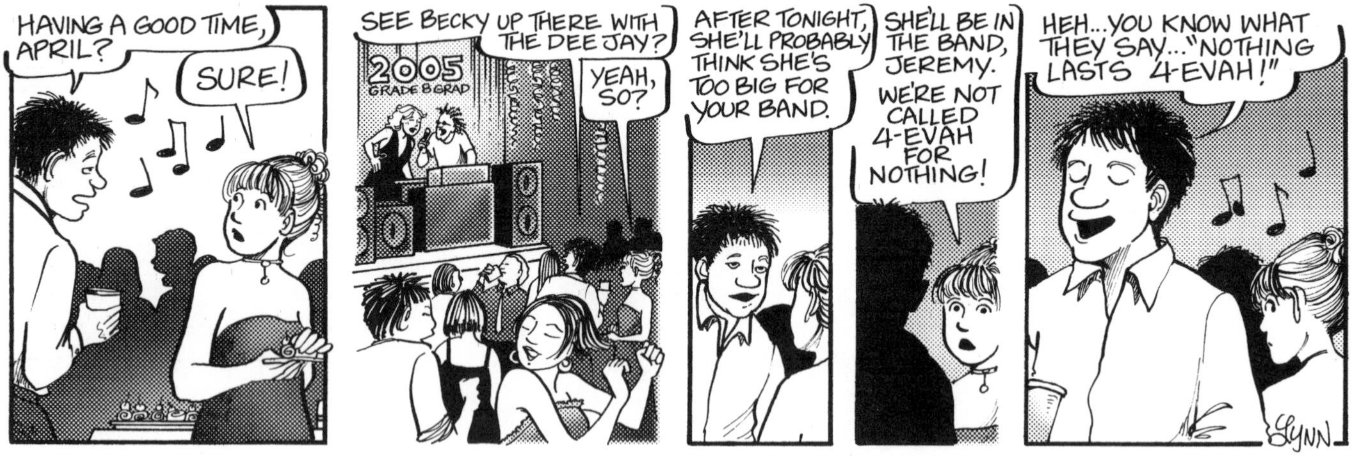
HAVING A GOOD TIME, APRIL?
SURE!
SEE BECKY UP THERE WITH THE DEE JAY?
2005 GRADE 8 GRAD
YEAH, SO?
AFTER TONIGHT, SHE'LL PROBABLY THINK SHE'S TOO BIG FOR YOUR BAND.
SHE'LL BE IN THE BAND, JEREMY.
WE'RE NOT CALLED 4-EVAH FOR NOTHING!
HEH...YOU KNOW WHAT THEY SAY..."NOTHING LASTS 4-EVAH!"
LYNN

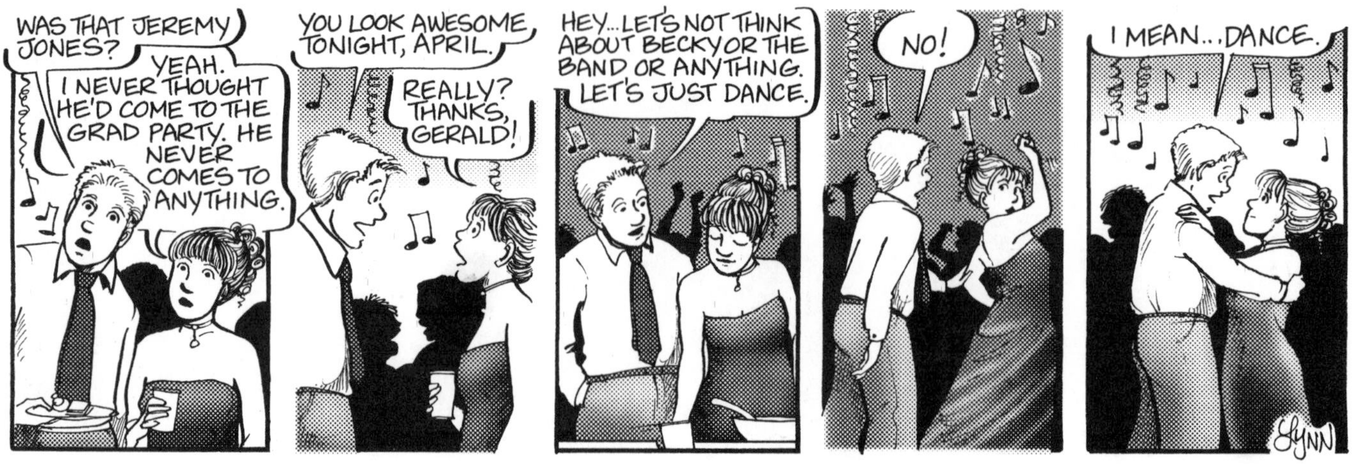
WAS THAT JEREMY JONES?
YEAH. I NEVER THOUGHT HE'D COME TO THE GRAD PARTY. HE NEVER COMES TO ANYTHING.
YOU LOOK AWESOME TONIGHT, APRIL.
REALLY? THANKS, GERALD!
HEY... LET'S NOT THINK ABOUT BECKY OR THE BAND OR ANYTHING. LET'S JUST DANCE.
NO!
I MEAN... DANCE.
LYNN

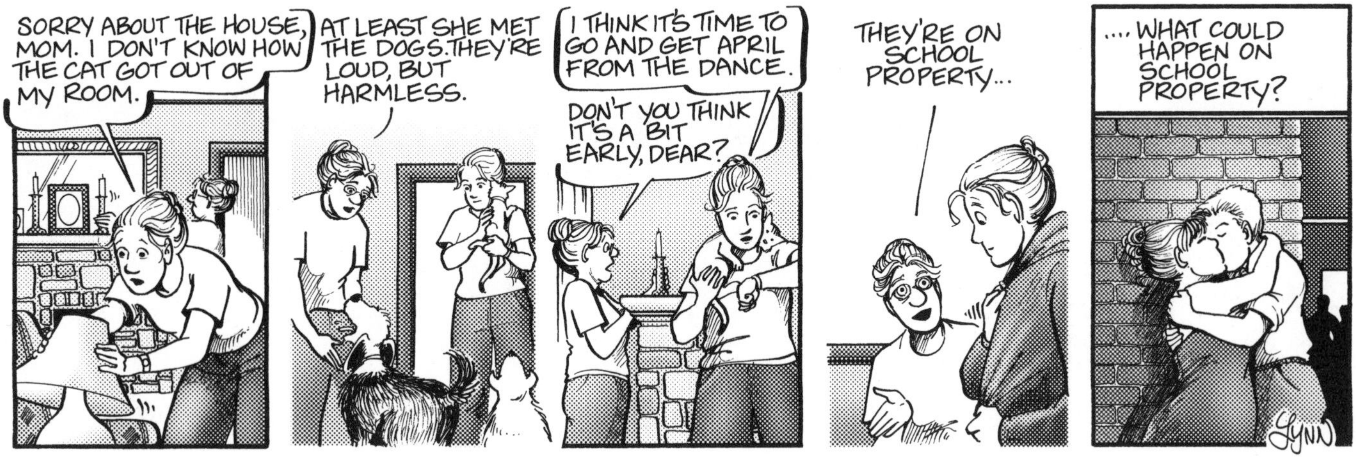
SORRY ABOUT THE HOUSE, MOM. I DON'T KNOW HOW THE CAT GOT OUT OF MY ROOM.
AT LEAST SHE MET THE DOGS. THEY'RE LOUD, BUT HARMLESS.
I THINK IT'S TIME TO GO AND GET APRIL FROM THE DANCE.
DON'T YOU THINK IT'S A BIT EARLY, DEAR?
THEY'RE ON SCHOOL PROPERTY...
....WHAT COULD HAPPEN ON SCHOOL PROPERTY?
LYNN

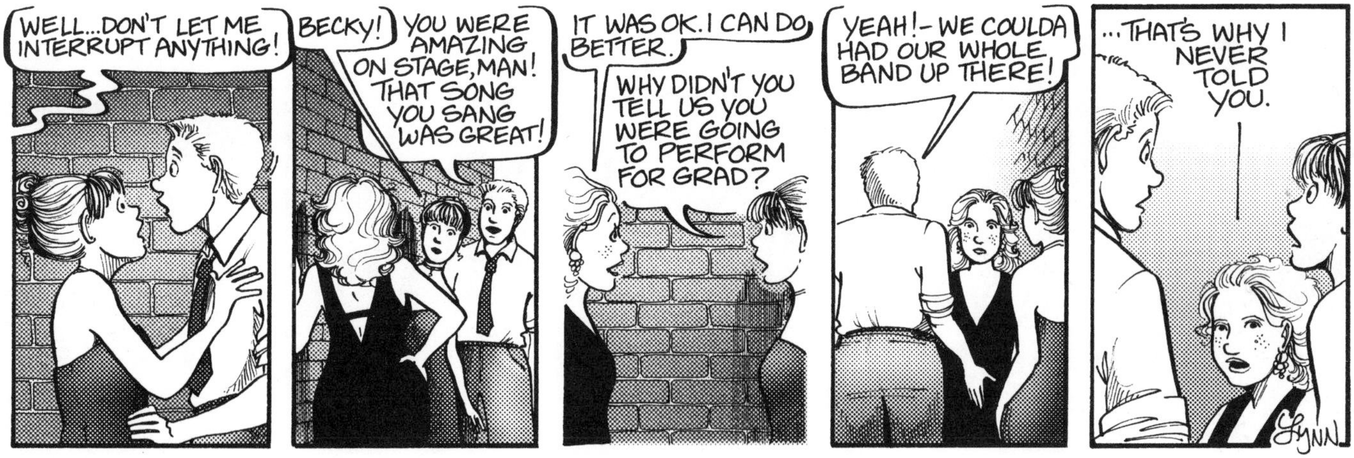
WELL...DON'T LET ME INTERRUPT ANYTHING!
BECKY!
YOU WERE AMAZING ON STAGE, MAN! THAT SONG YOU SANG WAS GREAT!
IT WAS OK. I CAN DO BETTER.
WHY DIDN'T YOU TELL US YOU WERE GOING TO PERFORM FOR GRAD?
YEAH! - WE COULDA HAD OUR WHOLE BAND UP THERE!
...THAT'S WHY I NEVER TOLD YOU.
LYNN

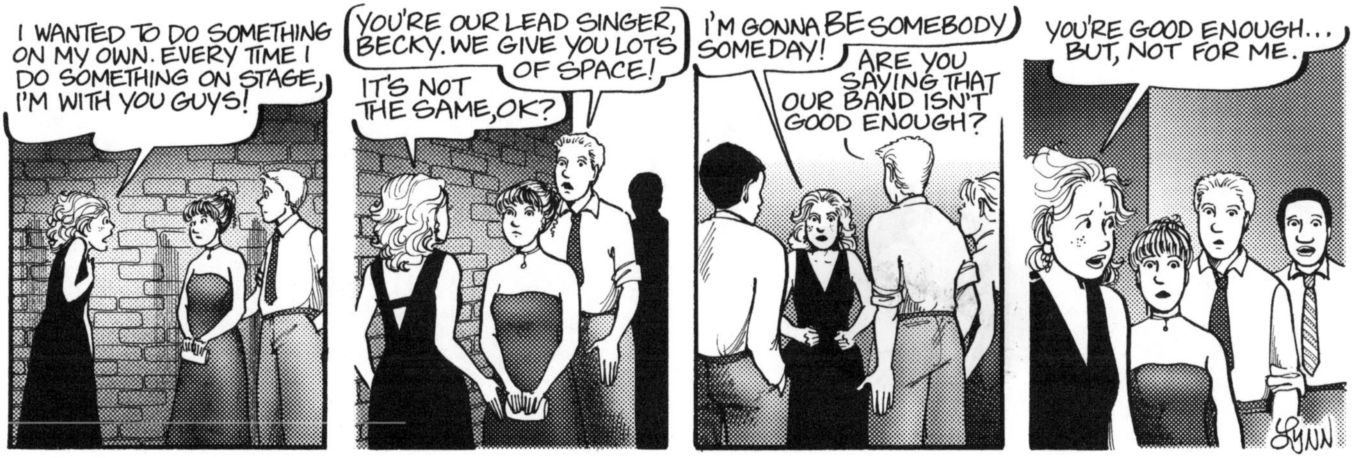
I WANTED TO DO SOMETHING ON MY OWN. EVERY TIME I DO SOMETHING ON STAGE, I'M WITH YOU GUYS!
YOU'RE OUR LEAD SINGER, BECKY. WE GIVE YOU LOTS OF SPACE!
IT'S NOT THE SAME, OK?
I'M GONNA BE SOMEBODY SOMEDAY!
ARE YOU SAYING THAT OUR BAND ISN'T GOOD ENOUGH?
YOU'RE GOOD ENOUGH... BUT, NOT FOR ME.
LYNN

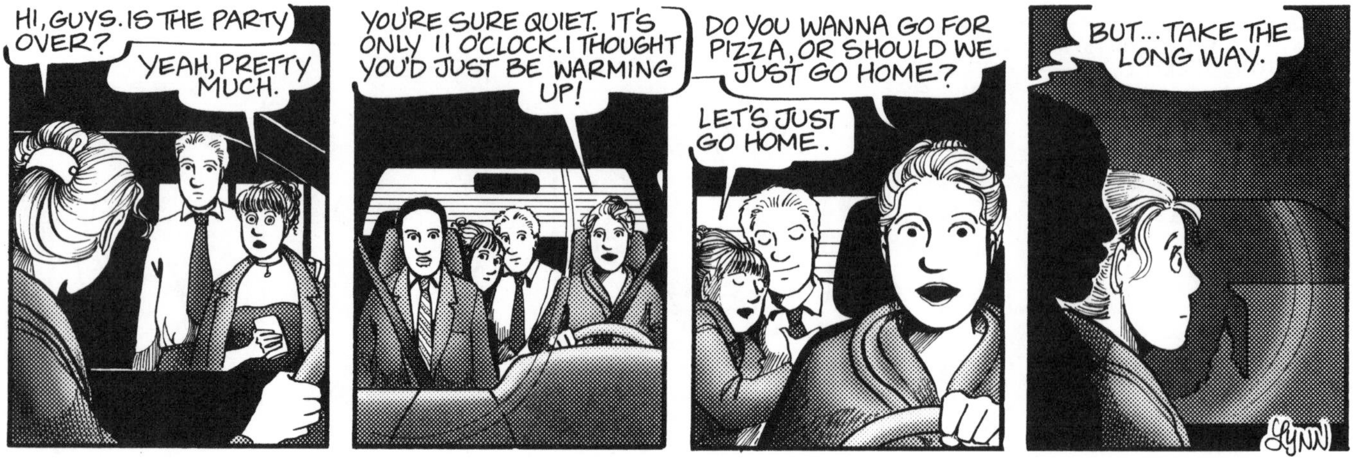
HI, GUYS. IS THE PARTY OVER?
YEAH, PRETTY MUCH.
YOU'RE SURE QUIET. IT'S ONLY 11 O'CLOCK. I THOUGHT YOU'D JUST BE WARMING UP!
DO YOU WANNA GO FOR PIZZA, OR SHOULD WE JUST GO HOME?
LET'S JUST GO HOME.
BUT... TAKE THE LONG WAY.
LYNN

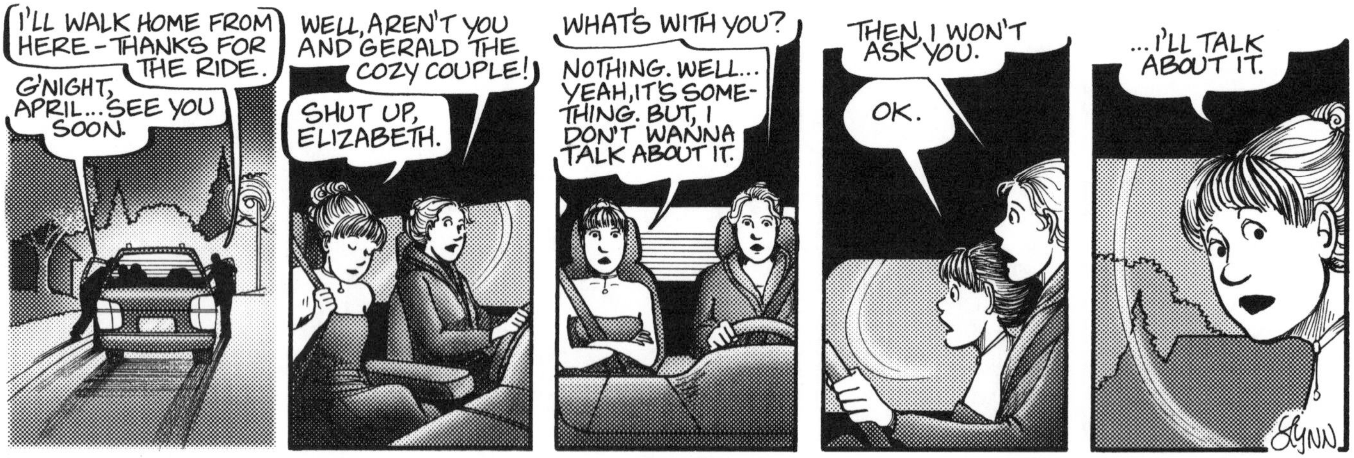
I'LL WALK HOME FROM HERE - THANKS FOR THE RIDE.
G'NIGHT, APRIL... SEE YOU SOON.
WELL, AREN'T YOU AND GERALD THE COZY COUPLE!
SHUT UP, ELIZABETH.
WHAT'S WITH YOU?
NOTHING. WELL... YEAH, IT'S SOME-THING. BUT, I DON'T WANNA TALK ABOUT IT.
THEN, I WON'T ASK YOU.
OK.
...I'LL TALK ABOUT IT.
LYNN

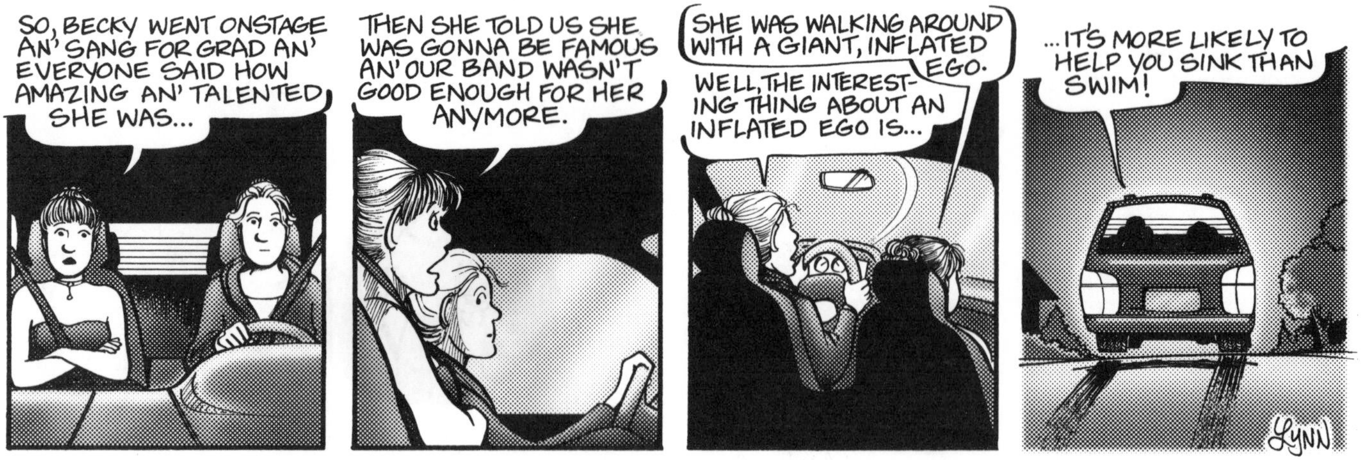
SO, BECKY WENT ONSTAGE AN' SANG FOR GRAD AN' EVERYONE SAID HOW AMAZING AN' TALENTED SHE WAS...
THEN SHE TOLD US SHE WAS GONNA BE FAMOUS AN' OUR BAND WASN'T GOOD ENOUGH FOR HER ANYMORE.
SHE WAS WALKING AROUND WITH A GIANT, INFLATED EGO.
WELL, THE INTEREST-ING THING ABOUT AN INFLATED EGO IS...
...IT'S MORE LIKELY TO HELP YOU SINK THAN SWIM!
LYNN

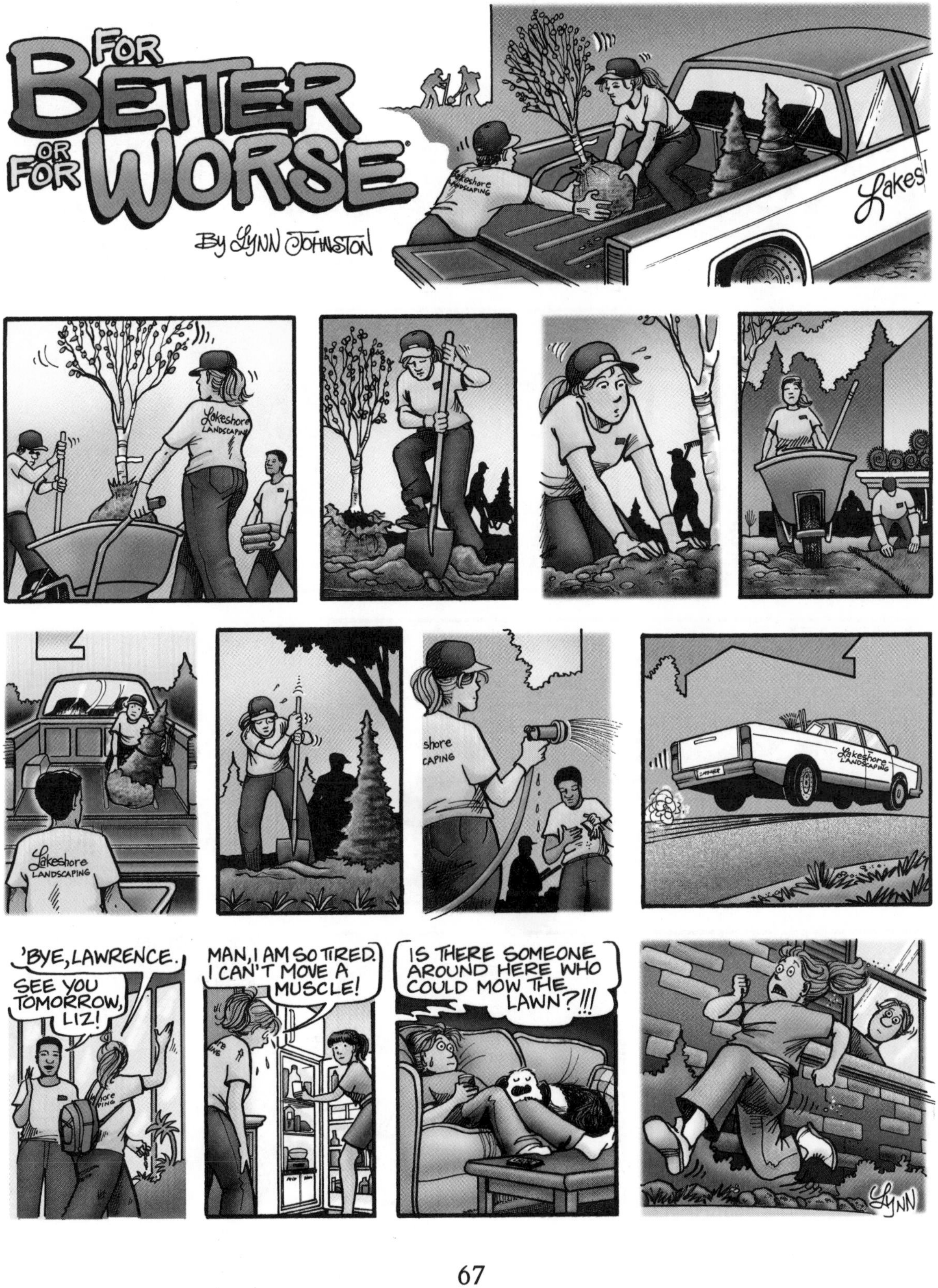
FOR BETTER OR FOR WORSE
By LYNN JOHNSTON
Lakeshore LANDSCAPING
'BYE, LAWRENCE.
SEE YOU TOMORROW, LIZ!
MAN, I AM SO TIRED. I CAN'T MOVE A MUSCLE!
IS THERE SOMEONE AROUND HERE WHO COULD MOW THE LAWN?!!!
LYNN

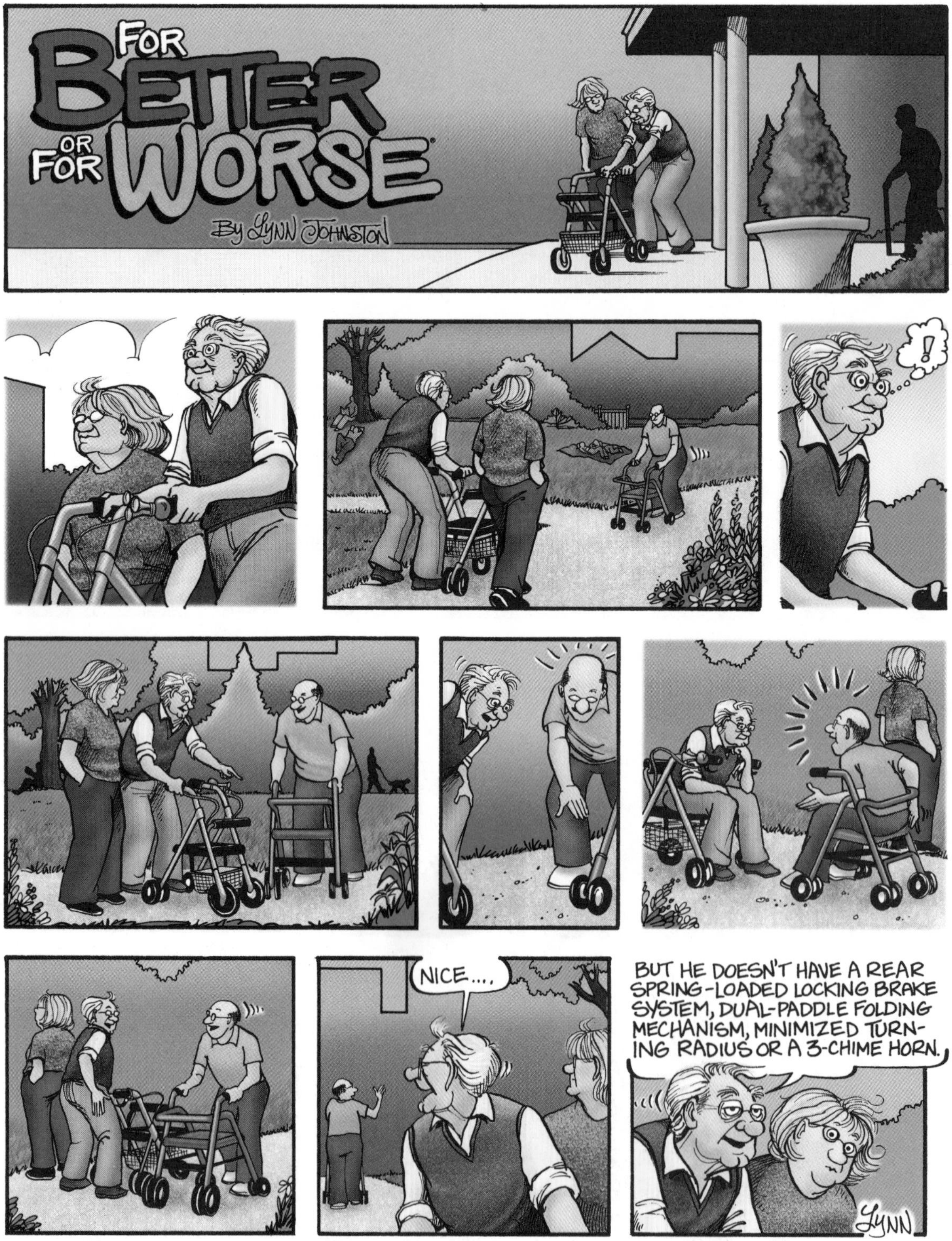
FOR BETTER OR FOR WORSE
BY LYNN JOHNSTON
!
NICE....
BUT HE DOESN'T HAVE A REAR SPRING-LOADED LOCKING BRAKE SYSTEM, DUAL-PADDLE FOLDING MECHANISM, MINIMIZED TURNING RADIUS OR A 3-CHIME HORN.
LYNN

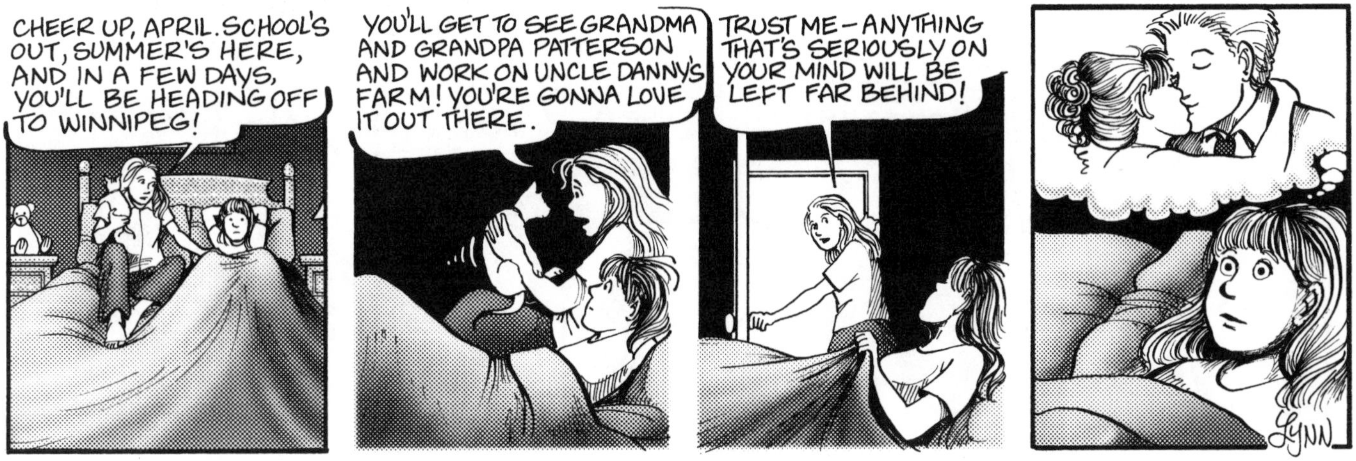
CHEER UP, APRIL. SCHOOL'S OUT, SUMMER'S HERE, AND IN A FEW DAYS, YOU'LL BE HEADING OFF TO WINNIPEG!
YOU'LL GET TO SEE GRANDMA AND GRANDPA PATTERSON AND WORK ON UNCLE DANNY'S FARM! YOU'RE GONNA LOVE IT OUT THERE.
TRUST ME – ANYTHING THAT'S SERIOUSLY ON YOUR MIND WILL BE LEFT FAR BEHIND!
LYNN

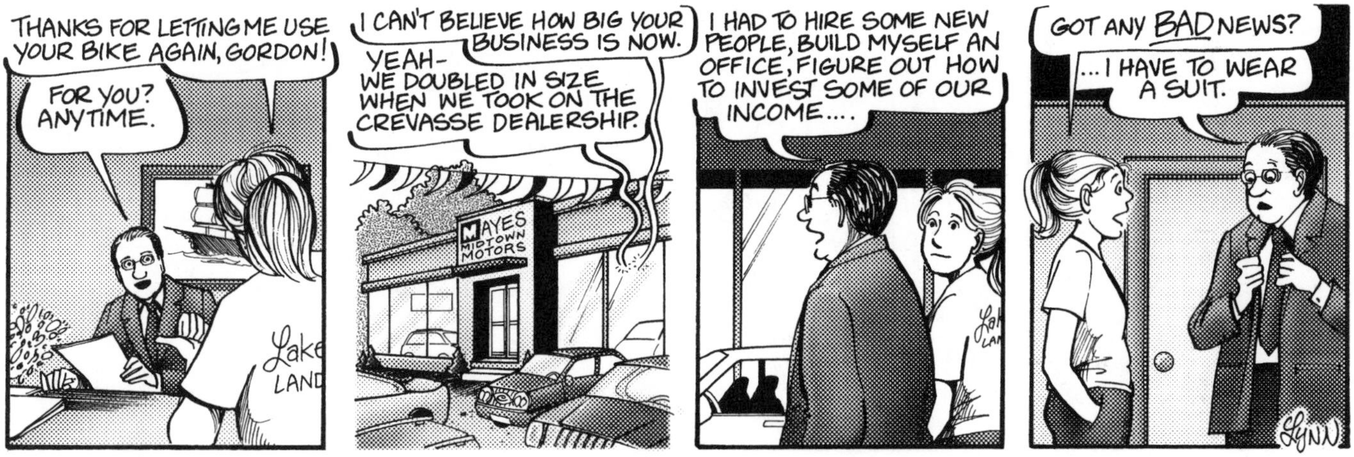
THANKS FOR LETTING ME USE YOUR BIKE AGAIN, GORDON!
FOR YOU? ANYTIME.
LAKE LAND
I CAN'T BELIEVE HOW BIG YOUR BUSINESS IS NOW.
YEAH– WE DOUBLED IN SIZE WHEN WE TOOK ON THE CREVASSE DEALERSHIP.
MAYES MIDTOWN MOTORS
I HAD TO HIRE SOME NEW PEOPLE, BUILD MYSELF AN OFFICE, FIGURE OUT HOW TO INVEST SOME OF OUR INCOME....
GOT ANY BAD NEWS?
...I HAVE TO WEAR A SUIT.
LYNN

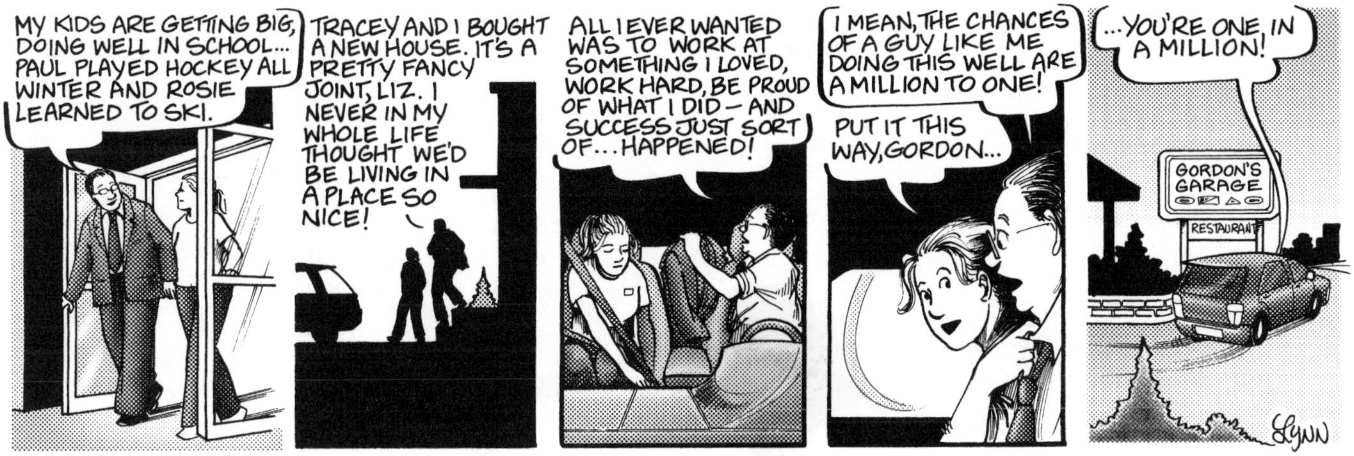
MY KIDS ARE GETTING BIG, DOING WELL IN SCHOOL... PAUL PLAYED HOCKEY ALL WINTER AND ROSIE LEARNED TO SKI.
TRACEY AND I BOUGHT A NEW HOUSE. IT'S A PRETTY FANCY JOINT, LIZ. I NEVER IN MY WHOLE LIFE THOUGHT WE'D BE LIVING IN A PLACE SO NICE!
ALL I EVER WANTED WAS TO WORK AT SOMETHING I LOVED, WORK HARD, BE PROUD OF WHAT I DID – AND SUCCESS JUST SORT OF... HAPPENED!
I MEAN, THE CHANCES OF A GUY LIKE ME DOING THIS WELL ARE A MILLION TO ONE!
PUT IT THIS WAY, GORDON...
...YOU'RE ONE IN A MILLION!
GORDON'S GARAGE
RESTAURANT
LYNN

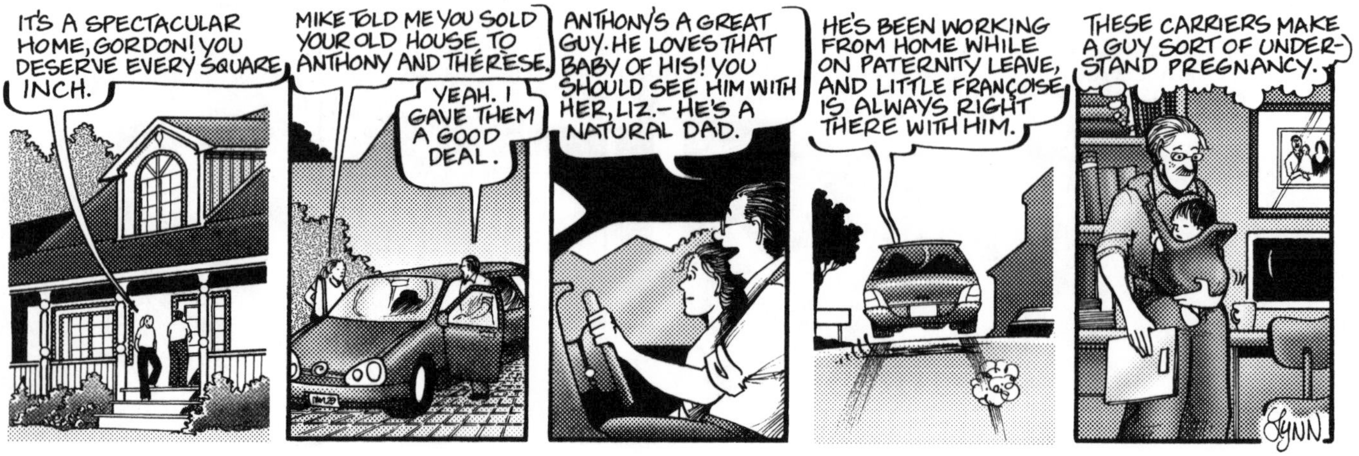
IT'S A SPECTACULAR HOME, GORDON! YOU DESERVE EVERY SQUARE INCH.
MIKE TOLD ME YOU SOLD YOUR OLD HOUSE TO ANTHONY AND THÉRÈSE.
YEAH. I GAVE THEM A GOOD DEAL.
ANTHONY'S A GREAT GUY. HE LOVES THAT BABY OF HIS! YOU SHOULD SEE HIM WITH HER, LIZ.– HE'S A NATURAL DAD.
HE'S BEEN WORKING FROM HOME WHILE ON PATERNITY LEAVE, AND LITTLE FRANÇOISE IS ALWAYS RIGHT THERE WITH HIM.
THESE CARRIERS MAKE A GUY SORT OF UNDER-STAND PREGNANCY.
LYNN

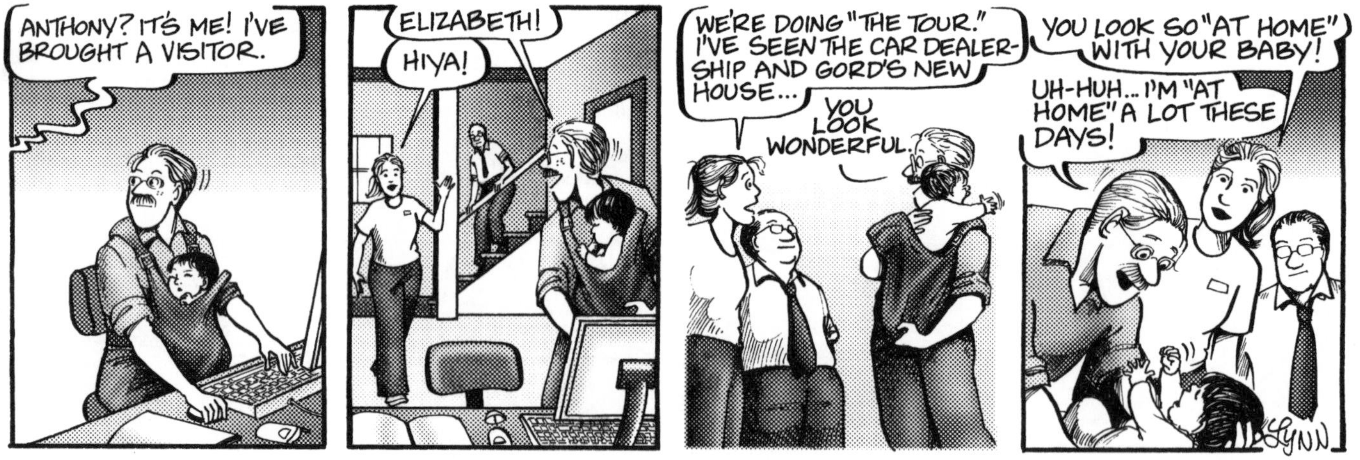
ANTHONY? IT'S ME! I'VE BROUGHT A VISITOR.
ELIZABETH!
HIYA!
WE'RE DOING "THE TOUR." I'VE SEEN THE CAR DEALER-SHIP AND GORD'S NEW HOUSE...
YOU LOOK WONDERFUL.
YOU LOOK SO "AT HOME" WITH YOUR BABY!
UH-HUH... I'M "AT HOME" A LOT THESE DAYS!
LYNN

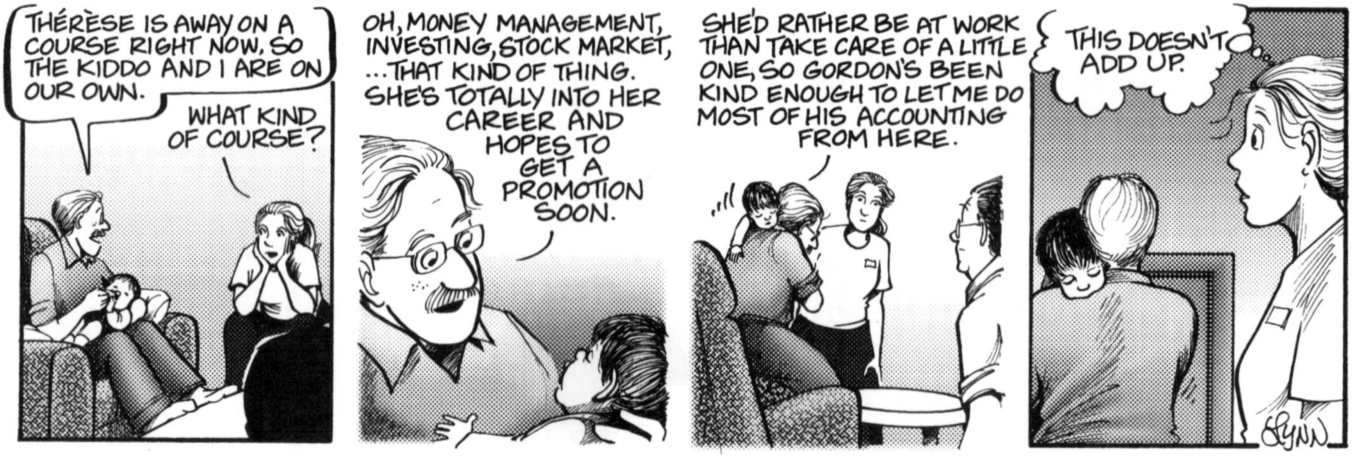
THÉRÈSE IS AWAY ON A COURSE RIGHT NOW, SO THE KIDDO AND I ARE ON OUR OWN.
WHAT KIND OF COURSE?
OH, MONEY MANAGEMENT, INVESTING, STOCK MARKET, ...THAT KIND OF THING. SHE'S TOTALLY INTO HER CAREER AND HOPES TO GET A PROMOTION SOON.
SHE'D RATHER BE AT WORK THAN TAKE CARE OF A LITTLE ONE, SO GORDON'S BEEN KIND ENOUGH TO LET ME DO MOST OF HIS ACCOUNTING FROM HERE.
THIS DOESN'T ADD UP.
LYNN

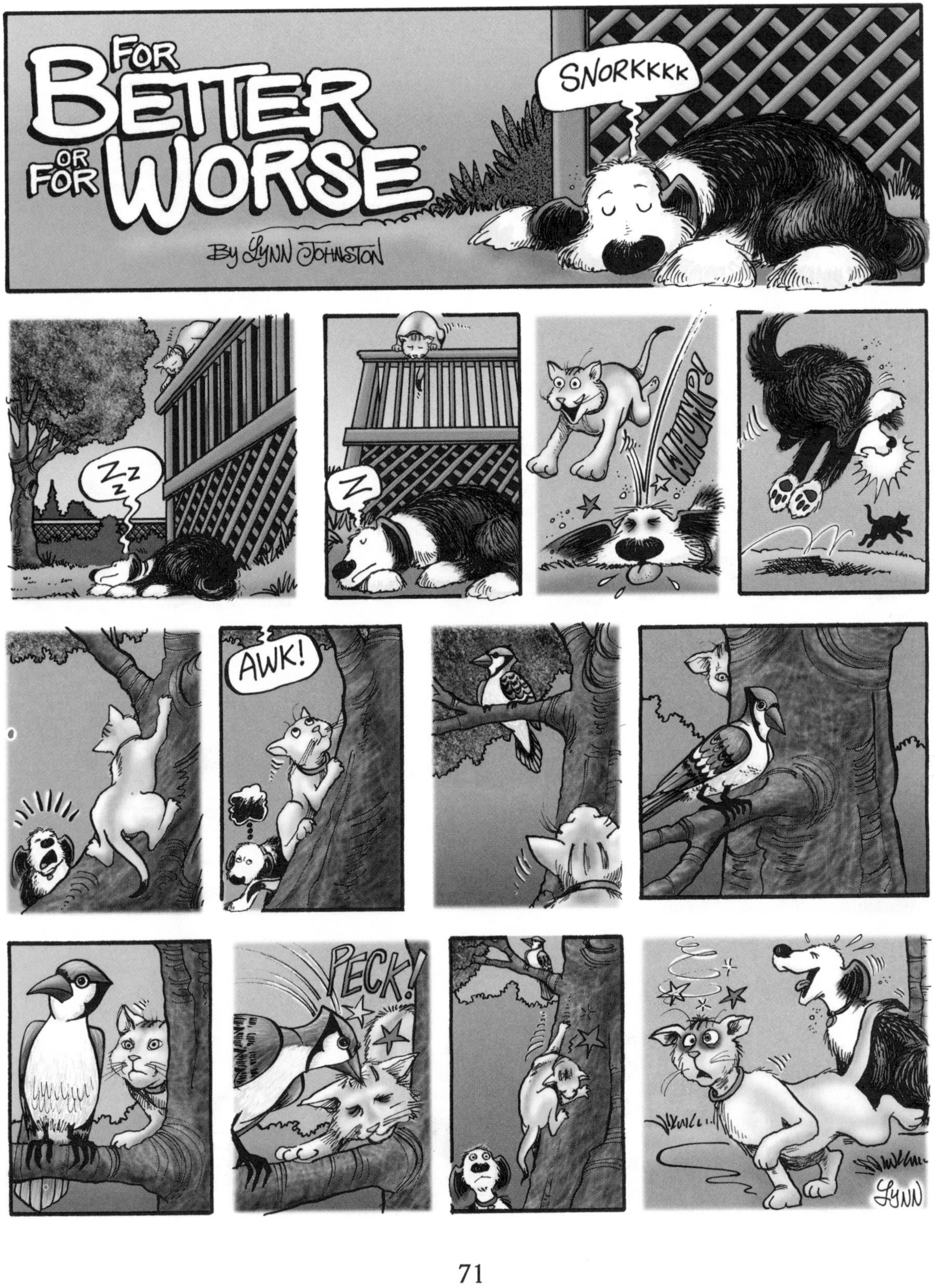
FOR BETTER OR FOR WORSE
BY LYNN JOHNSTON
SNORKKKK
ZZZ
Z
WHUMP!
AWK!
PECK!
LYNN

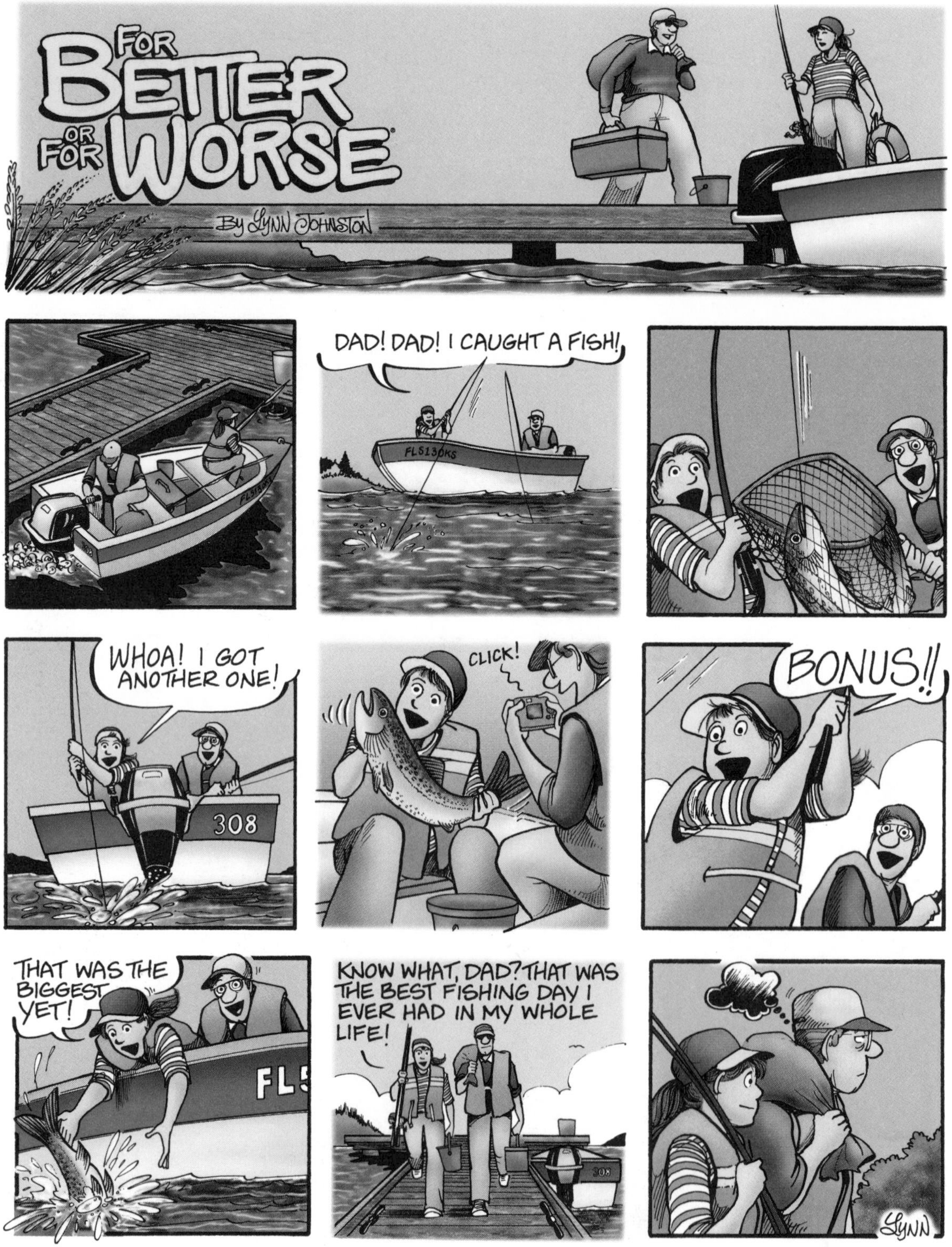
FOR BETTER OR FOR WORSE
BY LYNN JOHNSTON
DAD! DAD! I CAUGHT A FISH!
WHOA! I GOT ANOTHER ONE!
308
CLICK!
BONUS!!
THAT WAS THE BIGGEST YET!
FL5
KNOW WHAT, DAD? THAT WAS THE BEST FISHING DAY I EVER HAD IN MY WHOLE LIFE!
308
LYNN

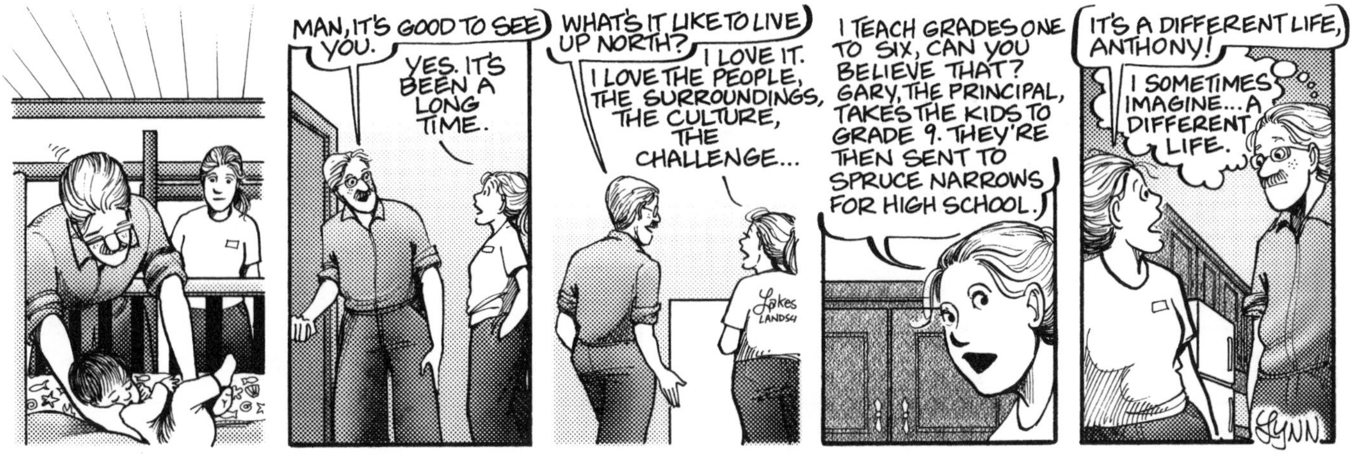
MAN, IT'S GOOD TO SEE YOU.
YES. IT'S BEEN A LONG TIME.
WHAT'S IT LIKE TO LIVE UP NORTH?
I LOVE IT. I LOVE THE PEOPLE, THE SURROUNDINGS, THE CULTURE, THE CHALLENGE...
I TEACH GRADES ONE TO SIX, CAN YOU BELIEVE THAT? GARY, THE PRINCIPAL, TAKES THE KIDS TO GRADE 9. THEY'RE THEN SENT TO SPRUCE NARROWS FOR HIGH SCHOOL.
IT'S A DIFFERENT LIFE, ANTHONY!
I SOMETIMES IMAGINE... A DIFFERENT LIFE.
LYNN

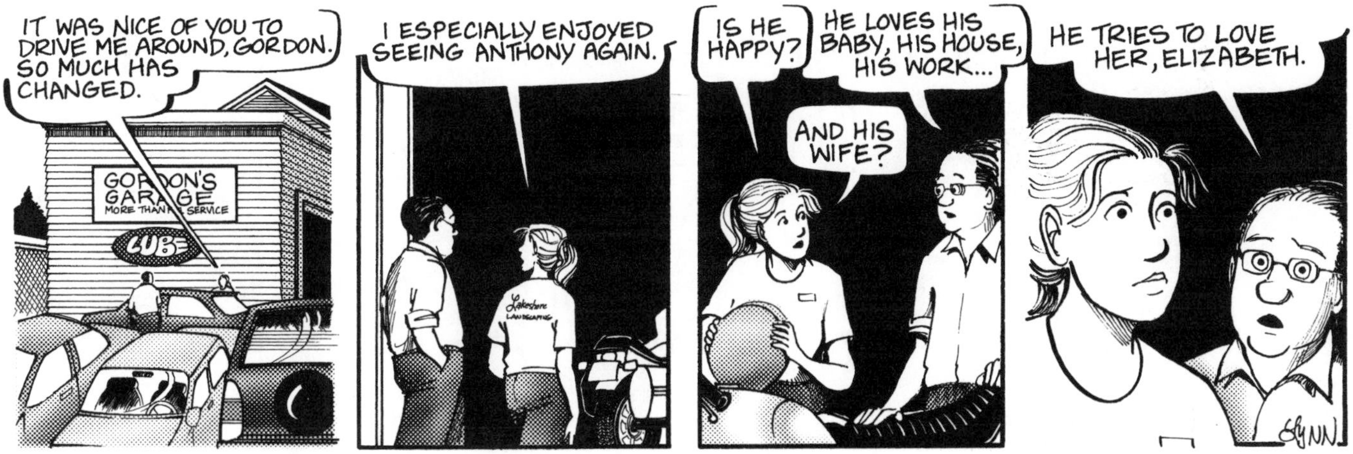
IT WAS NICE OF YOU TO DRIVE ME AROUND, GORDON. SO MUCH HAS CHANGED.
GORDON'S GARAGE
LUBE
I ESPECIALLY ENJOYED SEEING ANTHONY AGAIN.
IS HE HAPPY?
HE LOVES HIS BABY, HIS HOUSE, HIS WORK...
AND HIS WIFE?
HE TRIES TO LOVE HER, ELIZABETH.
LYNN

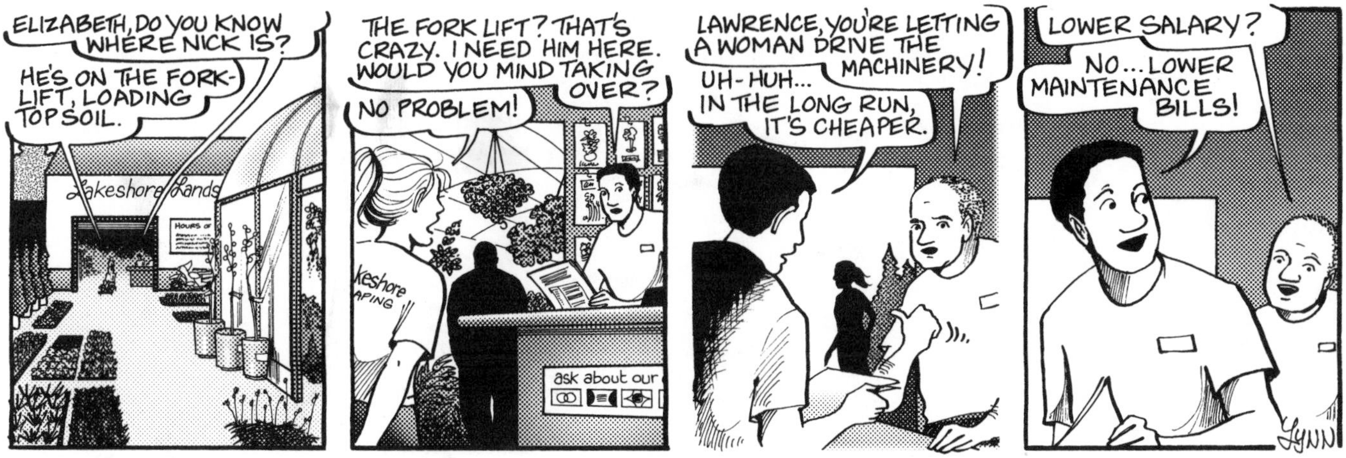
ELIZABETH, DO YOU KNOW WHERE NICK IS?
HE'S ON THE FORK-LIFT, LOADING TOPSOIL.
Lakeshore Lands
THE FORK LIFT? THAT'S CRAZY. I NEED HIM HERE. WOULD YOU MIND TAKING OVER?
NO PROBLEM!
ask about our
LAWRENCE, YOU'RE LETTING A WOMAN DRIVE THE MACHINERY!
UH-HUH... IN THE LONG RUN, IT'S CHEAPER.
LOWER SALARY?
NO... LOWER MAINTENANCE BILLS!
LYNN

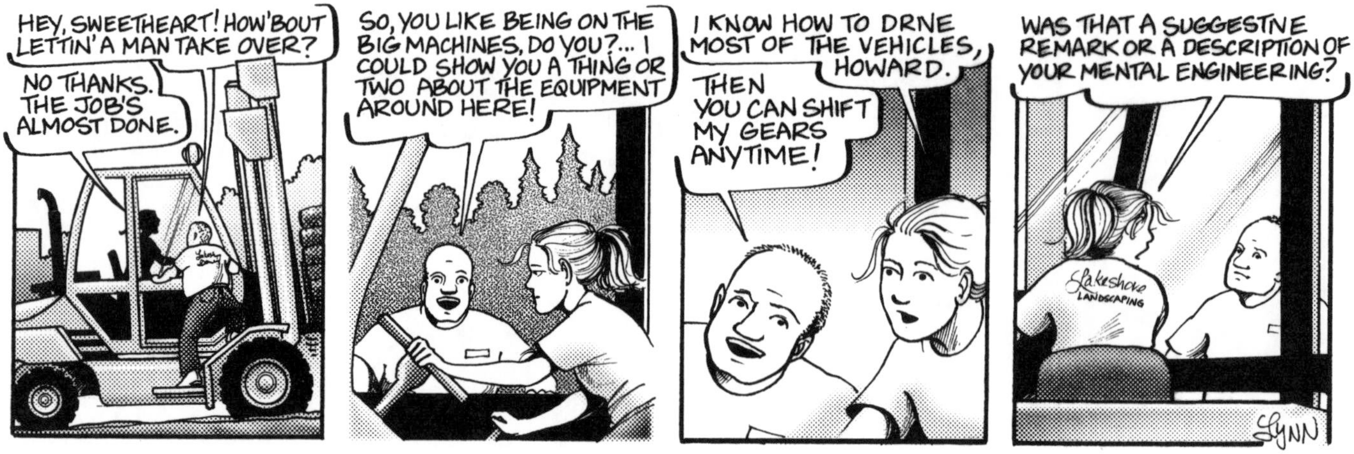
HEY, SWEETHEART! HOW'BOUT LETTIN' A MAN TAKE OVER?
NO THANKS. THE JOB'S ALMOST DONE.
SO, YOU LIKE BEING ON THE BIG MACHINES, DO YOU?... I COULD SHOW YOU A THING OR TWO ABOUT THE EQUIPMENT AROUND HERE!
I KNOW HOW TO DRIVE MOST OF THE VEHICLES, HOWARD.
THEN YOU CAN SHIFT MY GEARS ANYTIME!
WAS THAT A SUGGESTIVE REMARK OR A DESCRIPTION OF YOUR MENTAL ENGINEERING?
Lakeshore LANDSCAPING
LYNN

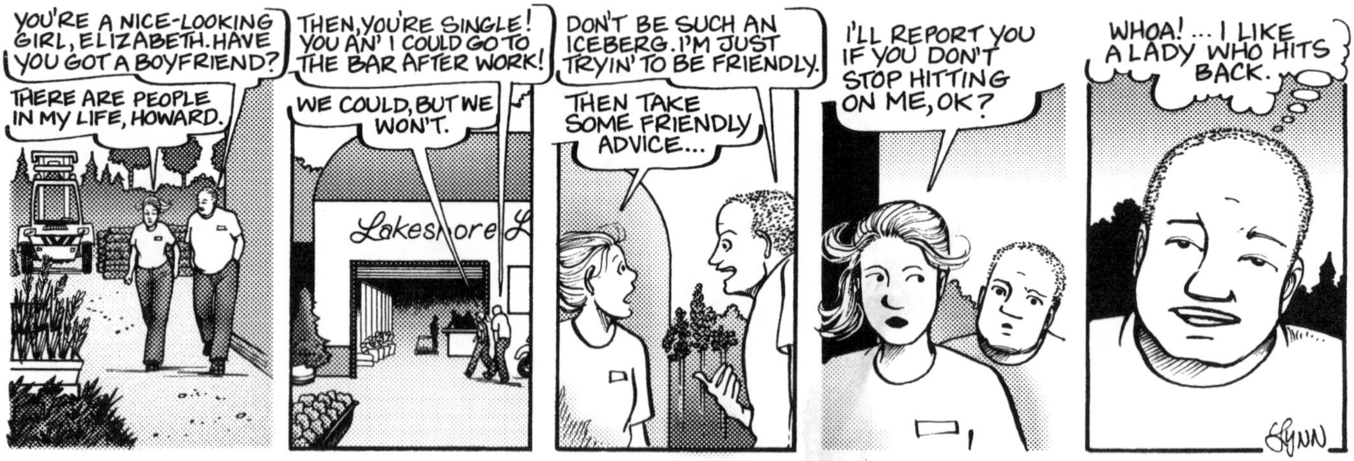
YOU'RE A NICE-LOOKING GIRL, ELIZABETH. HAVE YOU GOT A BOYFRIEND?
THERE ARE PEOPLE IN MY LIFE, HOWARD.
THEN, YOU'RE SINGLE! YOU AN' I COULD GO TO THE BAR AFTER WORK!
WE COULD, BUT WE WON'T.
Lakeshore L
DON'T BE SUCH AN ICEBERG. I'M JUST TRYIN' TO BE FRIENDLY.
THEN TAKE SOME FRIENDLY ADVICE...
I'LL REPORT YOU IF YOU DON'T STOP HITTING ON ME, OK?
WHOA! ... I LIKE A LADY WHO HITS BACK.
LYNN

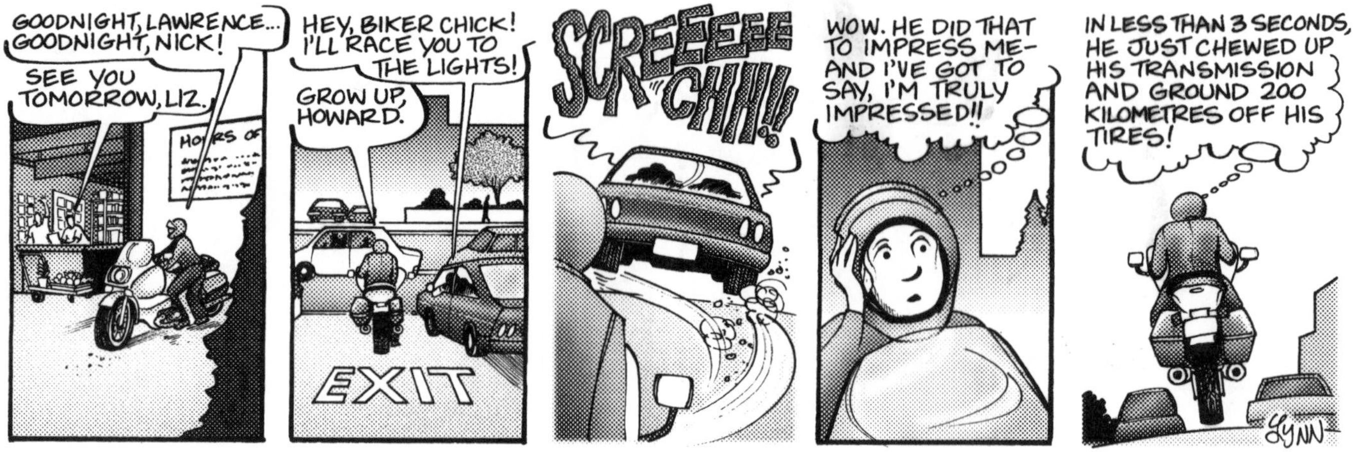
GOODNIGHT, LAWRENCE... GOODNIGHT, NICK!
SEE YOU TOMORROW, LIZ.
HEY, BIKER CHICK! I'LL RACE YOU TO THE LIGHTS!
GROW UP, HOWARD.
EXIT
SCREEEEE CHH!!
WOW. HE DID THAT TO IMPRESS ME- AND I'VE GOT TO SAY, I'M TRULY IMPRESSED!!
IN LESS THAN 3 SECONDS, HE JUST CHEWED UP HIS TRANSMISSION AND GROUND 200 KILOMETRES OFF HIS TIRES!
LYNN

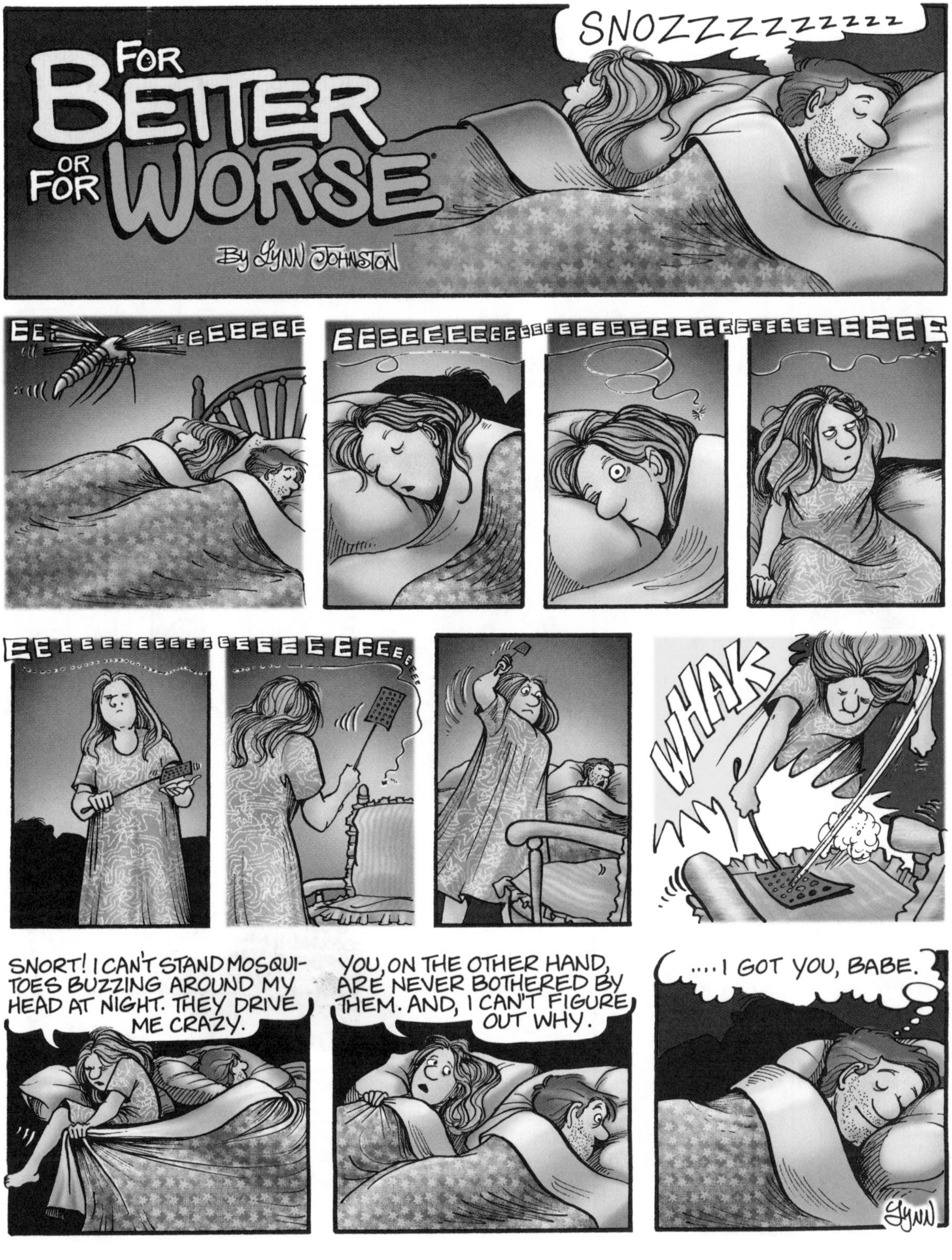
SNOZZZZZZZZZ
FOR BETTER OR FOR WORSE
BY LYNN JOHNSTON
EEEEEEEEE
EEEEEEEEEEEEEEEEEEEEEEEEEEEEEEEEE
EEEEEEEEEEEEEEEEEEEEEEEE
WHAK
SNORT! I CAN'T STAND MOSQUITOES BUZZING AROUND MY HEAD AT NIGHT. THEY DRIVE ME CRAZY.
YOU, ON THE OTHER HAND, ARE NEVER BOTHERED BY THEM. AND, I CAN'T FIGURE OUT WHY.
....I GOT YOU, BABE.
LYNN

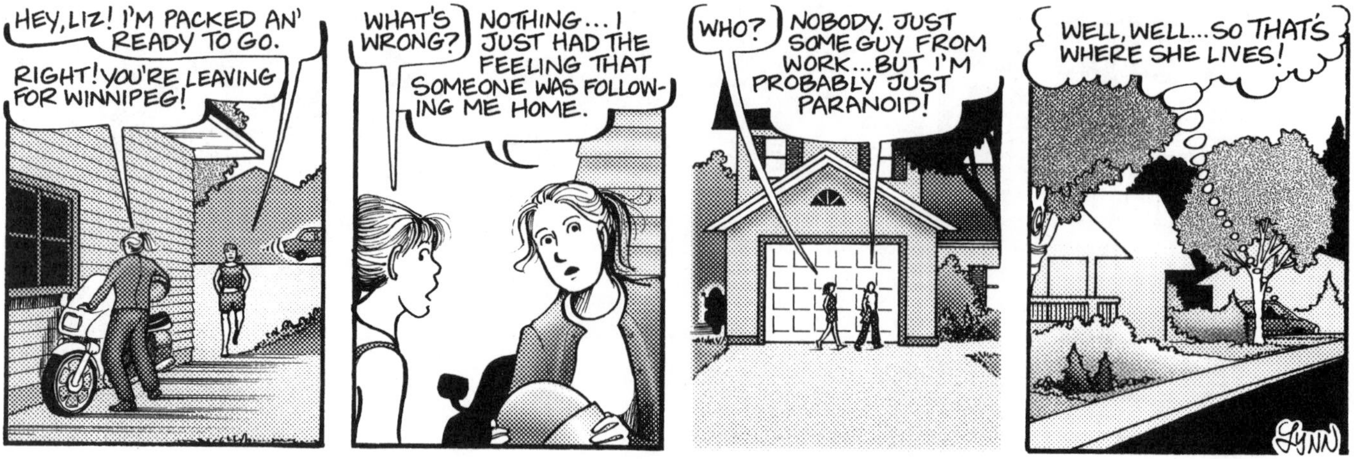
HEY, LIZ! I'M PACKED AN' READY TO GO.
RIGHT! YOU'RE LEAVING FOR WINNIPEG!
WHAT'S WRONG?
NOTHING... I JUST HAD THE FEELING THAT SOMEONE WAS FOLLOWING ME HOME.
WHO?
NOBODY. JUST SOME GUY FROM WORK... BUT I'M PROBABLY JUST PARANOID!
WELL, WELL... SO THAT'S WHERE SHE LIVES!
LYNN

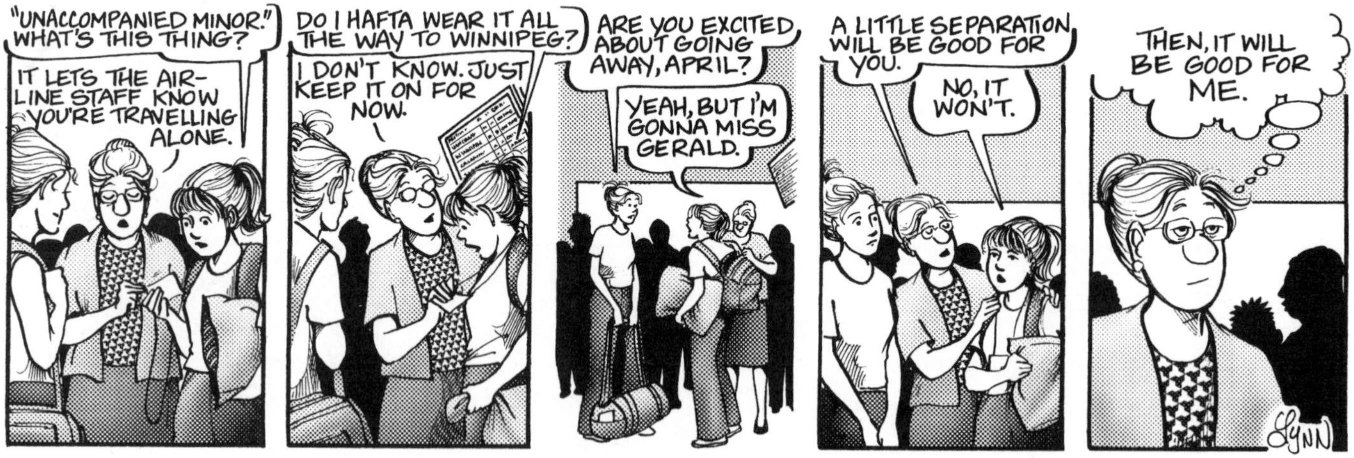
"UNACCOMPANIED MINOR." WHAT'S THIS THING?
IT LETS THE AIRLINE STAFF KNOW YOU'RE TRAVELLING ALONE.
DO I HAFTA WEAR IT ALL THE WAY TO WINNIPEG?
I DON'T KNOW. JUST KEEP IT ON FOR NOW.
ARE YOU EXCITED ABOUT GOING AWAY, APRIL?
YEAH, BUT I'M GONNA MISS GERALD.
A LITTLE SEPARATION WILL BE GOOD FOR YOU.
NO, IT WON'T.
THEN, IT WILL BE GOOD FOR ME.
LYNN

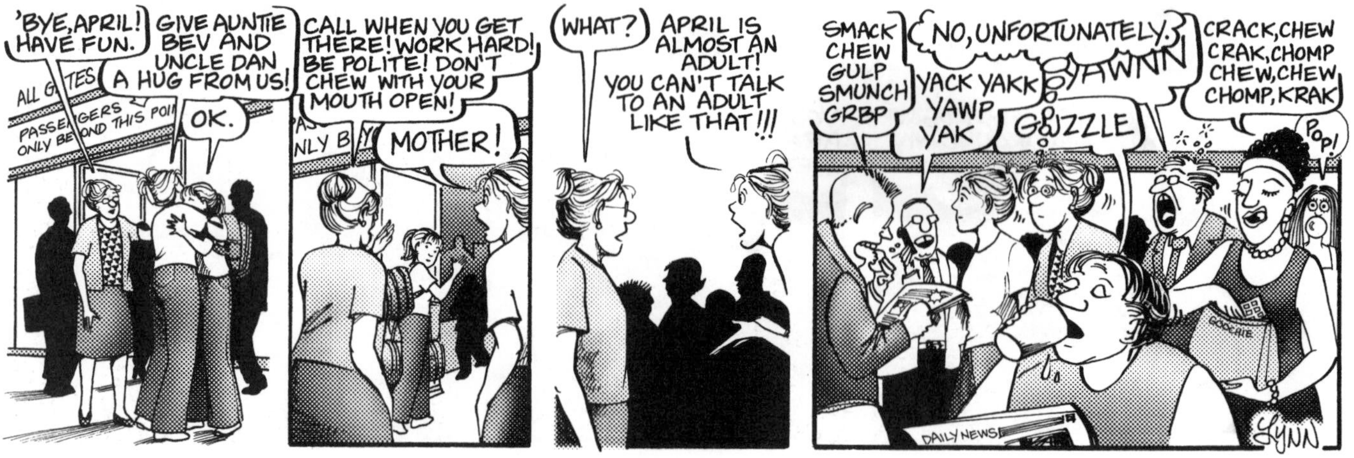
'BYE, APRIL! HAVE FUN.
GIVE AUNTIE BEV AND UNCLE DAN A HUG FROM US!
OK.
CALL WHEN YOU GET THERE! WORK HARD! BE POLITE! DON'T CHEW WITH YOUR MOUTH OPEN!
MOTHER!
WHAT?
APRIL IS ALMOST AN ADULT! YOU CAN'T TALK TO AN ADULT LIKE THAT!!!
SMACK CHEW GULP SMUNCH GRBP
NO, UNFORTUNATELY.
YACK YAKK YAWP YAK
YAWNN
GUZZLE
CRACK, CHEW CRAK, CHOMP CHEW, CHEW CHOMP, KRAK
POP!
LYNN

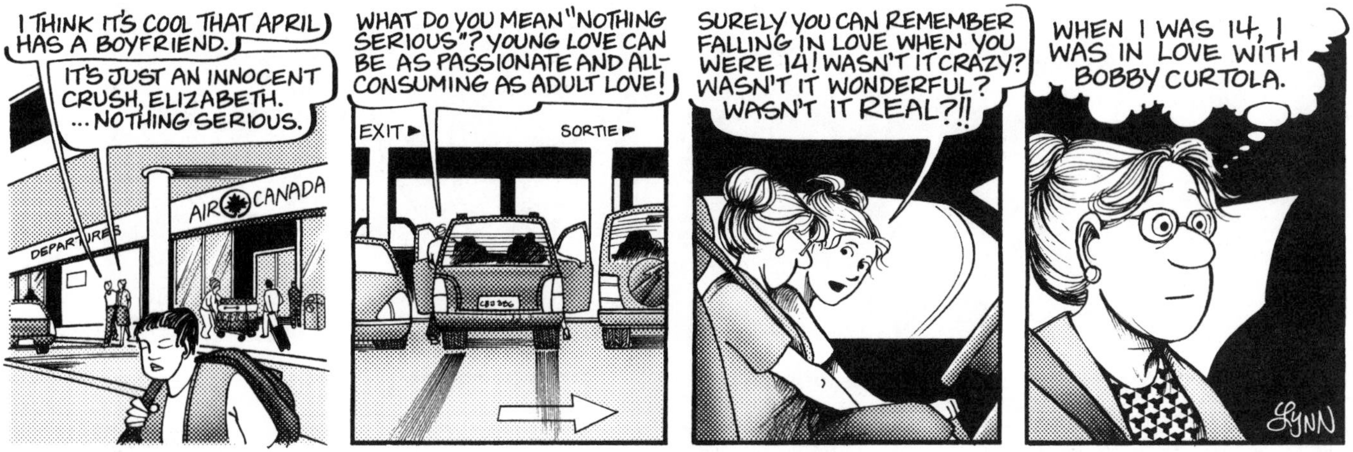
I THINK IT'S COOL THAT APRIL HAS A BOYFRIEND.
IT'S JUST AN INNOCENT CRUSH, ELIZABETH. ... NOTHING SERIOUS.
AIR CANADA
DEPARTURES
WHAT DO YOU MEAN "NOTHING SERIOUS"? YOUNG LOVE CAN BE AS PASSIONATE AND ALL-CONSUMING AS ADULT LOVE!
EXIT
SORTIE
SURELY YOU CAN REMEMBER FALLING IN LOVE WHEN YOU WERE 14! WASN'T IT CRAZY? WASN'T IT WONDERFUL? WASN'T IT REAL?!!
WHEN I WAS 14, I WAS IN LOVE WITH BOBBY CURTOLA.
LYNN

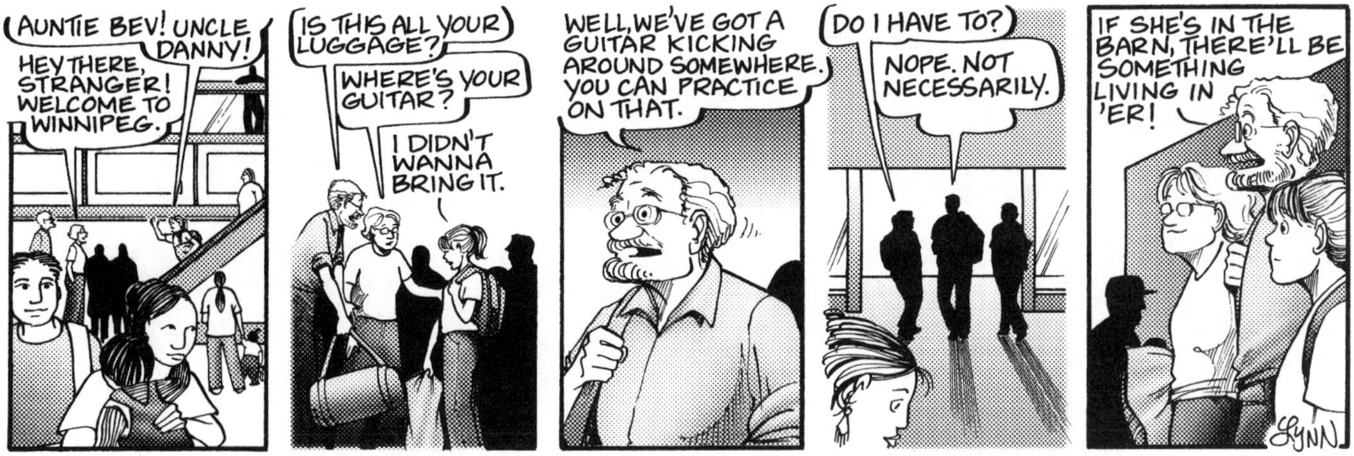
AUNTIE BEV! UNCLE DANNY!
HEY THERE, STRANGER! WELCOME TO WINNIPEG.
IS THIS ALL YOUR LUGGAGE?
WHERE'S YOUR GUITAR?
I DIDN'T WANNA BRING IT.
WELL, WE'VE GOT A GUITAR KICKING AROUND SOMEWHERE. YOU CAN PRACTICE ON THAT.
DO I HAVE TO?
NOPE. NOT NECESSARILY.
IF SHE'S IN THE BARN, THERE'LL BE SOMETHING LIVING IN 'ER!
LYNN

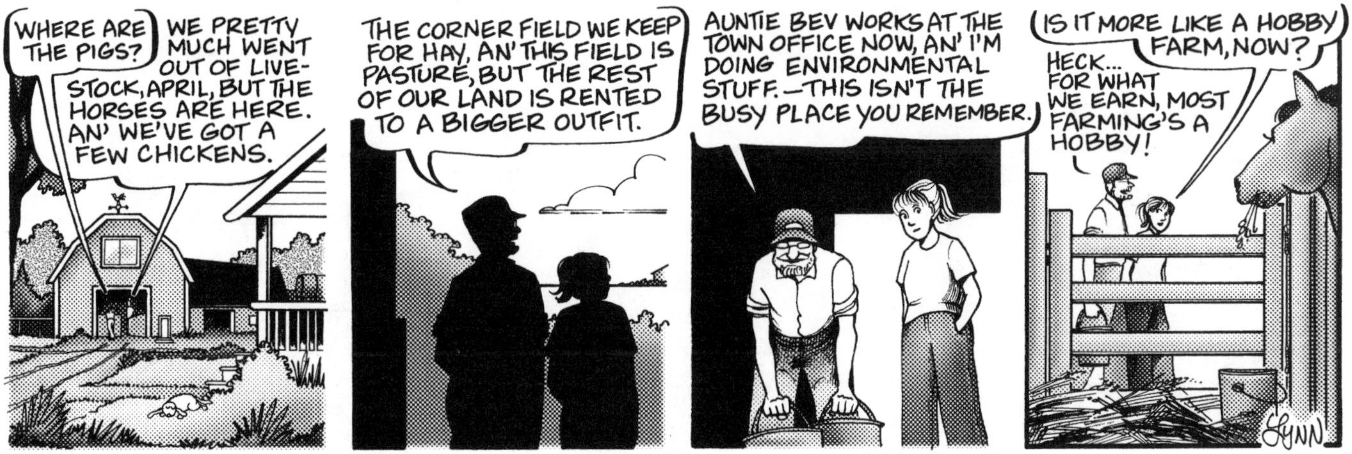
WHERE ARE THE PIGS?
WE PRETTY MUCH WENT OUT OF LIVE-STOCK, APRIL, BUT THE HORSES ARE HERE. AN' WE'VE GOT A FEW CHICKENS.
THE CORNER FIELD WE KEEP FOR HAY, AN' THIS FIELD IS PASTURE, BUT THE REST OF OUR LAND IS RENTED TO A BIGGER OUTFIT.
AUNTIE BEV WORKS AT THE TOWN OFFICE NOW, AN' I'M DOING ENVIRONMENTAL STUFF. —THIS ISN'T THE BUSY PLACE YOU REMEMBER.
IS IT MORE LIKE A HOBBY FARM, NOW?
HECK... FOR WHAT WE EARN, MOST FARMING'S A HOBBY!
LYNN

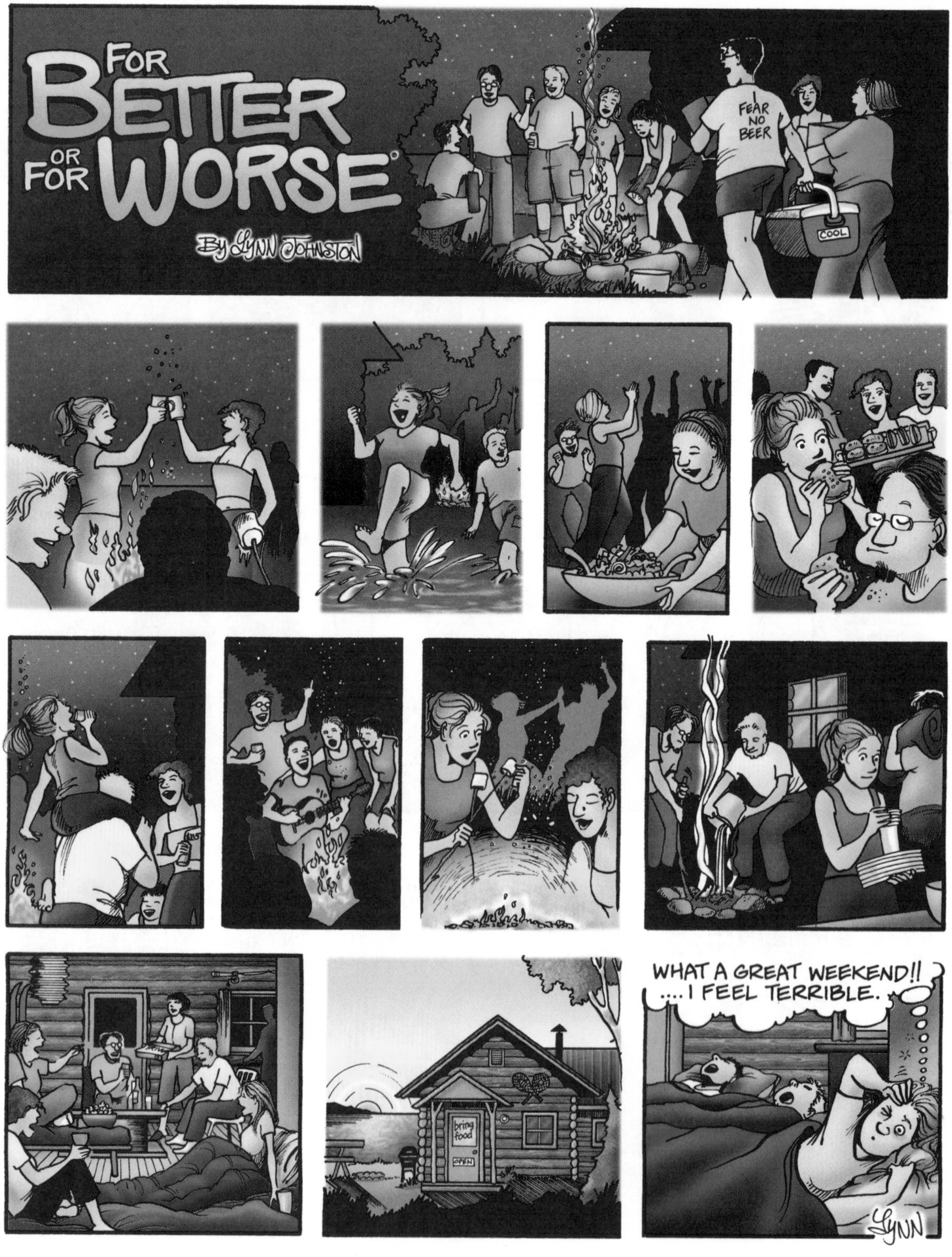
FOR BETTER OR FOR WORSE
By LYNN JOHNSTON
I FEAR NO BEER
COOL
bring food
OPEN
WHAT A GREAT WEEKEND!! ....I FEEL TERRIBLE.
LYNN

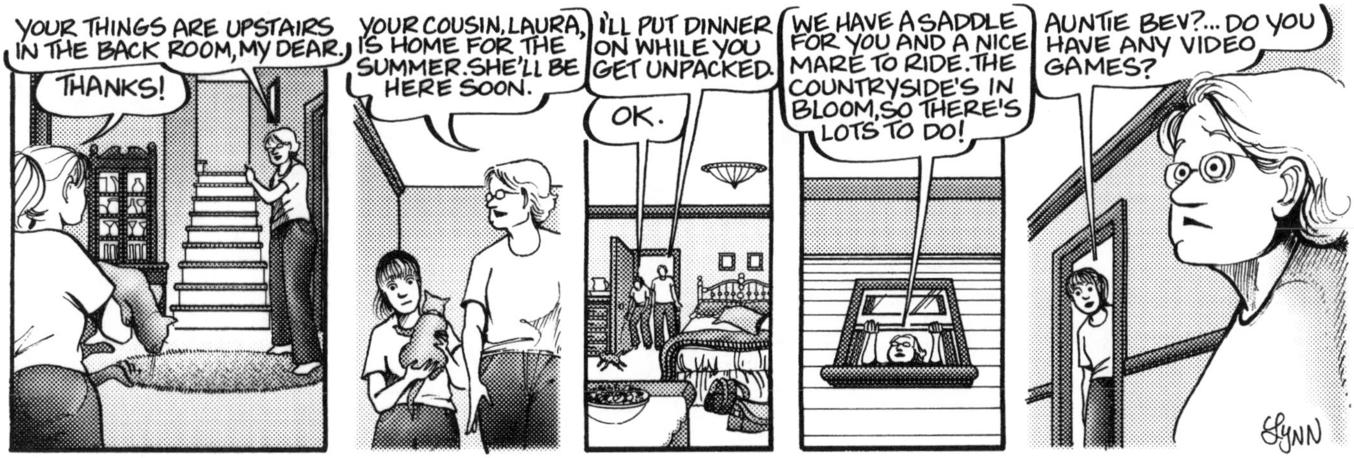
YOUR THINGS ARE UPSTAIRS IN THE BACK ROOM, MY DEAR.
THANKS!
YOUR COUSIN, LAURA, IS HOME FOR THE SUMMER. SHE'LL BE HERE SOON.
I'LL PUT DINNER ON WHILE YOU GET UNPACKED.
OK.
WE HAVE A SADDLE FOR YOU AND A NICE MARE TO RIDE. THE COUNTRYSIDE'S IN BLOOM, SO THERE'S LOTS TO DO!
AUNTIE BEV?... DO YOU HAVE ANY VIDEO GAMES?
LYNN

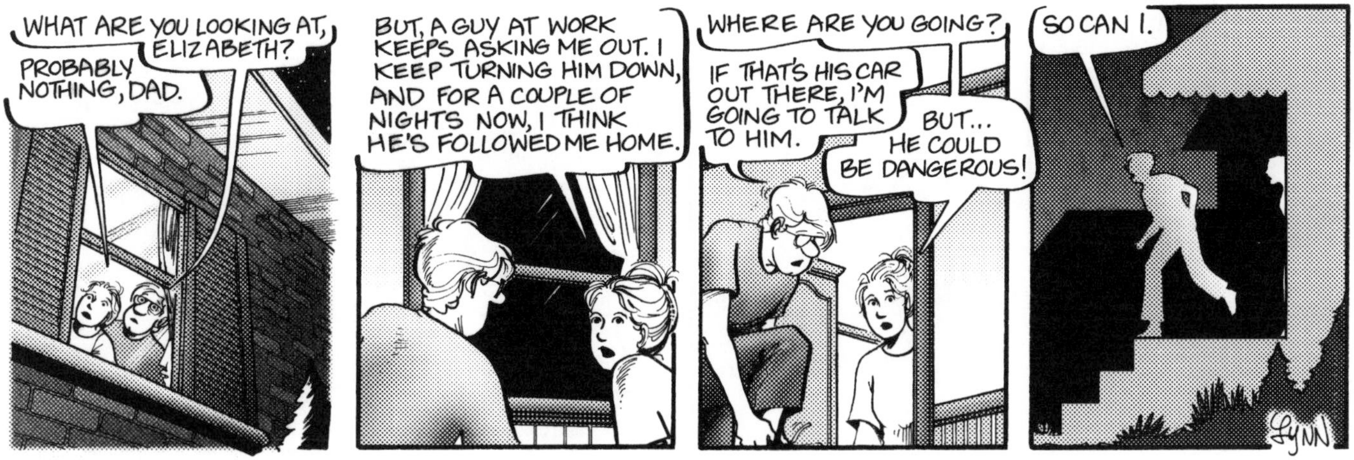
WHAT ARE YOU LOOKING AT, ELIZABETH?
PROBABLY NOTHING, DAD.
BUT, A GUY AT WORK KEEPS ASKING ME OUT. I KEEP TURNING HIM DOWN, AND FOR A COUPLE OF NIGHTS NOW, I THINK HE'S FOLLOWED ME HOME.
WHERE ARE YOU GOING?
IF THAT'S HIS CAR OUT THERE, I'M GOING TO TALK TO HIM.
BUT... HE COULD BE DANGEROUS!
SO CAN I.
LYNN

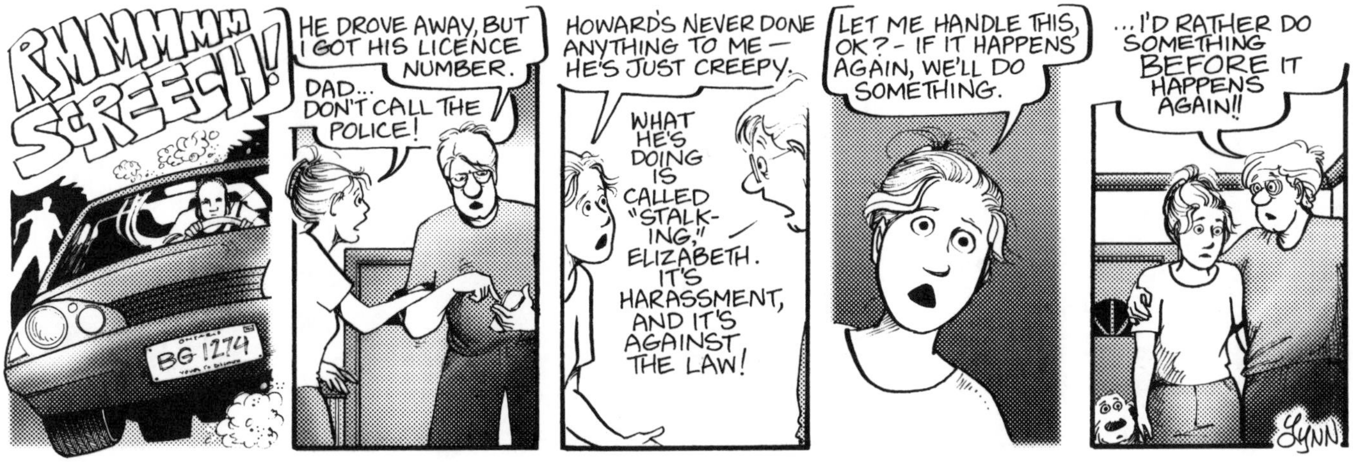
RMMMMM SCREECH!
BG 1274
HE DROVE AWAY, BUT I GOT HIS LICENCE NUMBER.
DAD... DON'T CALL THE POLICE!
HOWARD'S NEVER DONE ANYTHING TO ME — HE'S JUST CREEPY.
WHAT HE'S DOING IS CALLED "STALKING," ELIZABETH. IT'S HARASSMENT, AND IT'S AGAINST THE LAW!
LET ME HANDLE THIS, OK? - IF IT HAPPENS AGAIN, WE'LL DO SOMETHING.
...I'D RATHER DO SOMETHING BEFORE IT HAPPENS AGAIN!!
LYNN

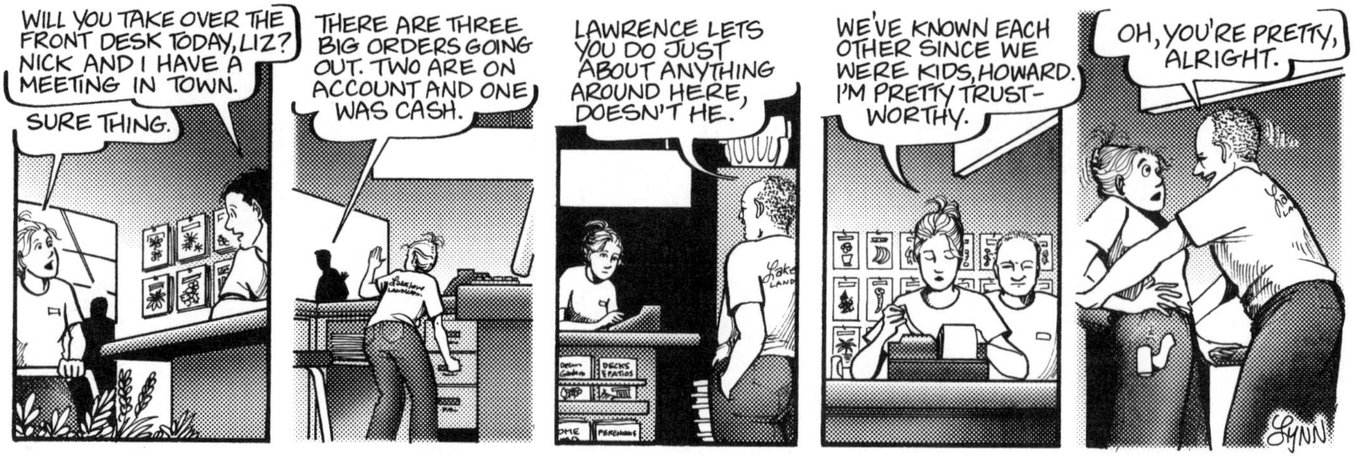
WILL YOU TAKE OVER THE FRONT DESK TODAY, LIZ? NICK AND I HAVE A MEETING IN TOWN.
SURE THING.
THERE ARE THREE BIG ORDERS GOING OUT. TWO ARE ON ACCOUNT AND ONE WAS CASH.
LAWRENCE LETS YOU DO JUST ABOUT ANYTHING AROUND HERE, DOESN'T HE.
WE'VE KNOWN EACH OTHER SINCE WE WERE KIDS, HOWARD. I'M PRETTY TRUST-WORTHY.
OH, YOU'RE PRETTY, ALRIGHT.
LYNN

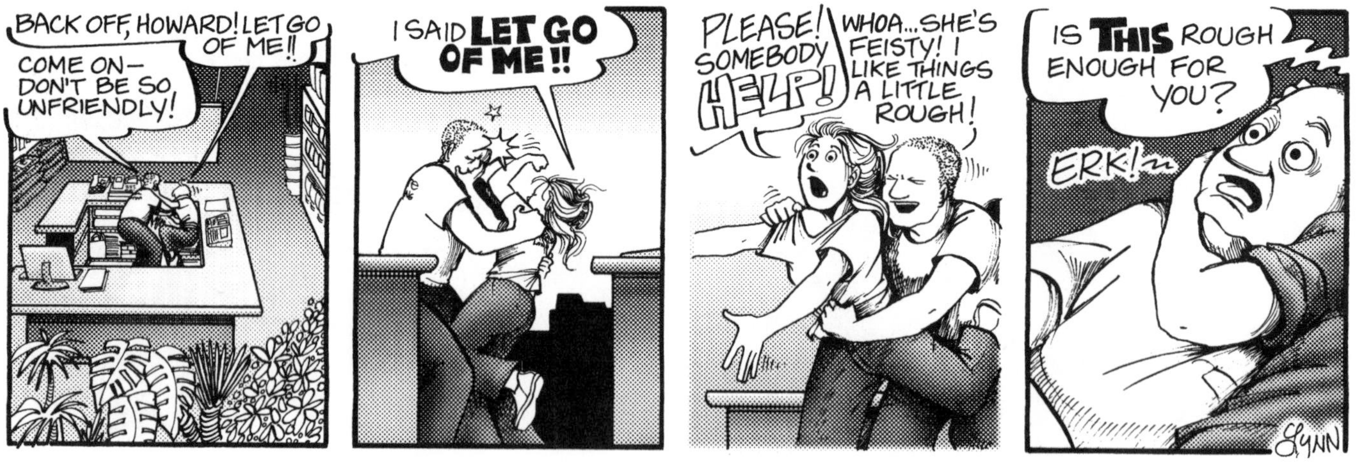
BACK OFF, HOWARD! LET GO OF ME!!
COME ON— DON'T BE SO UNFRIENDLY!
I SAID **LET GO OF ME!!**
PLEASE! SOMEBODY HELP!
WHOA...SHE'S FEISTY! I LIKE THINGS A LITTLE ROUGH!
IS **THIS** ROUGH ENOUGH FOR YOU?
ERK!
LYNN

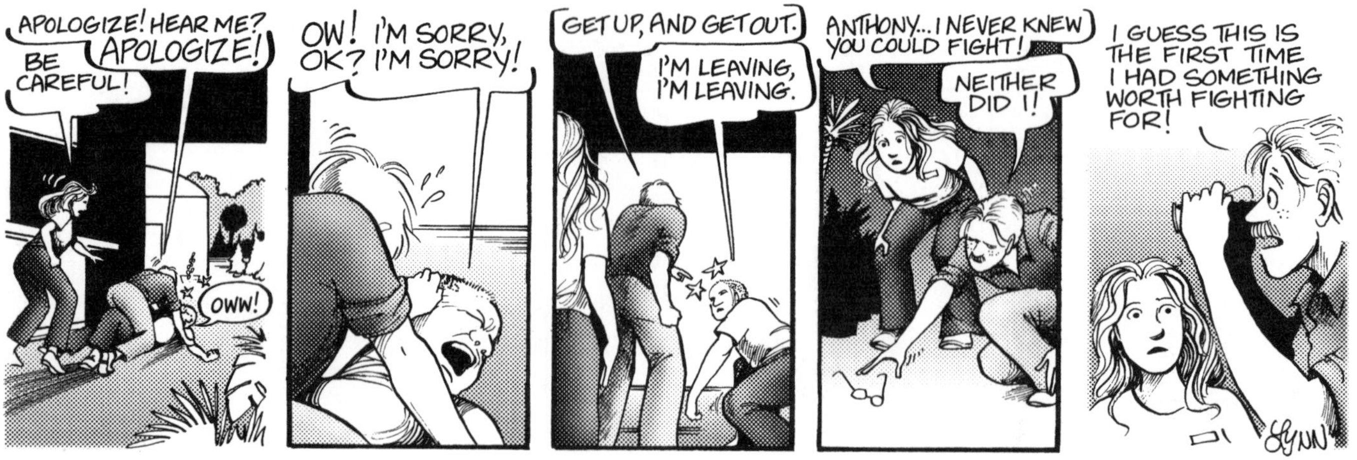
APOLOGIZE! HEAR ME? APOLOGIZE!
BE CAREFUL!
OWW!
OW! I'M SORRY, OK? I'M SORRY!
GET UP, AND GET OUT.
I'M LEAVING, I'M LEAVING.
ANTHONY... I NEVER KNEW YOU COULD FIGHT!
NEITHER DID I!
I GUESS THIS IS THE FIRST TIME I HAD SOMETHING WORTH FIGHTING FOR!
LYNN

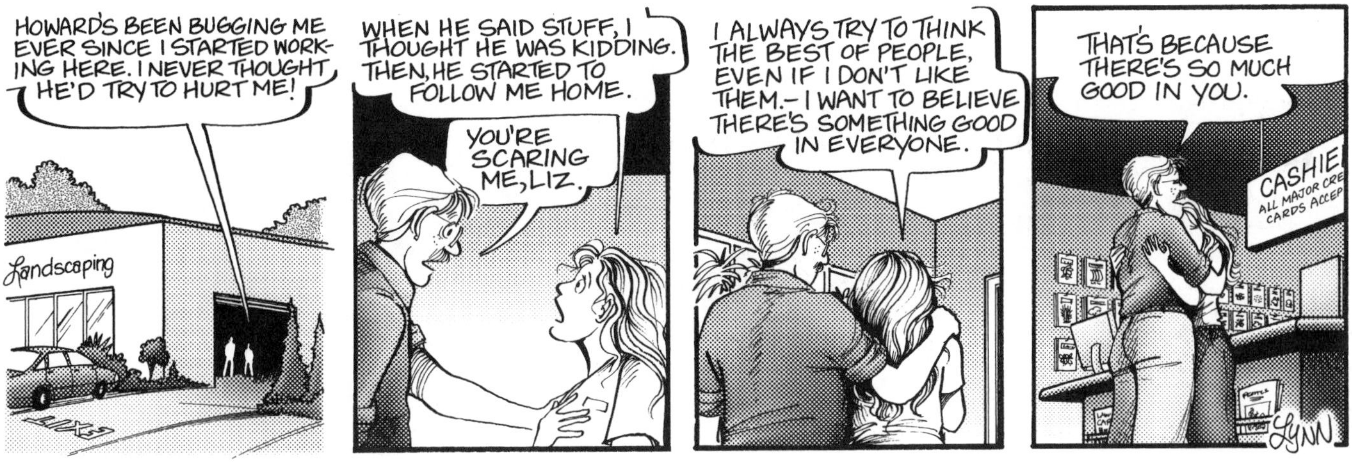
HOWARD'S BEEN BUGGING ME EVER SINCE I STARTED WORKING HERE. I NEVER THOUGHT HE'D TRY TO HURT ME!
Landscaping
WHEN HE SAID STUFF, I THOUGHT HE WAS KIDDING. THEN, HE STARTED TO FOLLOW ME HOME.
YOU'RE SCARING ME, LIZ.
I ALWAYS TRY TO THINK THE BEST OF PEOPLE, EVEN IF I DON'T LIKE THEM. – I WANT TO BELIEVE THERE'S SOMETHING GOOD IN EVERYONE.
THAT'S BECAUSE THERE'S SO MUCH GOOD IN YOU.
LYNN

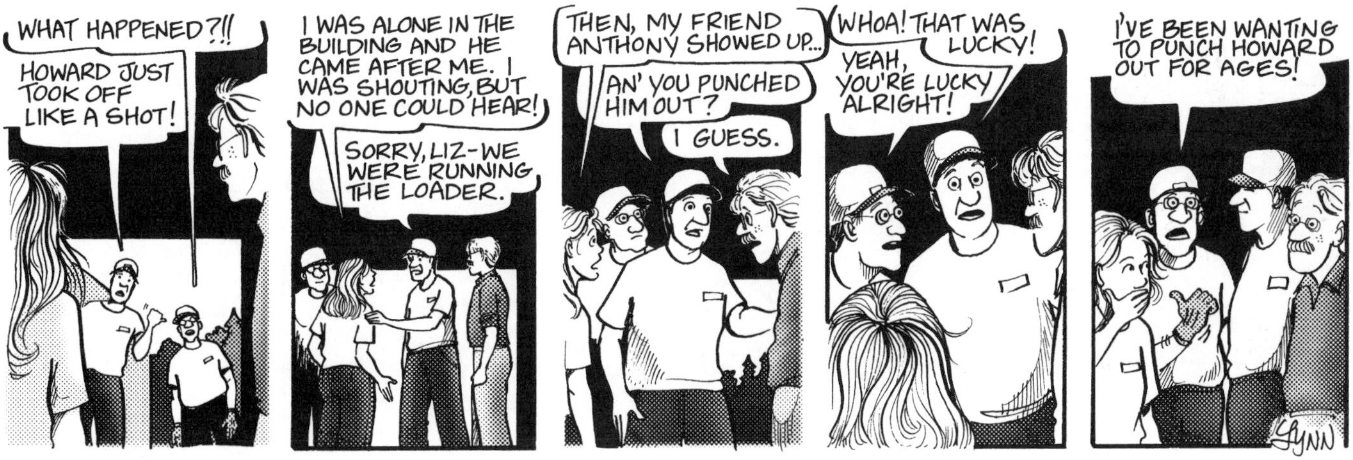
WHAT HAPPENED?!!
HOWARD JUST TOOK OFF LIKE A SHOT!
I WAS ALONE IN THE BUILDING AND HE CAME AFTER ME. I WAS SHOUTING, BUT NO ONE COULD HEAR!
SORRY, LIZ – WE WERE RUNNING THE LOADER.
THEN, MY FRIEND ANTHONY SHOWED UP...
AN' YOU PUNCHED HIM OUT?
I GUESS.
WHOA! THAT WAS LUCKY!
YEAH, YOU'RE LUCKY ALRIGHT!
I'VE BEEN WANTING TO PUNCH HOWARD OUT FOR AGES!
LYNN

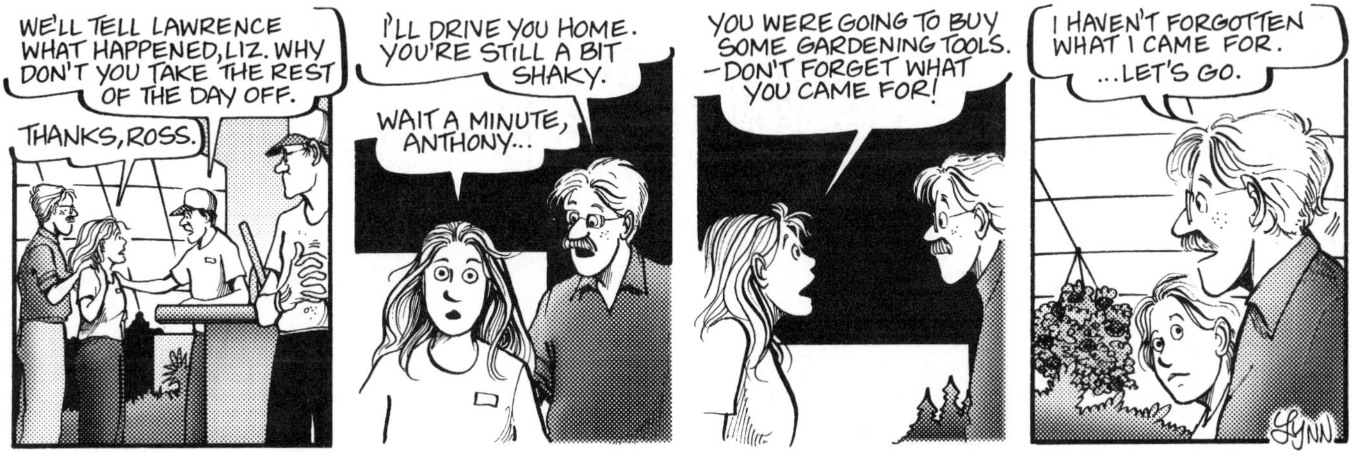
WE'LL TELL LAWRENCE WHAT HAPPENED, LIZ. WHY DON'T YOU TAKE THE REST OF THE DAY OFF.
THANKS, ROSS.
I'LL DRIVE YOU HOME. YOU'RE STILL A BIT SHAKY.
WAIT A MINUTE, ANTHONY...
YOU WERE GOING TO BUY SOME GARDENING TOOLS. – DON'T FORGET WHAT YOU CAME FOR!
I HAVEN'T FORGOTTEN WHAT I CAME FOR. ...LET'S GO.
LYNN

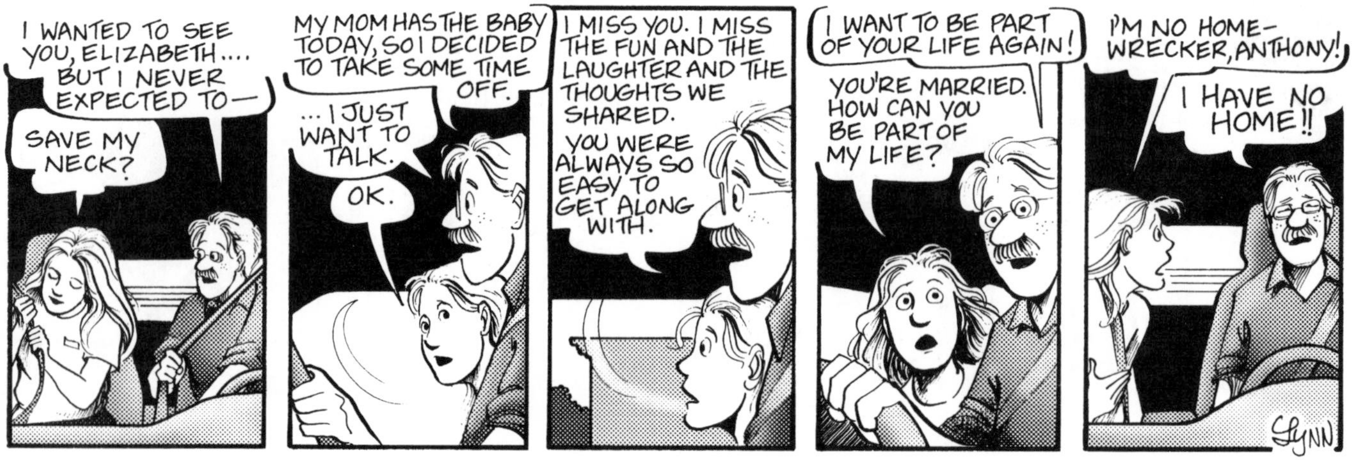
I WANTED TO SEE YOU, ELIZABETH.... BUT I NEVER EXPECTED TO—
SAVE MY NECK?
MY MOM HAS THE BABY TODAY, SO I DECIDED TO TAKE SOME TIME OFF.
... I JUST WANT TO TALK.
OK.
I MISS YOU. I MISS THE FUN AND THE LAUGHTER AND THE THOUGHTS WE SHARED.
YOU WERE ALWAYS SO EASY TO GET ALONG WITH.
I WANT TO BE PART OF YOUR LIFE AGAIN!
YOU'RE MARRIED. HOW CAN YOU BE PART OF MY LIFE?
I'M NO HOME-WRECKER, ANTHONY!
I HAVE NO HOME!!
LYNN

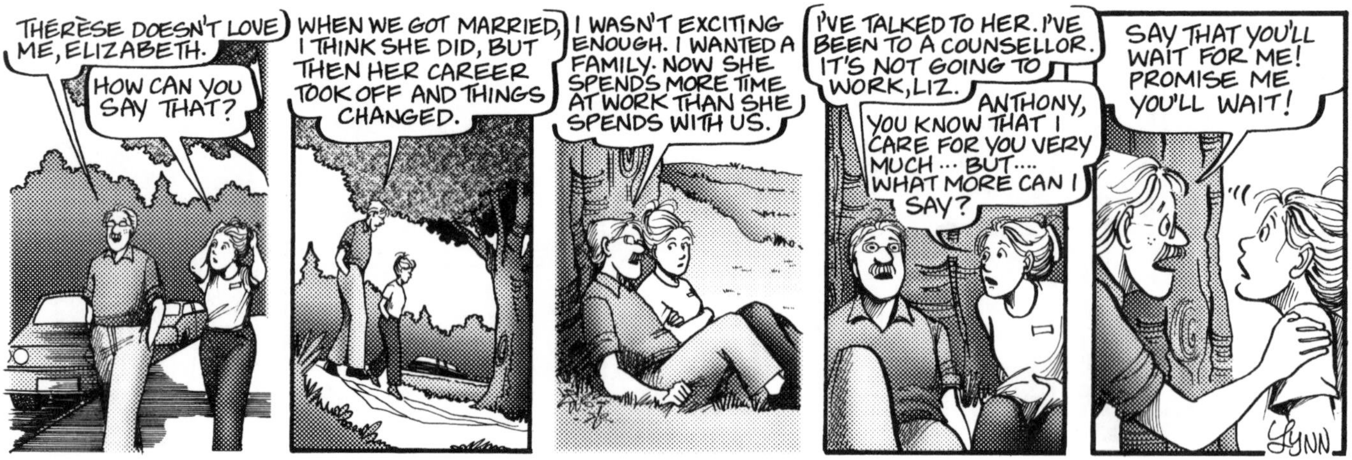
THERÈSE DOESN'T LOVE ME, ELIZABETH.
HOW CAN YOU SAY THAT?
WHEN WE GOT MARRIED, I THINK SHE DID, BUT THEN HER CAREER TOOK OFF AND THINGS CHANGED.
I WASN'T EXCITING ENOUGH. I WANTED A FAMILY. NOW SHE SPENDS MORE TIME AT WORK THAN SHE SPENDS WITH US.
I'VE TALKED TO HER. I'VE BEEN TO A COUNSELLOR. IT'S NOT GOING TO WORK, LIZ.
ANTHONY, YOU KNOW THAT I CARE FOR YOU VERY MUCH ... BUT.... WHAT MORE CAN I SAY?
SAY THAT YOU'LL WAIT FOR ME! PROMISE ME YOU'LL WAIT!
LYNN

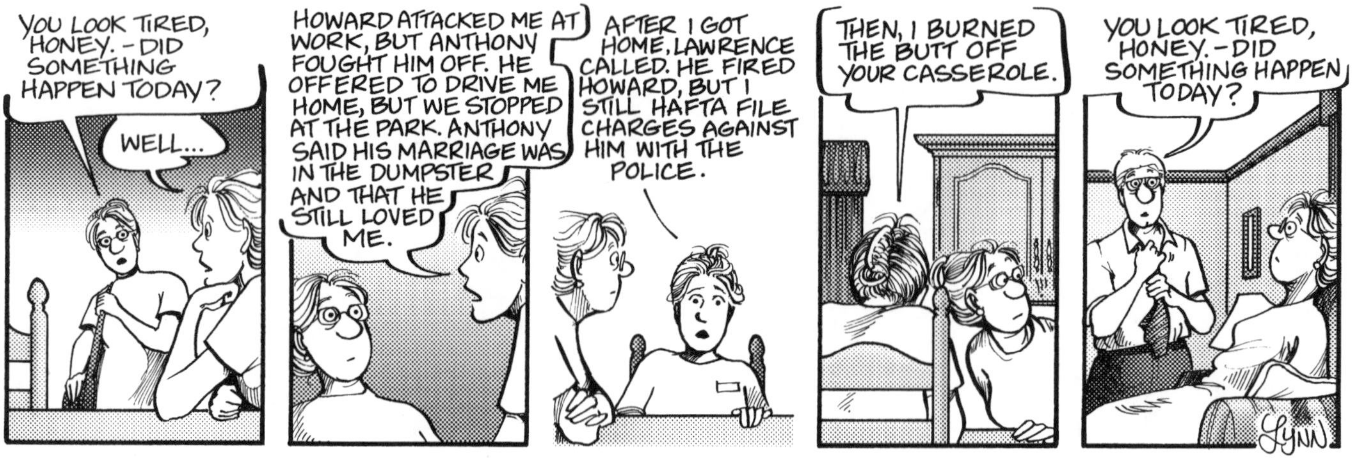
YOU LOOK TIRED, HONEY. - DID SOMETHING HAPPEN TODAY?
WELL...
HOWARD ATTACKED ME AT WORK, BUT ANTHONY FOUGHT HIM OFF. HE OFFERED TO DRIVE ME HOME, BUT WE STOPPED AT THE PARK. ANTHONY SAID HIS MARRIAGE WAS IN THE DUMPSTER AND THAT HE STILL LOVED ME.
AFTER I GOT HOME, LAWRENCE CALLED. HE FIRED HOWARD, BUT I STILL HAFTA FILE CHARGES AGAINST HIM WITH THE POLICE.
THEN, I BURNED THE BUTT OFF YOUR CASSEROLE.
YOU LOOK TIRED, HONEY. - DID SOMETHING HAPPEN TODAY?
LYNN

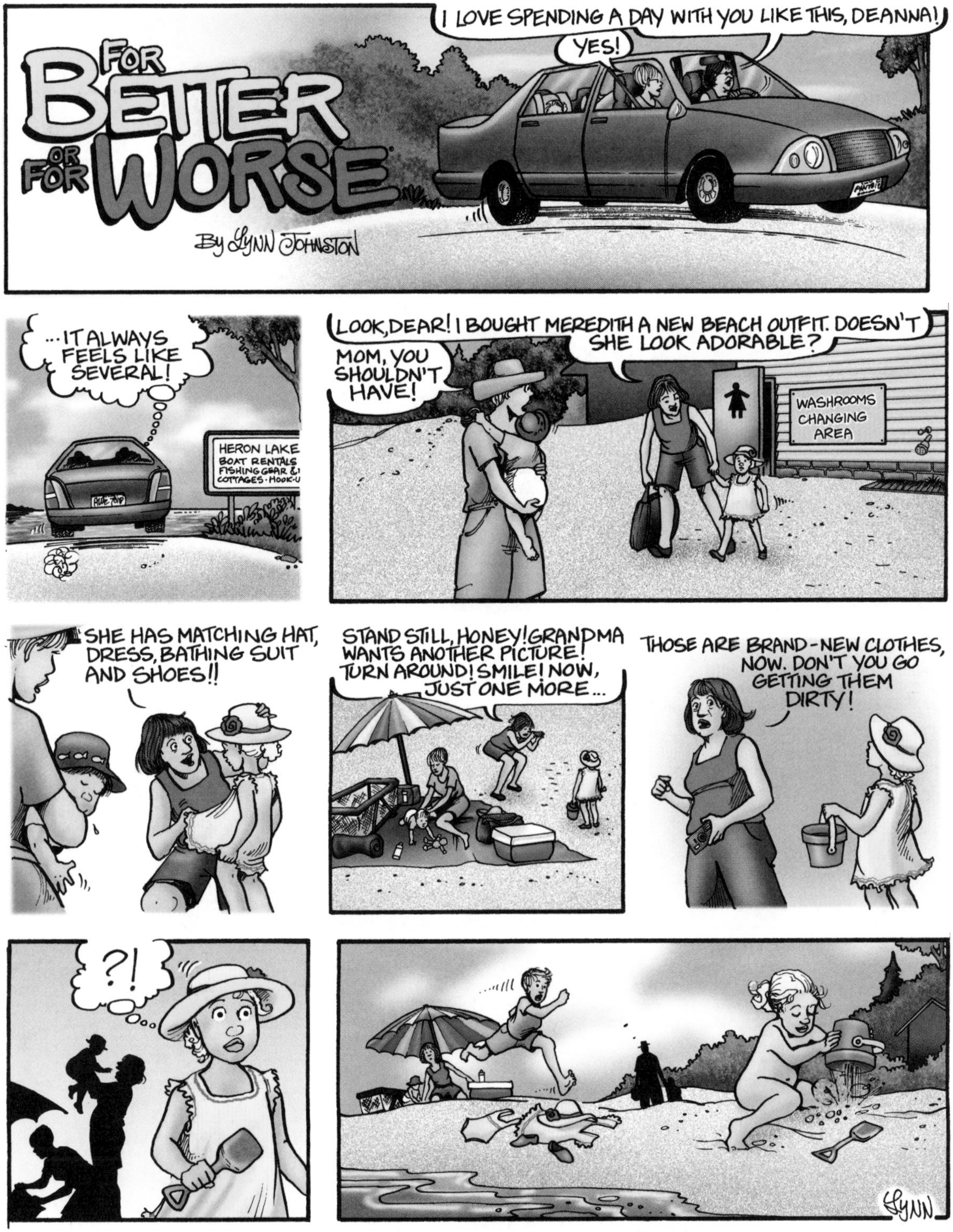
For Better or For Worse
By Lynn Johnston
I LOVE SPENDING A DAY WITH YOU LIKE THIS, DEANNA!
YES!
...IT ALWAYS FEELS LIKE SEVERAL!
HERON LAKE
BOAT RENTALS
FISHING GEAR &
COTTAGES · HOOK-U
LOOK, DEAR! I BOUGHT MEREDITH A NEW BEACH OUTFIT. DOESN'T SHE LOOK ADORABLE?
MOM, YOU SHOULDN'T HAVE!
WASHROOMS
CHANGING
AREA
SHE HAS MATCHING HAT, DRESS, BATHING SUIT AND SHOES!!
STAND STILL, HONEY! GRANDMA WANTS ANOTHER PICTURE! TURN AROUND! SMILE! NOW, JUST ONE MORE...
THOSE ARE BRAND-NEW CLOTHES, NOW. DON'T YOU GO GETTING THEM DIRTY!
?!
Lynn

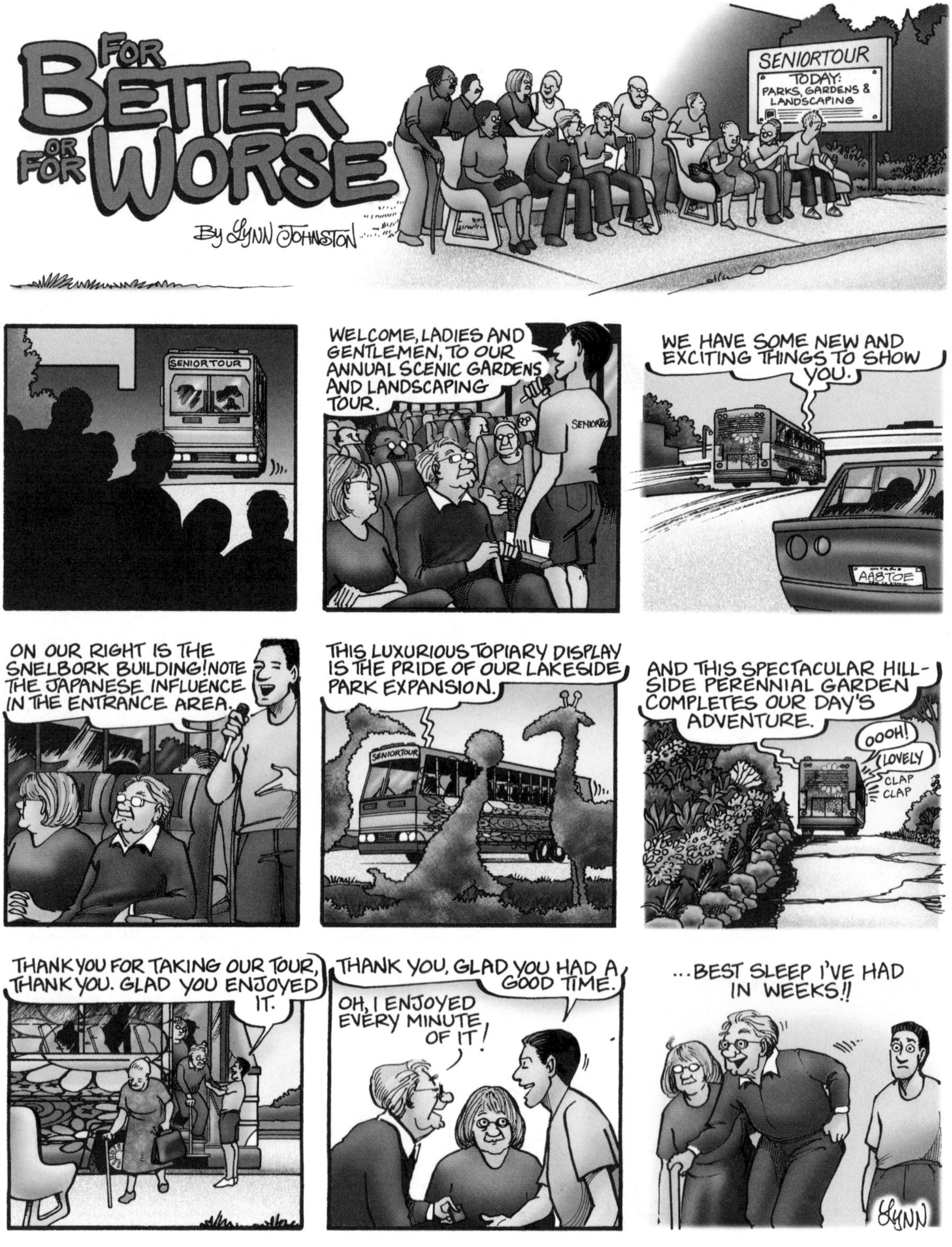
FOR BETTER OR FOR WORSE
By Lynn Johnston
SENIORTOUR
TODAY: PARKS, GARDENS & LANDSCAPING
SENIORTOUR
WELCOME, LADIES AND GENTLEMEN, TO OUR ANNUAL SCENIC GARDENS AND LANDSCAPING TOUR.
WE HAVE SOME NEW AND EXCITING THINGS TO SHOW YOU.
AA8TOE
ON OUR RIGHT IS THE SNELBORK BUILDING! NOTE THE JAPANESE INFLUENCE IN THE ENTRANCE AREA.
THIS LUXURIOUS TOPIARY DISPLAY IS THE PRIDE OF OUR LAKESIDE PARK EXPANSION.
SENIORTOUR
AND THIS SPECTACULAR HILL-SIDE PERENNIAL GARDEN COMPLETES OUR DAY'S ADVENTURE.
OOOH!
LOVELY
CLAP CLAP
THANK YOU FOR TAKING OUR TOUR, THANK YOU. GLAD YOU ENJOYED IT.
THANK YOU, GLAD YOU HAD A GOOD TIME.
OH, I ENJOYED EVERY MINUTE OF IT!
...BEST SLEEP I'VE HAD IN WEEKS!!
LYNN

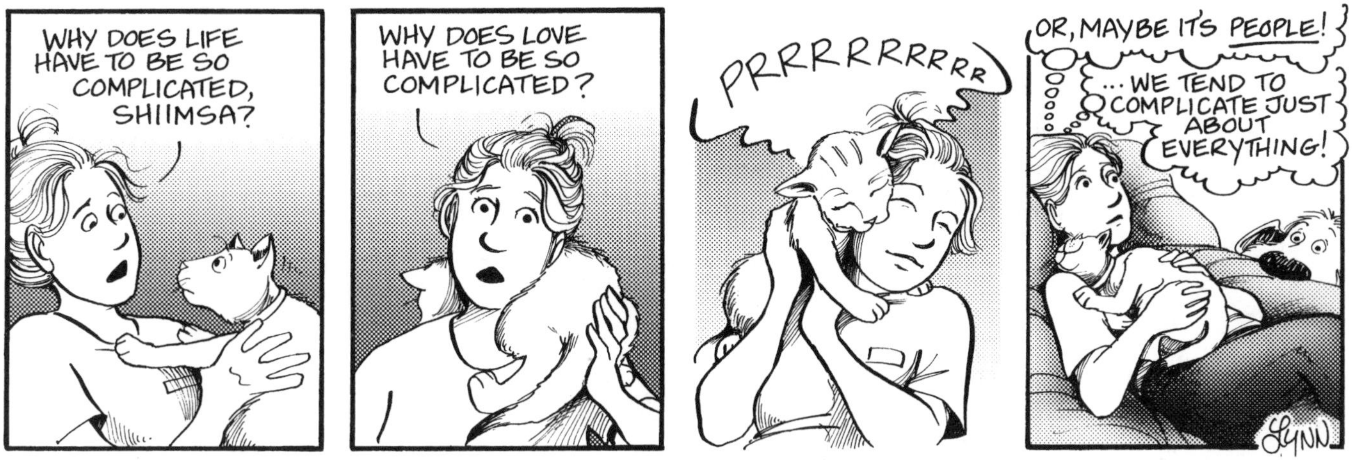
WHY DOES LIFE HAVE TO BE SO COMPLICATED, SHIIMSA?
WHY DOES LOVE HAVE TO BE SO COMPLICATED?
PRRRRRRRRRR
OR, MAYBE IT'S PEOPLE!
... WE TEND TO COMPLICATE JUST ABOUT EVERYTHING!
LYNN

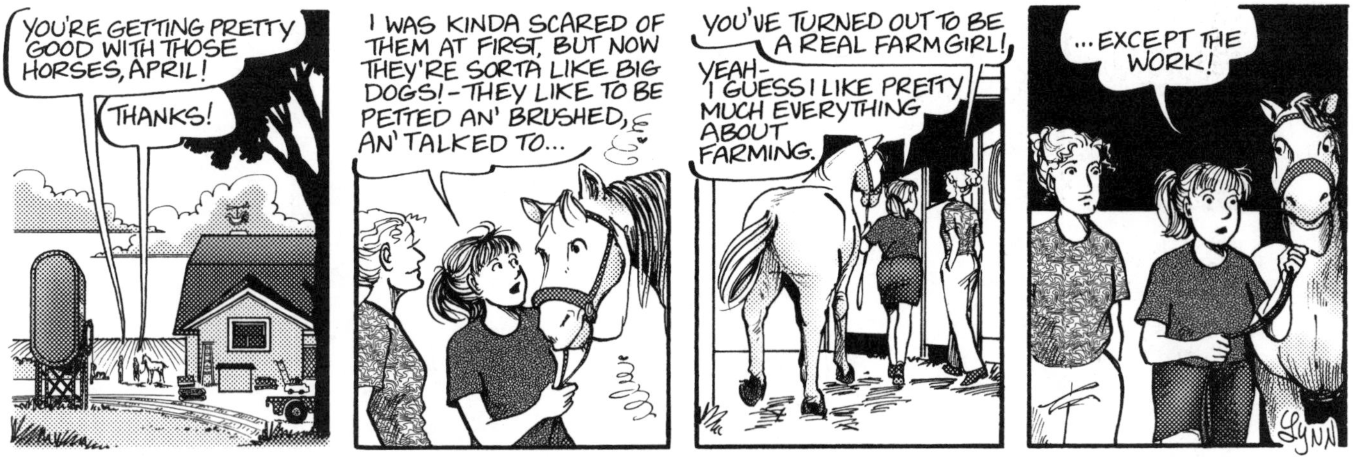
YOU'RE GETTING PRETTY GOOD WITH THOSE HORSES, APRIL!
THANKS!
I WAS KINDA SCARED OF THEM AT FIRST, BUT NOW THEY'RE SORTA LIKE BIG DOGS! - THEY LIKE TO BE PETTED AN' BRUSHED, AN' TALKED TO...
YOU'VE TURNED OUT TO BE A REAL FARM GIRL!
YEAH- I GUESS I LIKE PRETTY MUCH EVERYTHING ABOUT FARMING.
... EXCEPT THE WORK!
LYNN

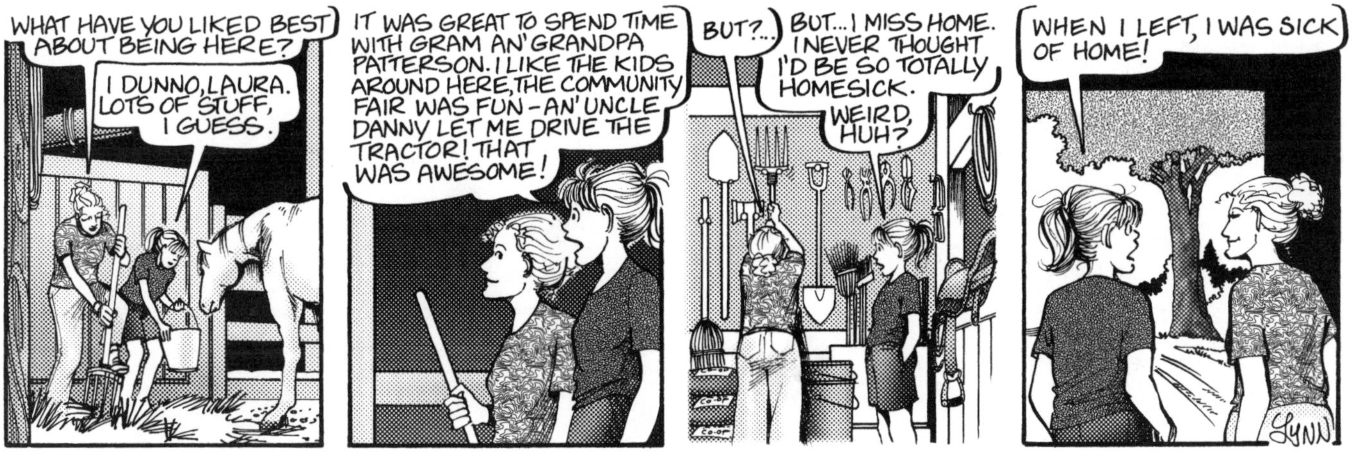
WHAT HAVE YOU LIKED BEST ABOUT BEING HERE?
I DUNNO, LAURA. LOTS OF STUFF, I GUESS.
IT WAS GREAT TO SPEND TIME WITH GRAM AN' GRANDPA PATTERSON. I LIKE THE KIDS AROUND HERE, THE COMMUNITY FAIR WAS FUN - AN' UNCLE DANNY LET ME DRIVE THE TRACTOR! THAT WAS AWESOME!
BUT?...
BUT... I MISS HOME. I NEVER THOUGHT I'D BE SO TOTALLY HOMESICK.
WEIRD, HUH?
WHEN I LEFT, I WAS SICK OF HOME!
LYNN

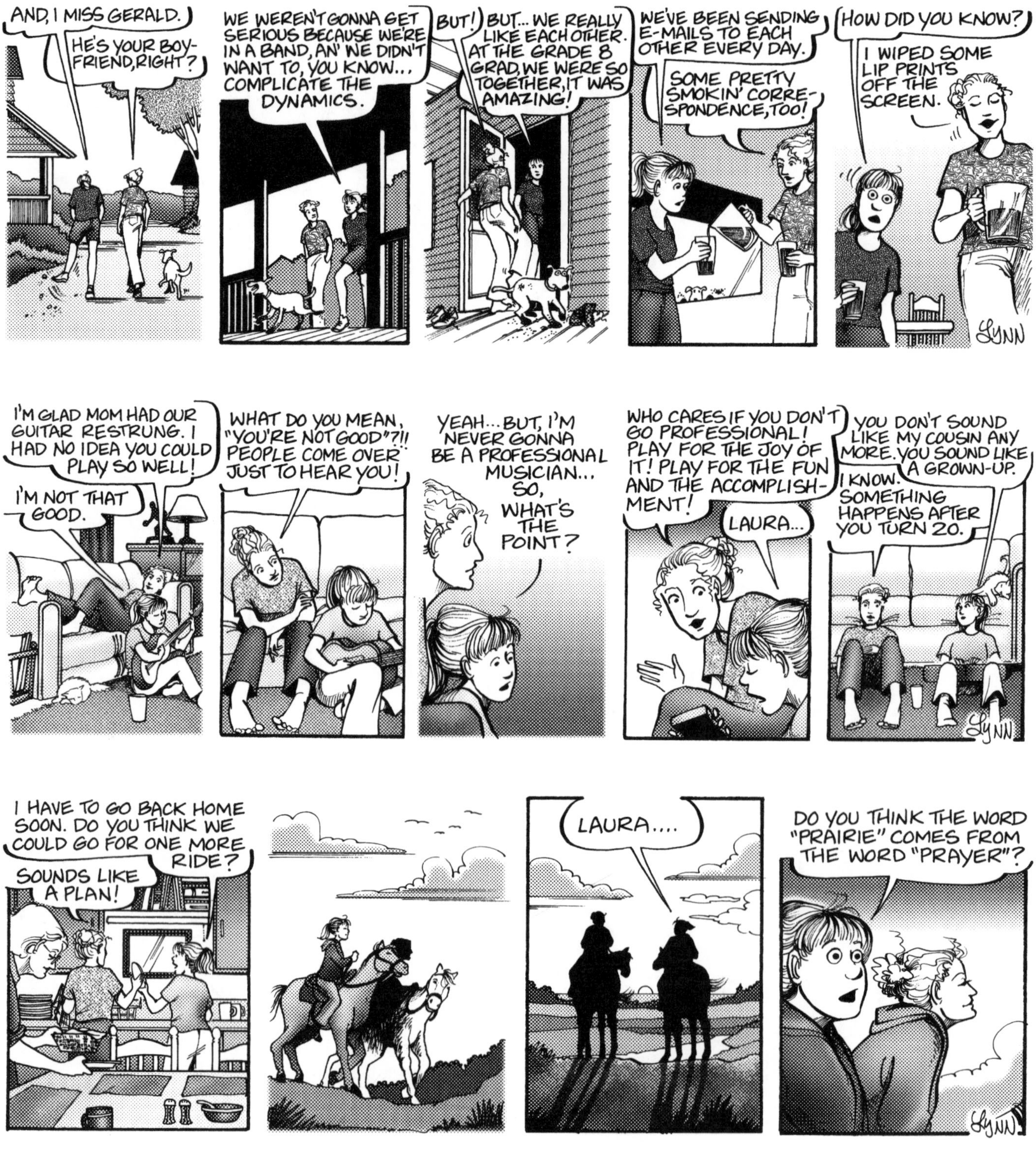
AND, I MISS GERALD.
HE'S YOUR BOY-FRIEND, RIGHT?
WE WEREN'T GONNA GET SERIOUS BECAUSE WE'RE IN A BAND, AN' WE DIDN'T WANT TO, YOU KNOW... COMPLICATE THE DYNAMICS.
BUT!
BUT... WE REALLY LIKE EACH OTHER. AT THE GRADE 8 GRAD, WE WERE SO TOGETHER, IT WAS AMAZING!
WE'VE BEEN SENDING E-MAILS TO EACH OTHER EVERY DAY.
SOME PRETTY SMOKIN' CORRE-SPONDENCE, TOO!
HOW DID YOU KNOW?
I WIPED SOME LIP PRINTS OFF THE SCREEN.
LYNN
I'M GLAD MOM HAD OUR GUITAR RESTRUNG. I HAD NO IDEA YOU COULD PLAY SO WELL!
I'M NOT THAT GOOD.
WHAT DO YOU MEAN, "YOU'RE NOT GOOD"?!! PEOPLE COME OVER JUST TO HEAR YOU!
YEAH... BUT, I'M NEVER GONNA BE A PROFESSIONAL MUSICIAN... SO, WHAT'S THE POINT?
WHO CARES IF YOU DON'T GO PROFESSIONAL! PLAY FOR THE JOY OF IT! PLAY FOR THE FUN AND THE ACCOMPLISH-MENT!
LAURA...
YOU DON'T SOUND LIKE MY COUSIN ANY MORE. YOU SOUND LIKE A GROWN-UP.
I KNOW. SOMETHING HAPPENS AFTER YOU TURN 20.
LYNN
I HAVE TO GO BACK HOME SOON. DO YOU THINK WE COULD GO FOR ONE MORE RIDE?
SOUNDS LIKE A PLAN!
LAURA....
DO YOU THINK THE WORD "PRAIRIE" COMES FROM THE WORD "PRAYER"?
LYNN

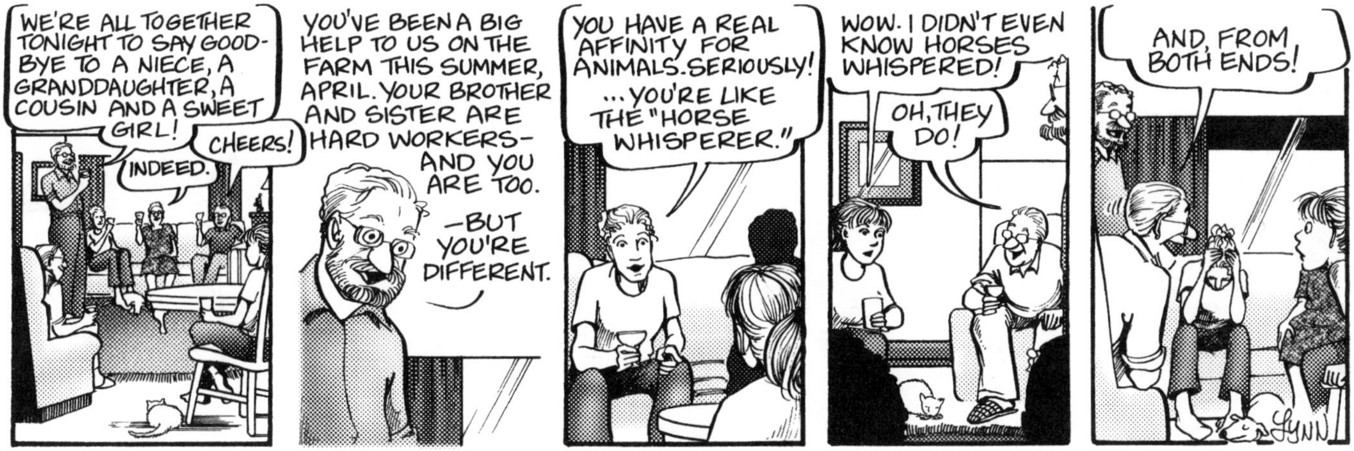
WE'RE ALL TOGETHER TONIGHT TO SAY GOOD-BYE TO A NIECE, A GRANDDAUGHTER, A COUSIN AND A SWEET GIRL!
INDEED.
CHEERS!
YOU'VE BEEN A BIG HELP TO US ON THE FARM THIS SUMMER, APRIL. YOUR BROTHER AND SISTER ARE HARD WORKERS- AND YOU ARE TOO.
-BUT YOU'RE DIFFERENT.
YOU HAVE A REAL AFFINITY FOR ANIMALS. SERIOUSLY!
...YOU'RE LIKE THE "HORSE WHISPERER."
WOW. I DIDN'T EVEN KNOW HORSES WHISPERED!
OH, THEY DO!
AND, FROM BOTH ENDS!
LYNN

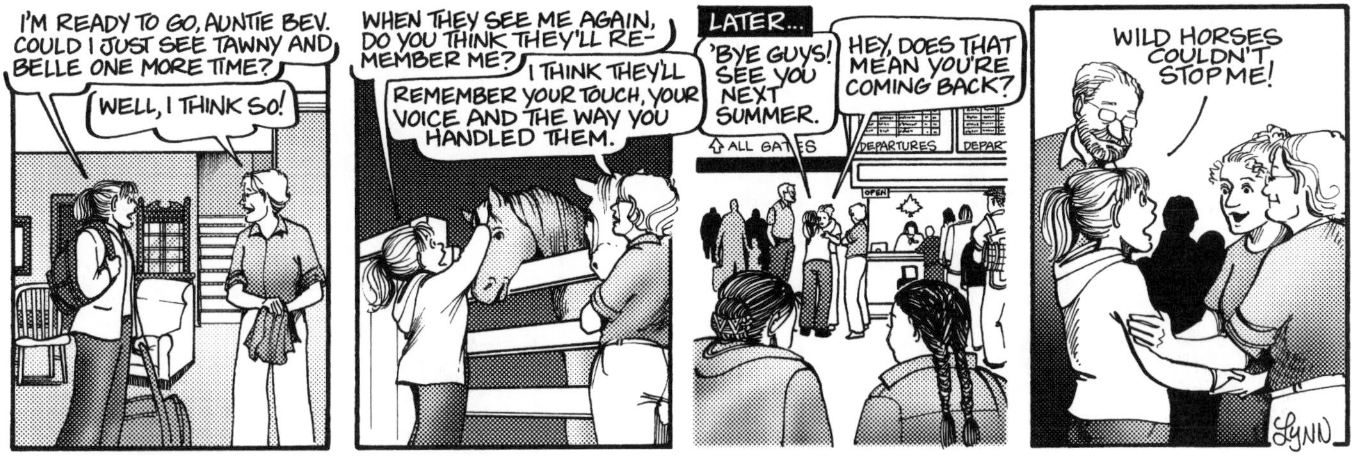
I'M READY TO GO, AUNTIE BEV. COULD I JUST SEE TAWNY AND BELLE ONE MORE TIME?
WELL, I THINK SO!
WHEN THEY SEE ME AGAIN, DO YOU THINK THEY'LL RE-MEMBER ME?
I THINK THEY'LL REMEMBER YOUR TOUCH, YOUR VOICE AND THE WAY YOU HANDLED THEM.
LATER...
'BYE GUYS! SEE YOU NEXT SUMMER.
HEY, DOES THAT MEAN YOU'RE COMING BACK?
ALL GATES
DEPARTURES
WILD HORSES COULDN'T STOP ME!
LYNN

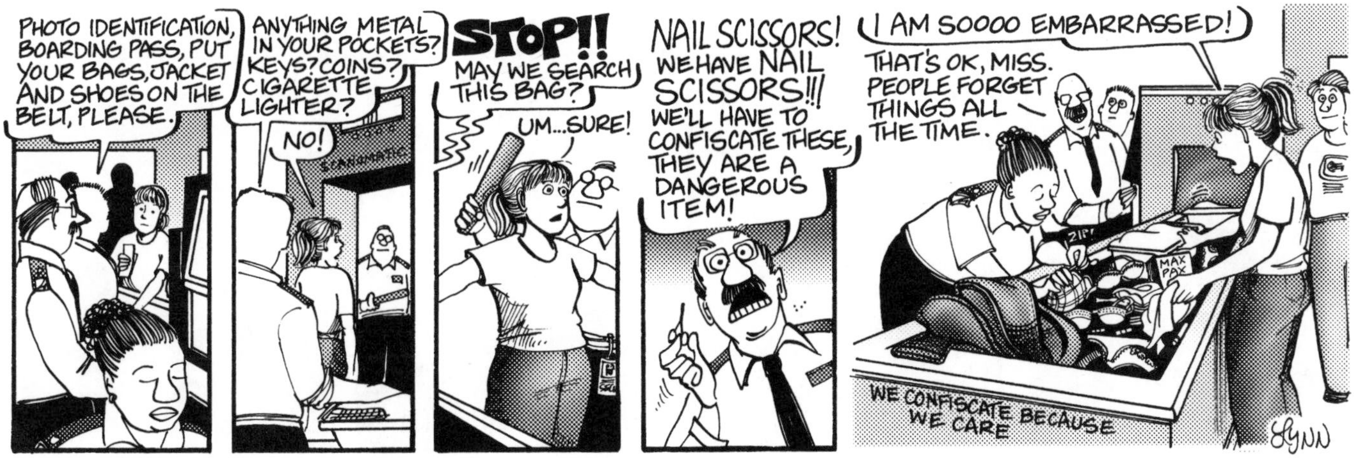
PHOTO IDENTIFICATION, BOARDING PASS, PUT YOUR BAGS, JACKET AND SHOES ON THE BELT, PLEASE.
ANYTHING METAL IN YOUR POCKETS? KEYS? COINS? CIGARETTE LIGHTER?
NO!
STOP!!
MAY WE SEARCH THIS BAG?
UM...SURE!
NAIL SCISSORS! WE HAVE NAIL SCISSORS!!! WE'LL HAVE TO CONFISCATE THESE, THEY ARE A DANGEROUS ITEM!
I AM SOOOO EMBARRASSED!
THAT'S OK, MISS. PEOPLE FORGET THINGS ALL THE TIME.
MAX PAX
WE CONFISCATE BECAUSE WE CARE
LYNN

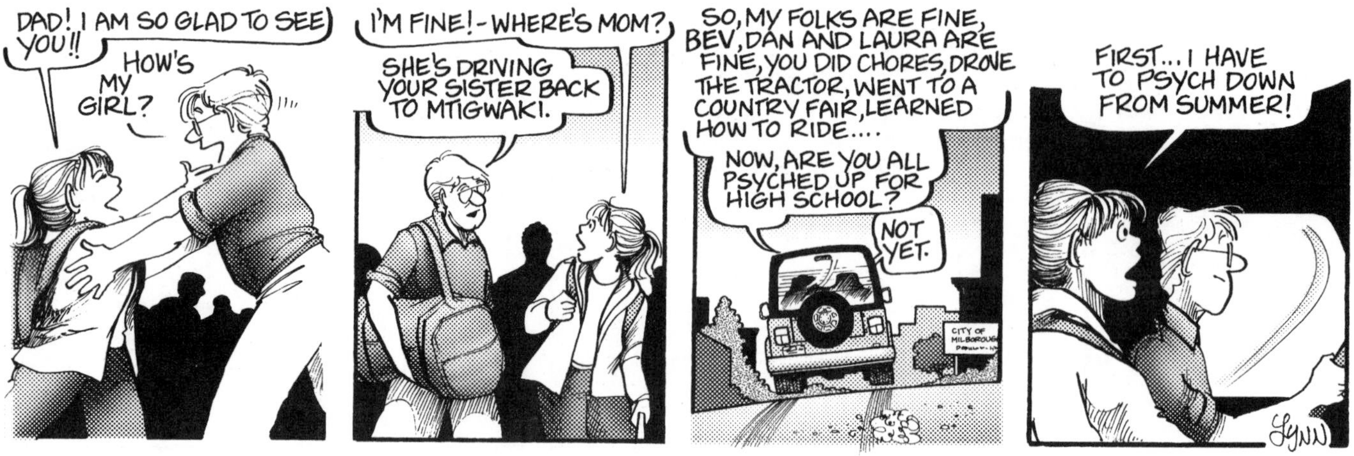
DAD! I AM SO GLAD TO SEE YOU!!
HOW'S MY GIRL?
I'M FINE! - WHERE'S MOM?
SHE'S DRIVING YOUR SISTER BACK TO MTIGWAKI.
SO, MY FOLKS ARE FINE, BEV, DAN AND LAURA ARE FINE, YOU DID CHORES, DROVE THE TRACTOR, WENT TO A COUNTRY FAIR, LEARNED HOW TO RIDE....
NOW, ARE YOU ALL PSYCHED UP FOR HIGH SCHOOL?
NOT YET.
FIRST... I HAVE TO PSYCH DOWN FROM SUMMER!
LYNN

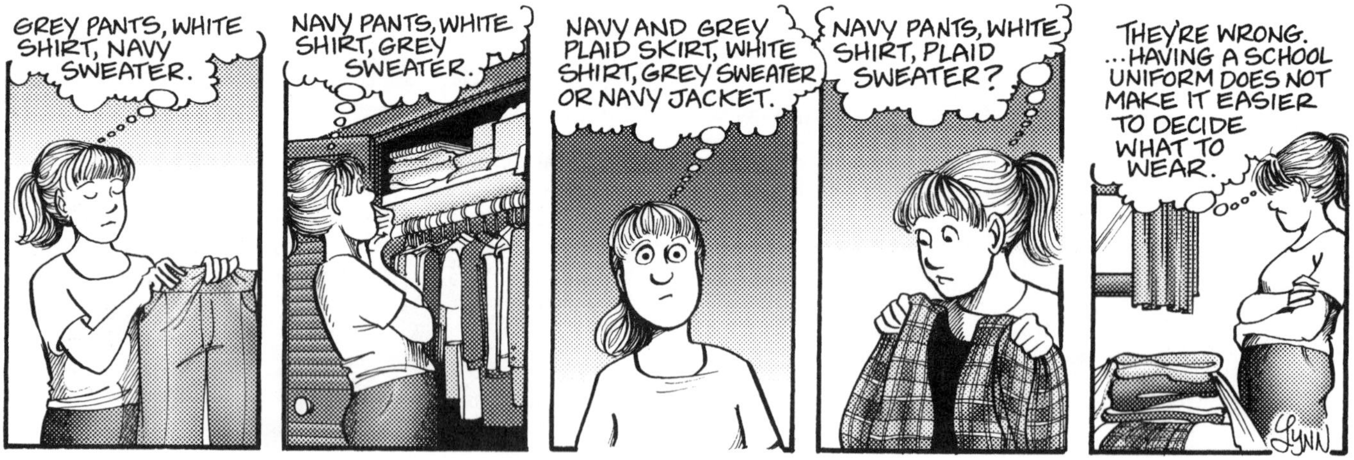
GREY PANTS, WHITE SHIRT, NAVY SWEATER.
NAVY PANTS, WHITE SHIRT, GREY SWEATER.
NAVY AND GREY PLAID SKIRT, WHITE SHIRT, GREY SWEATER OR NAVY JACKET.
NAVY PANTS, WHITE SHIRT, PLAID SWEATER?
THEY'RE WRONG. ...HAVING A SCHOOL UNIFORM DOES NOT MAKE IT EASIER TO DECIDE WHAT TO WEAR.
LYNN

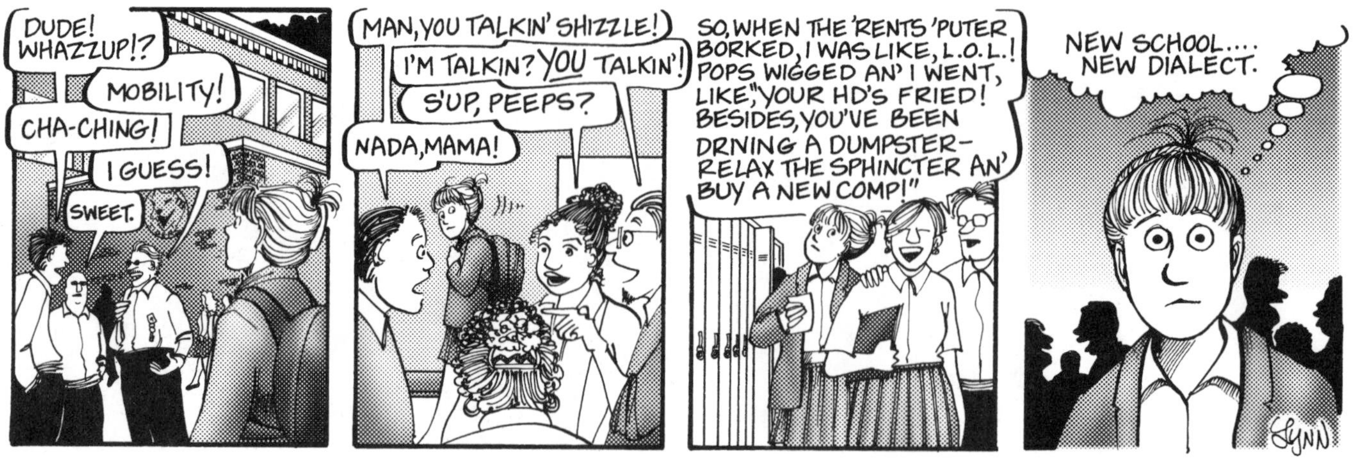
DUDE! WHAZZUP!?
MOBILITY!
CHA-CHING!
I GUESS!
SWEET.
MAN, YOU TALKIN' SHIZZLE!
I'M TALKIN? YOU TALKIN'!
S'UP, PEEPS?
NADA, MAMA!
SO, WHEN THE 'RENTS 'PUTER BORKED, I WAS LIKE, L.O.L.! POPS WIGGED AN' I WENT, LIKE, "YOUR HD'S FRIED! BESIDES, YOU'VE BEEN DRIVING A DUMPSTER- RELAX THE SPHINCTER AN' BUY A NEW COMP!"
NEW SCHOOL.... NEW DIALECT.
LYNN

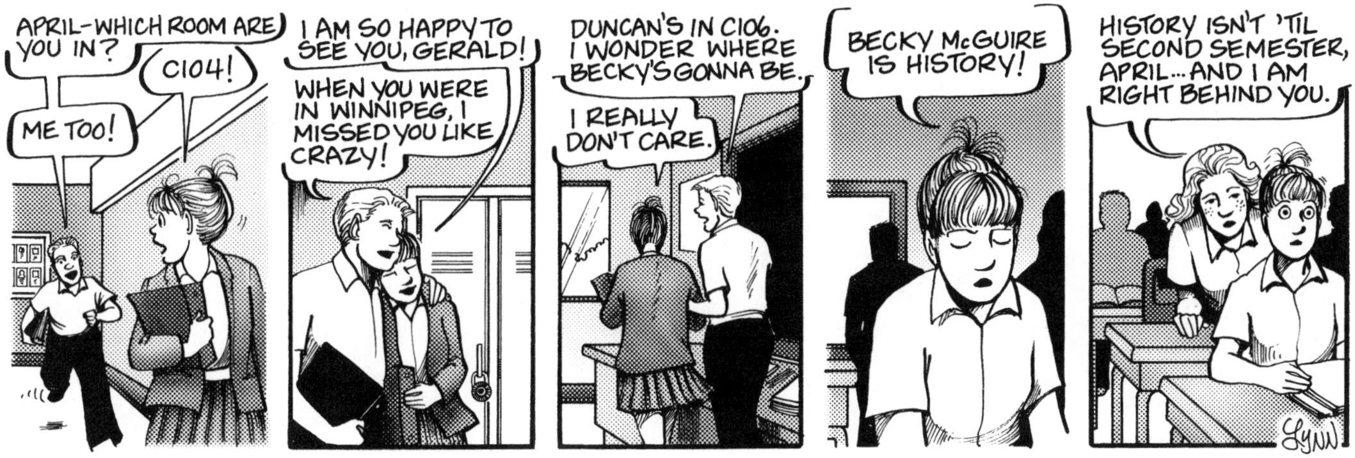
APRIL-WHICH ROOM ARE YOU IN?
C104!
ME TOO!
I AM SO HAPPY TO SEE YOU, GERALD!
WHEN YOU WERE IN WINNIPEG, I MISSED YOU LIKE CRAZY!
DUNCAN'S IN C106. I WONDER WHERE BECKY'S GONNA BE.
I REALLY DON'T CARE.
BECKY McGUIRE IS HISTORY!
HISTORY ISN'T 'TIL SECOND SEMESTER, APRIL... AND I AM RIGHT BEHIND YOU.
LYNN

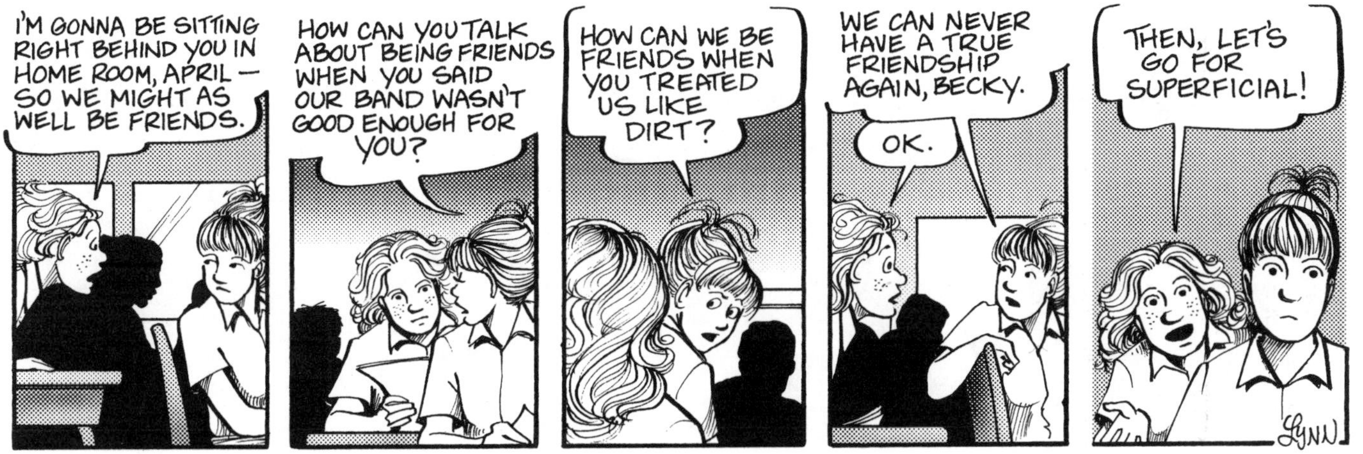
I'M GONNA BE SITTING RIGHT BEHIND YOU IN HOME ROOM, APRIL — SO WE MIGHT AS WELL BE FRIENDS.
HOW CAN YOU TALK ABOUT BEING FRIENDS WHEN YOU SAID OUR BAND WASN'T GOOD ENOUGH FOR YOU?
HOW CAN WE BE FRIENDS WHEN YOU TREATED US LIKE DIRT?
WE CAN NEVER HAVE A TRUE FRIENDSHIP AGAIN, BECKY.
OK.
THEN, LET'S GO FOR SUPERFICIAL!
LYNN

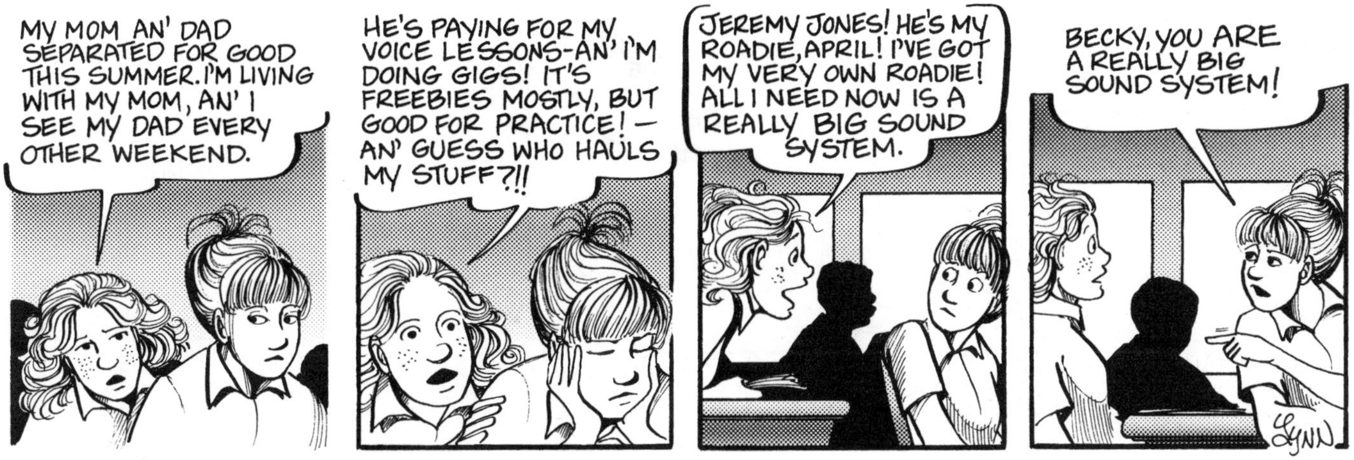
MY MOM AN' DAD SEPARATED FOR GOOD THIS SUMMER. I'M LIVING WITH MY MOM, AN' I SEE MY DAD EVERY OTHER WEEKEND.
HE'S PAYING FOR MY VOICE LESSONS-AN' I'M DOING GIGS! IT'S FREEBIES MOSTLY, BUT GOOD FOR PRACTICE! — AN' GUESS WHO HAULS MY STUFF?!!
JEREMY JONES! HE'S MY ROADIE, APRIL! I'VE GOT MY VERY OWN ROADIE! ALL I NEED NOW IS A REALLY BIG SOUND SYSTEM.
BECKY, YOU ARE A REALLY BIG SOUND SYSTEM!
LYNN

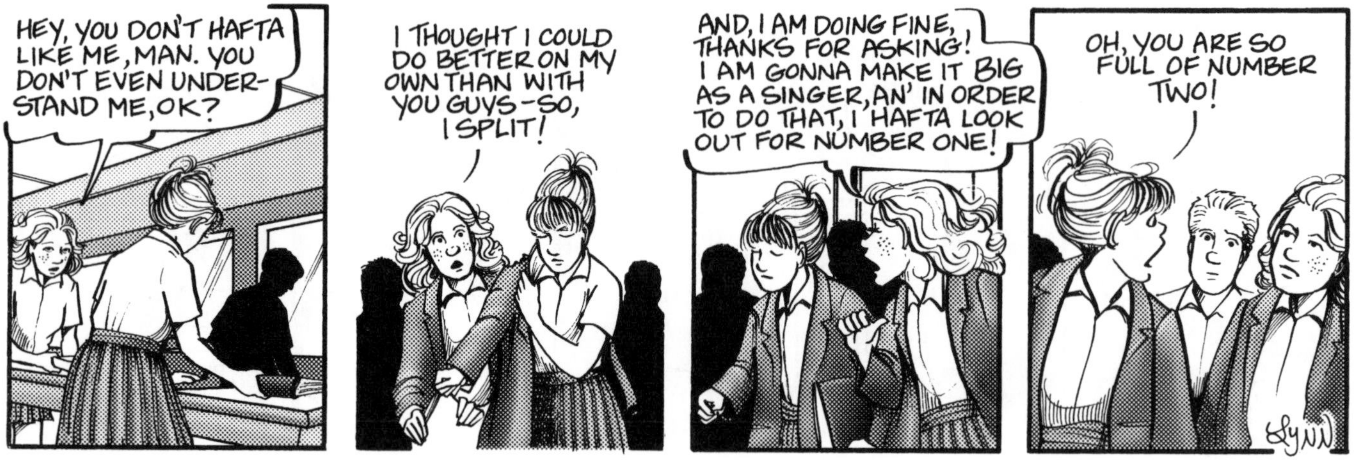
HEY, YOU DON'T HAFTA LIKE ME, MAN. YOU DON'T EVEN UNDERSTAND ME, OK?
I THOUGHT I COULD DO BETTER ON MY OWN THAN WITH YOU GUYS - SO, I SPLIT!
AND, I AM DOING FINE, THANKS FOR ASKING! I AM GONNA MAKE IT BIG AS A SINGER, AN' IN ORDER TO DO THAT, I HAFTA LOOK OUT FOR NUMBER ONE!
OH, YOU ARE SO FULL OF NUMBER TWO!

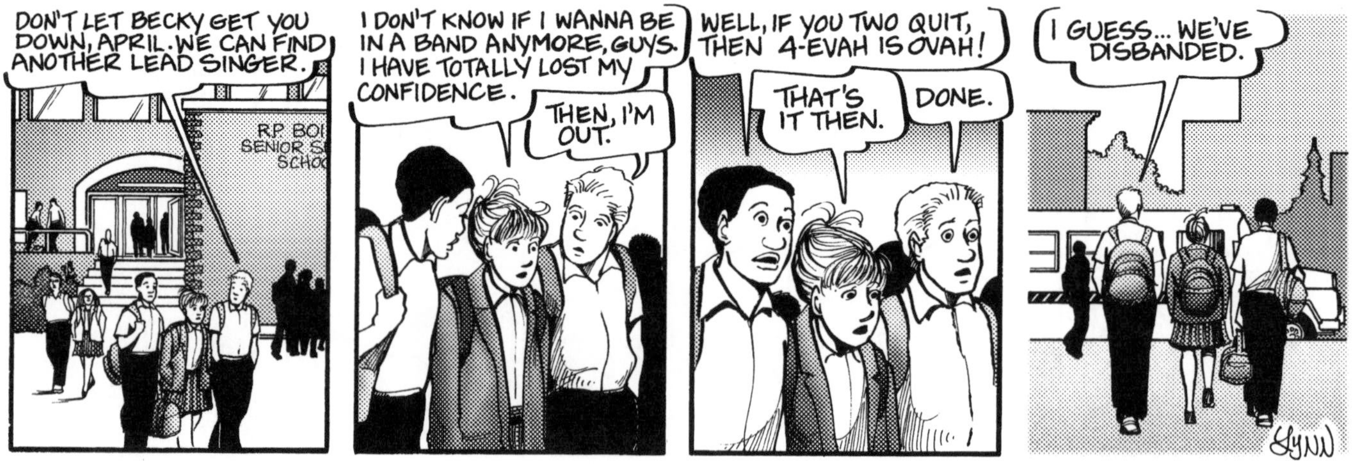
DON'T LET BECKY GET YOU DOWN, APRIL. WE CAN FIND ANOTHER LEAD SINGER.
I DON'T KNOW IF I WANNA BE IN A BAND ANYMORE, GUYS. I HAVE TOTALLY LOST MY CONFIDENCE.
THEN, I'M OUT.
WELL, IF YOU TWO QUIT, THEN 4-EVAH IS OVAH!
THAT'S IT THEN.
DONE.
I GUESS... WE'VE DISBANDED.

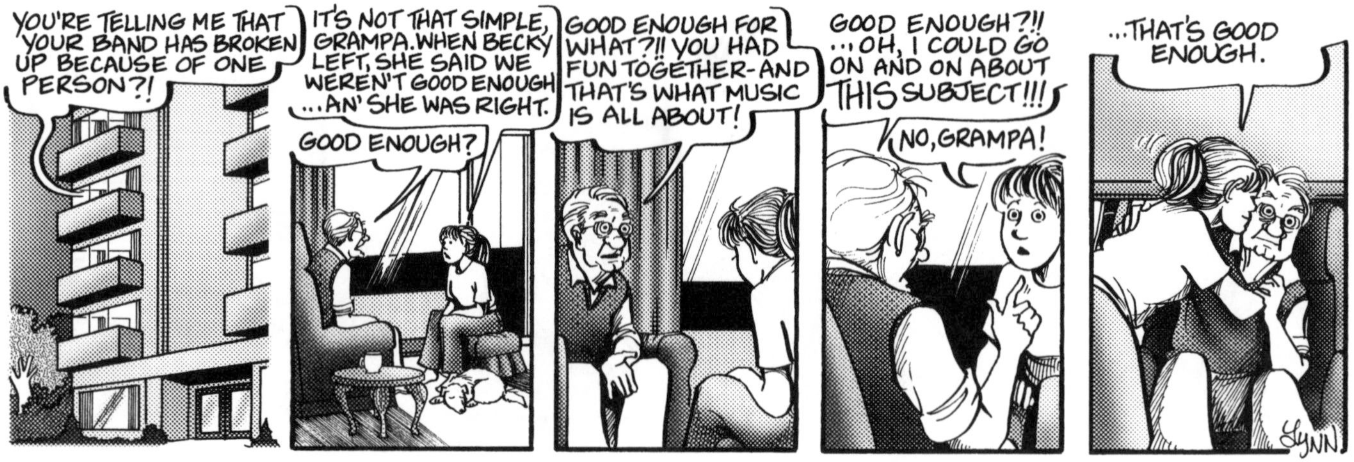
YOU'RE TELLING ME THAT YOUR BAND HAS BROKEN UP BECAUSE OF ONE PERSON?!
IT'S NOT THAT SIMPLE, GRAMPA. WHEN BECKY LEFT, SHE SAID WE WEREN'T GOOD ENOUGH ...AN' SHE WAS RIGHT.
GOOD ENOUGH?
GOOD ENOUGH FOR WHAT?!! YOU HAD FUN TOGETHER - AND THAT'S WHAT MUSIC IS ALL ABOUT!
GOOD ENOUGH?!! ...OH, I COULD GO ON AND ON ABOUT THIS SUBJECT!!!
NO, GRAMPA!
...THAT'S GOOD ENOUGH.

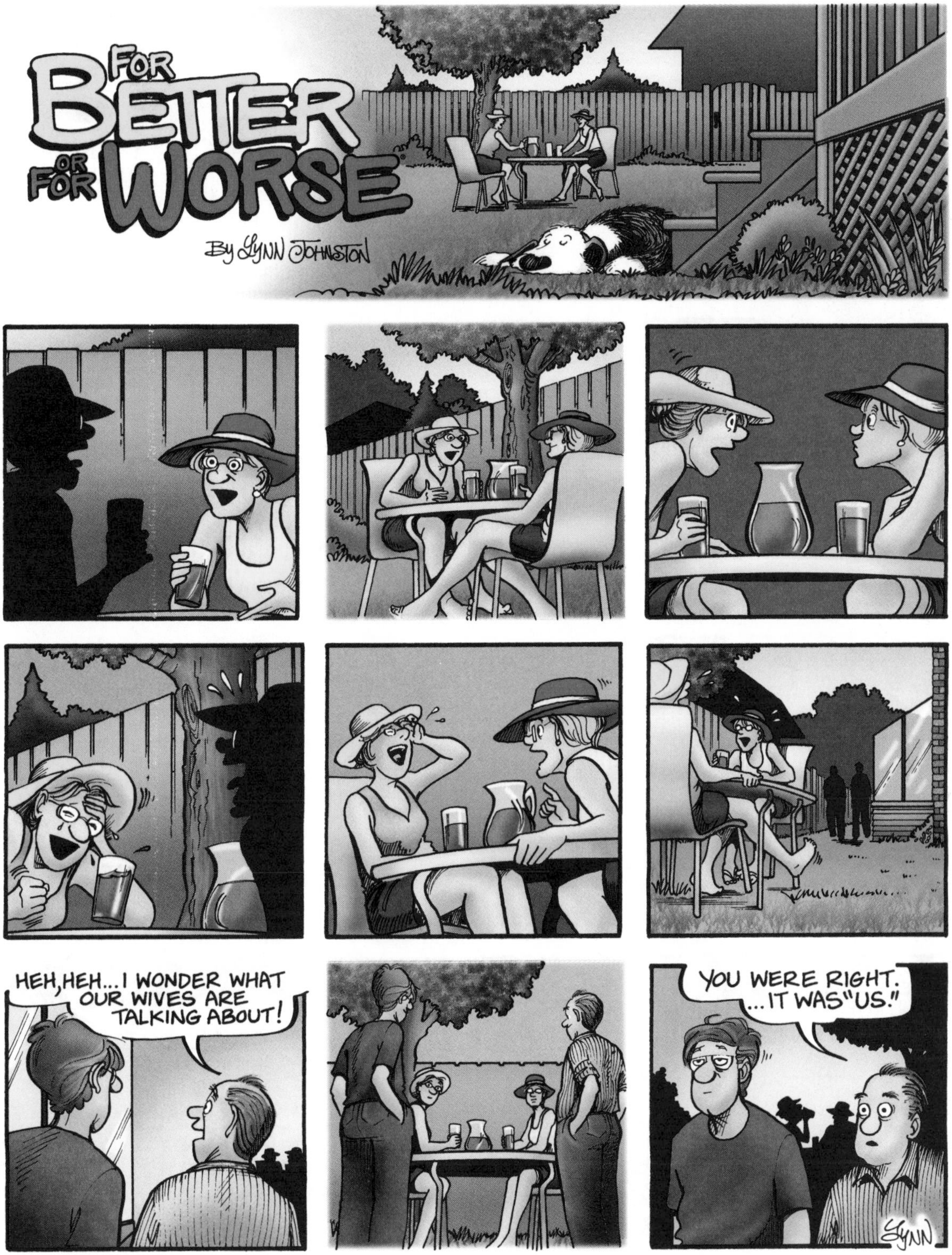
FOR BETTER OR FOR WORSE
By Lynn Johnston
HEH, HEH... I WONDER WHAT OUR WIVES ARE TALKING ABOUT!
YOU WERE RIGHT. ...IT WAS "US."
LYNN

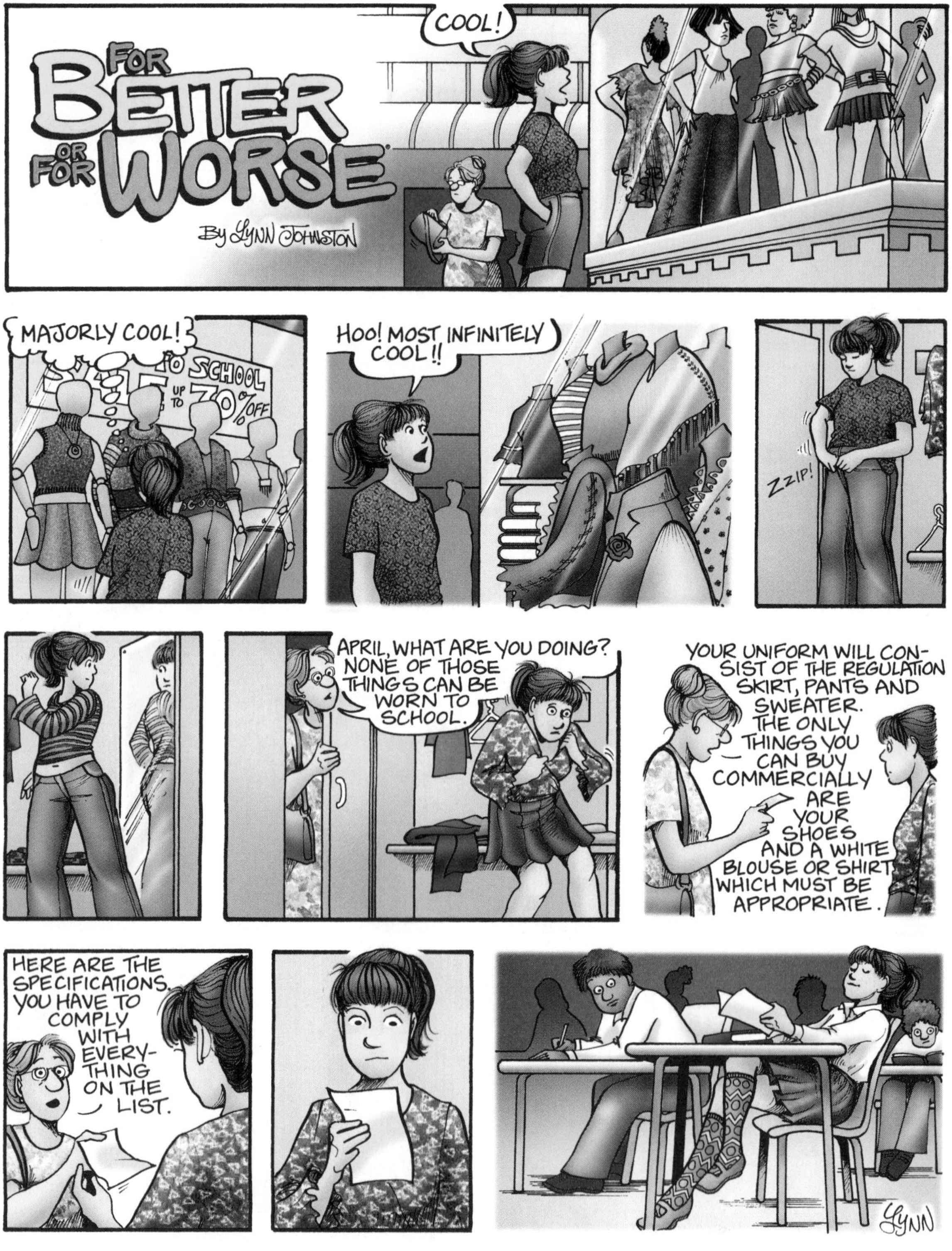
FOR BETTER OR FOR WORSE
By Lynn Johnston
COOL!
MAJORLY COOL!
BACK TO SCHOOL
UP TO 70% OFF
HOO! MOST INFINITELY COOL!!
ZZIP!
APRIL, WHAT ARE YOU DOING? NONE OF THOSE THINGS CAN BE WORN TO SCHOOL.
YOUR UNIFORM WILL CONSIST OF THE REGULATION SKIRT, PANTS AND SWEATER. THE ONLY THINGS YOU CAN BUY COMMERCIALLY ARE YOUR SHOES AND A WHITE BLOUSE OR SHIRT WHICH MUST BE APPROPRIATE.
HERE ARE THE SPECIFICATIONS. YOU HAVE TO COMPLY WITH EVERYTHING ON THE LIST.
LYNN

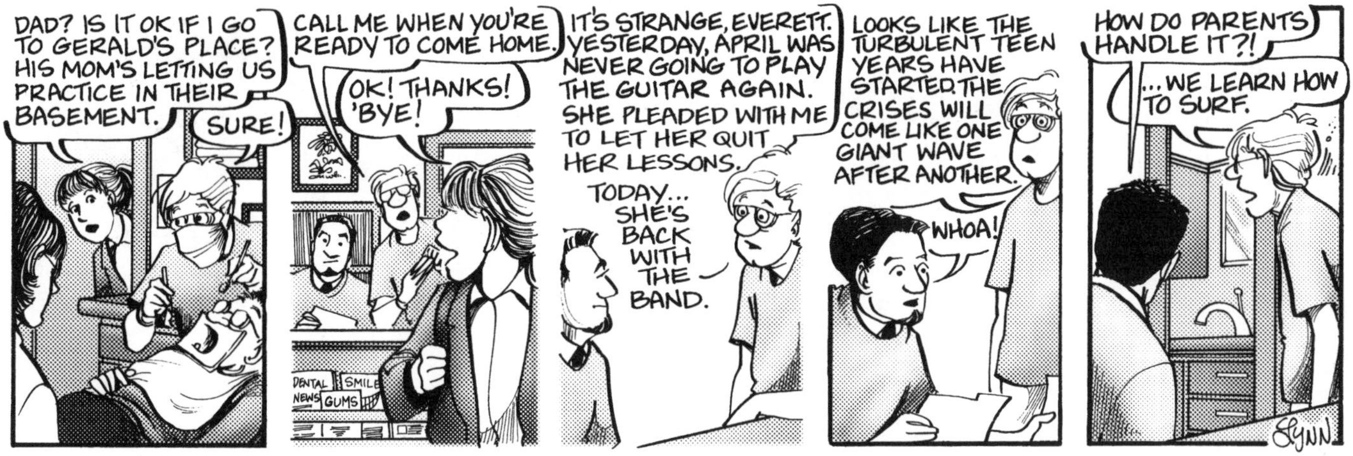
DAD? IS IT OK IF I GO TO GERALD'S PLACE? HIS MOM'S LETTING US PRACTICE IN THEIR BASEMENT.
SURE!
CALL ME WHEN YOU'RE READY TO COME HOME.
OK! THANKS! 'BYE!
DENTAL NEWS
SMILE
GUMS
IT'S STRANGE, EVERETT. YESTERDAY, APRIL WAS NEVER GOING TO PLAY THE GUITAR AGAIN. SHE PLEADED WITH ME TO LET HER QUIT HER LESSONS.
TODAY... SHE'S BACK WITH THE BAND.
LOOKS LIKE THE TURBULENT TEEN YEARS HAVE STARTED. THE CRISES WILL COME LIKE ONE GIANT WAVE AFTER ANOTHER.
WHOA!
HOW DO PARENTS HANDLE IT?!
...WE LEARN HOW TO SURF.
LYNN

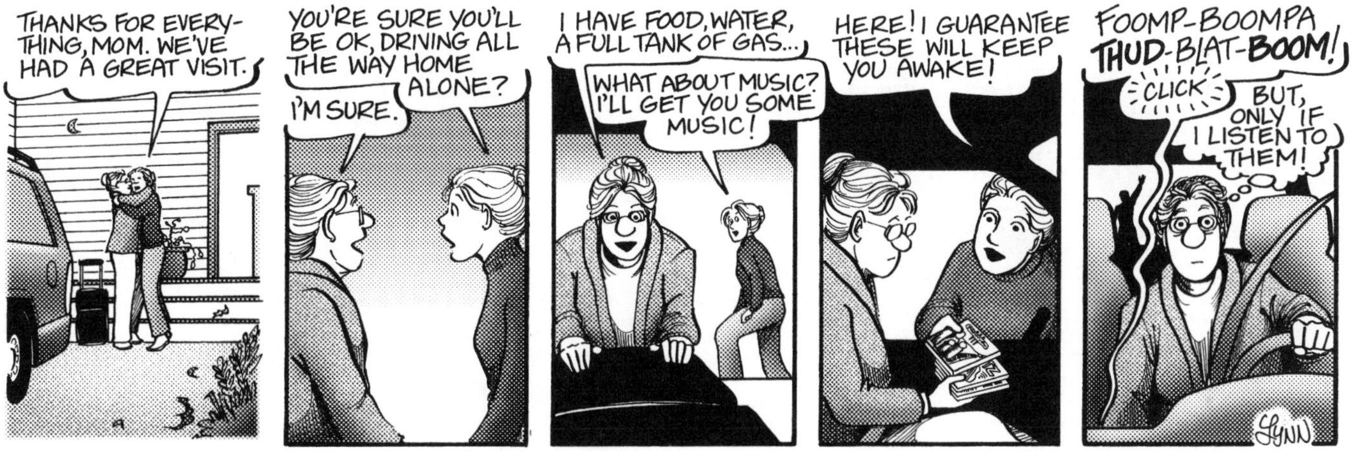
THANKS FOR EVERYTHING, MOM. WE'VE HAD A GREAT VISIT.
YOU'RE SURE YOU'LL BE OK, DRIVING ALL THE WAY HOME ALONE?
I'M SURE.
I HAVE FOOD, WATER, A FULL TANK OF GAS...
WHAT ABOUT MUSIC? I'LL GET YOU SOME MUSIC!
HERE! I GUARANTEE THESE WILL KEEP YOU AWAKE!
FOOMP-BOOMPA THUD-BLAT-BOOM!
CLICK
BUT, ONLY IF I LISTEN TO THEM!
LYNN

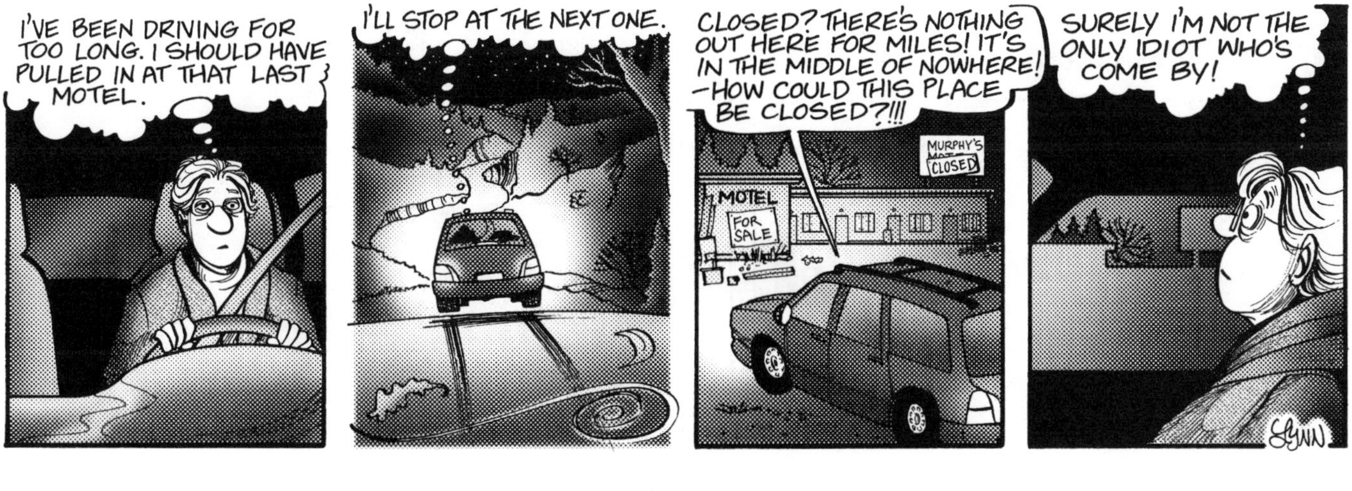
I'VE BEEN DRIVING FOR TOO LONG. I SHOULD HAVE PULLED IN AT THAT LAST MOTEL.
I'LL STOP AT THE NEXT ONE.
CLOSED? THERE'S NOTHING OUT HERE FOR MILES! IT'S IN THE MIDDLE OF NOWHERE! —HOW COULD THIS PLACE BE CLOSED?!!!
MURPHY'S
CLOSED
MOTEL
FOR SALE
SURELY I'M NOT THE ONLY IDIOT WHO'S COME BY!
LYNN

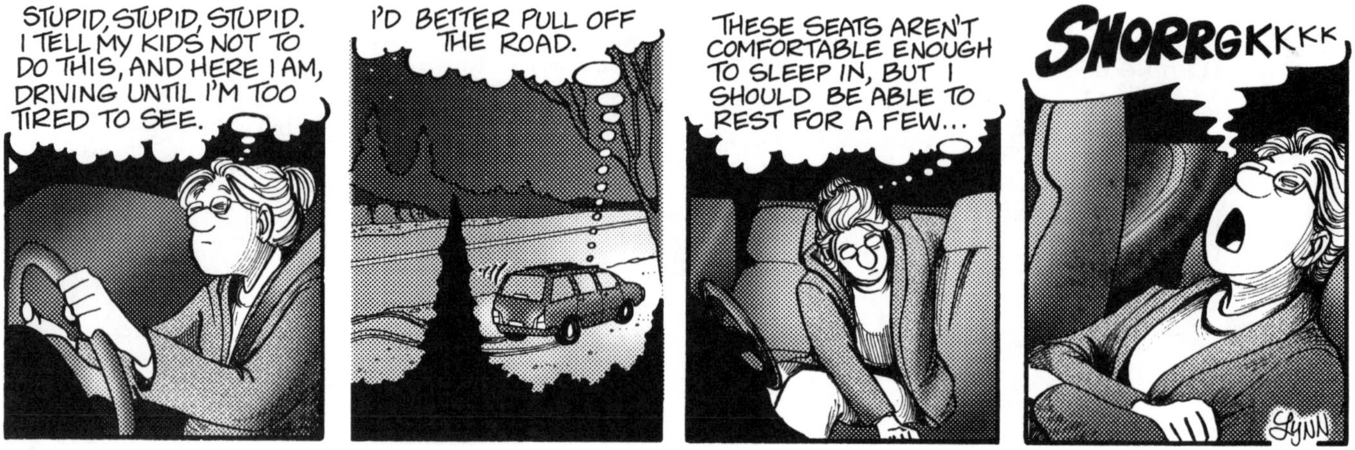
STUPID, STUPID, STUPID. I TELL MY KIDS NOT TO DO THIS, AND HERE I AM, DRIVING UNTIL I'M TOO TIRED TO SEE.
I'D BETTER PULL OFF THE ROAD.
THESE SEATS AREN'T COMFORTABLE ENOUGH TO SLEEP IN, BUT I SHOULD BE ABLE TO REST FOR A FEW...
SNORRGKKKK
LYNN

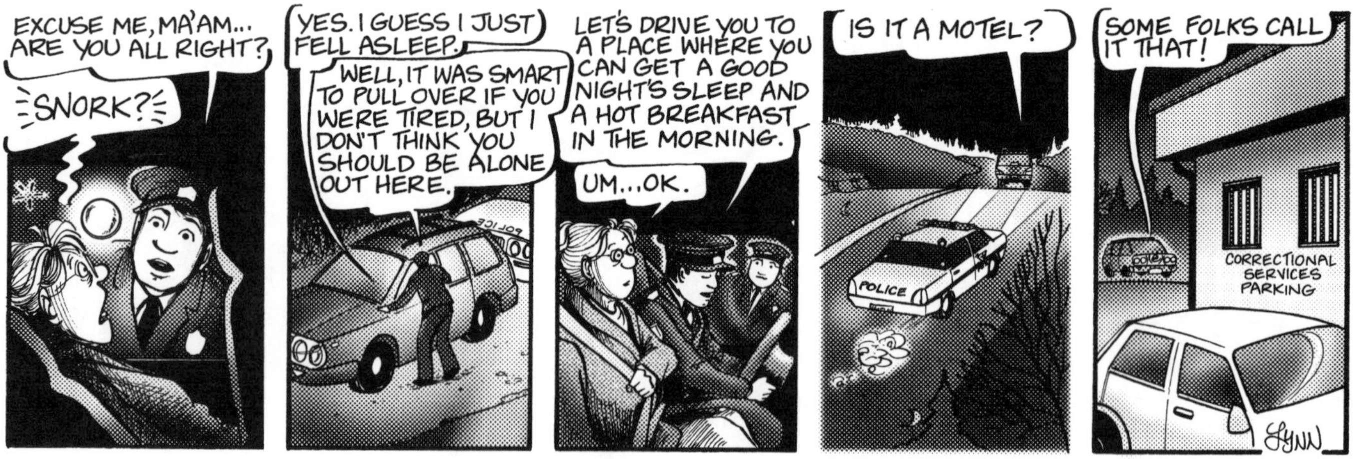
EXCUSE ME, MA'AM... ARE YOU ALL RIGHT?
SNORK?
YES. I GUESS I JUST FELL ASLEEP.
WELL, IT WAS SMART TO PULL OVER IF YOU WERE TIRED, BUT I DON'T THINK YOU SHOULD BE ALONE OUT HERE.
LET'S DRIVE YOU TO A PLACE WHERE YOU CAN GET A GOOD NIGHT'S SLEEP AND A HOT BREAKFAST IN THE MORNING.
UM...OK.
IS IT A MOTEL?
POLICE
SOME FOLKS CALL IT THAT!
CORRECTIONAL SERVICES PARKING
LYNN

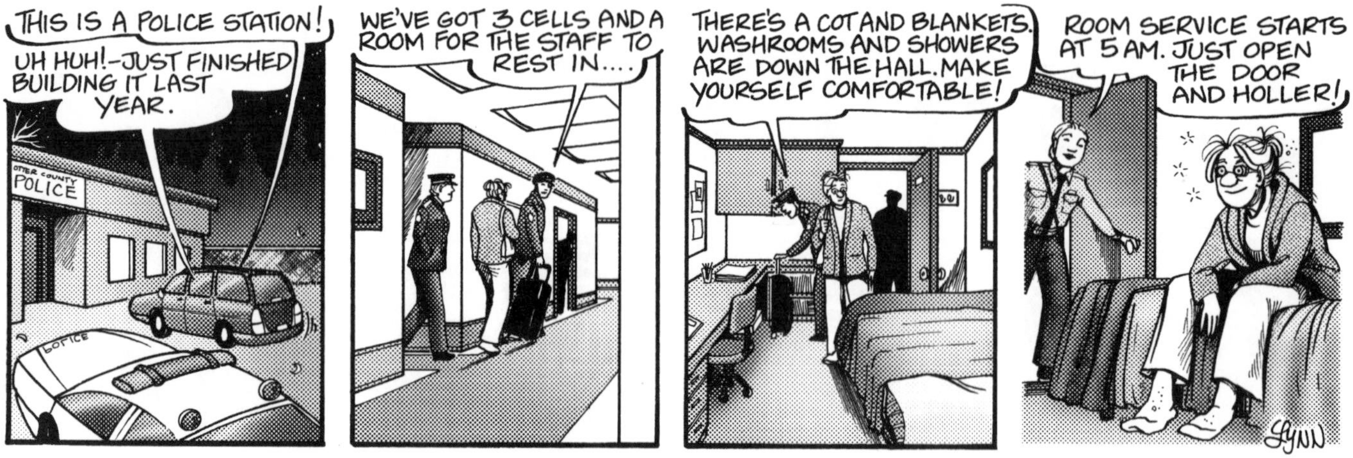
THIS IS A POLICE STATION!
UH HUH! - JUST FINISHED BUILDING IT LAST YEAR.
POLICE
WE'VE GOT 3 CELLS AND A ROOM FOR THE STAFF TO REST IN....
THERE'S A COT AND BLANKETS. WASHROOMS AND SHOWERS ARE DOWN THE HALL. MAKE YOURSELF COMFORTABLE!
ROOM SERVICE STARTS AT 5 AM. JUST OPEN THE DOOR AND HOLLER!
LYNN

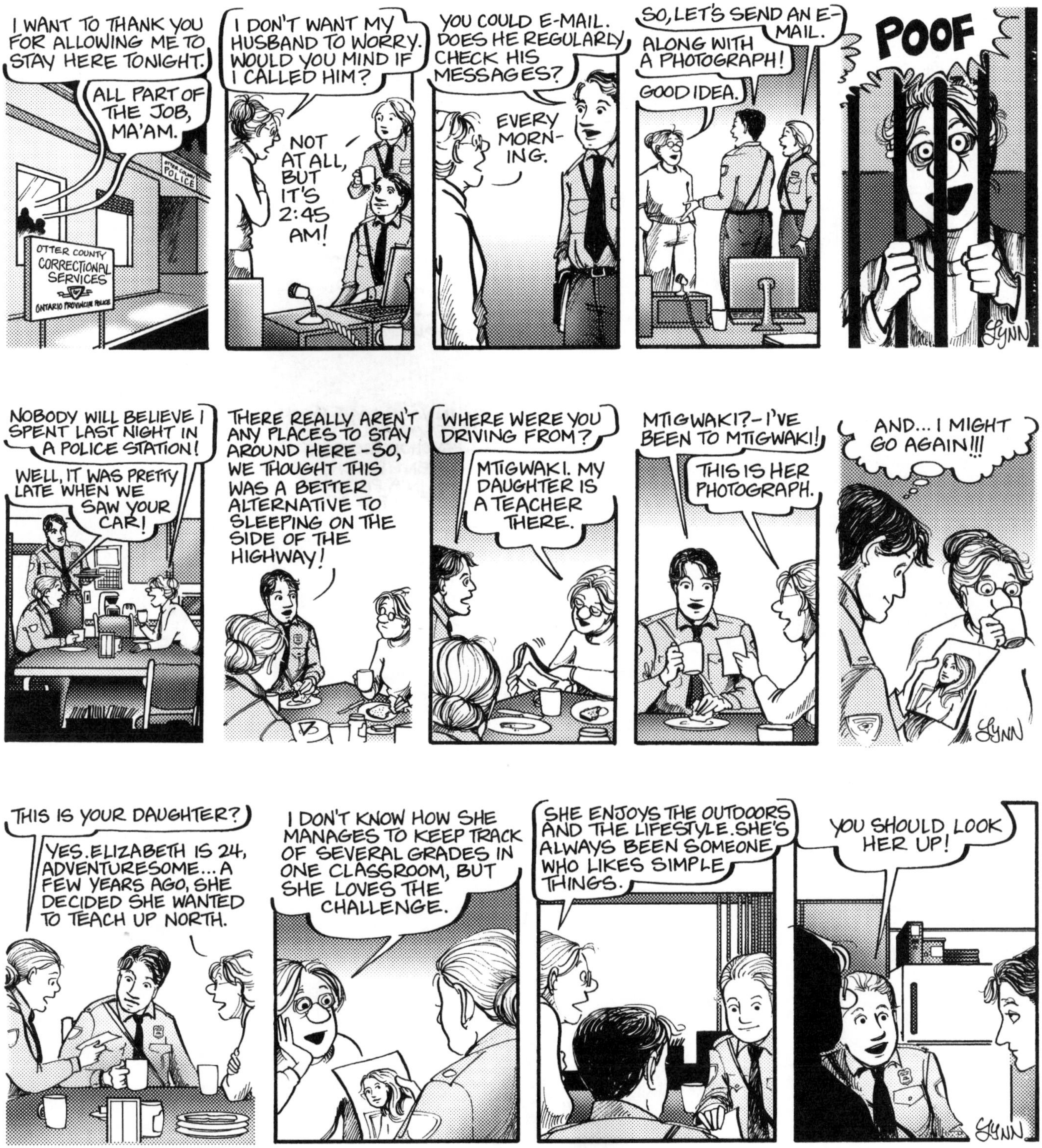
I WANT TO THANK YOU FOR ALLOWING ME TO STAY HERE TONIGHT.
ALL PART OF THE JOB, MA'AM.
OTTER COUNTY POLICE
OTTER COUNTY CORRECTIONAL SERVICES
ONTARIO PROVINCIAL POLICE
I DON'T WANT MY HUSBAND TO WORRY. WOULD YOU MIND IF I CALLED HIM?
NOT AT ALL, BUT IT'S 2:45 AM!
YOU COULD E-MAIL. DOES HE REGULARLY CHECK HIS MESSAGES?
EVERY MORNING.
SO, LET'S SEND AN E-MAIL.
ALONG WITH A PHOTOGRAPH!
GOOD IDEA.
POOF
LYNN
NOBODY WILL BELIEVE I SPENT LAST NIGHT IN A POLICE STATION!
WELL, IT WAS PRETTY LATE WHEN WE SAW YOUR CAR!
THERE REALLY AREN'T ANY PLACES TO STAY AROUND HERE - SO, WE THOUGHT THIS WAS A BETTER ALTERNATIVE TO SLEEPING ON THE SIDE OF THE HIGHWAY!
WHERE WERE YOU DRIVING FROM?
MTIGWAKI. MY DAUGHTER IS A TEACHER THERE.
MTIGWAKI?- I'VE BEEN TO MTIGWAKI!
THIS IS HER PHOTOGRAPH.
AND... I MIGHT GO AGAIN!!!
LYNN
THIS IS YOUR DAUGHTER?
YES. ELIZABETH IS 24, ADVENTURESOME... A FEW YEARS AGO, SHE DECIDED SHE WANTED TO TEACH UP NORTH.
I DON'T KNOW HOW SHE MANAGES TO KEEP TRACK OF SEVERAL GRADES IN ONE CLASSROOM, BUT SHE LOVES THE CHALLENGE.
SHE ENJOYS THE OUTDOORS AND THE LIFESTYLE. SHE'S ALWAYS BEEN SOMEONE WHO LIKES SIMPLE THINGS.
YOU SHOULD LOOK HER UP!
LYNN

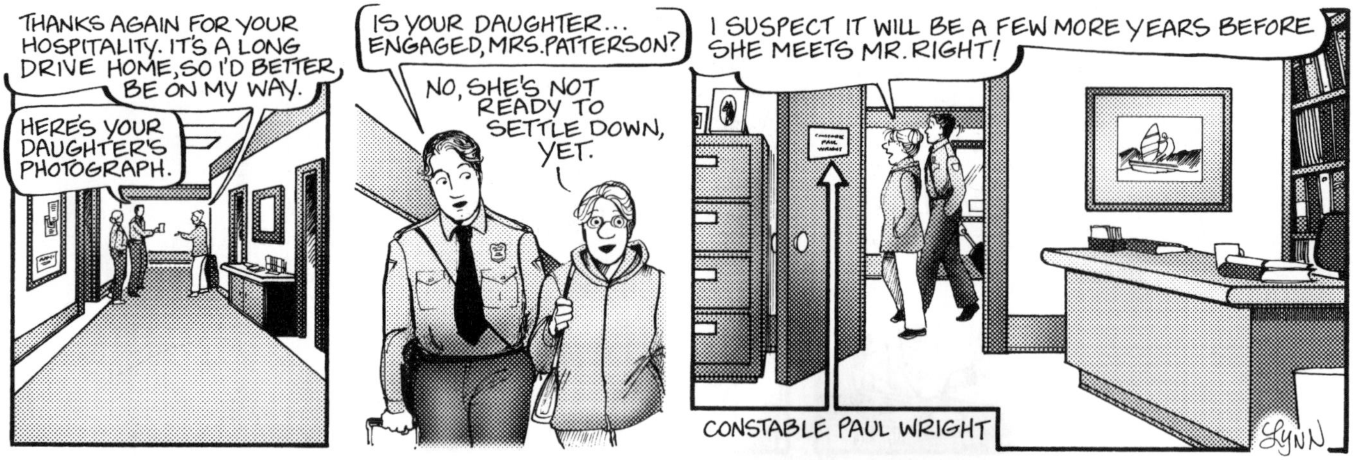
THANKS AGAIN FOR YOUR HOSPITALITY. IT'S A LONG DRIVE HOME, SO I'D BETTER BE ON MY WAY.
HERE'S YOUR DAUGHTER'S PHOTOGRAPH.
IS YOUR DAUGHTER... ENGAGED, MRS. PATTERSON?
NO, SHE'S NOT READY TO SETTLE DOWN, YET.
I SUSPECT IT WILL BE A FEW MORE YEARS BEFORE SHE MEETS MR. RIGHT!
CONSTABLE PAUL WRIGHT
LYNN

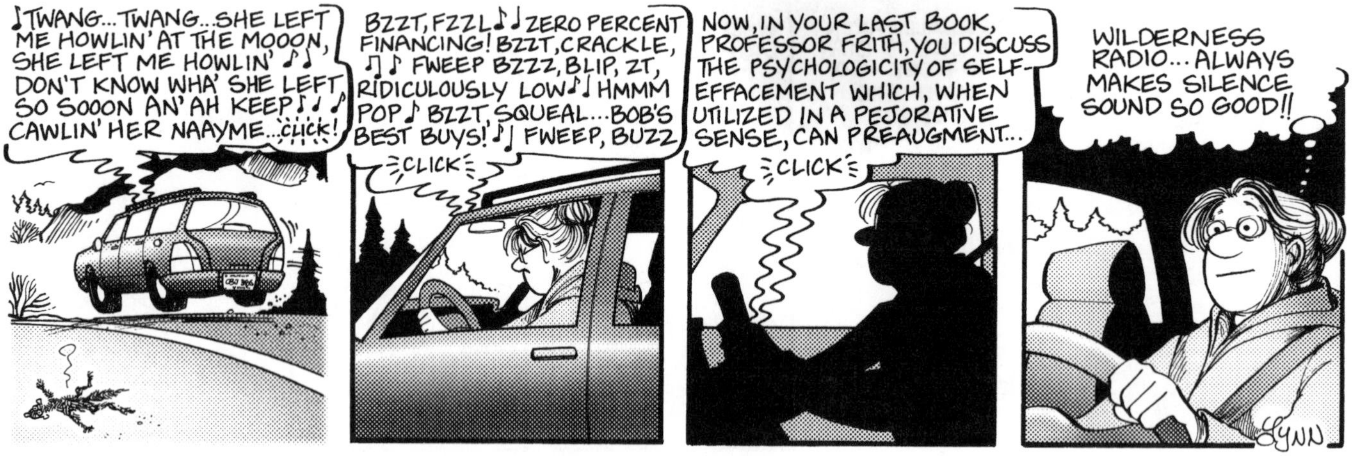
♩TWANG... TWANG... SHE LEFT ME HOWLIN' AT THE MOOON, SHE LEFT ME HOWLIN' ♪♩ DON'T KNOW WHA' SHE LEFT SO SOOON AN' AH KEEP ♪♩♪ CAWLIN' HER NAAYME... CLICK!
BZZT, FZZL ♪♩ ZERO PERCENT FINANCING! BZZT, CRACKLE, ♫♪ FWEEP BZZZ, BLIP, ZT, RIDICULOUSLY LOW ♪♩ HMMM POP ♪ BZZT, SQUEAL... BOB'S BEST BUYS! ♪♩ FWEEP, BUZZ
CLICK
NOW, IN YOUR LAST BOOK, PROFESSOR FRITH, YOU DISCUSS THE PSYCHOLOGICITY OF SELF-EFFACEMENT WHICH, WHEN UTILIZED IN A PEJORATIVE SENSE, CAN PREAUGMENT...
CLICK
WILDERNESS RADIO... ALWAYS MAKES SILENCE SOUND SO GOOD!!
LYNN

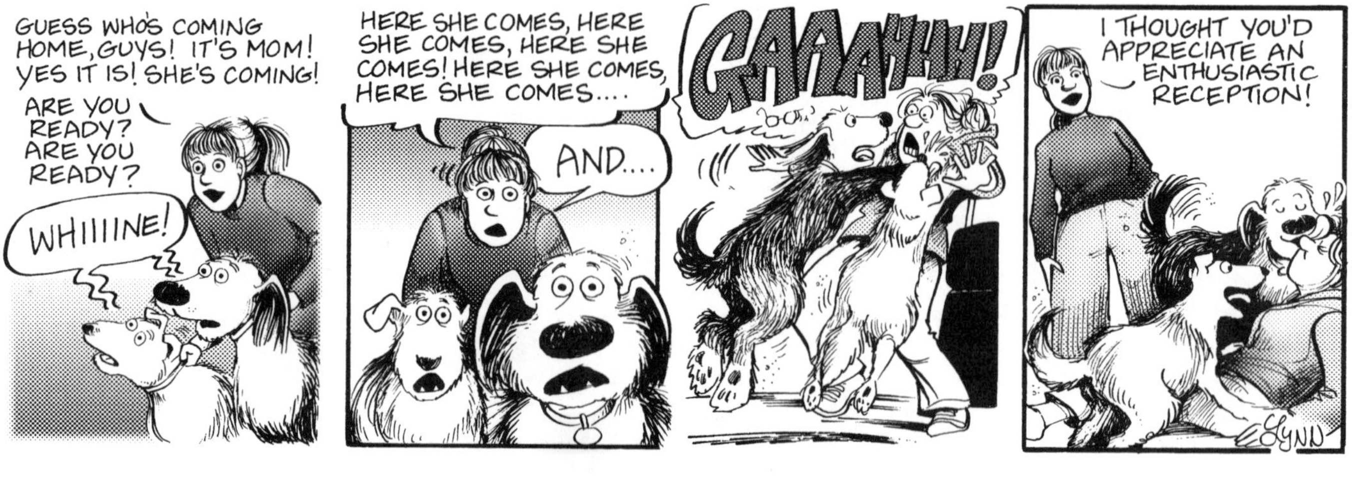
GUESS WHO'S COMING HOME, GUYS! IT'S MOM! YES IT IS! SHE'S COMING!
ARE YOU READY? ARE YOU READY?
WHIIIINE!
HERE SHE COMES, HERE SHE COMES, HERE SHE COMES! HERE SHE COMES, HERE SHE COMES....
AND....
GAAAAHHH!
I THOUGHT YOU'D APPRECIATE AN ENTHUSIASTIC RECEPTION!
LYNN

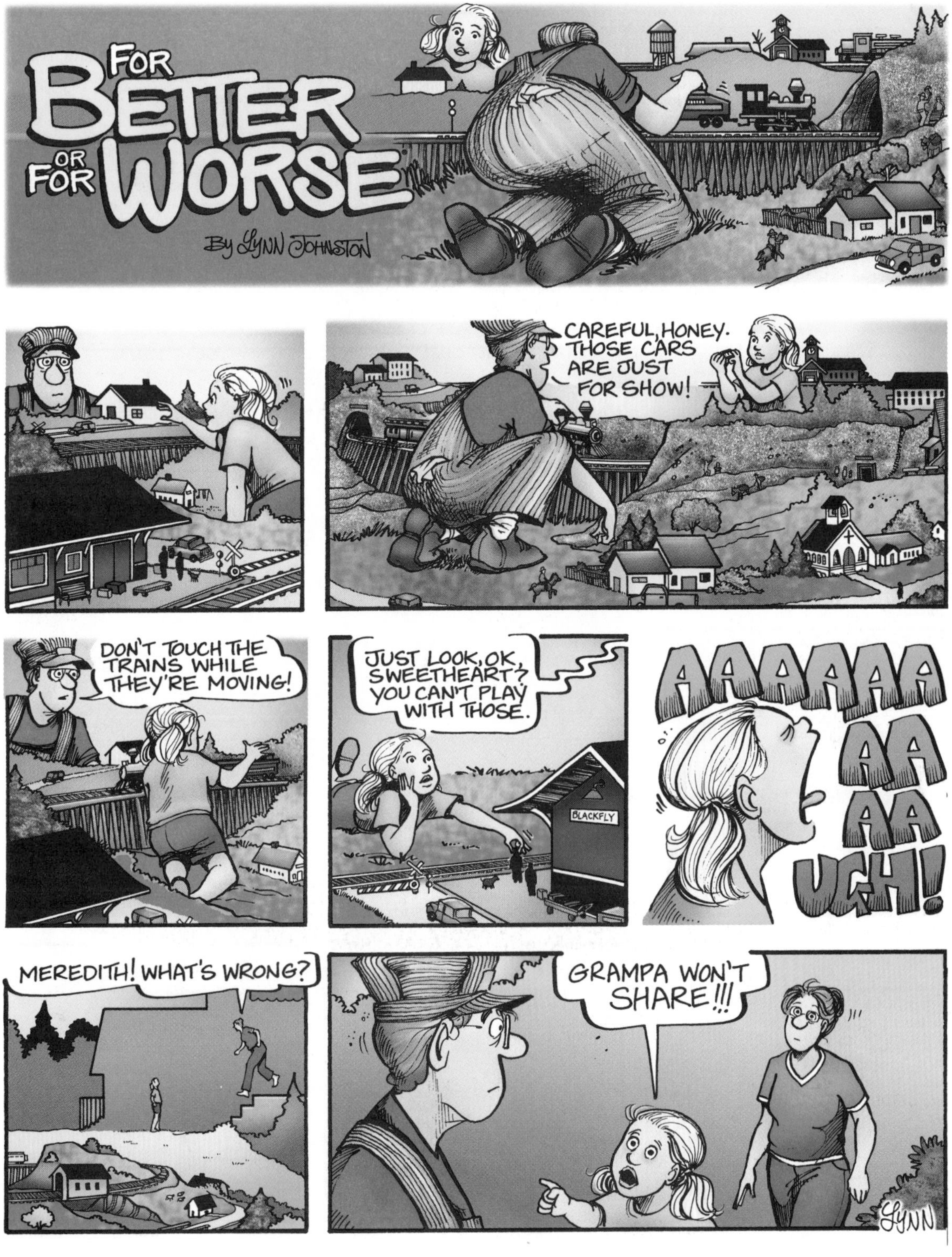
FOR BETTER OR FOR WORSE
BY LYNN JOHNSTON
CAREFUL, HONEY. THOSE CARS ARE JUST FOR SHOW!
DON'T TOUCH THE TRAINS WHILE THEY'RE MOVING!
JUST LOOK, OK, SWEETHEART? YOU CAN'T PLAY WITH THOSE.
BLACKFLY
AAAAAA AA AA UGH!
MEREDITH! WHAT'S WRONG?
GRAMPA WON'T SHARE!!!
LYNN

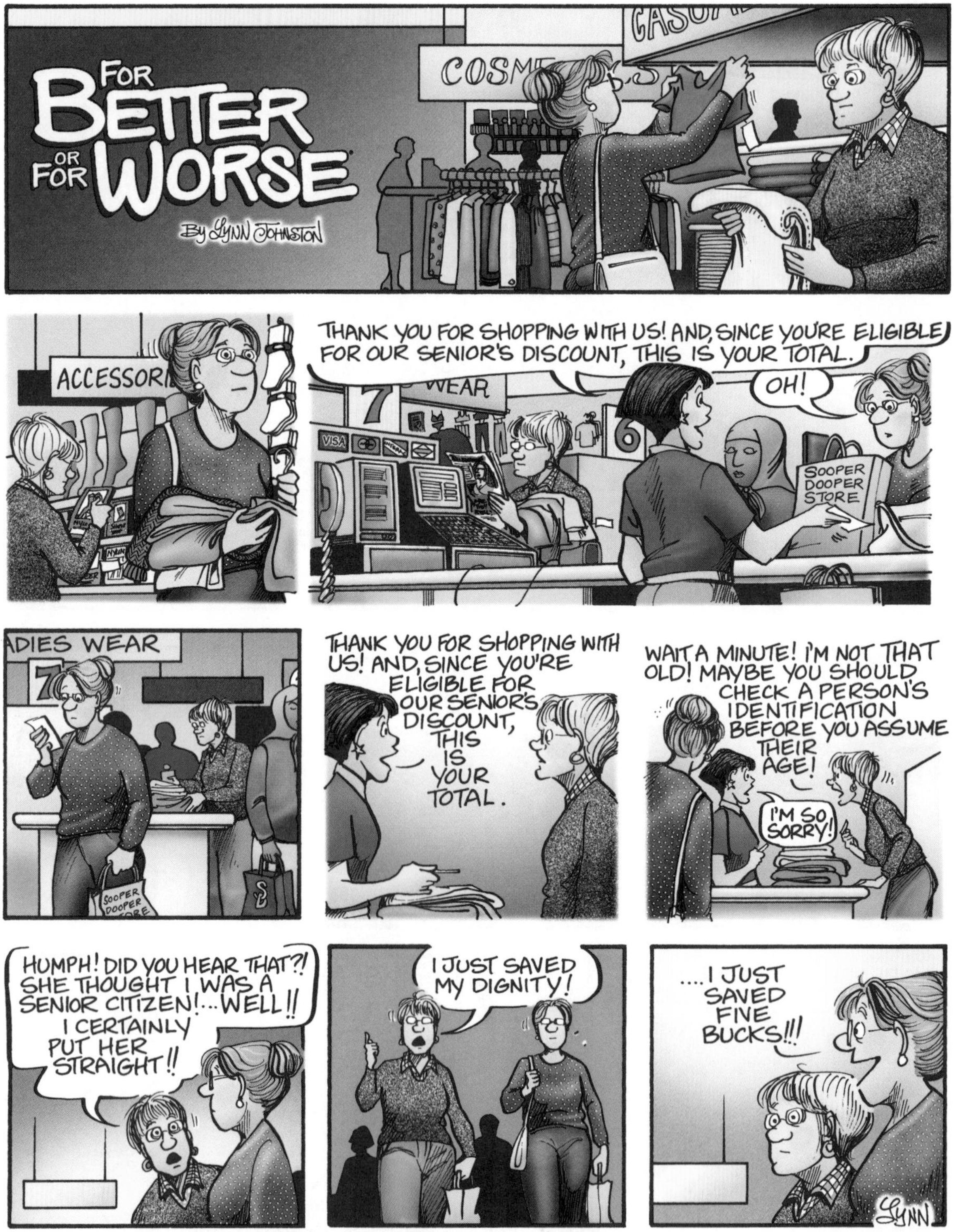
FOR BETTER OR FOR WORSE
By Lynn Johnston
CASUAL
COSMETICS
ACCESSORIES
THANK YOU FOR SHOPPING WITH US! AND, SINCE YOU'RE ELIGIBLE FOR OUR SENIOR'S DISCOUNT, THIS IS YOUR TOTAL.
OH!
WEAR
VISA
SOOPER DOOPER STORE
LADIES WEAR
THANK YOU FOR SHOPPING WITH US! AND, SINCE YOU'RE ELIGIBLE FOR OUR SENIOR'S DISCOUNT, THIS IS YOUR TOTAL.
WAIT A MINUTE! I'M NOT THAT OLD! MAYBE YOU SHOULD CHECK A PERSON'S IDENTIFICATION BEFORE YOU ASSUME THEIR AGE!
I'M SO SORRY!
HUMPH! DID YOU HEAR THAT?! SHE THOUGHT I WAS A SENIOR CITIZEN!...WELL!! I CERTAINLY PUT HER STRAIGHT!!
I JUST SAVED MY DIGNITY!
....I JUST SAVED FIVE BUCKS!!!
LYNN

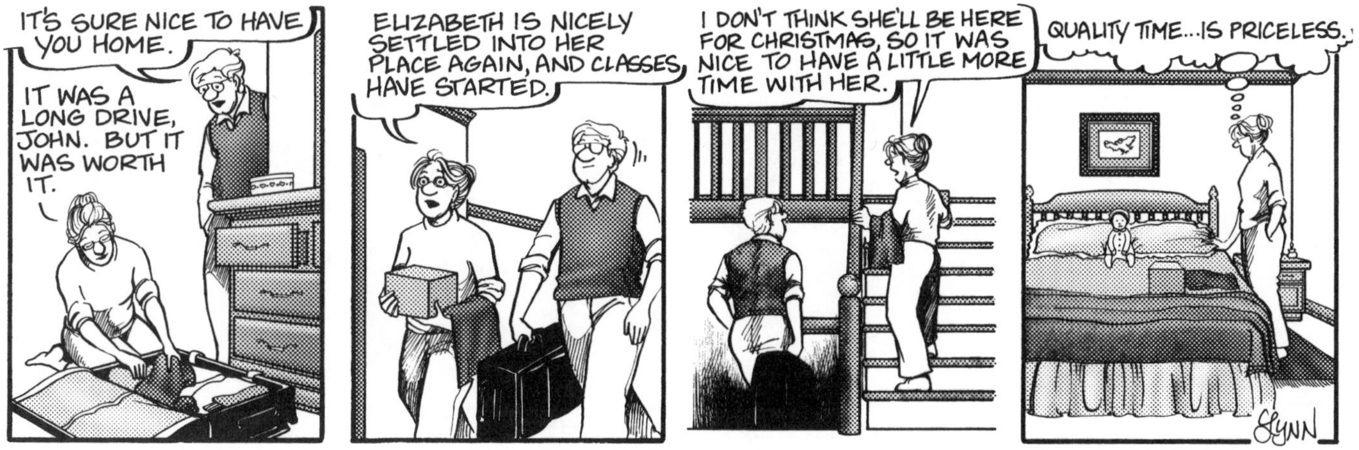
IT'S SURE NICE TO HAVE YOU HOME.
IT WAS A LONG DRIVE, JOHN. BUT IT WAS WORTH IT.
ELIZABETH IS NICELY SETTLED INTO HER PLACE AGAIN, AND CLASSES HAVE STARTED.
I DON'T THINK SHE'LL BE HERE FOR CHRISTMAS, SO IT WAS NICE TO HAVE A LITTLE MORE TIME WITH HER.
QUALITY TIME...IS PRICELESS.
LYNN

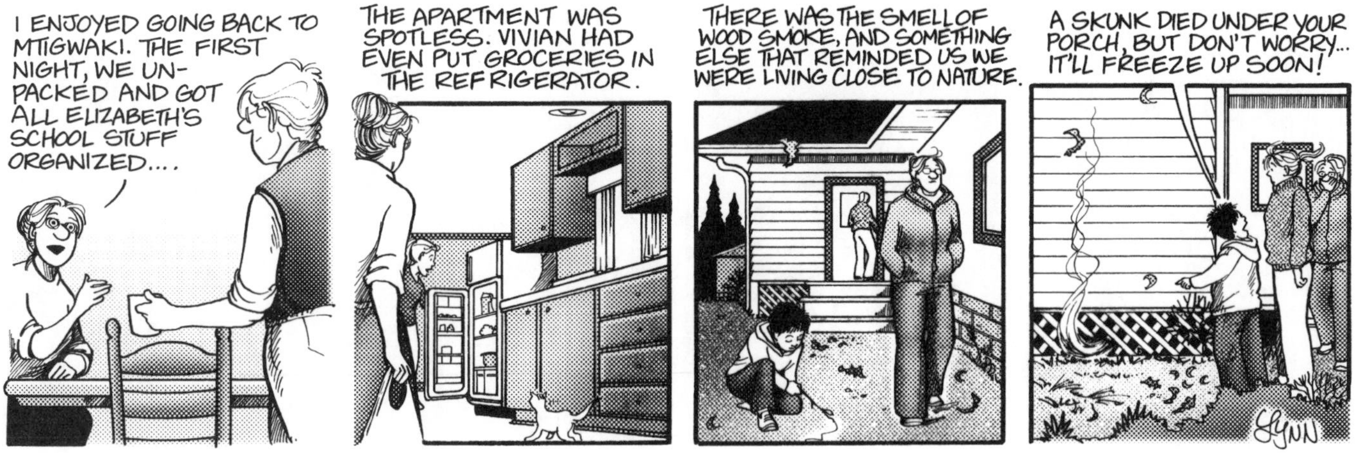
I ENJOYED GOING BACK TO MTIGWAKI. THE FIRST NIGHT, WE UNPACKED AND GOT ALL ELIZABETH'S SCHOOL STUFF ORGANIZED....
THE APARTMENT WAS SPOTLESS. VIVIAN HAD EVEN PUT GROCERIES IN THE REFRIGERATOR.
THERE WAS THE SMELL OF WOOD SMOKE, AND SOMETHING ELSE THAT REMINDED US WE WERE LIVING CLOSE TO NATURE.
A SKUNK DIED UNDER YOUR PORCH, BUT DON'T WORRY... IT'LL FREEZE UP SOON!
LYNN

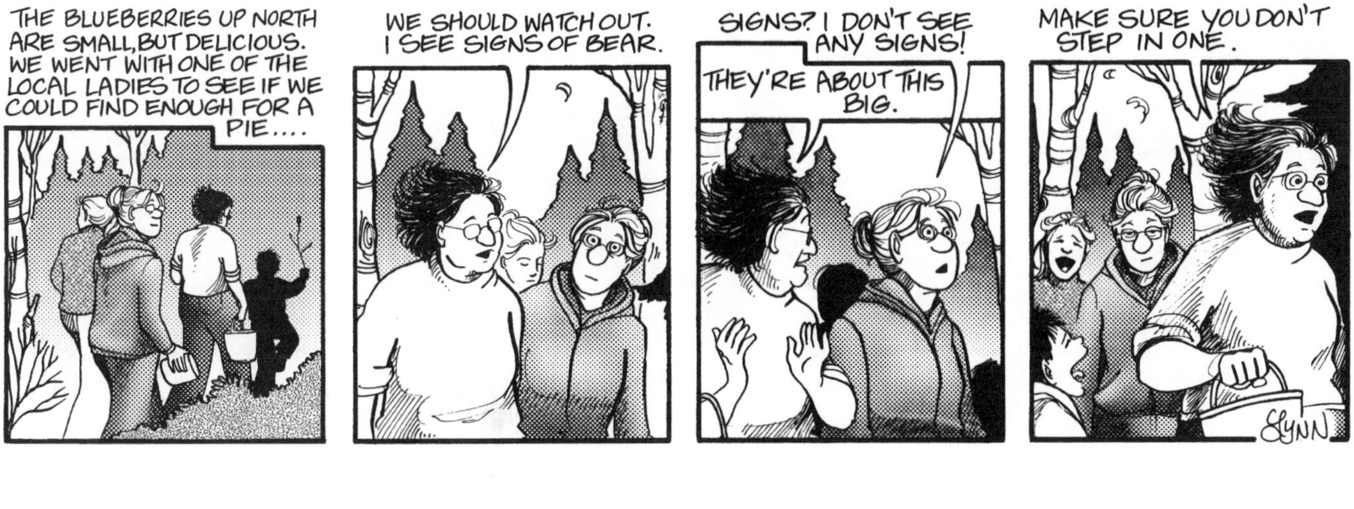
THE BLUEBERRIES UP NORTH ARE SMALL, BUT DELICIOUS. WE WENT WITH ONE OF THE LOCAL LADIES TO SEE IF WE COULD FIND ENOUGH FOR A PIE....
WE SHOULD WATCH OUT. I SEE SIGNS OF BEAR.
SIGNS? I DON'T SEE ANY SIGNS!
THEY'RE ABOUT THIS BIG.
MAKE SURE YOU DON'T STEP IN ONE.
LYNN

MTIGWAKI HAS BEEN AN ESTABLISHED COMMUNITY FOR AS LONG AS THE OJIBWAY PEOPLE CAN REMEMBER.

THE ORIGINAL STRUCTURES ARE LONG GONE, BUT THE POWWOW GROUNDS REMAIN VERY MUCH THE SAME.

THE SACRED FIRE IS LIT WITHIN THE SAME CIRCLE OF STONES PLACED THERE BY THE ANCESTORS.

IN EVERY WAY, IT IS A PLACE OF WORSHIP.

IF WE CAN RAISE A BIT MORE MONEY, WE CAN FIX THE ROOF.

A POWWOW WAS HELD, AND PEOPLE CAME FROM EVERY-WHERE! THERE WAS A FEAST!

THERE WAS DANCING AND SINGING AND EVERY-ONE WAS WELCOME.

ELIZABETH SAID THAT NATIVE GATHERINGS ALWAYS INCLUDE A TRADITIONAL GIVING OF GIFTS.

AN iPOD! .... COOL !!

CORN SOUP & SCONE ... 4.00
BUFFALO BURGER 5.00
INDIAN TACO 6.00
BALONEY & BANNOCK... 4.00
.... 4.00

THE DANCING GOES ON FOR HOURS, CLOCKWISE AROUND THE CENTRAL ARBOR. IT BEGINS WITH THE GRASS DANCERS.

THESE YOUNG PEOPLE WEAR OUTFITS MADE OF RICH COLORED FABRICS AND LONG FLOWING YARN.

THEIR JOB IS TO PRESS DOWN THE GRASS TO MAKE WAY FOR THE OTHER DANCERS.

HEH... AND THEY THINK CROP CIRCLES ARE MADE BY ALIENS!

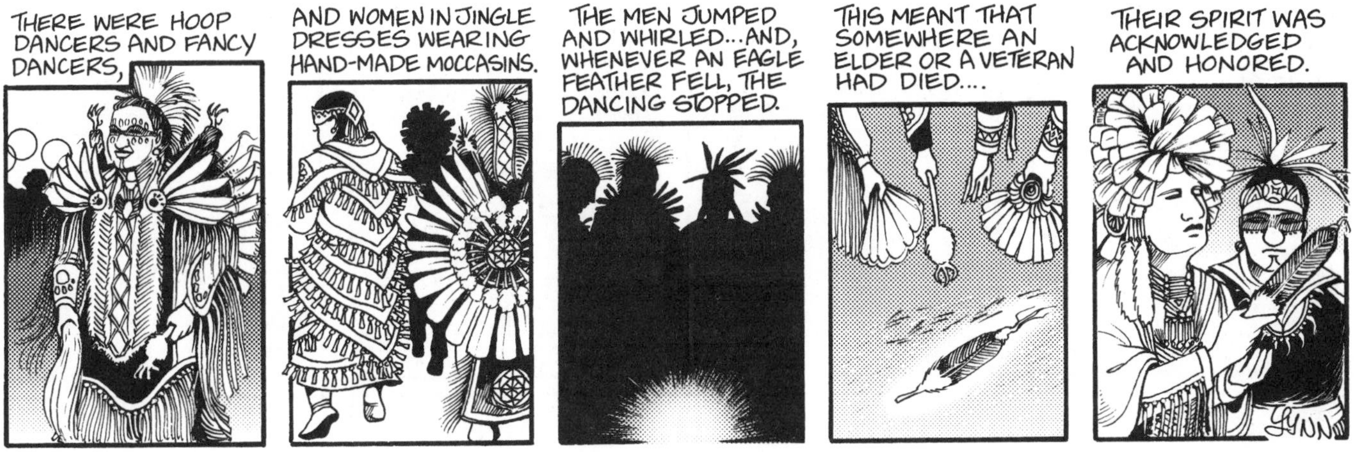
THERE WERE HOOP DANCERS AND FANCY DANCERS,
AND WOMEN IN JINGLE DRESSES WEARING HAND-MADE MOCCASINS.
THE MEN JUMPED AND WHIRLED...AND, WHENEVER AN EAGLE FEATHER FELL, THE DANCING STOPPED.
THIS MEANT THAT SOMEWHERE AN ELDER OR A VETERAN HAD DIED....
THEIR SPIRIT WAS ACKNOWLEDGED AND HONORED.
LYNN

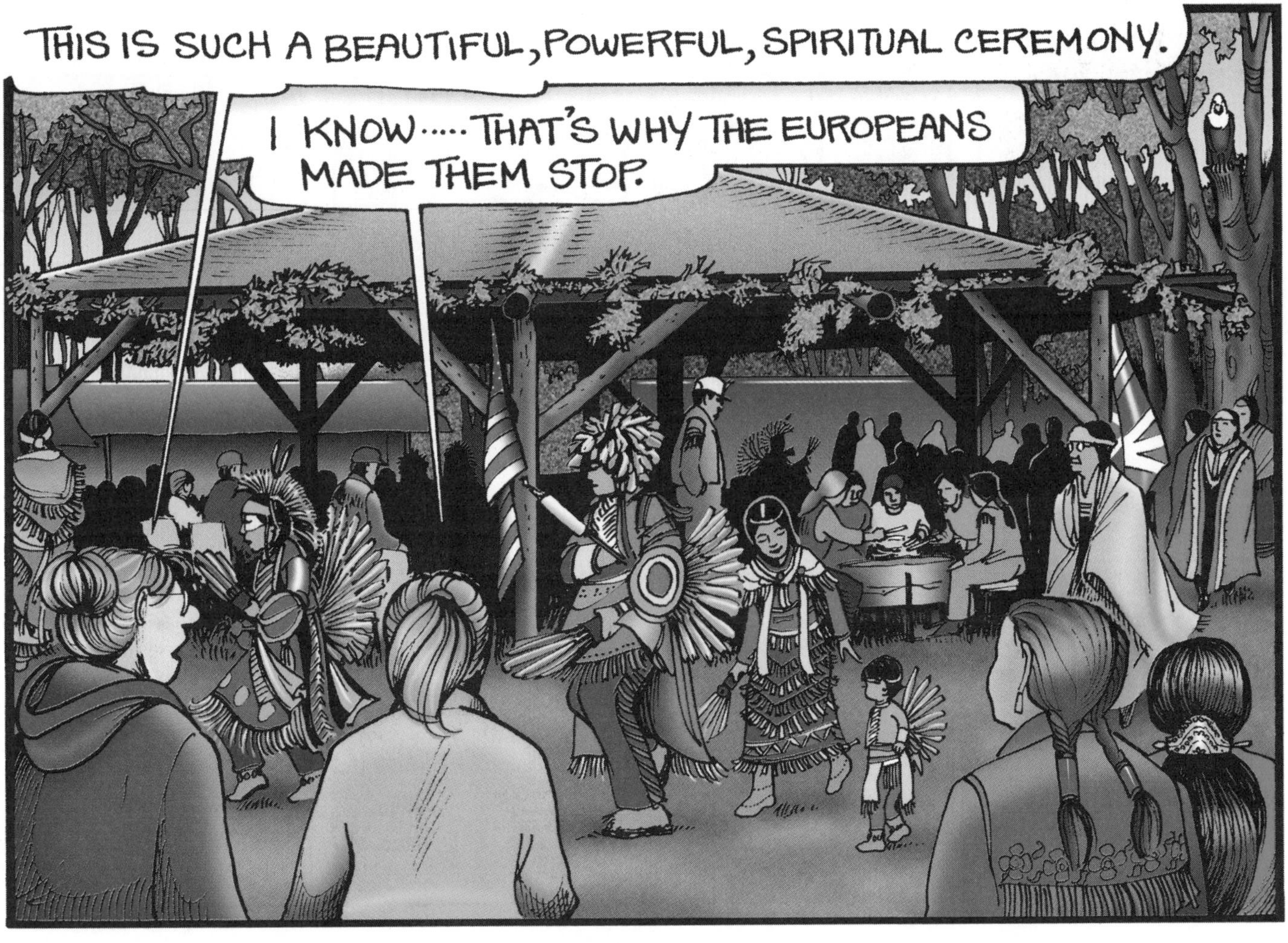
THIS IS SUCH A BEAUTIFUL, POWERFUL, SPIRITUAL CEREMONY.
I KNOW..... THAT'S WHY THE EUROPEANS MADE THEM STOP.

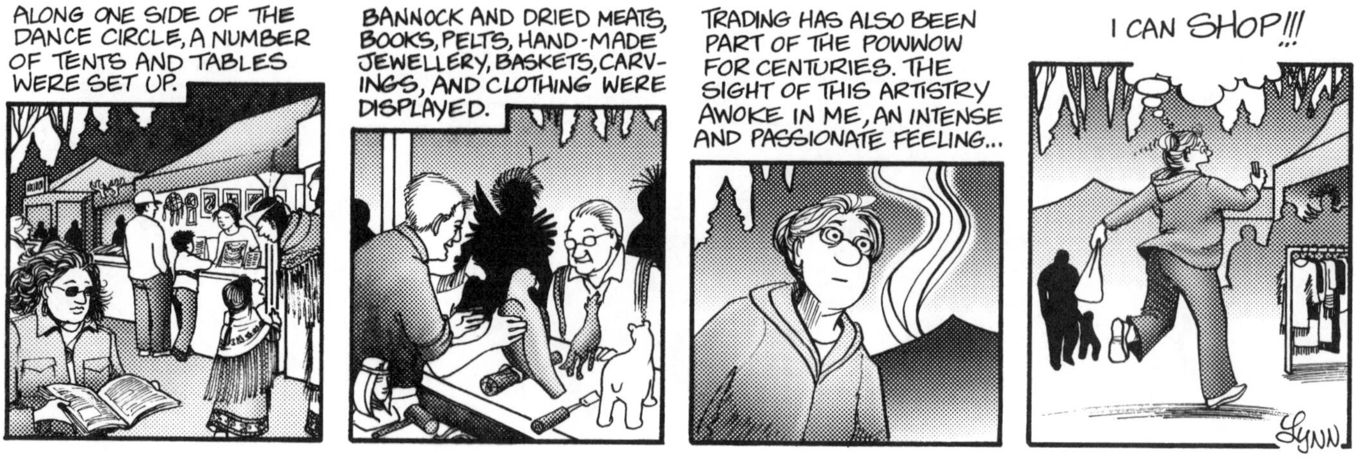
ALONG ONE SIDE OF THE DANCE CIRCLE, A NUMBER OF TENTS AND TABLES WERE SET UP.
BANNOCK AND DRIED MEATS, BOOKS, PELTS, HAND-MADE JEWELLERY, BASKETS, CARVINGS, AND CLOTHING WERE DISPLAYED.
TRADING HAS ALSO BEEN PART OF THE POWWOW FOR CENTURIES. THE SIGHT OF THIS ARTISTRY AWOKE IN ME, AN INTENSE AND PASSIONATE FEELING...
I CAN SHOP!!!
Lynn

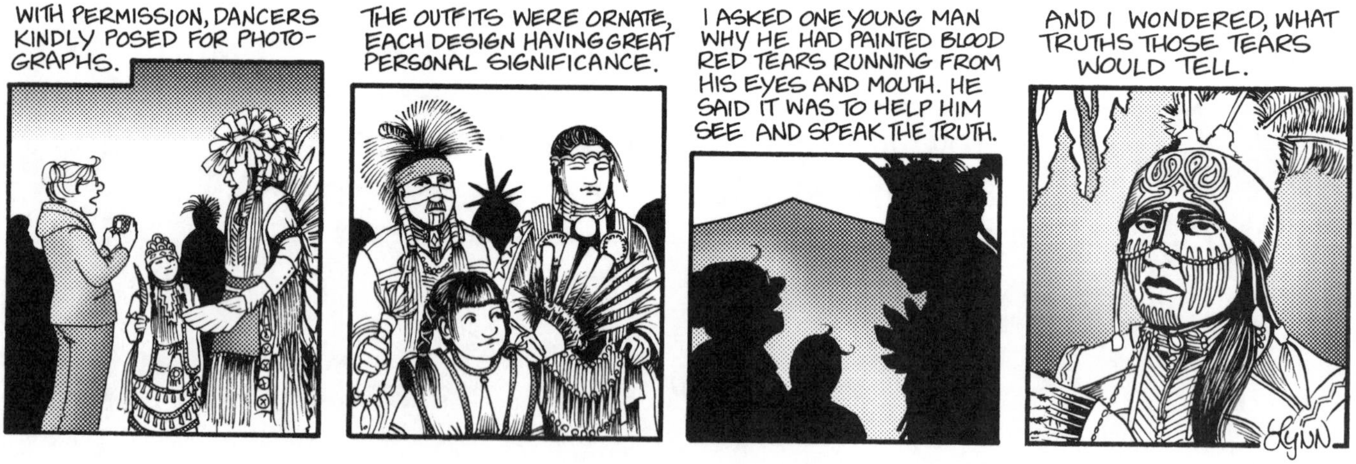
WITH PERMISSION, DANCERS KINDLY POSED FOR PHOTOGRAPHS.
THE OUTFITS WERE ORNATE, EACH DESIGN HAVING GREAT PERSONAL SIGNIFICANCE.
I ASKED ONE YOUNG MAN WHY HE HAD PAINTED BLOOD RED TEARS RUNNING FROM HIS EYES AND MOUTH. HE SAID IT WAS TO HELP HIM SEE AND SPEAK THE TRUTH.
AND I WONDERED, WHAT TRUTHS THOSE TEARS WOULD TELL.
Lynn

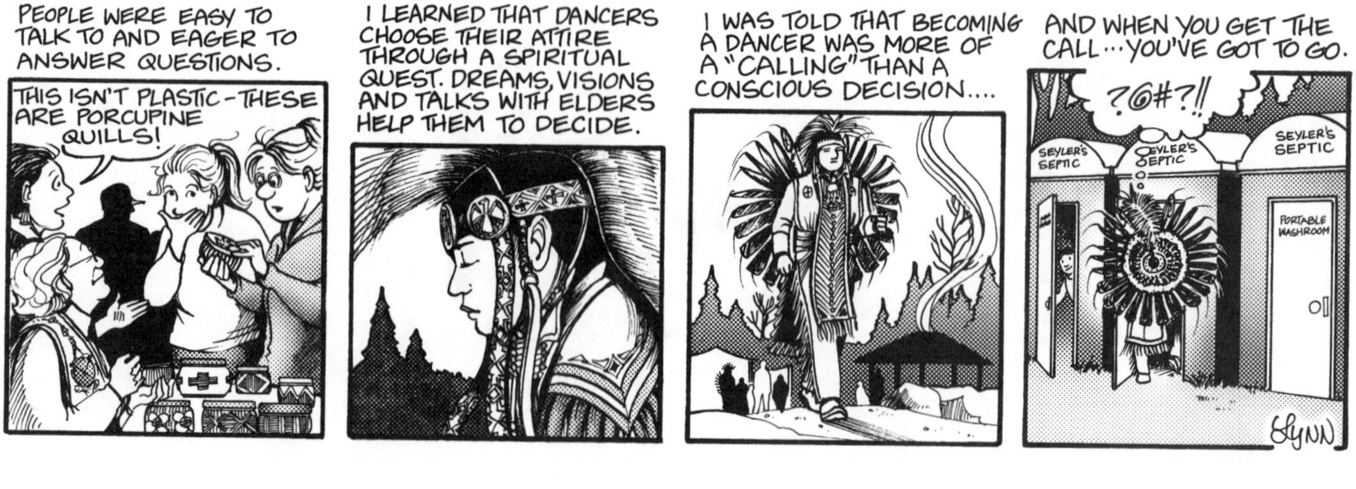
PEOPLE WERE EASY TO TALK TO AND EAGER TO ANSWER QUESTIONS.
THIS ISN'T PLASTIC - THESE ARE PORCUPINE QUILLS!
I LEARNED THAT DANCERS CHOOSE THEIR ATTIRE THROUGH A SPIRITUAL QUEST. DREAMS, VISIONS AND TALKS WITH ELDERS HELP THEM TO DECIDE.
I WAS TOLD THAT BECOMING A DANCER WAS MORE OF A "CALLING" THAN A CONSCIOUS DECISION....
AND WHEN YOU GET THE CALL ··· YOU'VE GOT TO GO.
?@#?!!
SEYLER'S SEPTIC
SEYLER'S SEPTIC
SEYLER'S SEPTIC
PORTABLE WASHROOM
Lynn

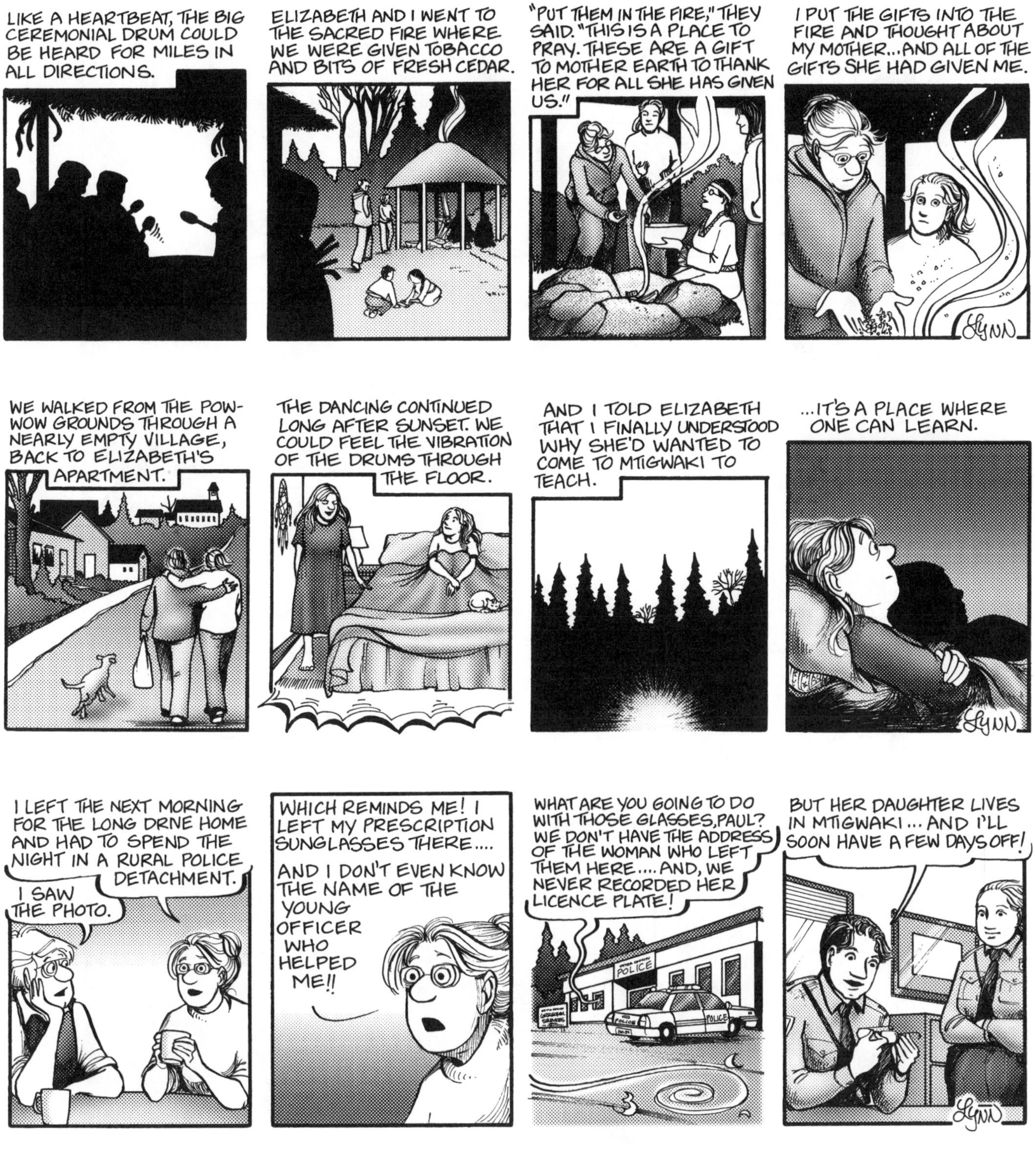
LIKE A HEARTBEAT, THE BIG CEREMONIAL DRUM COULD BE HEARD FOR MILES IN ALL DIRECTIONS.
ELIZABETH AND I WENT TO THE SACRED FIRE WHERE WE WERE GIVEN TOBACCO AND BITS OF FRESH CEDAR.
"PUT THEM IN THE FIRE," THEY SAID. "THIS IS A PLACE TO PRAY. THESE ARE A GIFT TO MOTHER EARTH TO THANK HER FOR ALL SHE HAS GIVEN US."
I PUT THE GIFTS INTO THE FIRE AND THOUGHT ABOUT MY MOTHER... AND ALL OF THE GIFTS SHE HAD GIVEN ME.
LYNN
WE WALKED FROM THE POW-WOW GROUNDS THROUGH A NEARLY EMPTY VILLAGE, BACK TO ELIZABETH'S APARTMENT.
THE DANCING CONTINUED LONG AFTER SUNSET. WE COULD FEEL THE VIBRATION OF THE DRUMS THROUGH THE FLOOR.
AND I TOLD ELIZABETH THAT I FINALLY UNDERSTOOD WHY SHE'D WANTED TO COME TO MTIGWAKI TO TEACH.
...IT'S A PLACE WHERE ONE CAN LEARN.
LYNN
I LEFT THE NEXT MORNING FOR THE LONG DRIVE HOME AND HAD TO SPEND THE NIGHT IN A RURAL POLICE DETACHMENT.
I SAW THE PHOTO.
WHICH REMINDS ME! I LEFT MY PRESCRIPTION SUNGLASSES THERE....
AND I DON'T EVEN KNOW THE NAME OF THE YOUNG OFFICER WHO HELPED ME!!
WHAT ARE YOU GOING TO DO WITH THOSE GLASSES, PAUL? WE DON'T HAVE THE ADDRESS OF THE WOMAN WHO LEFT THEM HERE.... AND, WE NEVER RECORDED HER LICENCE PLATE!
POLICE
BUT HER DAUGHTER LIVES IN MTIGWAKI... AND I'LL SOON HAVE A FEW DAYS OFF!
LYNN

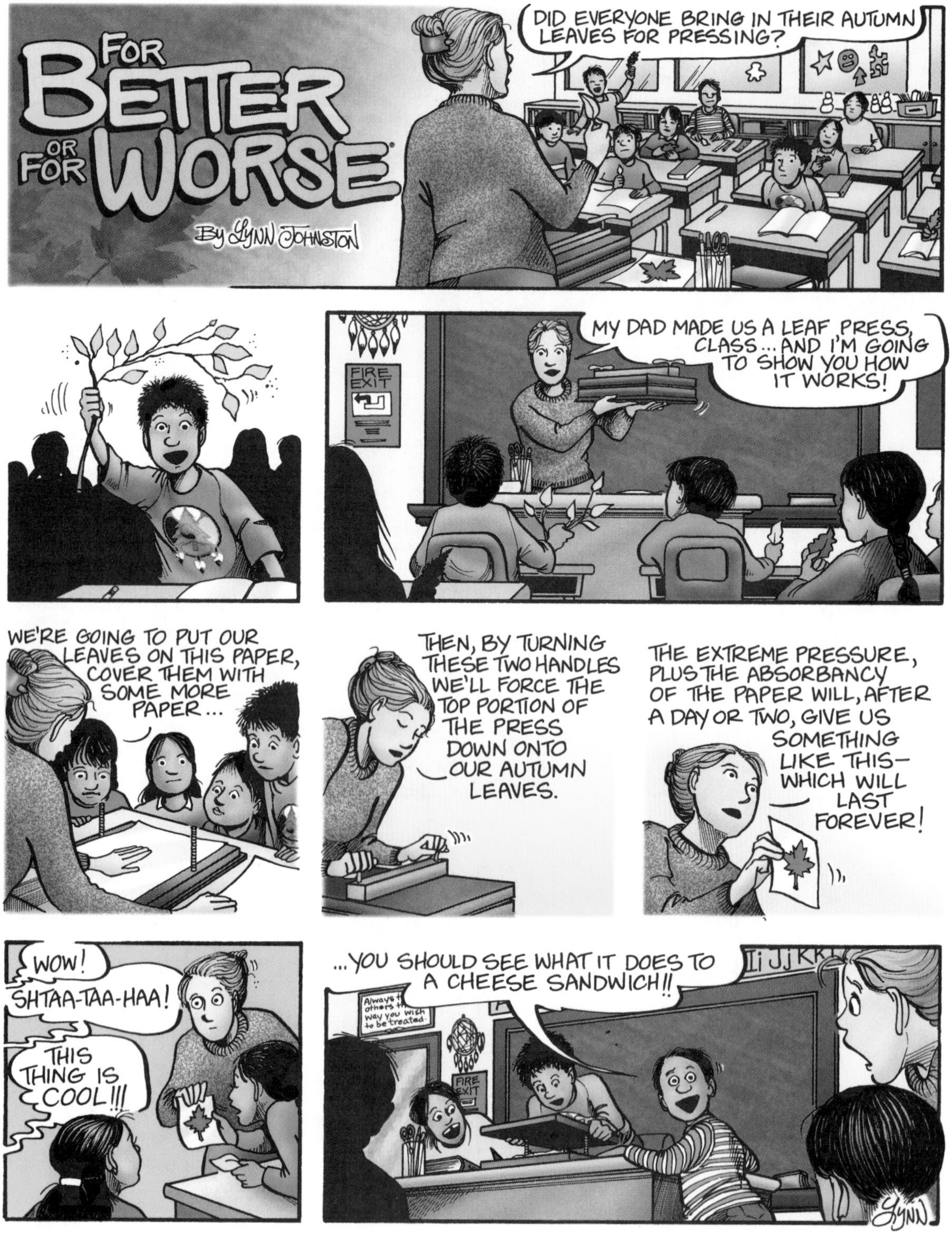
FOR BETTER OR FOR WORSE
BY LYNN JOHNSTON
DID EVERYONE BRING IN THEIR AUTUMN LEAVES FOR PRESSING?
MY DAD MADE US A LEAF PRESS, CLASS... AND I'M GOING TO SHOW YOU HOW IT WORKS!
FIRE EXIT
WE'RE GOING TO PUT OUR LEAVES ON THIS PAPER, COVER THEM WITH SOME MORE PAPER...
THEN, BY TURNING THESE TWO HANDLES WE'LL FORCE THE TOP PORTION OF THE PRESS DOWN ONTO OUR AUTUMN LEAVES.
THE EXTREME PRESSURE, PLUS THE ABSORBANCY OF THE PAPER WILL, AFTER A DAY OR TWO, GIVE US SOMETHING LIKE THIS— WHICH WILL LAST FOREVER!
WOW!
SHTAA-TAA-HAA!
THIS THING IS COOL!!!
...YOU SHOULD SEE WHAT IT DOES TO A CHEESE SANDWICH!!
FIRE EXIT
LYNN

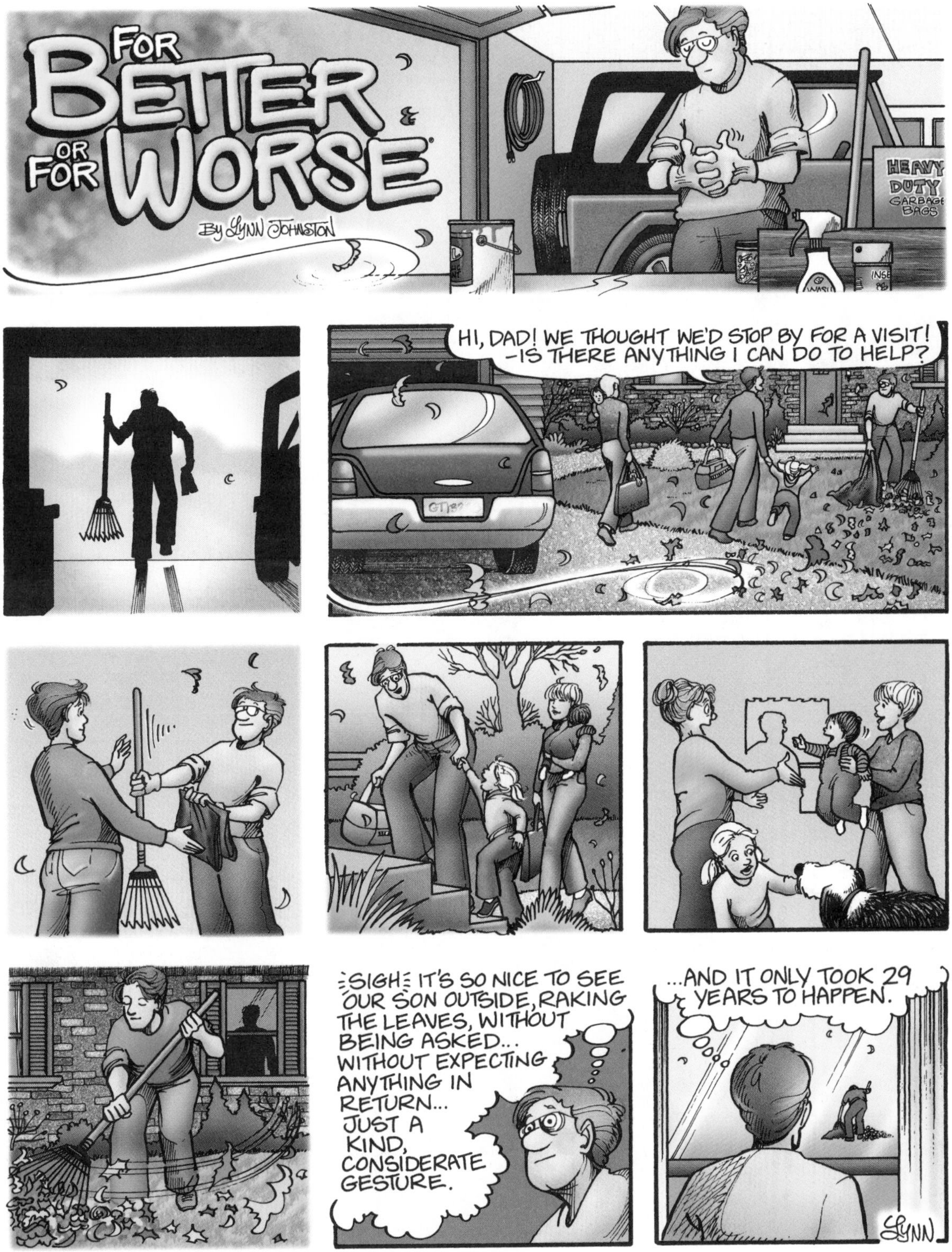
FOR BETTER OR FOR WORSE
BY LYNN JOHNSTON
HEAVY DUTY GARBAGE BAGS
HI, DAD! WE THOUGHT WE'D STOP BY FOR A VISIT! -IS THERE ANYTHING I CAN DO TO HELP?
SIGH IT'S SO NICE TO SEE OUR SON OUTSIDE, RAKING THE LEAVES, WITHOUT BEING ASKED... WITHOUT EXPECTING ANYTHING IN RETURN... JUST A KIND, CONSIDERATE GESTURE.
...AND IT ONLY TOOK 29 YEARS TO HAPPEN.
LYNN

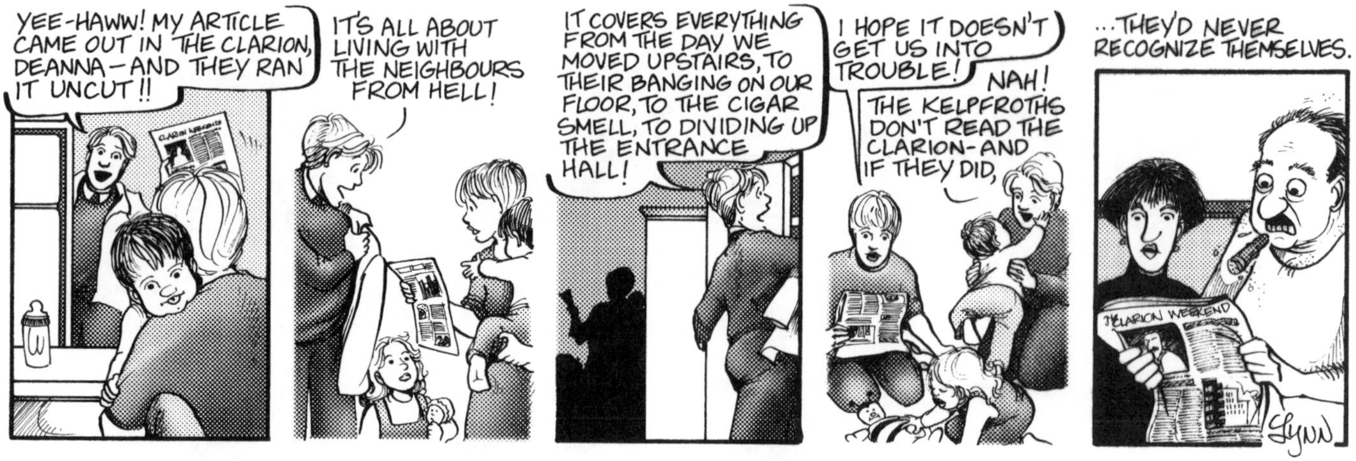
YEE-HAWW! MY ARTICLE CAME OUT IN THE CLARION, DEANNA—AND THEY RAN IT UNCUT!!
IT'S ALL ABOUT LIVING WITH THE NEIGHBOURS FROM HELL!
IT COVERS EVERYTHING FROM THE DAY WE MOVED UPSTAIRS, TO THEIR BANGING ON OUR FLOOR, TO THE CIGAR SMELL, TO DIVIDING UP THE ENTRANCE HALL!
I HOPE IT DOESN'T GET US INTO TROUBLE!
NAH! THE KELPFROTHS DON'T READ THE CLARION—AND IF THEY DID,
...THEY'D NEVER RECOGNIZE THEMSELVES.
THE CLARION WEEKEND

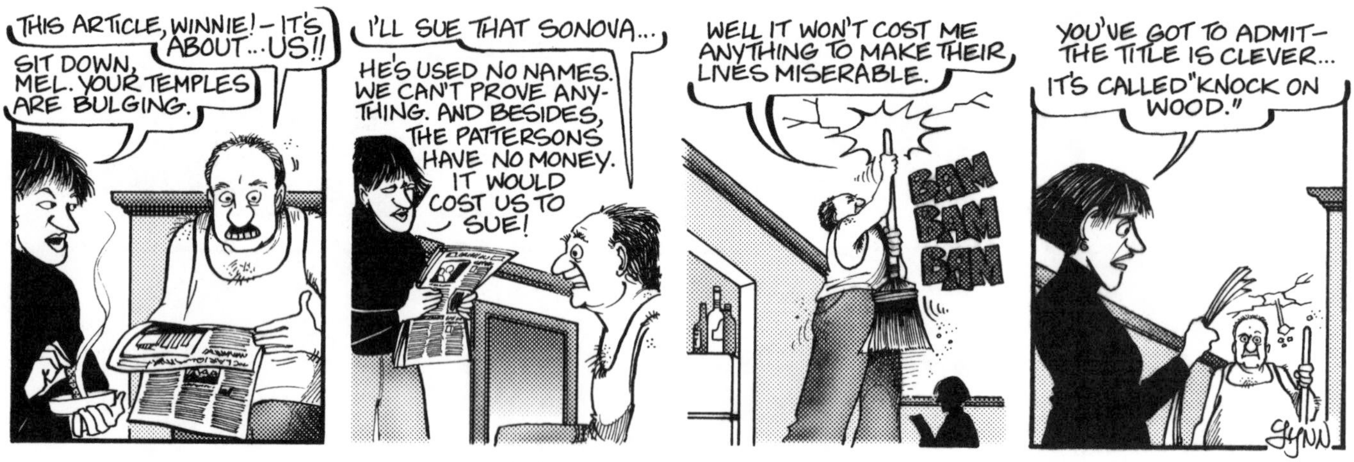
THIS ARTICLE, WINNIE!—IT'S ABOUT...US!!
SIT DOWN, MEL. YOUR TEMPLES ARE BULGING.
I'LL SUE THAT SONOVA...
HE'S USED NO NAMES. WE CAN'T PROVE ANYTHING. AND BESIDES, THE PATTERSONS HAVE NO MONEY. IT WOULD COST US TO SUE!
WELL IT WON'T COST ME ANYTHING TO MAKE THEIR LIVES MISERABLE.
BAM BAM BAM
YOU'VE GOT TO ADMIT—THE TITLE IS CLEVER...
IT'S CALLED "KNOCK ON WOOD."

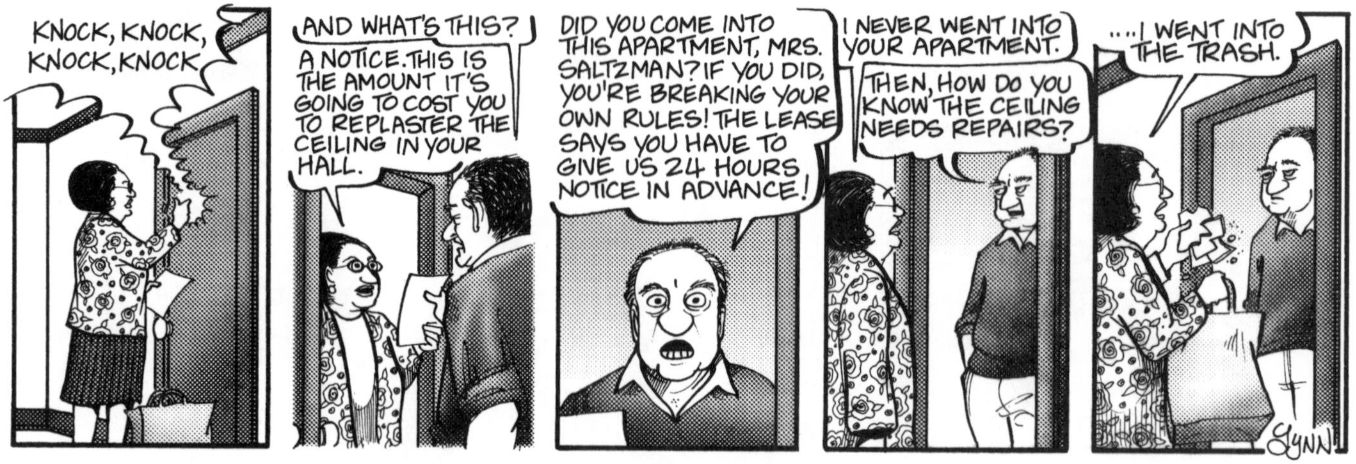
KNOCK, KNOCK, KNOCK, KNOCK
AND WHAT'S THIS?
A NOTICE. THIS IS THE AMOUNT IT'S GOING TO COST YOU TO REPLASTER THE CEILING IN YOUR HALL.
DID YOU COME INTO THIS APARTMENT, MRS. SALTZMAN? IF YOU DID, YOU'RE BREAKING YOUR OWN RULES! THE LEASE SAYS YOU HAVE TO GIVE US 24 HOURS NOTICE IN ADVANCE!
I NEVER WENT INTO YOUR APARTMENT.
THEN, HOW DO YOU KNOW THE CEILING NEEDS REPAIRS?
....I WENT INTO THE TRASH.

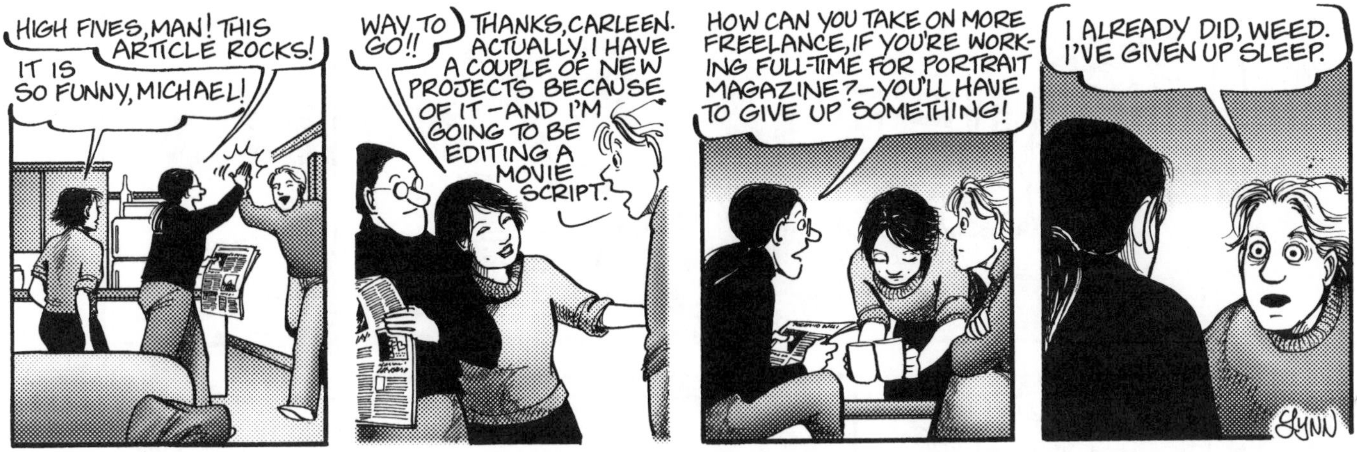
HIGH FIVES, MAN! THIS ARTICLE ROCKS!
IT IS SO FUNNY, MICHAEL!
WAY TO GO!!
THANKS, CARLEEN. ACTUALLY, I HAVE A COUPLE OF NEW PROJECTS BECAUSE OF IT–AND I'M GOING TO BE EDITING A MOVIE SCRIPT.
HOW CAN YOU TAKE ON MORE FREELANCE, IF YOU'RE WORKING FULL-TIME FOR PORTRAIT MAGAZINE?–YOU'LL HAVE TO GIVE UP SOMETHING!
I ALREADY DID, WEED. I'VE GIVEN UP SLEEP.

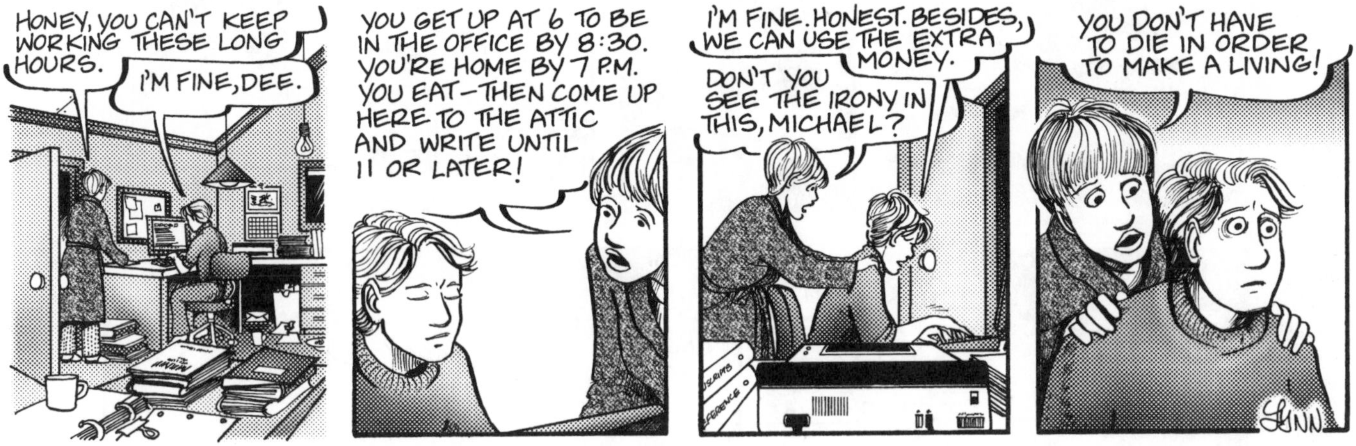
HONEY, YOU CAN'T KEEP WORKING THESE LONG HOURS.
I'M FINE, DEE.
YOU GET UP AT 6 TO BE IN THE OFFICE BY 8:30. YOU'RE HOME BY 7 P.M. YOU EAT–THEN COME UP HERE TO THE ATTIC AND WRITE UNTIL 11 OR LATER!
I'M FINE. HONEST. BESIDES, WE CAN USE THE EXTRA MONEY.
DON'T YOU SEE THE IRONY IN THIS, MICHAEL?
YOU DON'T HAVE TO DIE IN ORDER TO MAKE A LIVING!

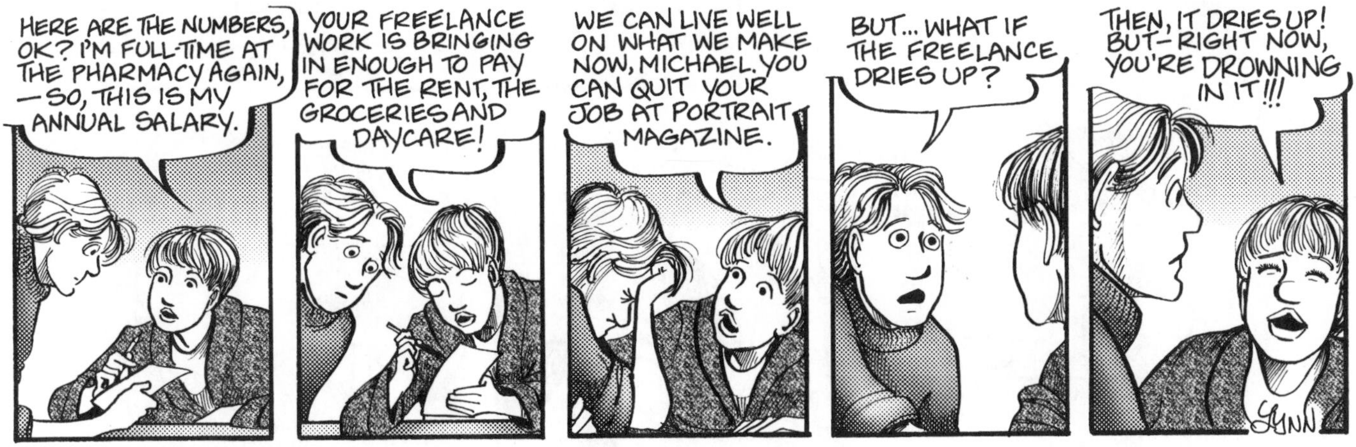
HERE ARE THE NUMBERS, OK? I'M FULL-TIME AT THE PHARMACY AGAIN, –SO, THIS IS MY ANNUAL SALARY.
YOUR FREELANCE WORK IS BRINGING IN ENOUGH TO PAY FOR THE RENT, THE GROCERIES AND DAYCARE!
WE CAN LIVE WELL ON WHAT WE MAKE NOW, MICHAEL. YOU CAN QUIT YOUR JOB AT PORTRAIT MAGAZINE.
BUT... WHAT IF THE FREELANCE DRIES UP?
THEN, IT DRIES UP! BUT–RIGHT NOW, YOU'RE DROWNING IN IT!!!

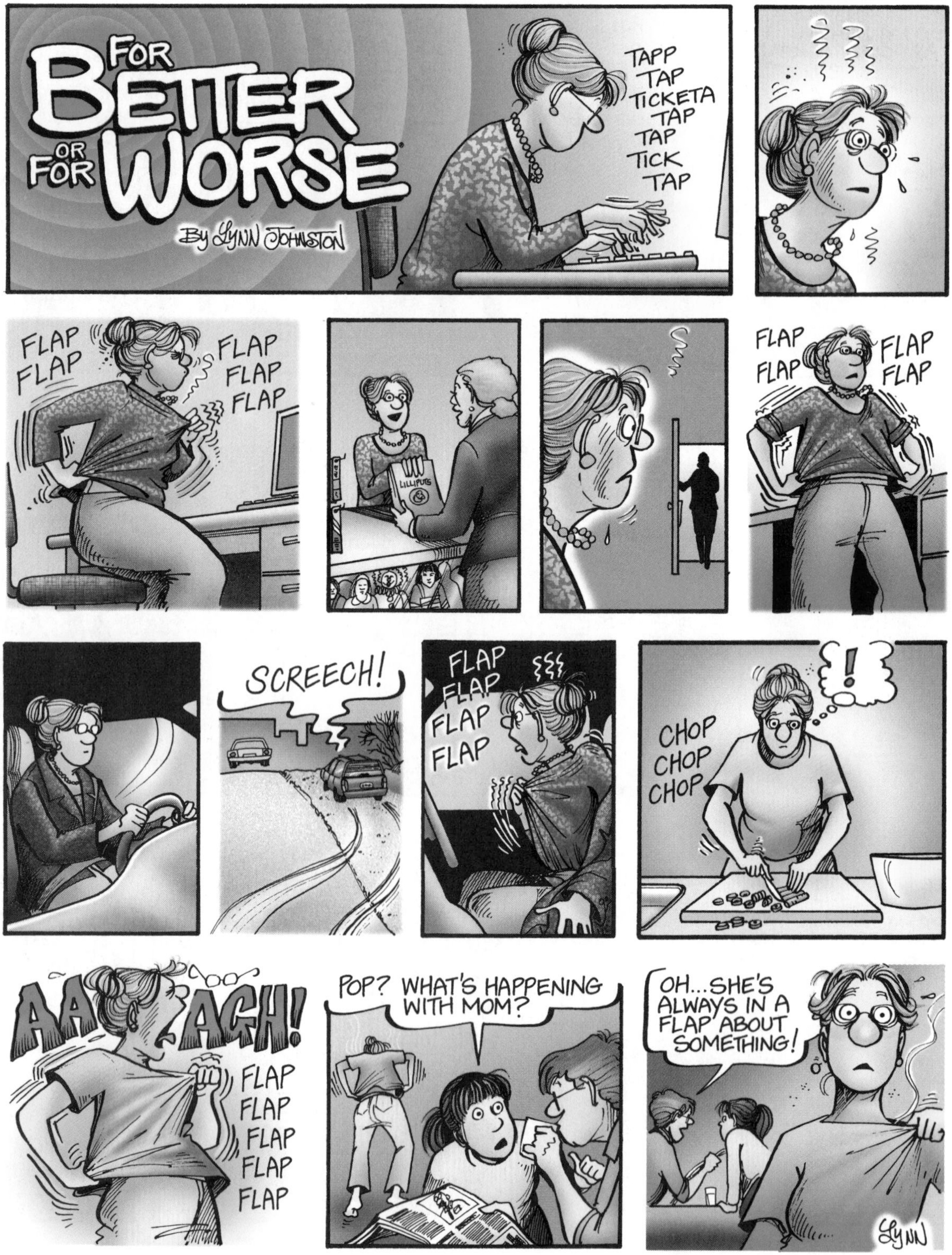
FOR BETTER OR FOR WORSE
BY LYNN JOHNSTON
TAPP TAP TICKETA TAP TAP TICK TAP
FLAP FLAP FLAP FLAP FLAP
LILLIPUTS
FLAP FLAP FLAP FLAP
SCREECH!
FLAP FLAP FLAP FLAP FLAP
CHOP CHOP CHOP
!
AAAGH!
FLAP FLAP FLAP FLAP FLAP
POP? WHAT'S HAPPENING WITH MOM?
OH...SHE'S ALWAYS IN A FLAP ABOUT SOMETHING!
LYNN

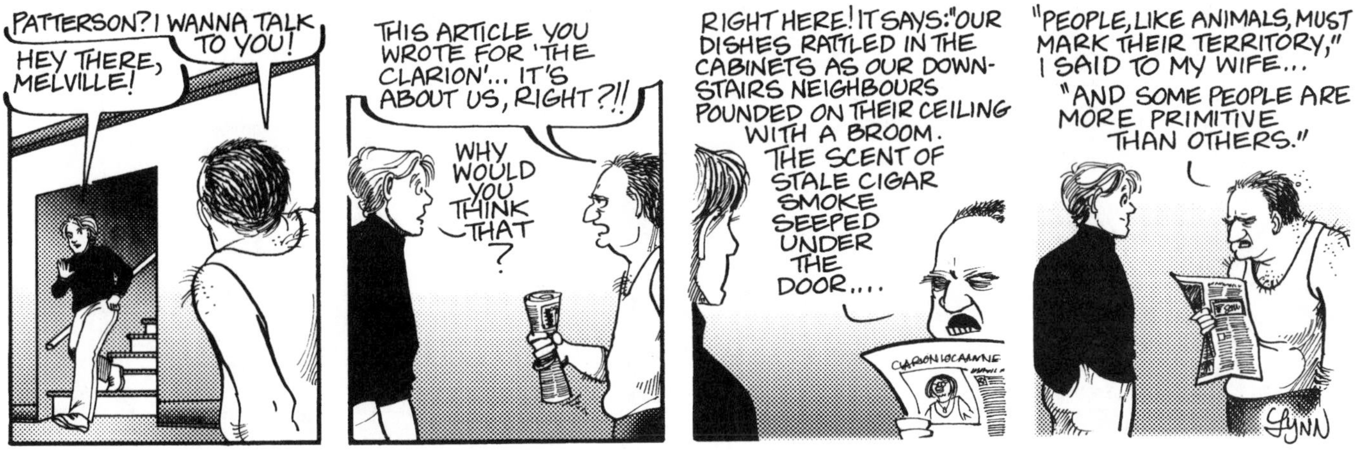
PATTERSON?! WANNA TALK TO YOU!
HEY THERE, MELVILLE!
THIS ARTICLE YOU WROTE FOR 'THE CLARION'... IT'S ABOUT US, RIGHT?!!
WHY WOULD YOU THINK THAT?
RIGHT HERE! IT SAYS: "OUR DISHES RATTLED IN THE CABINETS AS OUR DOWN-STAIRS NEIGHBOURS POUNDED ON THEIR CEILING WITH A BROOM. THE SCENT OF STALE CIGAR SMOKE SEEPED UNDER THE DOOR....
"PEOPLE, LIKE ANIMALS, MUST MARK THEIR TERRITORY," I SAID TO MY WIFE...
"AND SOME PEOPLE ARE MORE PRIMITIVE THAN OTHERS."
LYNN

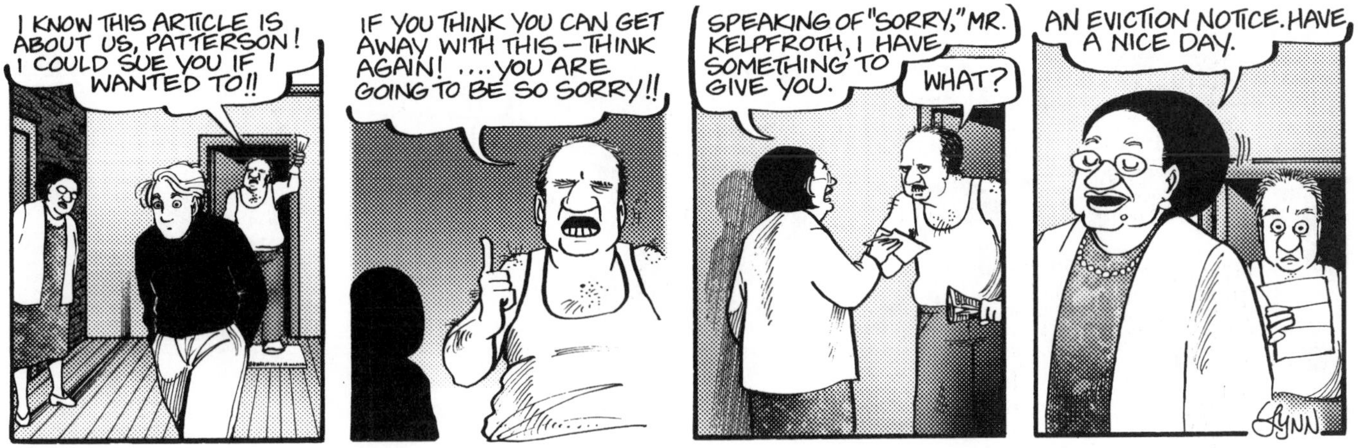
I KNOW THIS ARTICLE IS ABOUT US, PATTERSON! I COULD SUE YOU IF I WANTED TO!!
IF YOU THINK YOU CAN GET AWAY WITH THIS – THINK AGAIN! ....YOU ARE GOING TO BE SO SORRY!!
SPEAKING OF "SORRY," MR. KELPFROTH, I HAVE SOMETHING TO GIVE YOU.
WHAT?
AN EVICTION NOTICE. HAVE A NICE DAY.
LYNN

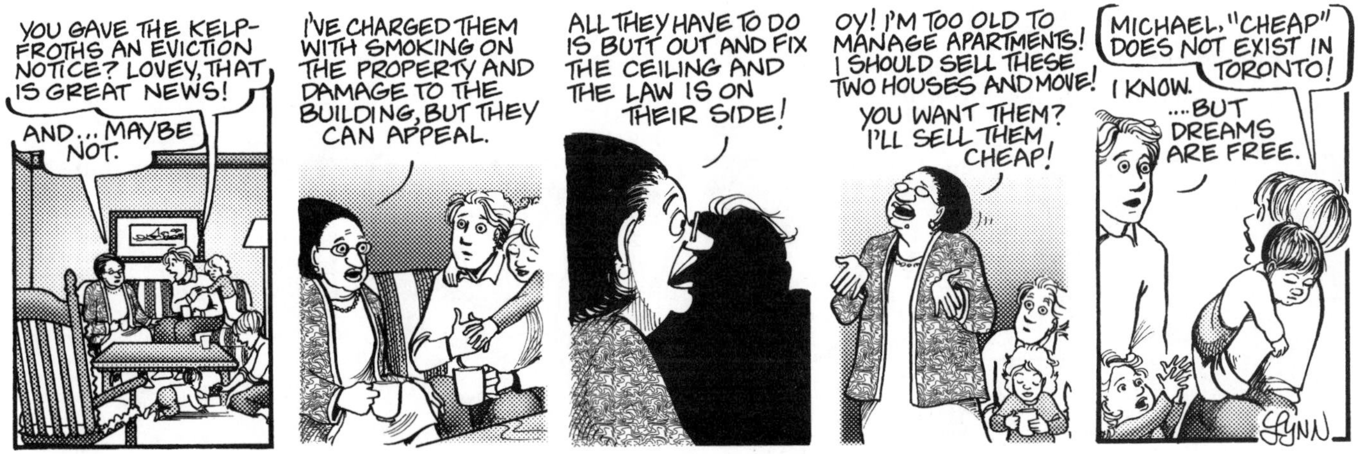
YOU GAVE THE KELP-FROTHS AN EVICTION NOTICE? LOVEY, THAT IS GREAT NEWS!
AND... MAYBE NOT.
I'VE CHARGED THEM WITH SMOKING ON THE PROPERTY AND DAMAGE TO THE BUILDING, BUT THEY CAN APPEAL.
ALL THEY HAVE TO DO IS BUTT OUT AND FIX THE CEILING AND THE LAW IS ON THEIR SIDE!
OY! I'M TOO OLD TO MANAGE APARTMENTS! I SHOULD SELL THESE TWO HOUSES AND MOVE!
YOU WANT THEM? I'LL SELL THEM CHEAP!
MICHAEL, "CHEAP" DOES NOT EXIST IN TORONTO!
I KNOW.
...BUT DREAMS ARE FREE.
LYNN

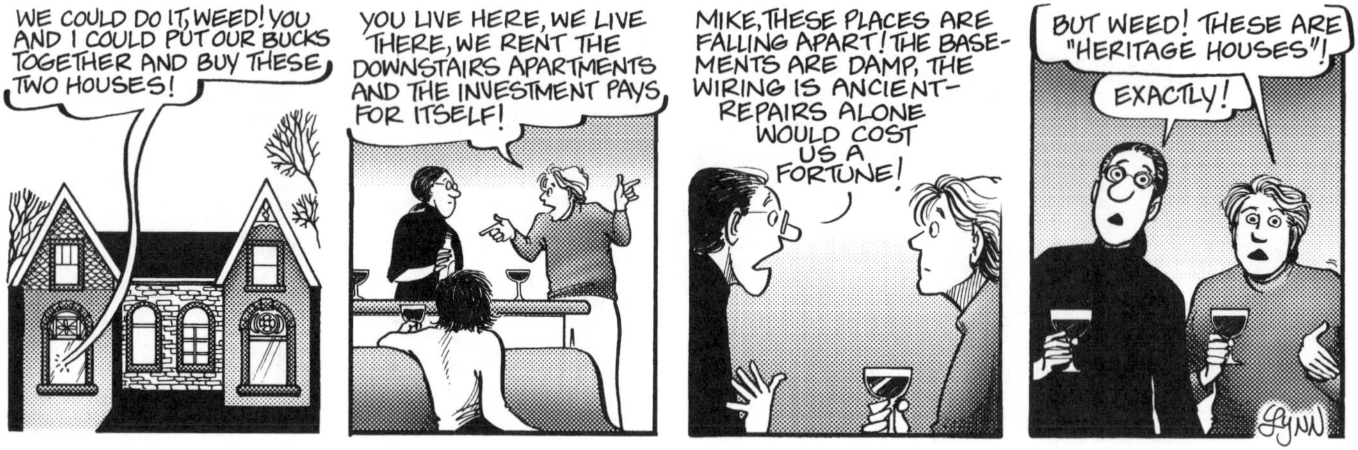
WE COULD DO IT, WEED! YOU AND I COULD PUT OUR BUCKS TOGETHER AND BUY THESE TWO HOUSES!
YOU LIVE HERE, WE LIVE THERE, WE RENT THE DOWNSTAIRS APARTMENTS AND THE INVESTMENT PAYS FOR ITSELF!
MIKE, THESE PLACES ARE FALLING APART! THE BASEMENTS ARE DAMP, THE WIRING IS ANCIENT– REPAIRS ALONE WOULD COST US A FORTUNE!
BUT WEED! THESE ARE "HERITAGE HOUSES"!
EXACTLY!
LYNN

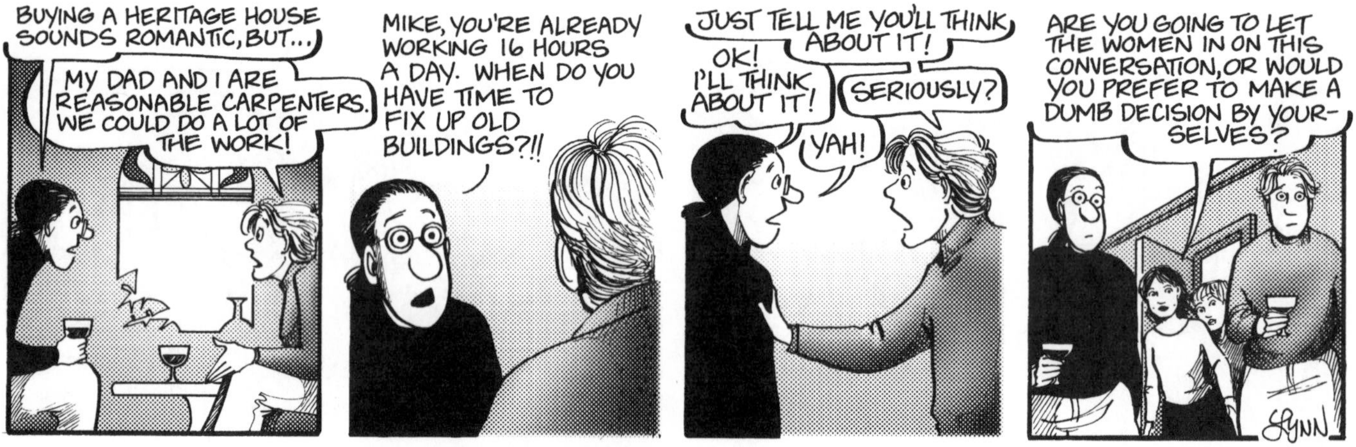
BUYING A HERITAGE HOUSE SOUNDS ROMANTIC, BUT...
MY DAD AND I ARE REASONABLE CARPENTERS. WE COULD DO A LOT OF THE WORK!
MIKE, YOU'RE ALREADY WORKING 16 HOURS A DAY. WHEN DO YOU HAVE TIME TO FIX UP OLD BUILDINGS?!!
JUST TELL ME YOU'LL THINK ABOUT IT!
OK! I'LL THINK ABOUT IT!
SERIOUSLY?
YAH!
ARE YOU GOING TO LET THE WOMEN IN ON THIS CONVERSATION, OR WOULD YOU PREFER TO MAKE A DUMB DECISION BY YOURSELVES?
LYNN

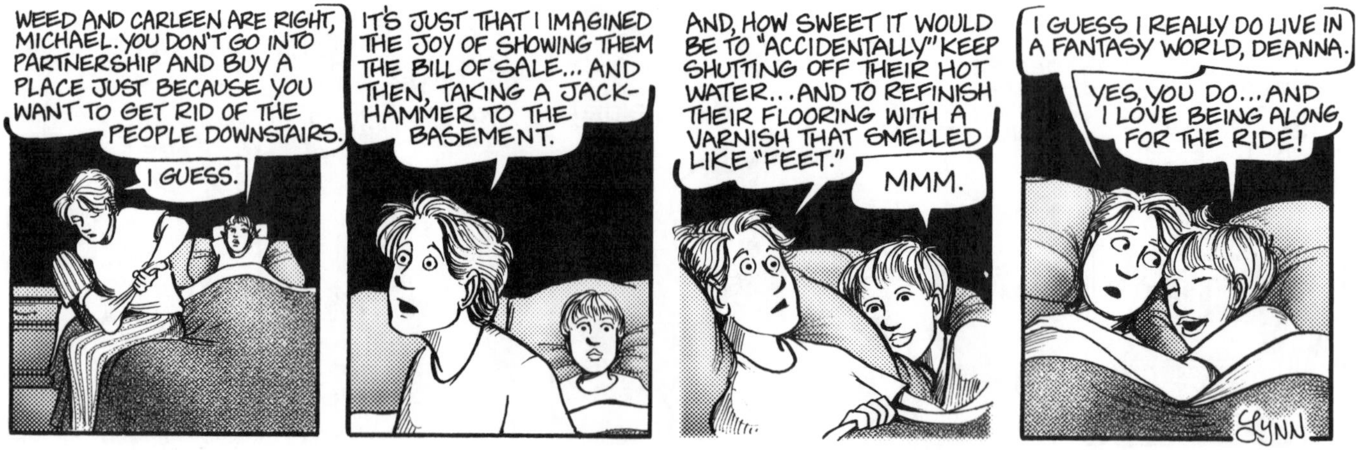
WEED AND CARLEEN ARE RIGHT, MICHAEL. YOU DON'T GO INTO PARTNERSHIP AND BUY A PLACE JUST BECAUSE YOU WANT TO GET RID OF THE PEOPLE DOWNSTAIRS.
I GUESS.
IT'S JUST THAT I IMAGINED THE JOY OF SHOWING THEM THE BILL OF SALE... AND THEN, TAKING A JACKHAMMER TO THE BASEMENT.
AND, HOW SWEET IT WOULD BE TO "ACCIDENTALLY" KEEP SHUTTING OFF THEIR HOT WATER...AND TO REFINISH THEIR FLOORING WITH A VARNISH THAT SMELLED LIKE "FEET."
MMM.
I GUESS I REALLY DO LIVE IN A FANTASY WORLD, DEANNA.
YES, YOU DO...AND I LOVE BEING ALONG FOR THE RIDE!
LYNN

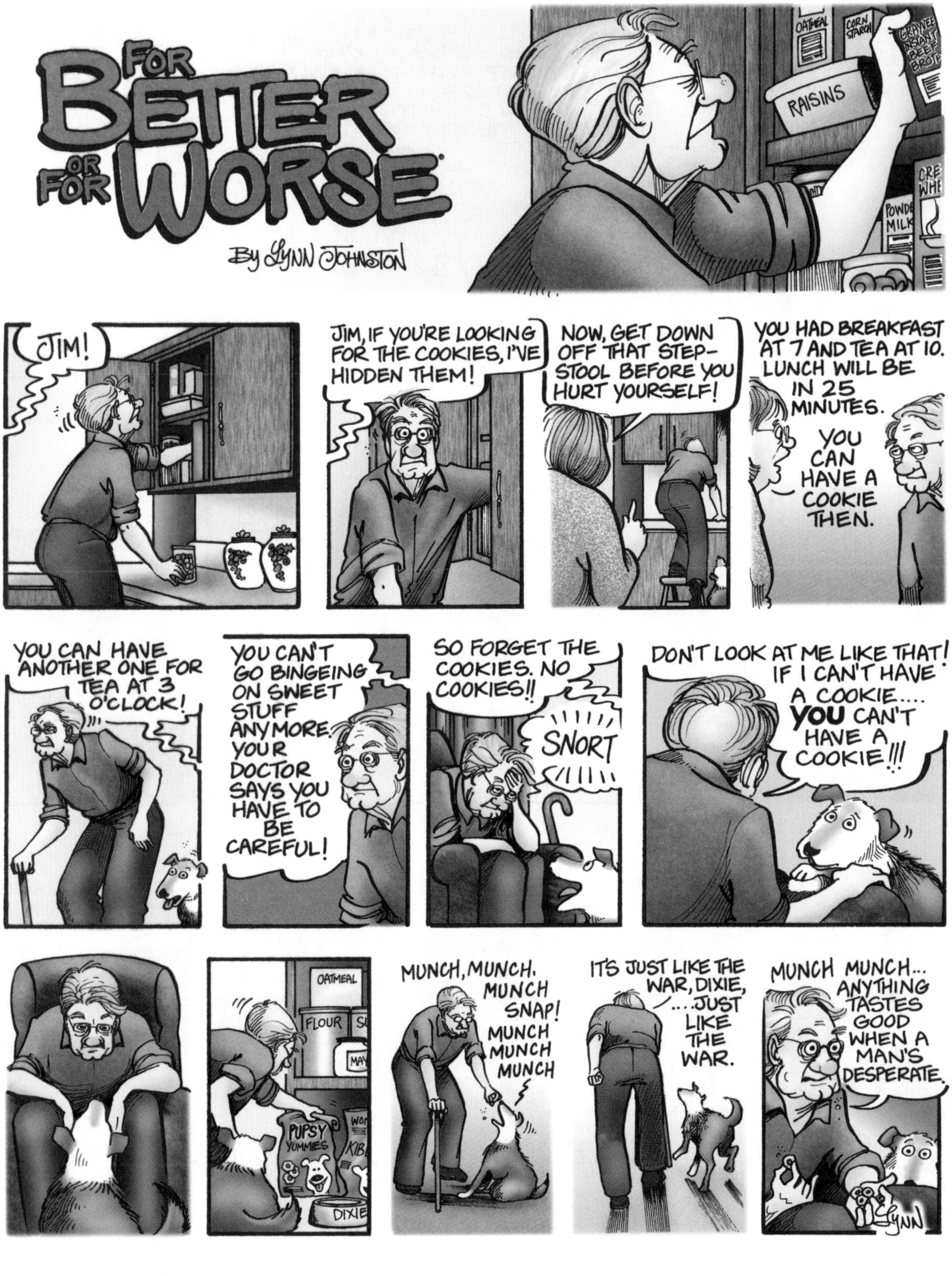
FOR BETTER OR FOR WORSE
BY LYNN JOHNSTON
OATMEAL
CORN STARCH
RAISINS
JIM!
JIM, IF YOU'RE LOOKING FOR THE COOKIES, I'VE HIDDEN THEM!
NOW, GET DOWN OFF THAT STEP-STOOL BEFORE YOU HURT YOURSELF!
YOU HAD BREAKFAST AT 7 AND TEA AT 10. LUNCH WILL BE IN 25 MINUTES.
YOU CAN HAVE A COOKIE THEN.
YOU CAN HAVE ANOTHER ONE FOR TEA AT 3 O'CLOCK!
YOU CAN'T GO BINGEING ON SWEET STUFF ANYMORE. YOUR DOCTOR SAYS YOU HAVE TO BE CAREFUL!
SO FORGET THE COOKIES. NO COOKIES!!
SNORT
DON'T LOOK AT ME LIKE THAT! IF I CAN'T HAVE A COOKIE.... YOU CAN'T HAVE A COOKIE!!!
OATMEAL
FLOUR
PUPSY YUMMIES
DIXIE
MUNCH, MUNCH. MUNCH SNAP! MUNCH MUNCH MUNCH
IT'S JUST LIKE THE WAR, DIXIE, ...JUST LIKE THE WAR.
MUNCH MUNCH... ANYTHING TASTES GOOD WHEN A MAN'S DESPERATE.
LYNN

COFFEE! I NEED MORE COFFEE!!

POWER BLEND
THE BEAN WITH THE BUZZ

I'VE GOT A CURRICULUM TO FOLLOW FOR FIVE GRADES—AND I'M RUNNING OUT OF IDEAS!

THEY'RE ALL DIFFERENT AGES. THEY'RE ALL AT DIFFERENT LEVELS OF UNDERSTANDING ...HOW DO I HOLD THE INTEREST OF THESE KIDS?

IF I DON'T GET A GOOD LESSON PLAN READY FOR TOMORROW, I'M GOING TO FREAK OUT IN FRONT OF THE WHOLE CLASS!

THAT WOULD HOLD THEIR INTEREST!

WHEN THEY WERE FAR OUT AT SEA, WITH NO LAND-MARKS...HOW DID ANCIENT SAILORS KNOW WHERE THEY WERE?

THERE ARE NO LINES OR NUMBERS ON THE EARTH, SO WHAT DID THEY USE TO HELP THEM NAVIGATE?

THE SUN!

THE STARS!

EXACTLY!

THIS WEEK, WE ARE GOING TO IMAGINE WHAT LIFE WAS LIKE ON AN ANCIENT SAILING SHIP!

AND, JESSE...PRETENDING TO BARF OVER THE RAILING IS NOT ONE OF THE EXERCISES.

WE KNOW THAT THE EARTH REVOLVES AROUND THE SUN. ANCIENT SAILORS KNEW THE DIRECTIONS EAST AND WEST BECAUSE...

sun
earth
moon

BECAUSE THE SUN RISES IN THE EAST AND SETS IN THE WEST!

GOOD WORK!

BUT, MORE PRECISE NAVIGATION WAS DONE USING THE STARS! NOW...WHAT DO YOU THINK OF WHEN YOU HEAR THE WORD, "POLARIS"?

north POLE
earth
south POLE

SNOW MACHINES!!

AS MY SCIENCE PROF. SAID, "THE BEST WAY TO LEARN IS BY WORD ASSOCIATION."

north POLE
earth
south POLE

the earth revolve around the sun

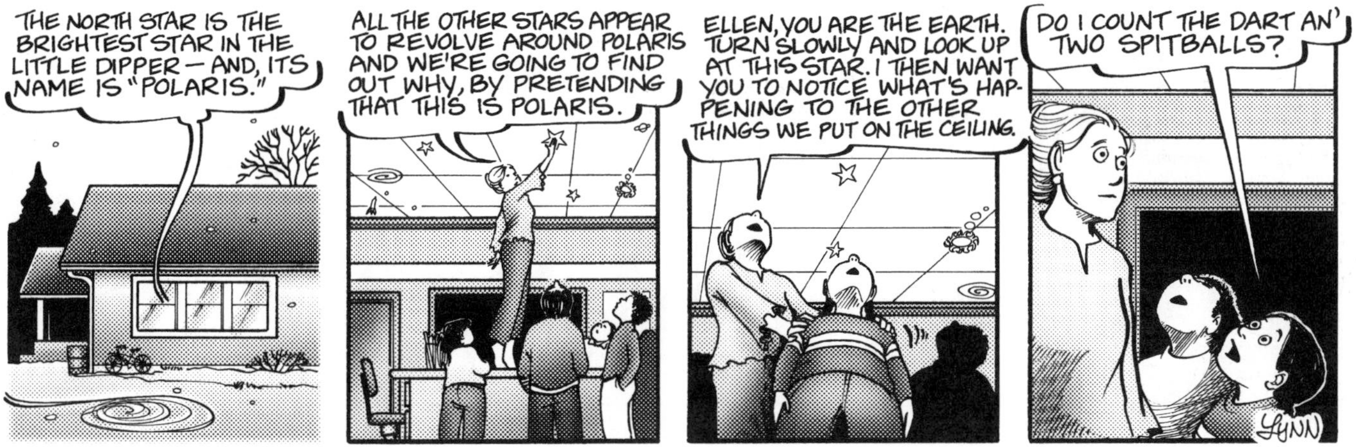

THE NORTH STAR IS THE BRIGHTEST STAR IN THE LITTLE DIPPER — AND, ITS NAME IS "POLARIS."
ALL THE OTHER STARS APPEAR TO REVOLVE AROUND POLARIS AND WE'RE GOING TO FIND OUT WHY, BY PRETENDING THAT THIS IS POLARIS.
ELLEN, YOU ARE THE EARTH. TURN SLOWLY AND LOOK UP AT THIS STAR. I THEN WANT YOU TO NOTICE WHAT'S HAPPENING TO THE OTHER THINGS WE PUT ON THE CEILING.
DO I COUNT THE DART AN' TWO SPITBALLS?
LYNN

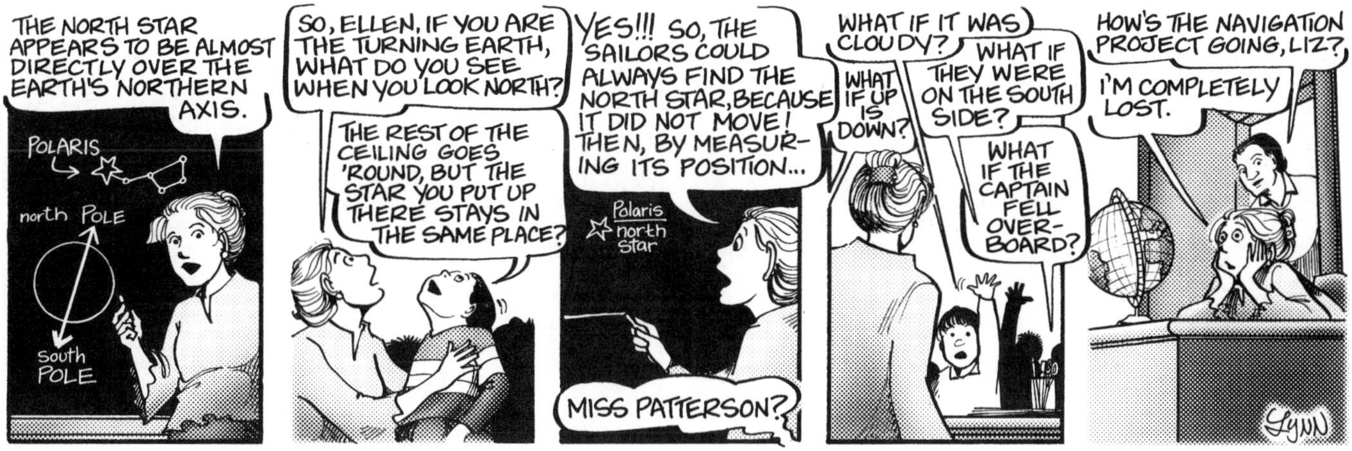

THE NORTH STAR APPEARS TO BE ALMOST DIRECTLY OVER THE EARTH'S NORTHERN AXIS.
POLARIS
north POLE
south POLE
SO, ELLEN, IF YOU ARE THE TURNING EARTH, WHAT DO YOU SEE WHEN YOU LOOK NORTH?
THE REST OF THE CEILING GOES 'ROUND, BUT THE STAR YOU PUT UP THERE STAYS IN THE SAME PLACE?
YES!!! SO, THE SAILORS COULD ALWAYS FIND THE NORTH STAR, BECAUSE IT DID NOT MOVE! THEN, BY MEASURING ITS POSITION...
Polaris north star
MISS PATTERSON?
WHAT IF IT WAS CLOUDY?
WHAT IF UP IS DOWN?
WHAT IF THEY WERE ON THE SOUTH SIDE?
WHAT IF THE CAPTAIN FELL OVERBOARD?
HOW'S THE NAVIGATION PROJECT GOING, LIZ?
I'M COMPLETELY LOST.
LYNN

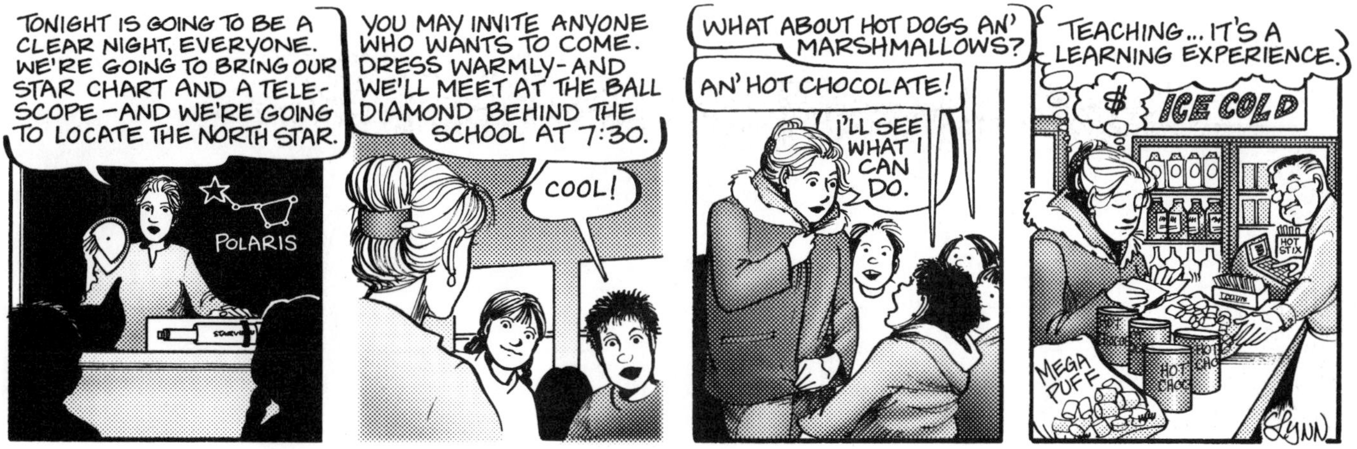

TONIGHT IS GOING TO BE A CLEAR NIGHT, EVERYONE. WE'RE GOING TO BRING OUR STAR CHART AND A TELESCOPE — AND WE'RE GOING TO LOCATE THE NORTH STAR.
POLARIS
YOU MAY INVITE ANYONE WHO WANTS TO COME. DRESS WARMLY — AND WE'LL MEET AT THE BALL DIAMOND BEHIND THE SCHOOL AT 7:30.
COOL!
WHAT ABOUT HOT DOGS AN' MARSHMALLOWS?
AN' HOT CHOCOLATE!
I'LL SEE WHAT I CAN DO.
TEACHING... IT'S A LEARNING EXPERIENCE.
$
ICE COLD
HOT STIX
MEGA PUFF
HOT CHOC
LYNN

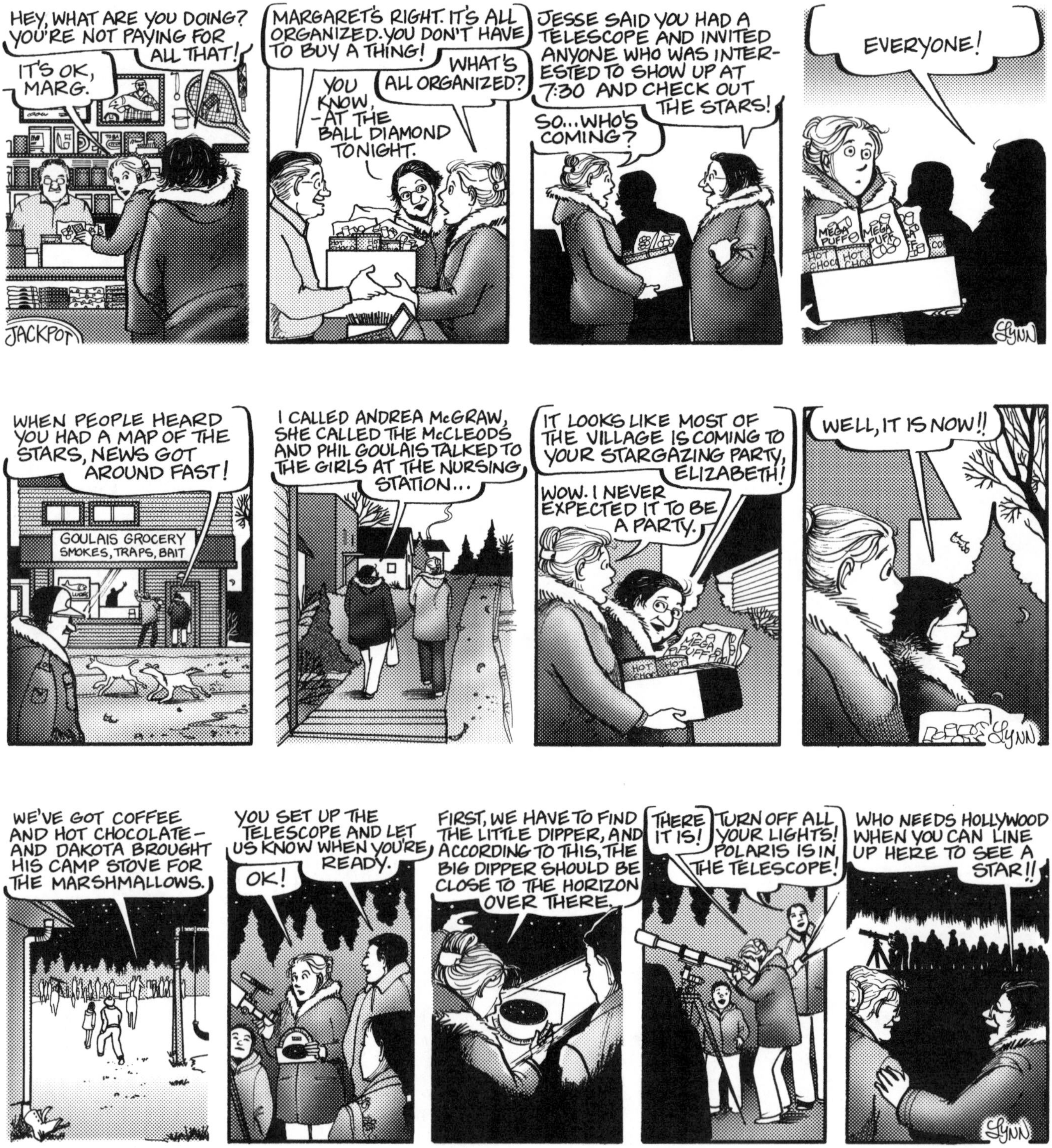
HEY, WHAT ARE YOU DOING? YOU'RE NOT PAYING FOR ALL THAT!
IT'S OK, MARG.
JACKPOT
MARGARET'S RIGHT. IT'S ALL ORGANIZED. YOU DON'T HAVE TO BUY A THING!
WHAT'S ALL ORGANIZED?
YOU KNOW, -AT THE BALL DIAMOND TONIGHT.
JESSE SAID YOU HAD A TELESCOPE AND INVITED ANYONE WHO WAS INTERESTED TO SHOW UP AT 7:30 AND CHECK OUT THE STARS!
SO...WHO'S COMING?
EVERYONE!
MEGA PUFF
HOT CHOC
LYNN
WHEN PEOPLE HEARD YOU HAD A MAP OF THE STARS, NEWS GOT AROUND FAST!
GOULAIS GROCERY SMOKES, TRAPS, BAIT
I CALLED ANDREA McGRAW, SHE CALLED THE McCLEODS AND PHIL GOULAIS TALKED TO THE GIRLS AT THE NURSING STATION...
IT LOOKS LIKE MOST OF THE VILLAGE IS COMING TO YOUR STARGAZING PARTY, ELIZABETH!
WOW. I NEVER EXPECTED IT TO BE A PARTY.
WELL, IT IS NOW!!
LYNN
WE'VE GOT COFFEE AND HOT CHOCOLATE - AND DAKOTA BROUGHT HIS CAMP STOVE FOR THE MARSHMALLOWS.
YOU SET UP THE TELESCOPE AND LET US KNOW WHEN YOU'RE READY.
OK!
FIRST, WE HAVE TO FIND THE LITTLE DIPPER, AND ACCORDING TO THIS, THE BIG DIPPER SHOULD BE CLOSE TO THE HORIZON OVER THERE.
THERE IT IS!
TURN OFF ALL YOUR LIGHTS! POLARIS IS IN THE TELESCOPE!
WHO NEEDS HOLLYWOOD WHEN YOU CAN LINE UP HERE TO SEE A STAR!!
LYNN

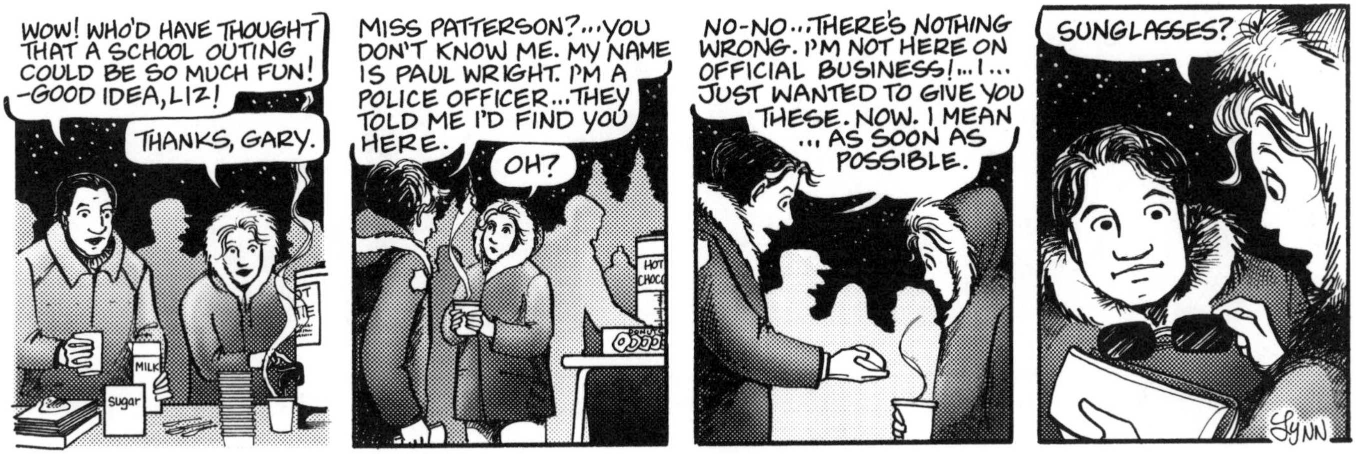
WOW! WHO'D HAVE THOUGHT THAT A SCHOOL OUTING COULD BE SO MUCH FUN! -GOOD IDEA, LIZ!
THANKS, GARY.
MILK
sugar
MISS PATTERSON?...YOU DON'T KNOW ME. MY NAME IS PAUL WRIGHT. I'M A POLICE OFFICER...THEY TOLD ME I'D FIND YOU HERE.
OH?
NO-NO...THERE'S NOTHING WRONG. I'M NOT HERE ON OFFICIAL BUSINESS!...I... JUST WANTED TO GIVE YOU THESE. NOW. I MEAN ...AS SOON AS POSSIBLE.
SUNGLASSES?
LYNN

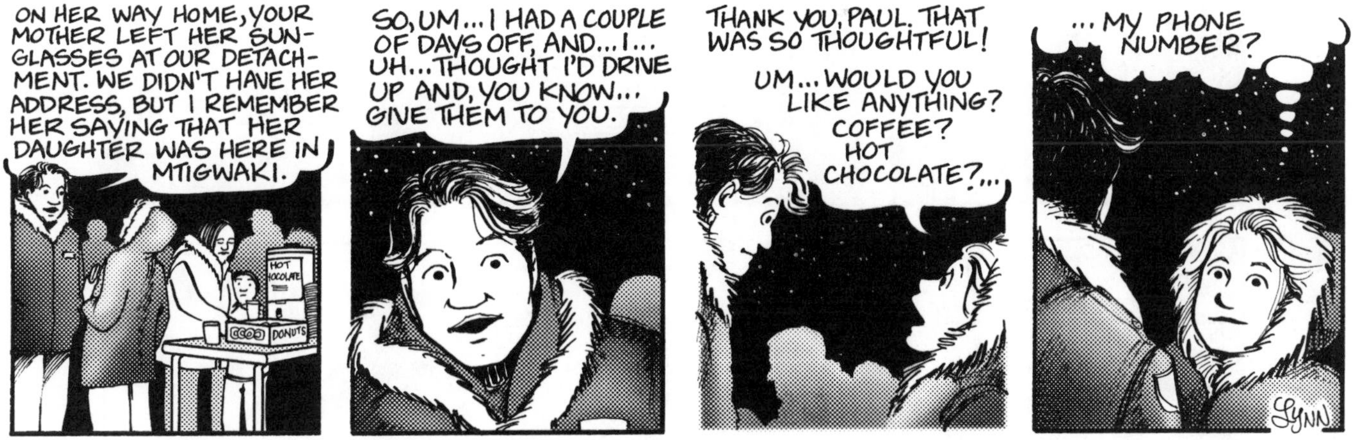
ON HER WAY HOME, YOUR MOTHER LEFT HER SUN-GLASSES AT OUR DETACH-MENT. WE DIDN'T HAVE HER ADDRESS, BUT I REMEMBER HER SAYING THAT HER DAUGHTER WAS HERE IN MTIGWAKI.
HOT CHOCOLATE
DONUTS
SO, UM...I HAD A COUPLE OF DAYS OFF, AND...I... UH...THOUGHT I'D DRIVE UP AND, YOU KNOW... GIVE THEM TO YOU.
THANK YOU, PAUL. THAT WAS SO THOUGHTFUL!
UM...WOULD YOU LIKE ANYTHING? COFFEE? HOT CHOCOLATE?...
...MY PHONE NUMBER?
LYNN

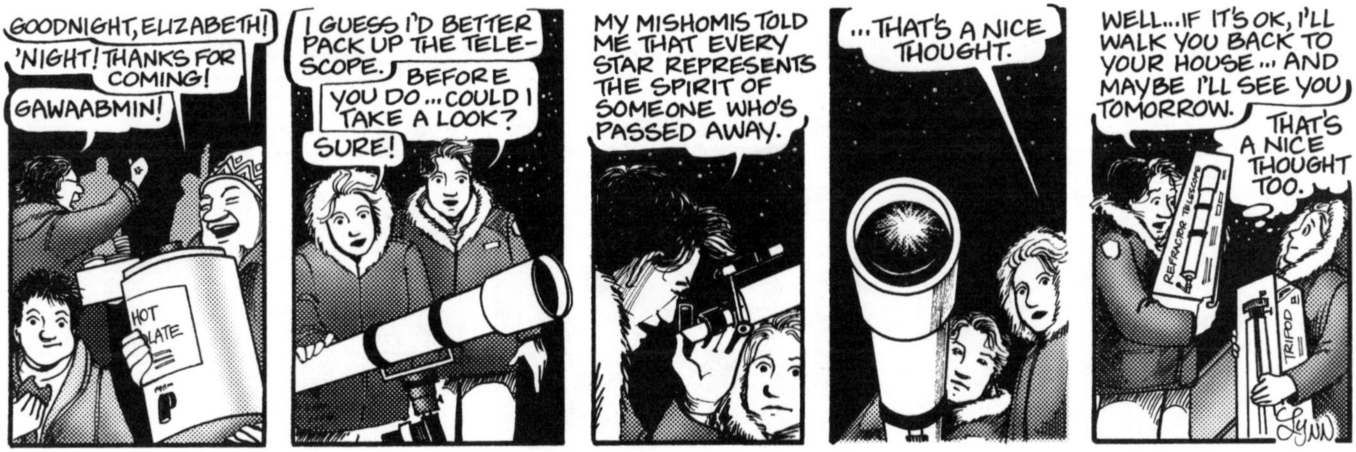
GOODNIGHT, ELIZABETH!
'NIGHT! THANKS FOR COMING!
GAWAABMIN!
I GUESS I'D BETTER PACK UP THE TELE-SCOPE.
BEFORE YOU DO...COULD I TAKE A LOOK?
SURE!
MY MISHOMIS TOLD ME THAT EVERY STAR REPRESENTS THE SPIRIT OF SOMEONE WHO'S PASSED AWAY.
...THAT'S A NICE THOUGHT.
WELL...IF IT'S OK, I'LL WALK YOU BACK TO YOUR HOUSE...AND MAYBE I'LL SEE YOU TOMORROW.
THAT'S A NICE THOUGHT TOO.
REFRACTOR TELESCOPE
TRIPOD
LYNN

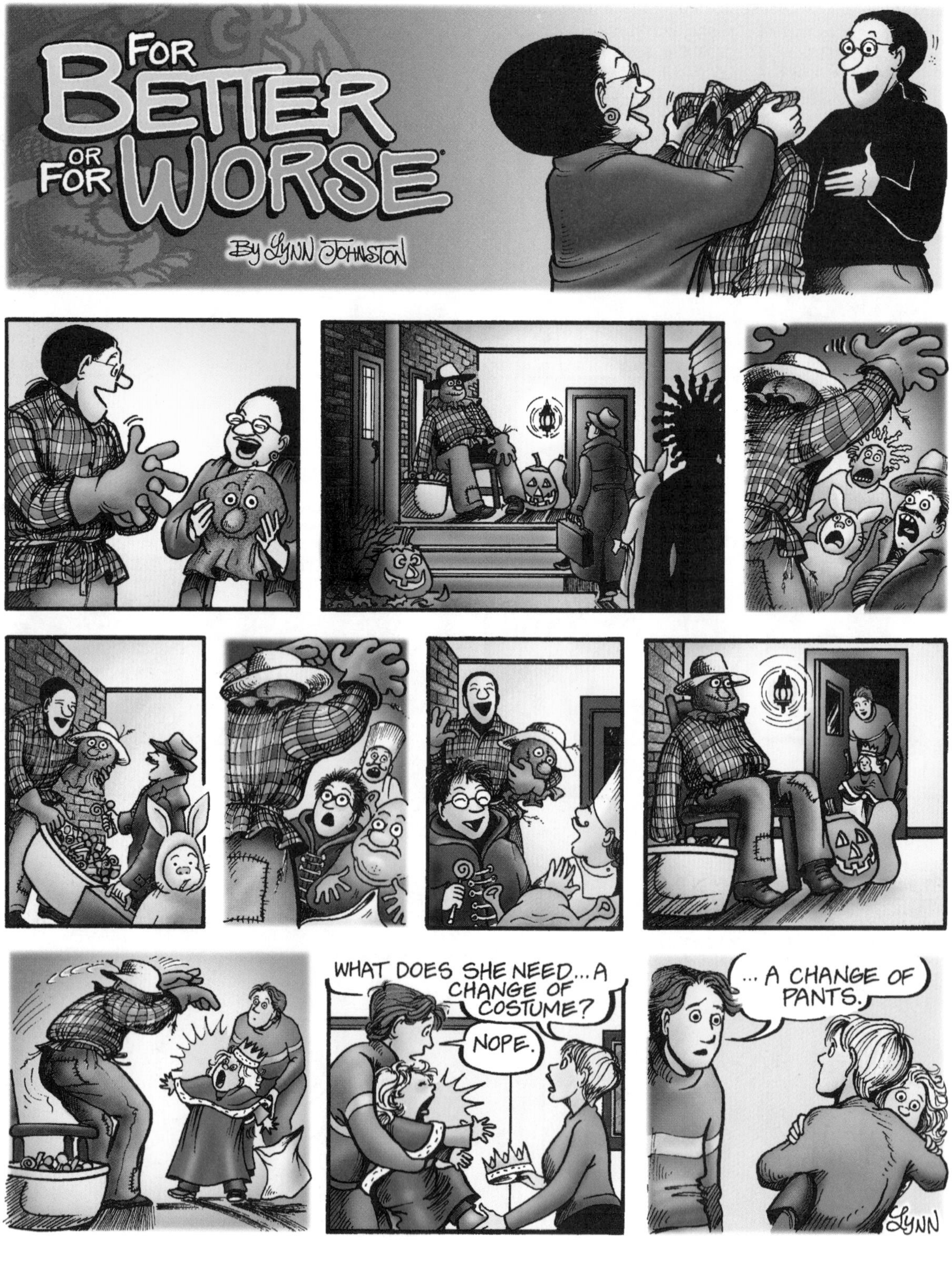
FOR BETTER OR FOR WORSE
By Lynn Johnston
WHAT DOES SHE NEED... A CHANGE OF COSTUME?
NOPE.
... A CHANGE OF PANTS.
LYNN

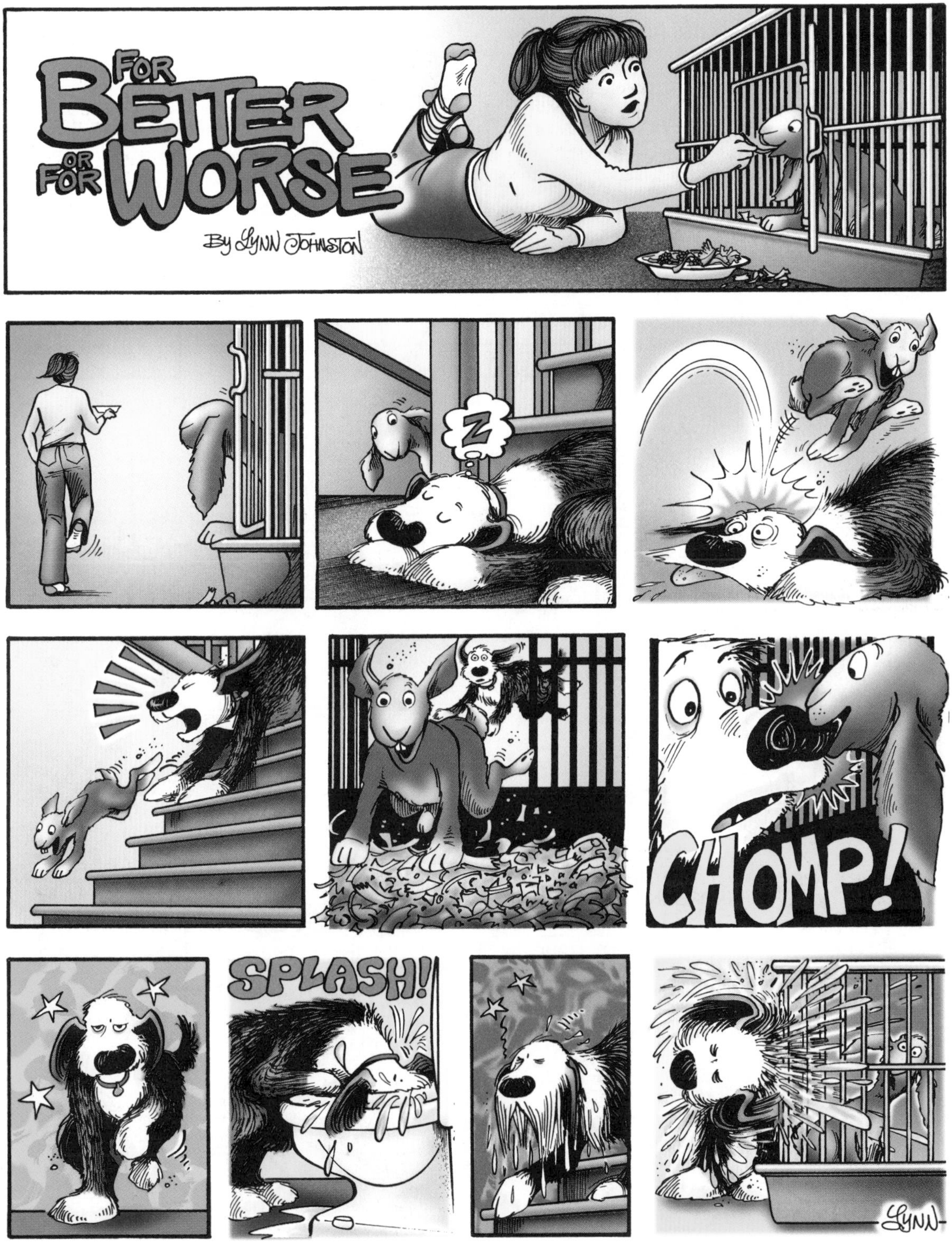
FOR BETTER OR FOR WORSE
By Lynn Johnston
Z
CHOMP!
SPLASH!
LYNN

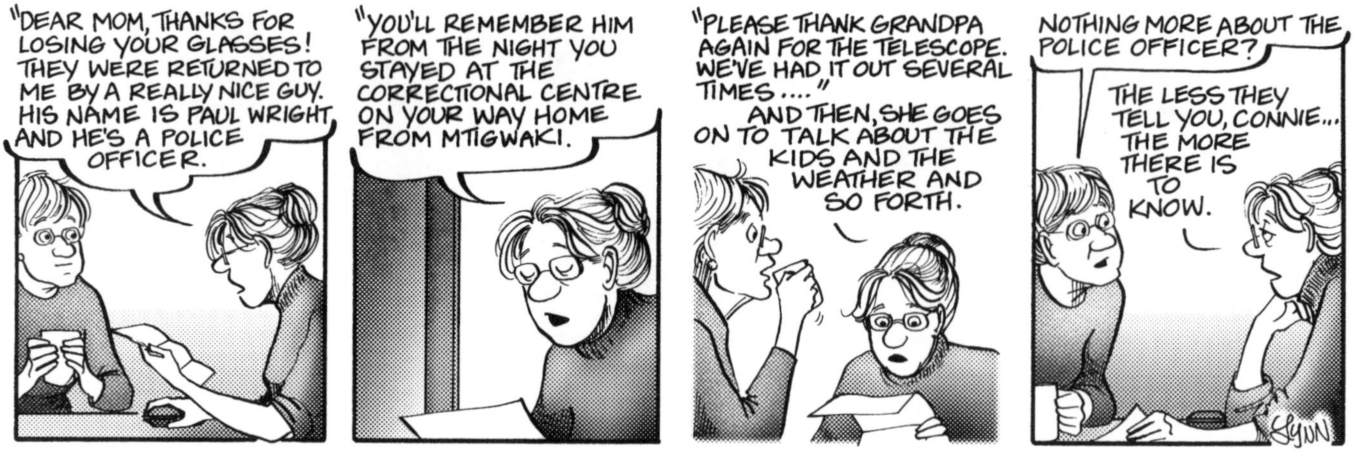
"DEAR MOM, THANKS FOR LOSING YOUR GLASSES! THEY WERE RETURNED TO ME BY A REALLY NICE GUY. HIS NAME IS PAUL WRIGHT, AND HE'S A POLICE OFFICER.
"YOU'LL REMEMBER HIM FROM THE NIGHT YOU STAYED AT THE CORRECTIONAL CENTRE ON YOUR WAY HOME FROM MTIGWAKI.
"PLEASE THANK GRANDPA AGAIN FOR THE TELESCOPE. WE'VE HAD IT OUT SEVERAL TIMES...."
AND THEN, SHE GOES ON TO TALK ABOUT THE KIDS AND THE WEATHER AND SO FORTH.
NOTHING MORE ABOUT THE POLICE OFFICER?
THE LESS THEY TELL YOU, CONNIE... THE MORE THERE IS TO KNOW.
Lynn

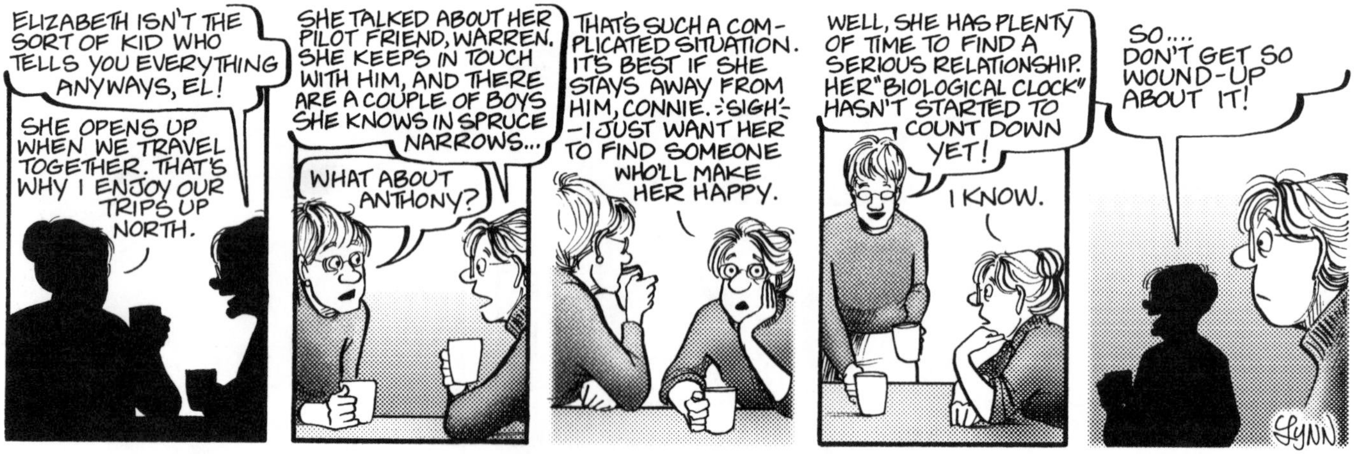
ELIZABETH ISN'T THE SORT OF KID WHO TELLS YOU EVERYTHING ANYWAYS, EL!
SHE OPENS UP WHEN WE TRAVEL TOGETHER. THAT'S WHY I ENJOY OUR TRIPS UP NORTH.
SHE TALKED ABOUT HER PILOT FRIEND, WARREN. SHE KEEPS IN TOUCH WITH HIM, AND THERE ARE A COUPLE OF BOYS SHE KNOWS IN SPRUCE NARROWS...
WHAT ABOUT ANTHONY?
THAT'S SUCH A COMPLICATED SITUATION. IT'S BEST IF SHE STAYS AWAY FROM HIM, CONNIE. -SIGH- -I JUST WANT HER TO FIND SOMEONE WHO'LL MAKE HER HAPPY.
WELL, SHE HAS PLENTY OF TIME TO FIND A SERIOUS RELATIONSHIP. HER "BIOLOGICAL CLOCK" HASN'T STARTED TO COUNT DOWN YET!
I KNOW.
SO.... DON'T GET SO WOUND-UP ABOUT IT!
Lynn

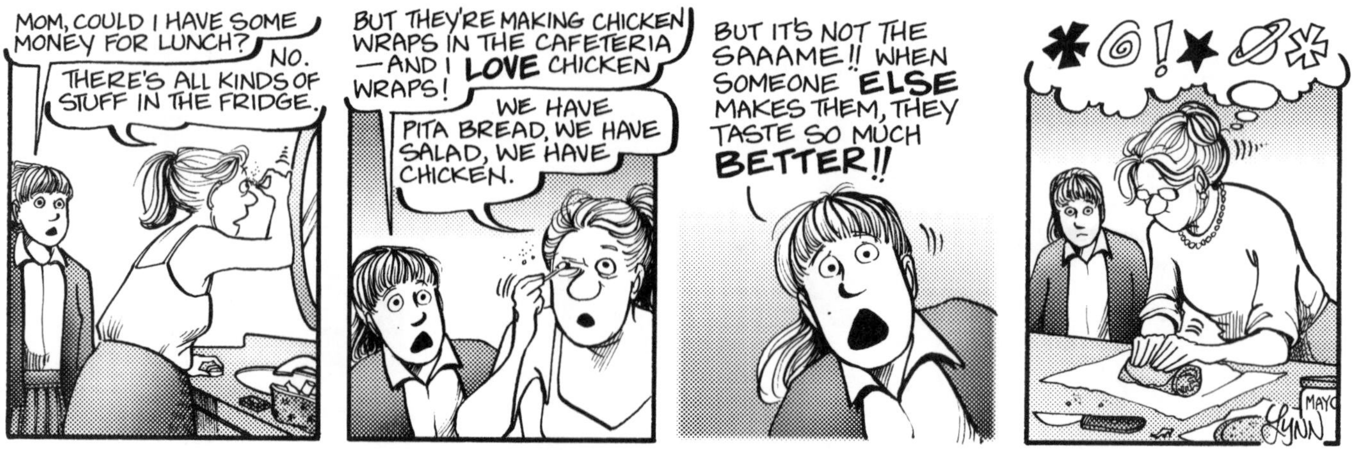
MOM, COULD I HAVE SOME MONEY FOR LUNCH?
NO. THERE'S ALL KINDS OF STUFF IN THE FRIDGE.
BUT THEY'RE MAKING CHICKEN WRAPS IN THE CAFETERIA —AND I LOVE CHICKEN WRAPS!
WE HAVE PITA BREAD, WE HAVE SALAD, WE HAVE CHICKEN.
BUT IT'S NOT THE SAAAME!! WHEN SOMEONE ELSE MAKES THEM, THEY TASTE SO MUCH BETTER!!
Lynn

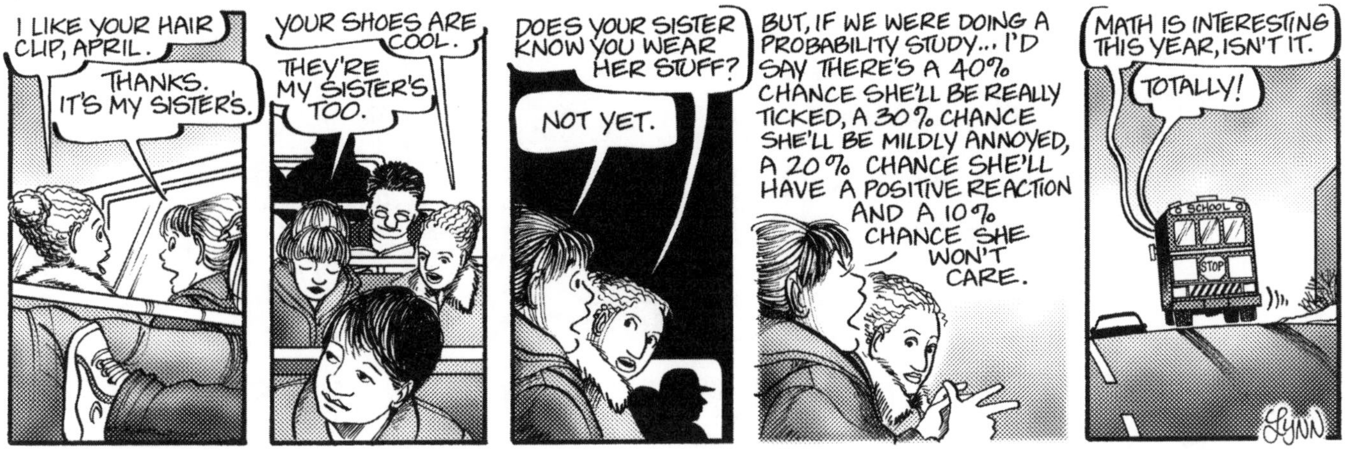
I LIKE YOUR HAIR CLIP, APRIL.
THANKS. IT'S MY SISTER'S.
YOUR SHOES ARE COOL.
THEY'RE MY SISTER'S, TOO.
DOES YOUR SISTER KNOW YOU WEAR HER STUFF?
NOT YET.
BUT, IF WE WERE DOING A PROBABILITY STUDY... I'D SAY THERE'S A 40% CHANCE SHE'LL BE REALLY TICKED, A 30% CHANCE SHE'LL BE MILDLY ANNOYED, A 20% CHANCE SHE'LL HAVE A POSITIVE REACTION
AND A 10% CHANCE SHE WON'T CARE.
MATH IS INTERESTING THIS YEAR, ISN'T IT.
TOTALLY!
SCHOOL
STOP
LYNN

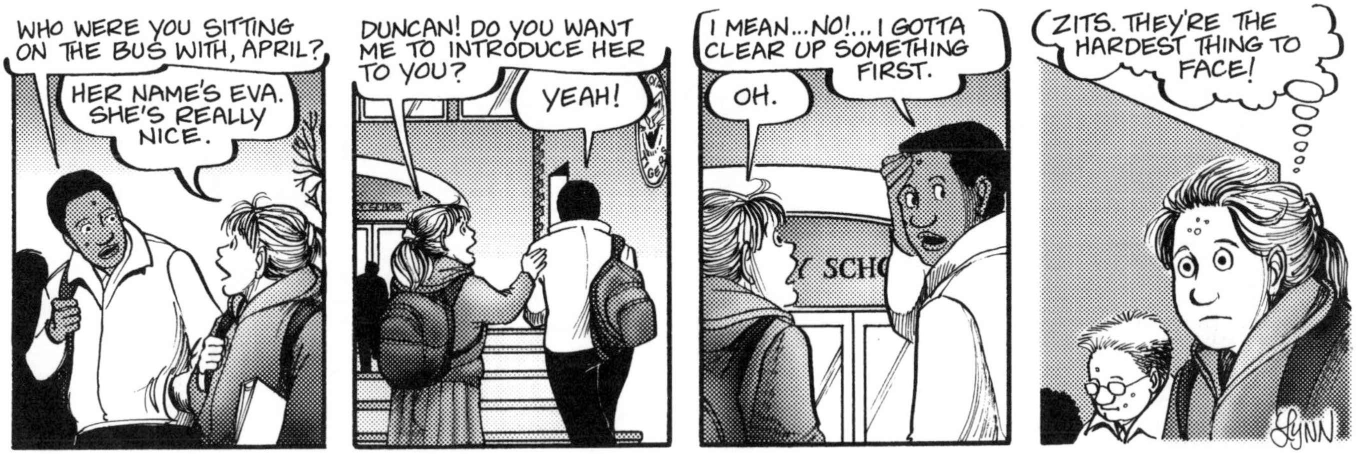
WHO WERE YOU SITTING ON THE BUS WITH, APRIL?
HER NAME'S EVA. SHE'S REALLY NICE.
DUNCAN! DO YOU WANT ME TO INTRODUCE HER TO YOU?
YEAH!
I MEAN...NO!... I GOTTA CLEAR UP SOMETHING FIRST.
OH.
ZITS. THEY'RE THE HARDEST THING TO FACE!
LYNN

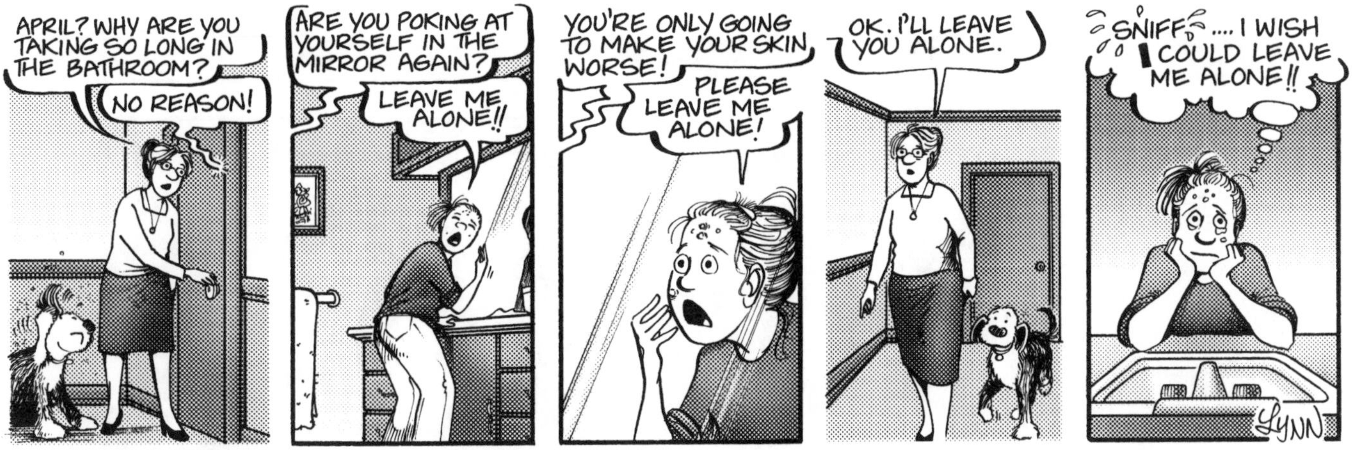
APRIL? WHY ARE YOU TAKING SO LONG IN THE BATHROOM?
NO REASON!
ARE YOU POKING AT YOURSELF IN THE MIRROR AGAIN?
LEAVE ME ALONE!!
YOU'RE ONLY GOING TO MAKE YOUR SKIN WORSE!
PLEASE LEAVE ME ALONE!
OK. I'LL LEAVE YOU ALONE.
SNIFF.... I WISH I COULD LEAVE ME ALONE!!
LYNN

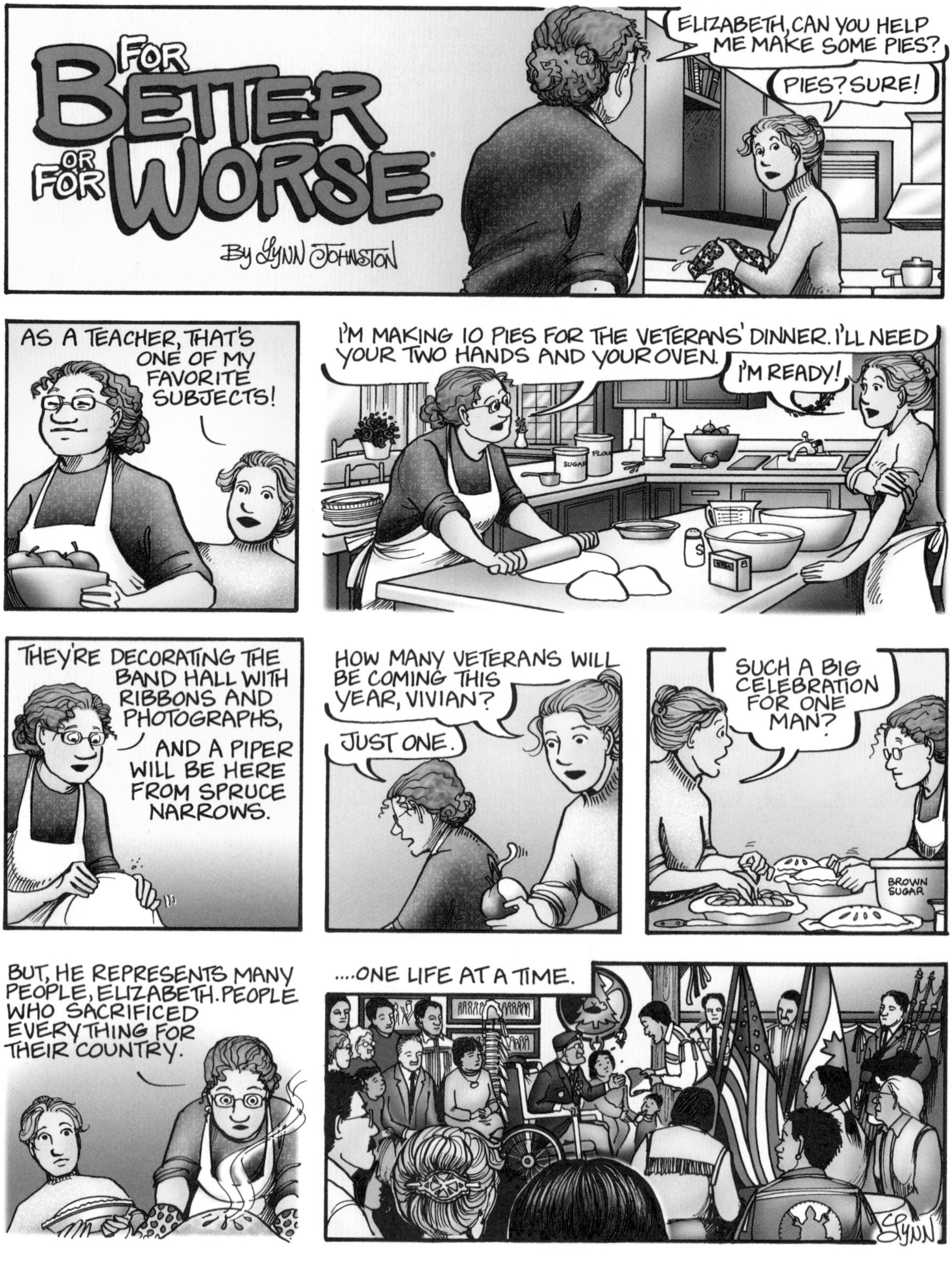

FOR BETTER OR FOR WORSE
By Lynn Johnston
ELIZABETH, CAN YOU HELP ME MAKE SOME PIES?
PIES? SURE!
AS A TEACHER, THAT'S ONE OF MY FAVORITE SUBJECTS!
I'M MAKING 10 PIES FOR THE VETERANS' DINNER. I'LL NEED YOUR TWO HANDS AND YOUR OVEN.
I'M READY!
THEY'RE DECORATING THE BAND HALL WITH RIBBONS AND PHOTOGRAPHS,
AND A PIPER WILL BE HERE FROM SPRUCE NARROWS.
HOW MANY VETERANS WILL BE COMING THIS YEAR, VIVIAN?
JUST ONE.
SUCH A BIG CELEBRATION FOR ONE MAN?
BROWN SUGAR
BUT, HE REPRESENTS MANY PEOPLE, ELIZABETH. PEOPLE WHO SACRIFICED EVERYTHING FOR THEIR COUNTRY.
....ONE LIFE AT A TIME.
LYNN

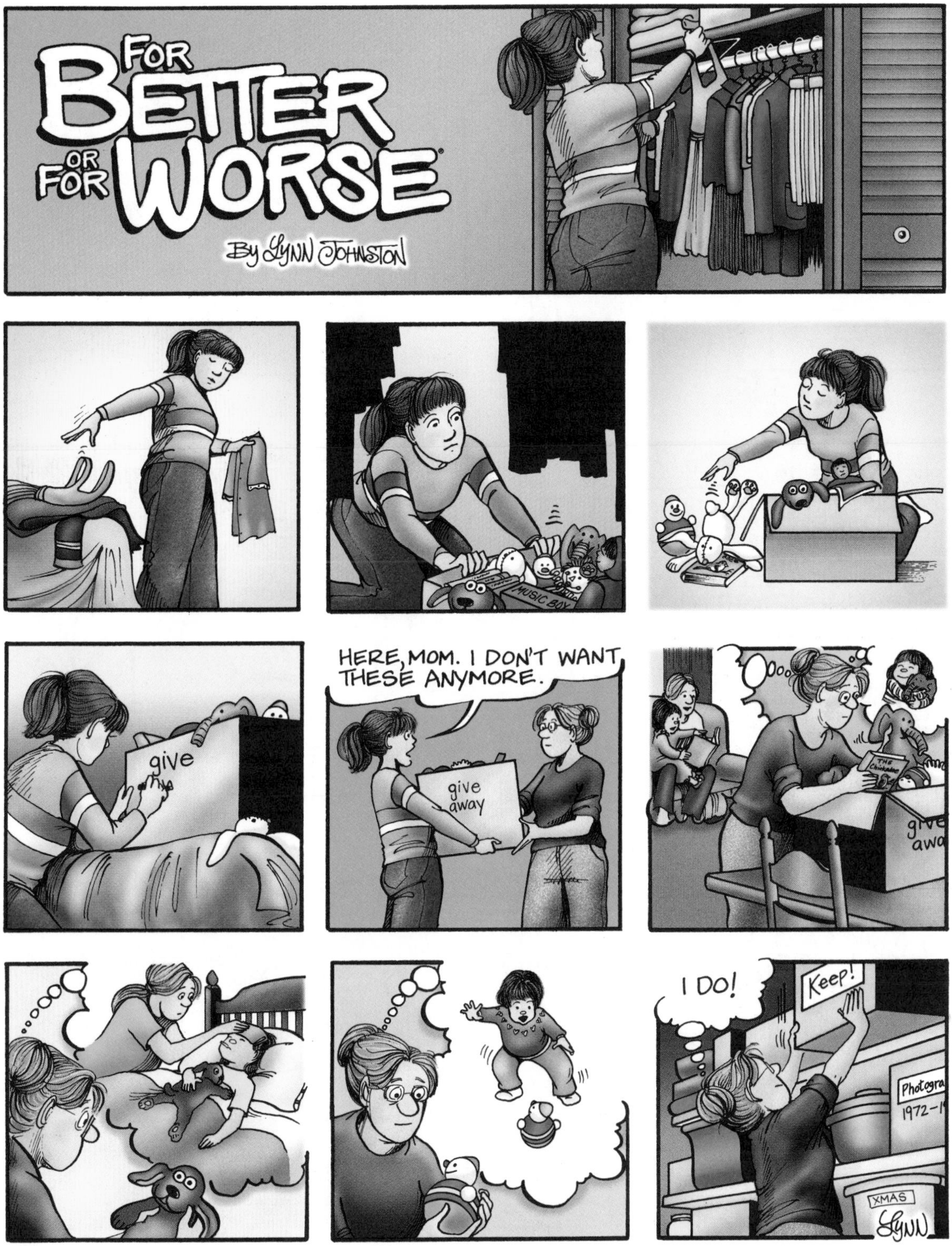
FOR BETTER OR FOR WORSE
BY LYNN JOHNSTON
MUSIC BOX
give
HERE, MOM. I DON'T WANT THESE ANYMORE.
give away
I DO!
Keep!
XMAS
LYNN

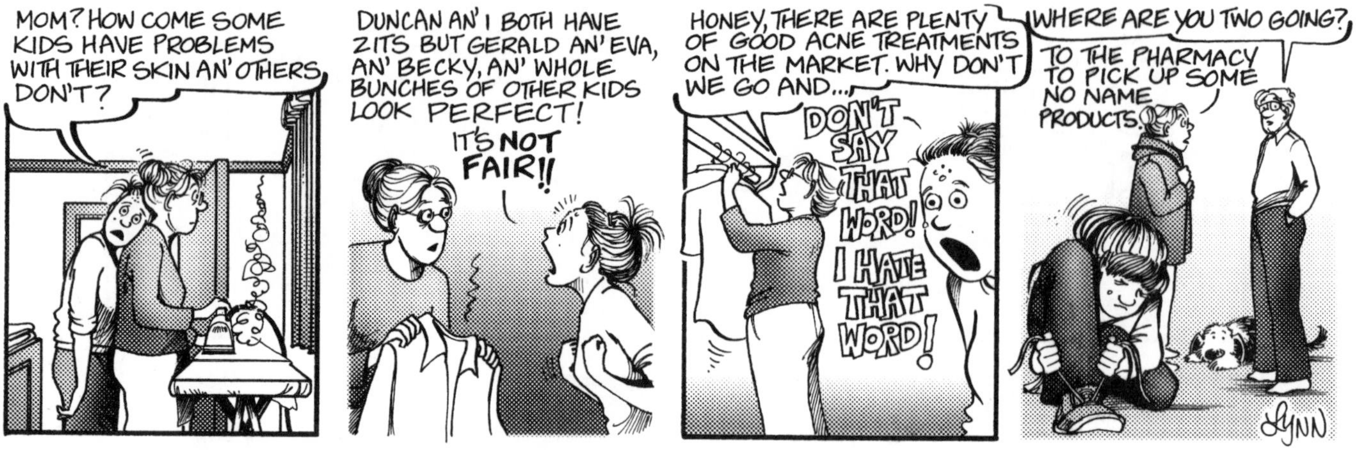

MOM? HOW COME SOME KIDS HAVE PROBLEMS WITH THEIR SKIN AN' OTHERS DON'T?
DUNCAN AN' I BOTH HAVE ZITS BUT GERALD AN' EVA, AN' BECKY, AN' WHOLE BUNCHES OF OTHER KIDS LOOK PERFECT!
IT'S NOT FAIR!!
HONEY, THERE ARE PLENTY OF GOOD ACNE TREATMENTS ON THE MARKET. WHY DON'T WE GO AND...
DON'T SAY THAT WORD! I HATE THAT WORD!
WHERE ARE YOU TWO GOING?
TO THE PHARMACY TO PICK UP SOME NO NAME PRODUCTS.
LYNN

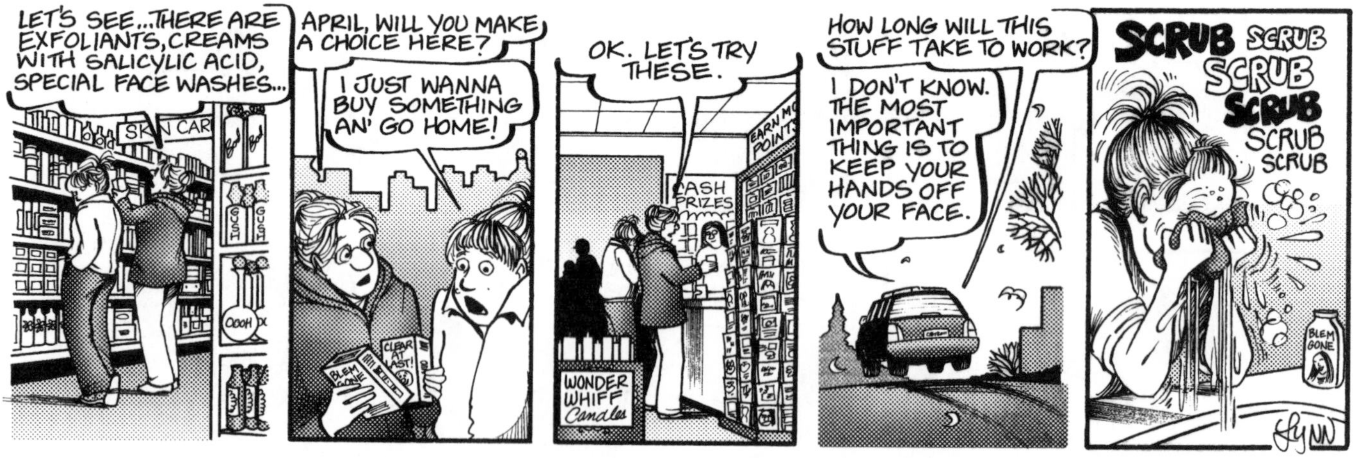

LET'S SEE...THERE ARE EXFOLIANTS, CREAMS WITH SALICYLIC ACID, SPECIAL FACE WASHES...
APRIL, WILL YOU MAKE A CHOICE HERE?
I JUST WANNA BUY SOMETHING AN' GO HOME!
BLEM GONE
OK. LET'S TRY THESE.
CASH PRIZES
WONDER WHIFF Candles
HOW LONG WILL THIS STUFF TAKE TO WORK?
I DON'T KNOW. THE MOST IMPORTANT THING IS TO KEEP YOUR HANDS OFF YOUR FACE.
SCRUB SCRUB SCRUB SCRUB SCRUB SCRUB
BLEM GONE
LYNN

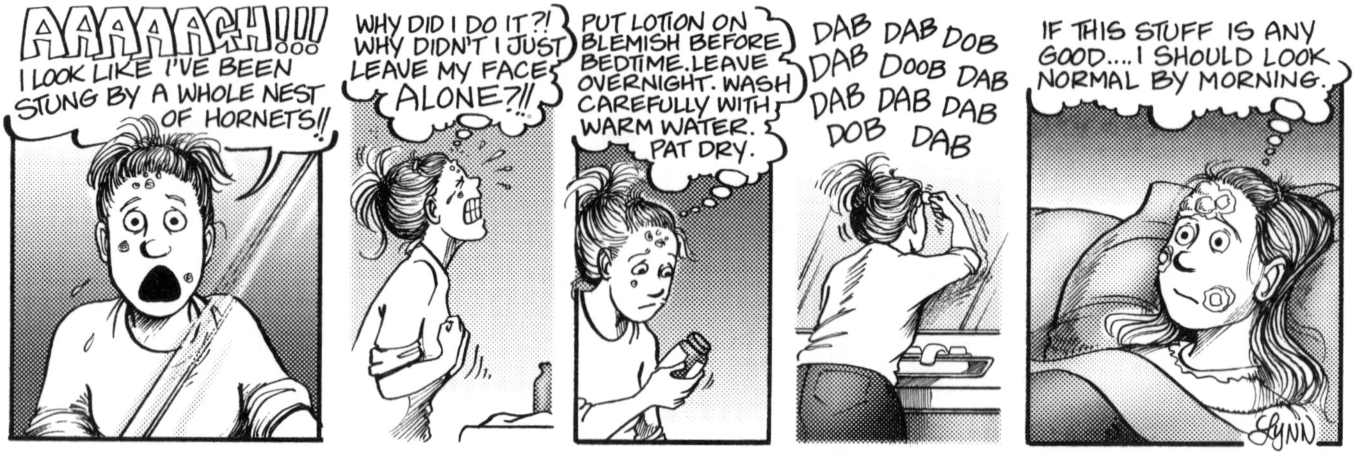

AAAAACH!!!
I LOOK LIKE I'VE BEEN STUNG BY A WHOLE NEST OF HORNETS!!
WHY DID I DO IT?! WHY DIDN'T I JUST LEAVE MY FACE ALONE?!!
PUT LOTION ON BLEMISH BEFORE BEDTIME. LEAVE OVERNIGHT. WASH CAREFULLY WITH WARM WATER. PAT DRY.
DAB DAB DOB DAB DOOB DAB DAB DAB DAB DOB DAB
IF THIS STUFF IS ANY GOOD.... I SHOULD LOOK NORMAL BY MORNING.
LYNN

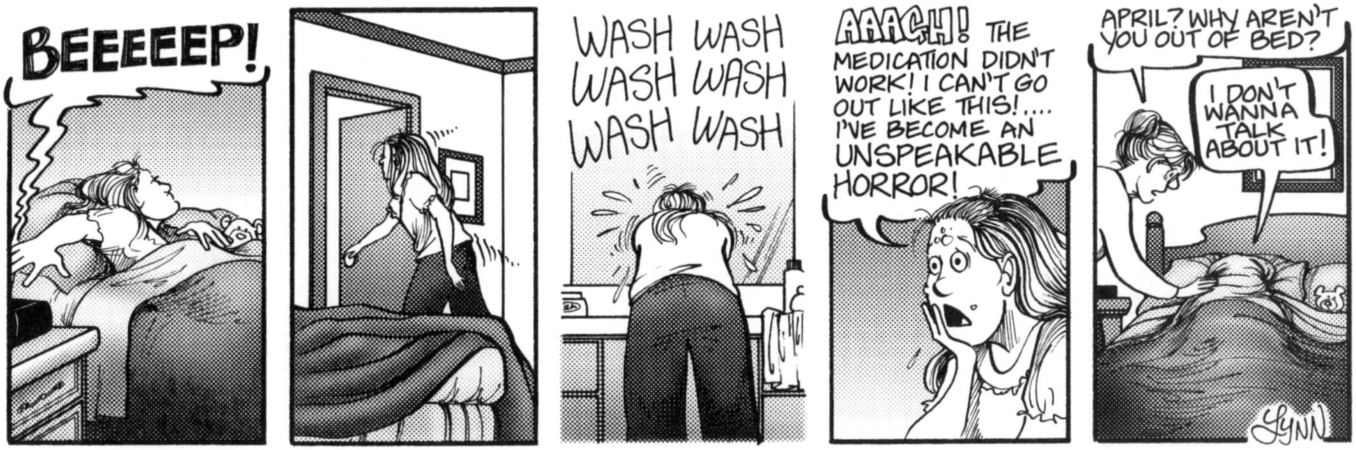
BEEEEEP!
WASH WASH
WASH WASH
WASH WASH
AAAGH! THE MEDICATION DIDN'T WORK! I CAN'T GO OUT LIKE THIS!.... I'VE BECOME AN UNSPEAKABLE HORROR!
APRIL? WHY AREN'T YOU OUT OF BED?
I DON'T WANNA TALK ABOUT IT!
LYNN

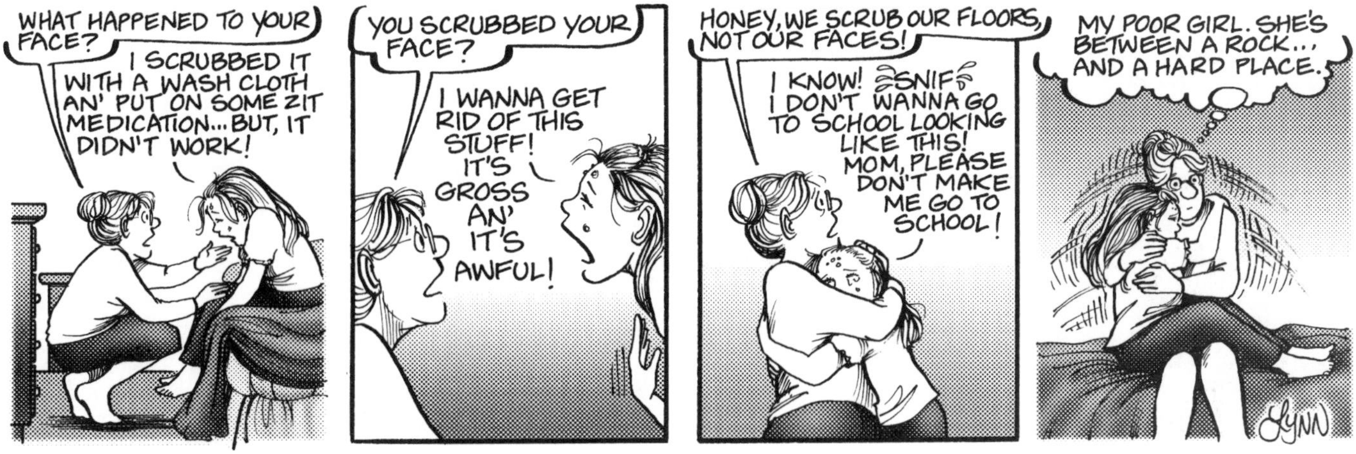
WHAT HAPPENED TO YOUR FACE?
I SCRUBBED IT WITH A WASH CLOTH AN' PUT ON SOME ZIT MEDICATION...BUT, IT DIDN'T WORK!
YOU SCRUBBED YOUR FACE?
I WANNA GET RID OF THIS STUFF! IT'S GROSS AN' IT'S AWFUL!
HONEY, WE SCRUB OUR FLOORS, NOT OUR FACES!
I KNOW! SNIF I DON'T WANNA GO TO SCHOOL LOOKING LIKE THIS! MOM, PLEASE DON'T MAKE ME GO TO SCHOOL!
MY POOR GIRL. SHE'S BETWEEN A ROCK... AND A HARD PLACE.
LYNN

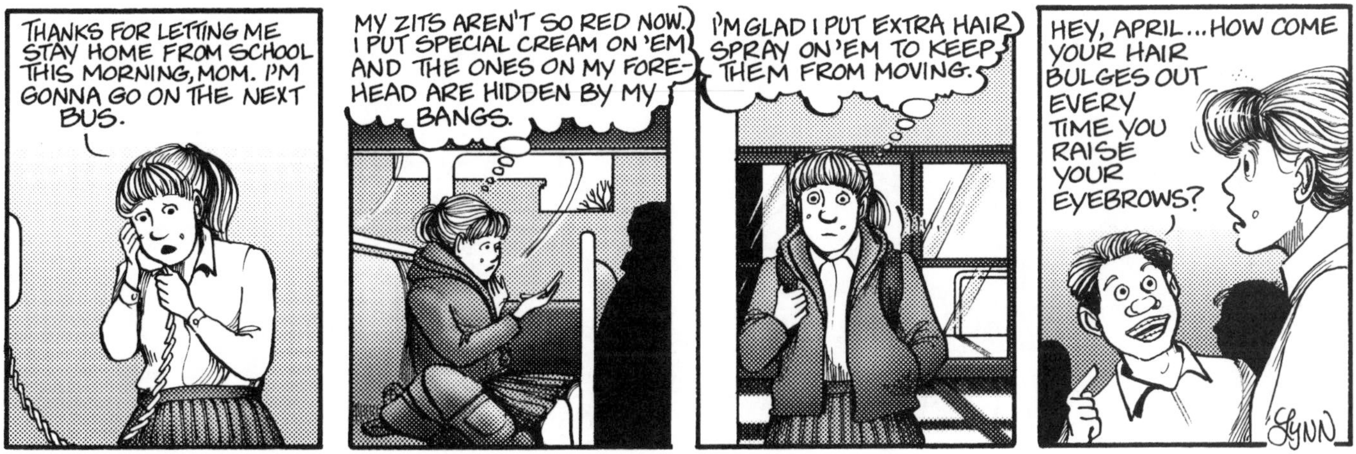
THANKS FOR LETTING ME STAY HOME FROM SCHOOL THIS MORNING, MOM. I'M GONNA GO ON THE NEXT BUS.
MY ZITS AREN'T SO RED NOW. I PUT SPECIAL CREAM ON 'EM AND THE ONES ON MY FORE-HEAD ARE HIDDEN BY MY BANGS.
I'M GLAD I PUT EXTRA HAIR SPRAY ON 'EM TO KEEP THEM FROM MOVING.
HEY, APRIL... HOW COME YOUR HAIR BULGES OUT EVERY TIME YOU RAISE YOUR EYEBROWS?
LYNN

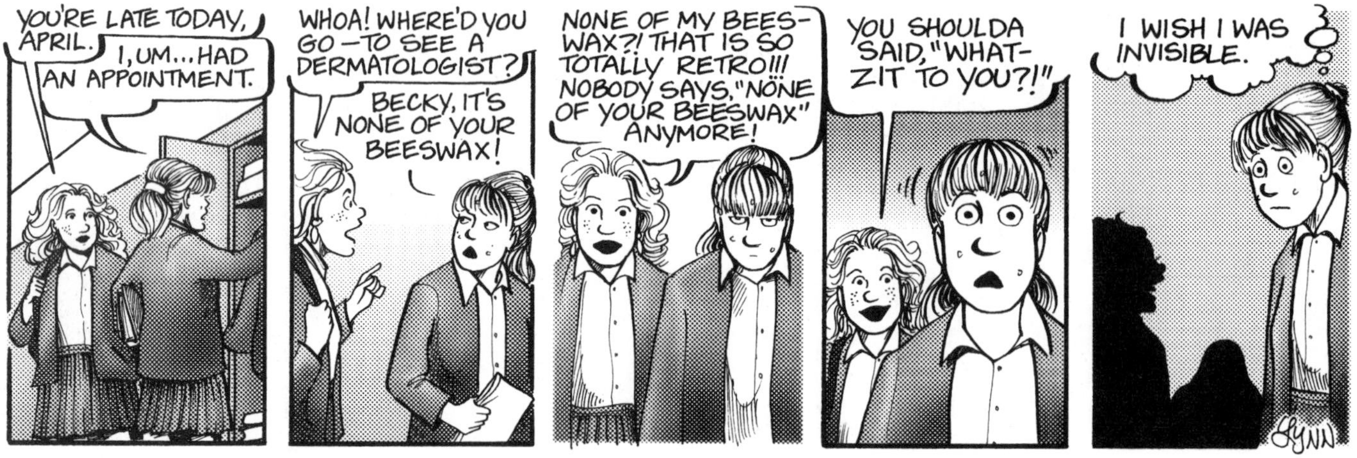

YOU'RE LATE TODAY, APRIL.
I, UM... HAD AN APPOINTMENT.
WHOA! WHERE'D YOU GO — TO SEE A DERMATOLOGIST?
BECKY, IT'S NONE OF YOUR BEESWAX!
NONE OF MY BEESWAX?! THAT IS SO TOTALLY RETRO!!! NOBODY SAYS, "NONE OF YOUR BEESWAX" ANYMORE!
YOU SHOULDA SAID, "WHAT-ZIT TO YOU?!"
I WISH I WAS INVISIBLE.
LYNN

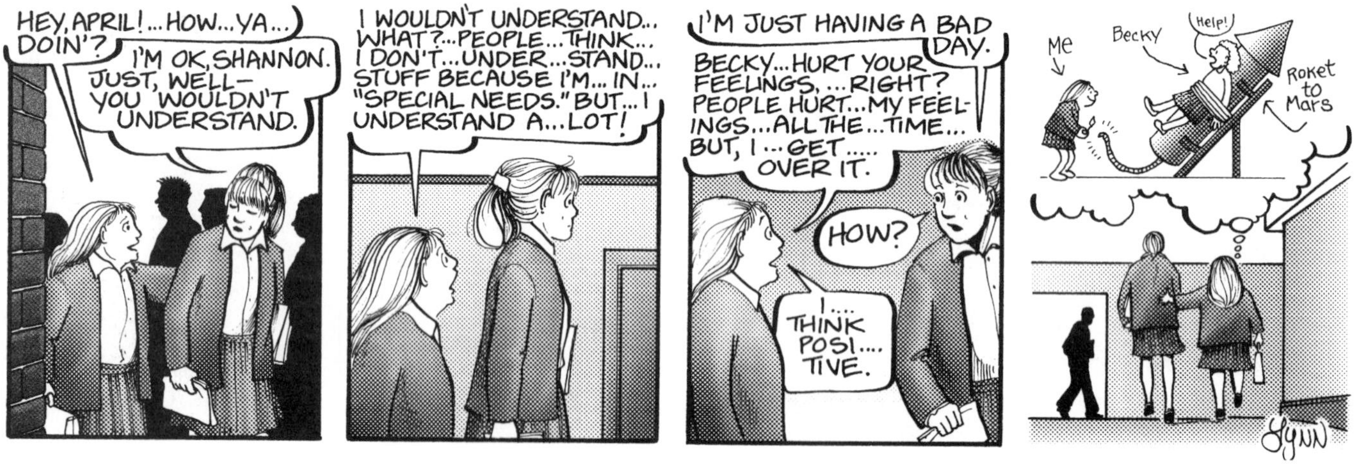

HEY, APRIL! ... HOW... YA... DOIN'?
I'M OK, SHANNON. JUST, WELL— YOU WOULDN'T UNDERSTAND.
I WOULDN'T UNDERSTAND... WHAT?... PEOPLE... THINK... I DON'T... UNDER... STAND... STUFF BECAUSE I'M... IN... "SPECIAL NEEDS." BUT... I UNDERSTAND A... LOT!
I'M JUST HAVING A BAD DAY.
BECKY... HURT YOUR FEELINGS, ... RIGHT? PEOPLE HURT... MY FEELINGS... ALL THE... TIME... BUT, I... GET..... OVER IT.
HOW?
I.... THINK POSI.... TIVE.
Me
Becky
Help!
Roket to Mars
LYNN

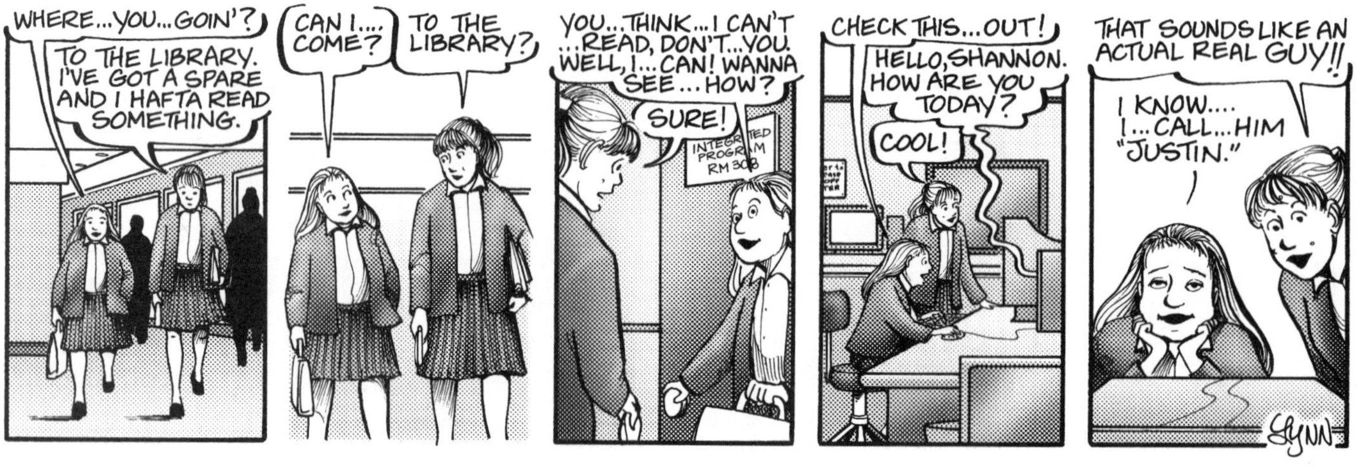

WHERE... YOU... GOIN'?
TO THE LIBRARY. I'VE GOT A SPARE AND I HAFTA READ SOMETHING.
CAN I.... COME?
TO THE LIBRARY?
YOU... THINK... I CAN'T ... READ, DON'T... YOU. WELL, I... CAN! WANNA SEE... HOW?
SURE!
INTEGRATED PROGRAM RM 308
CHECK THIS... OUT!
HELLO, SHANNON. HOW ARE YOU TODAY?
COOL!
THAT SOUNDS LIKE AN ACTUAL REAL GUY!!
I KNOW.... I... CALL... HIM "JUSTIN."
LYNN

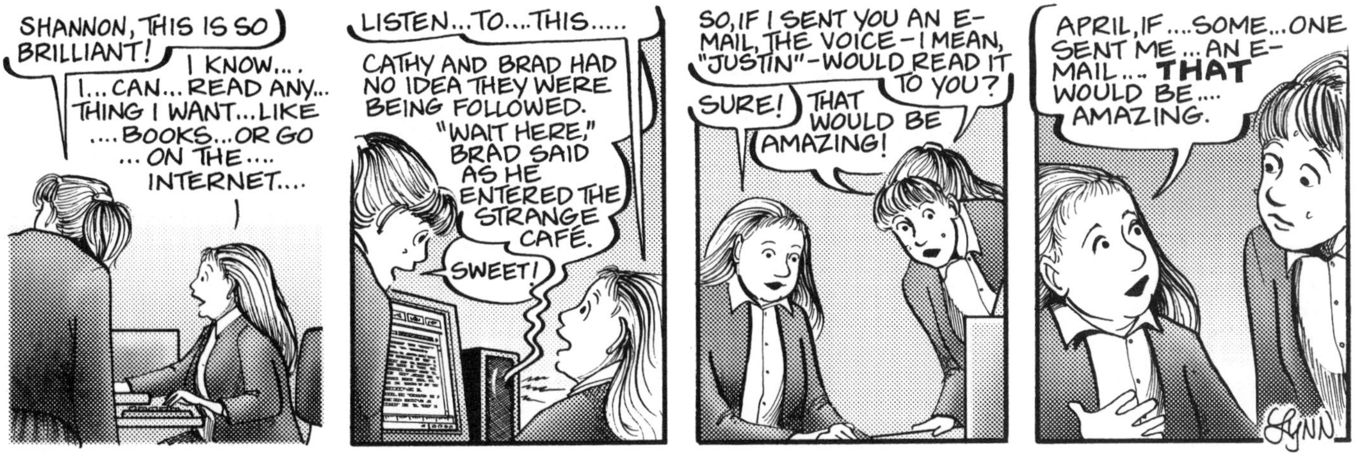
SHANNON, THIS IS SO BRILLIANT!
I KNOW.... I... CAN... READ ANY... THING I WANT... LIKE .... BOOKS... OR GO ... ON THE.... INTERNET....
LISTEN... TO.... THIS.....
CATHY AND BRAD HAD NO IDEA THEY WERE BEING FOLLOWED. "WAIT HERE," BRAD SAID AS HE ENTERED THE STRANGE CAFÉ.
SWEET!
SO, IF I SENT YOU AN E-MAIL, THE VOICE – I MEAN, "JUSTIN" – WOULD READ IT TO YOU?
SURE!
THAT WOULD BE AMAZING!
APRIL, IF .... SOME... ONE SENT ME ... AN E-MAIL.... **THAT** WOULD BE.... AMAZING.
LYNN

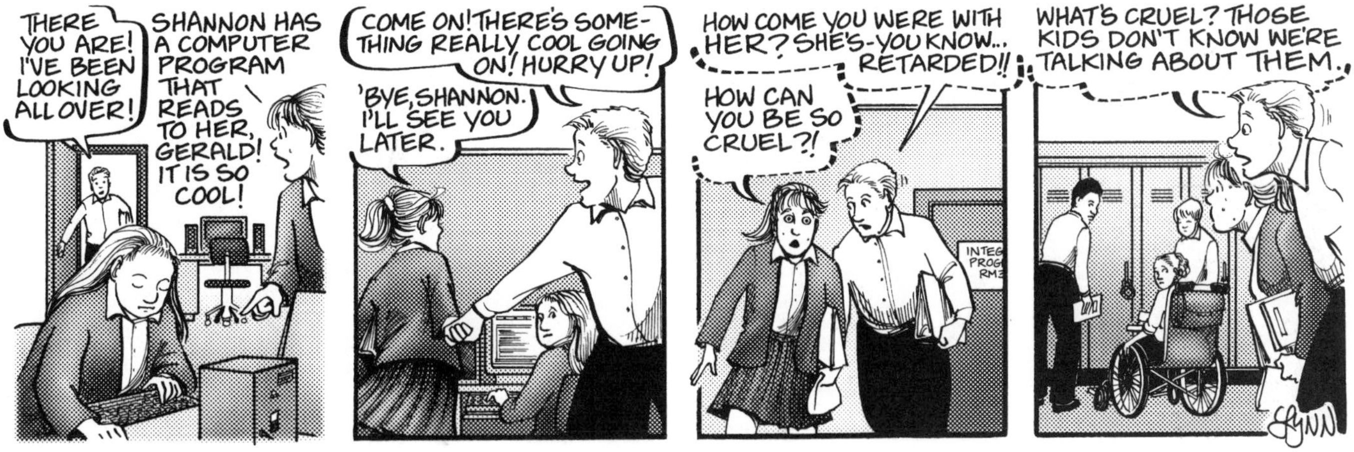
THERE YOU ARE! I'VE BEEN LOOKING ALL OVER!
SHANNON HAS A COMPUTER PROGRAM THAT READS TO HER, GERALD! IT IS SO COOL!
COME ON! THERE'S SOME-THING REALLY COOL GOING ON! HURRY UP!
'BYE, SHANNON. I'LL SEE YOU LATER.
HOW COME YOU WERE WITH HER? SHE'S - YOU KNOW... RETARDED!!
HOW CAN YOU BE SO CRUEL?!
INTEG PROG RM3
WHAT'S CRUEL? THOSE KIDS DON'T KNOW WE'RE TALKING ABOUT THEM.
LYNN

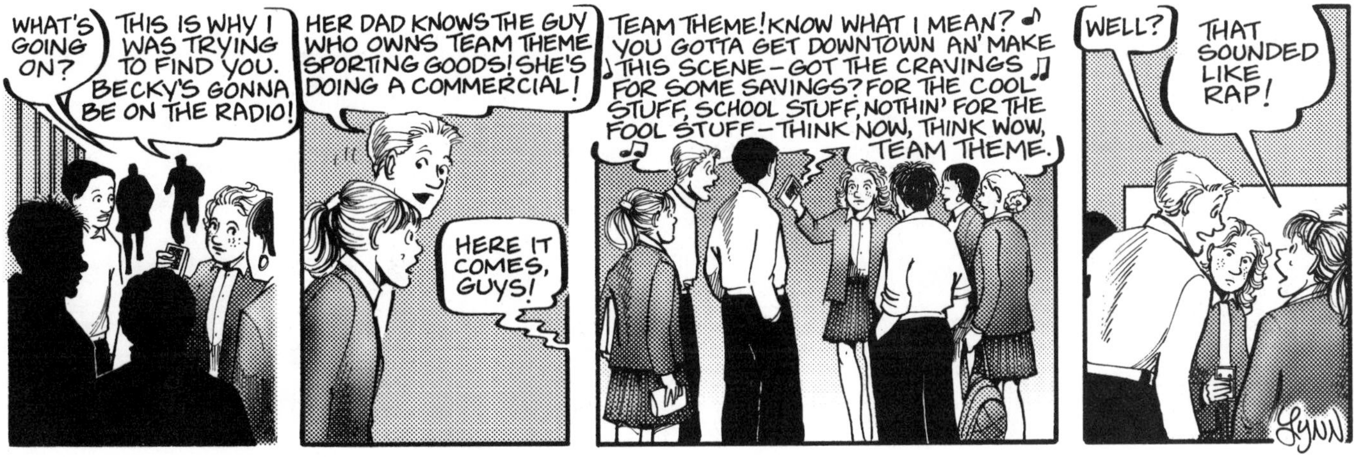
WHAT'S GOING ON?
THIS IS WHY I WAS TRYING TO FIND YOU. BECKY'S GONNA BE ON THE RADIO!
HER DAD KNOWS THE GUY WHO OWNS TEAM THEME SPORTING GOODS! SHE'S DOING A COMMERCIAL!
HERE IT COMES, GUYS!
TEAM THEME! KNOW WHAT I MEAN? YOU GOTTA GET DOWNTOWN AN' MAKE THIS SCENE – GOT THE CRAVINGS FOR SOME SAVINGS? FOR THE COOL STUFF, SCHOOL STUFF, NOTHIN' FOR THE FOOL STUFF – THINK NOW, THINK WOW, TEAM THEME.
WELL?
THAT SOUNDED LIKE RAP!
LYNN

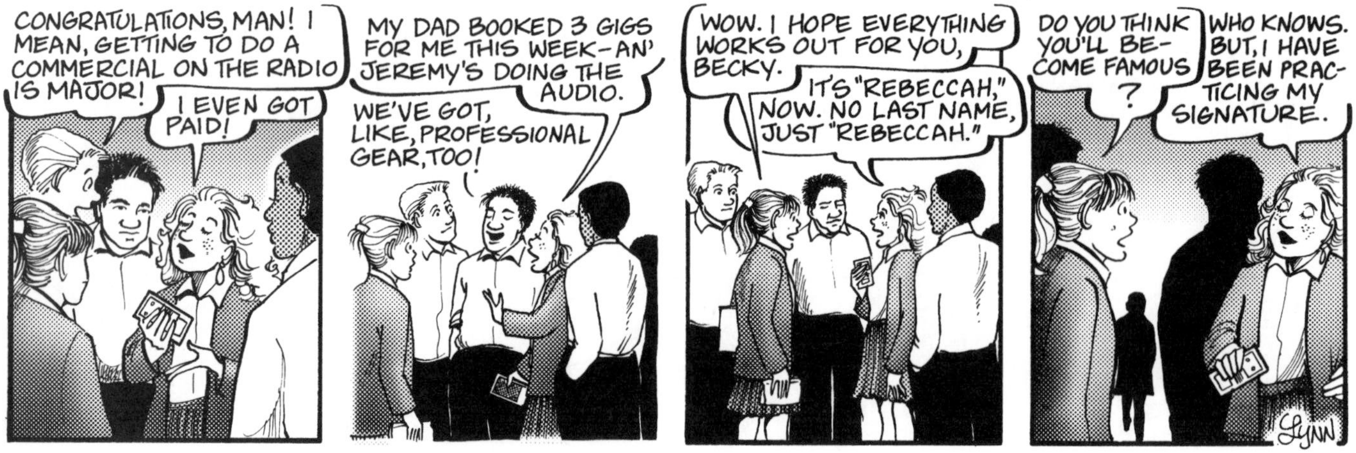
CONGRATULATIONS, MAN! I MEAN, GETTING TO DO A COMMERCIAL ON THE RADIO IS MAJOR!
I EVEN GOT PAID!
MY DAD BOOKED 3 GIGS FOR ME THIS WEEK–AN' JEREMY'S DOING THE AUDIO.
WE'VE GOT, LIKE, PROFESSIONAL GEAR, TOO!
WOW. I HOPE EVERYTHING WORKS OUT FOR YOU, BECKY.
IT'S "REBECCAH," NOW. NO LAST NAME, JUST "REBECCAH."
DO YOU THINK YOU'LL BECOME FAMOUS?
WHO KNOWS. BUT, I HAVE BEEN PRACTICING MY SIGNATURE.
LYNN

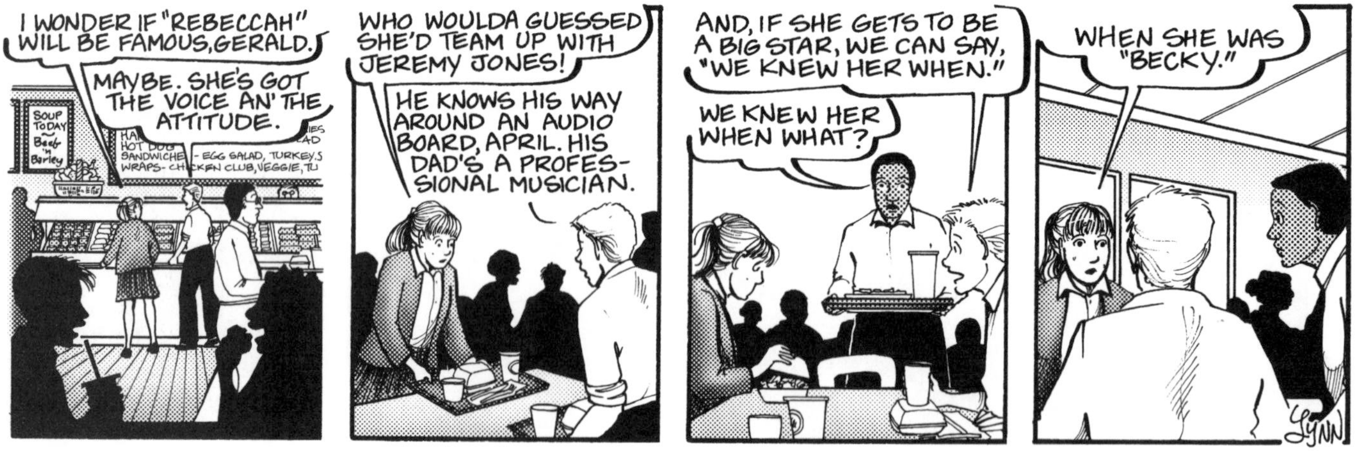
I WONDER IF "REBECCAH" WILL BE FAMOUS, GERALD.
MAYBE. SHE'S GOT THE VOICE AN' THE ATTITUDE.
SOUP TODAY Beef 'n Barley
WHO WOULDA GUESSED SHE'D TEAM UP WITH JEREMY JONES!
HE KNOWS HIS WAY AROUND AN AUDIO BOARD, APRIL. HIS DAD'S A PROFESSIONAL MUSICIAN.
AND, IF SHE GETS TO BE A BIG STAR, WE CAN SAY, "WE KNEW HER WHEN."
WE KNEW HER WHEN WHAT?
WHEN SHE WAS "BECKY."
LYNN

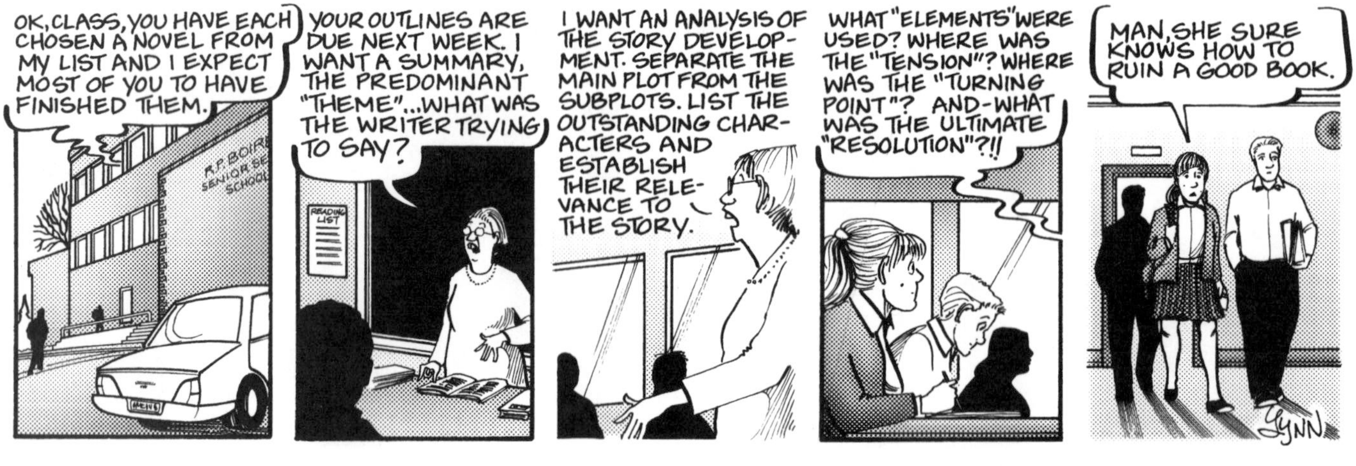
OK, CLASS, YOU HAVE EACH CHOSEN A NOVEL FROM MY LIST AND I EXPECT MOST OF YOU TO HAVE FINISHED THEM.
YOUR OUTLINES ARE DUE NEXT WEEK. I WANT A SUMMARY, THE PREDOMINANT "THEME"...WHAT WAS THE WRITER TRYING TO SAY?
I WANT AN ANALYSIS OF THE STORY DEVELOPMENT. SEPARATE THE MAIN PLOT FROM THE SUBPLOTS. LIST THE OUTSTANDING CHARACTERS AND ESTABLISH THEIR RELEVANCE TO THE STORY.
WHAT "ELEMENTS" WERE USED? WHERE WAS THE "TENSION"? WHERE WAS THE "TURNING POINT"? AND–WHAT WAS THE ULTIMATE "RESOLUTION"?!!
MAN, SHE SURE KNOWS HOW TO RUIN A GOOD BOOK.
LYNN

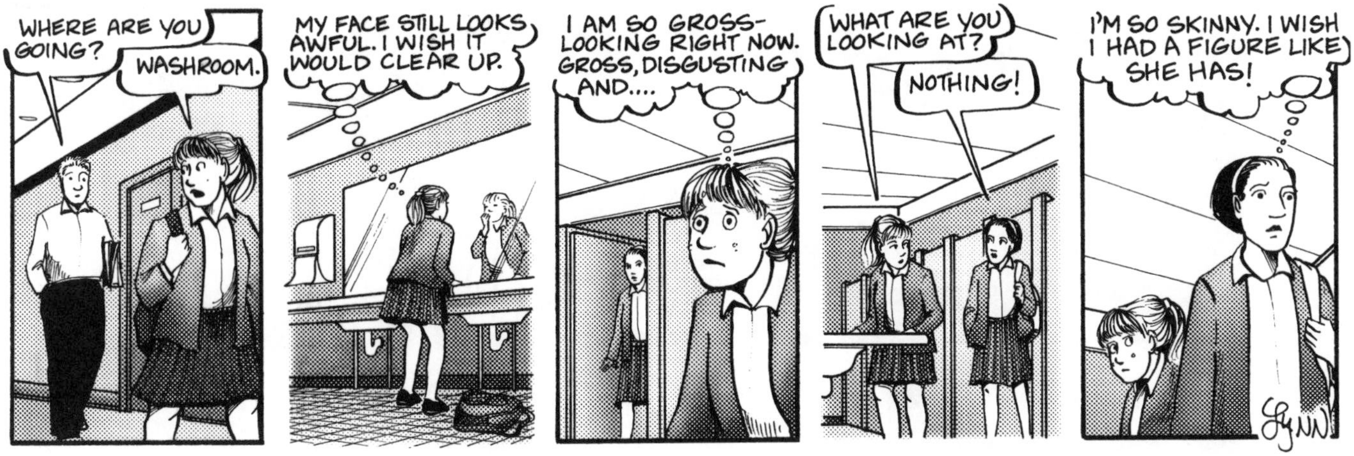
WHERE ARE YOU GOING?
WASHROOM.
MY FACE STILL LOOKS AWFUL. I WISH IT WOULD CLEAR UP.
I AM SO GROSS-LOOKING RIGHT NOW. GROSS, DISGUSTING AND....
WHAT ARE YOU LOOKING AT?
NOTHING!
I'M SO SKINNY. I WISH I HAD A FIGURE LIKE SHE HAS!
LYNN

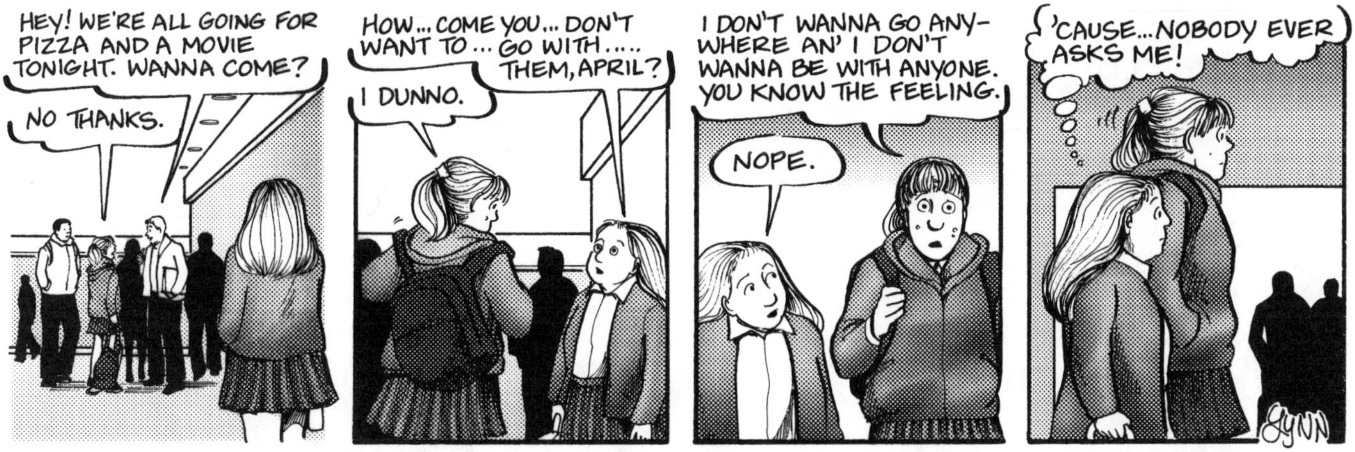
HEY! WE'RE ALL GOING FOR PIZZA AND A MOVIE TONIGHT. WANNA COME?
NO THANKS.
HOW... COME YOU... DON'T WANT TO ... GO WITH..... THEM, APRIL?
I DUNNO.
I DON'T WANNA GO ANY-WHERE AN' I DON'T WANNA BE WITH ANYONE. YOU KNOW THE FEELING.
NOPE.
'CAUSE...NOBODY EVER ASKS ME!
LYNN

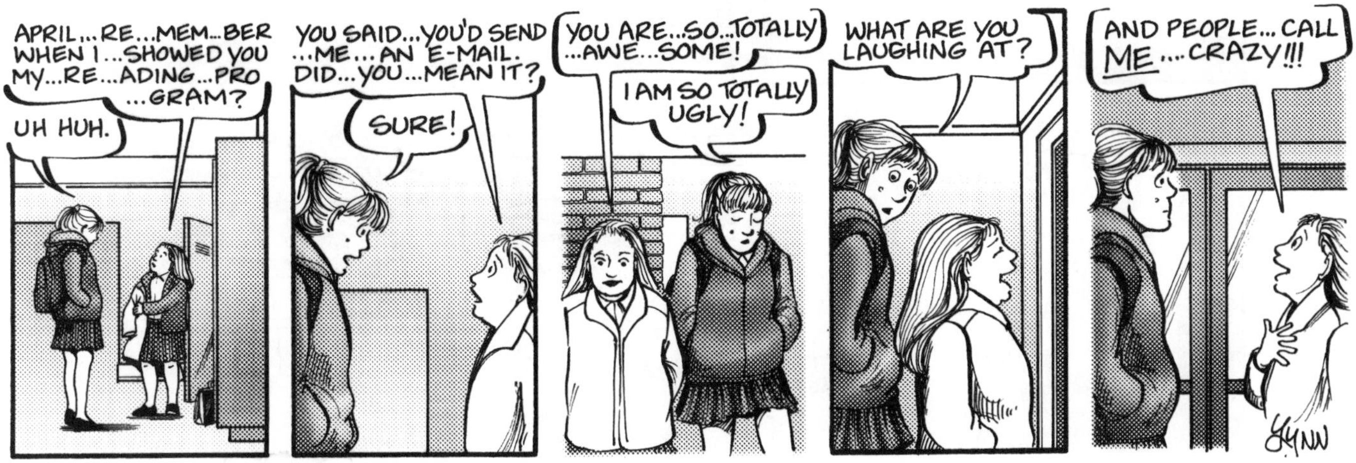
APRIL... RE... MEM... BER WHEN I... SHOWED YOU MY... RE... ADING... PRO ...GRAM?
UH HUH.
YOU SAID... YOU'D SEND ...ME... AN E-MAIL. DID... YOU... MEAN IT?
SURE!
YOU ARE... SO... TOTALLY ...AWE... SOME!
I AM SO TOTALLY UGLY!
WHAT ARE YOU LAUGHING AT?
AND PEOPLE... CALL ME.... CRAZY!!!
LYNN

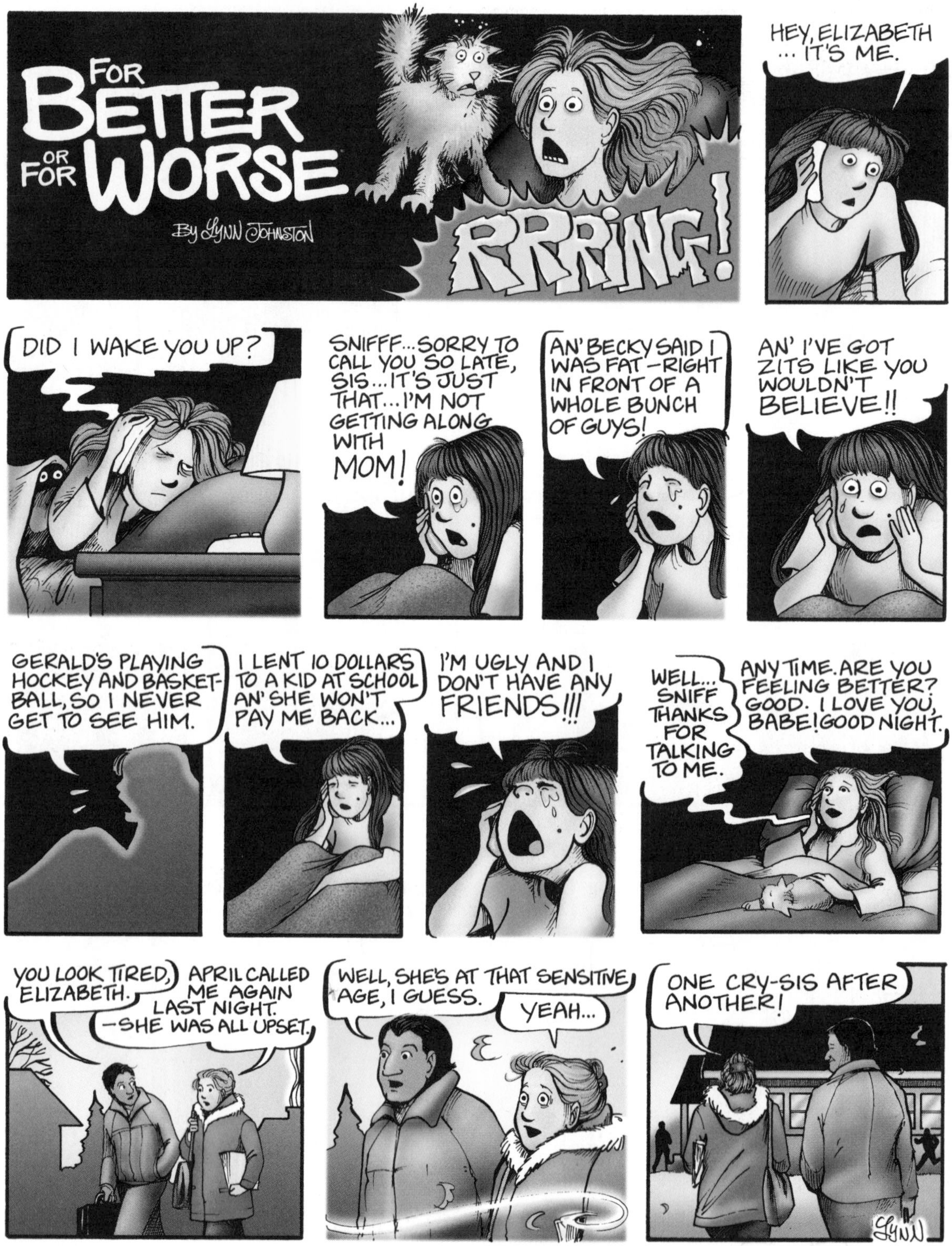
FOR BETTER OR FOR WORSE
BY LYNN JOHNSTON
RRRING!
HEY, ELIZABETH ... IT'S ME.
DID I WAKE YOU UP?
SNIFFF...SORRY TO CALL YOU SO LATE, SIS...IT'S JUST THAT...I'M NOT GETTING ALONG WITH MOM!
AN' BECKY SAID I WAS FAT—RIGHT IN FRONT OF A WHOLE BUNCH OF GUYS!
AN' I'VE GOT ZITS LIKE YOU WOULDN'T BELIEVE!!
GERALD'S PLAYING HOCKEY AND BASKET-BALL, SO I NEVER GET TO SEE HIM.
I LENT 10 DOLLARS TO A KID AT SCHOOL AN' SHE WON'T PAY ME BACK...
I'M UGLY AND I DON'T HAVE ANY FRIENDS!!!
WELL... SNIFF THANKS FOR TALKING TO ME.
ANY TIME. ARE YOU FEELING BETTER? GOOD. I LOVE YOU, BABE! GOOD NIGHT.
YOU LOOK TIRED, ELIZABETH.
APRIL CALLED ME AGAIN LAST NIGHT. —SHE WAS ALL UPSET.
WELL, SHE'S AT THAT SENSITIVE AGE, I GUESS.
YEAH...
ONE CRY-SIS AFTER ANOTHER!
LYNN

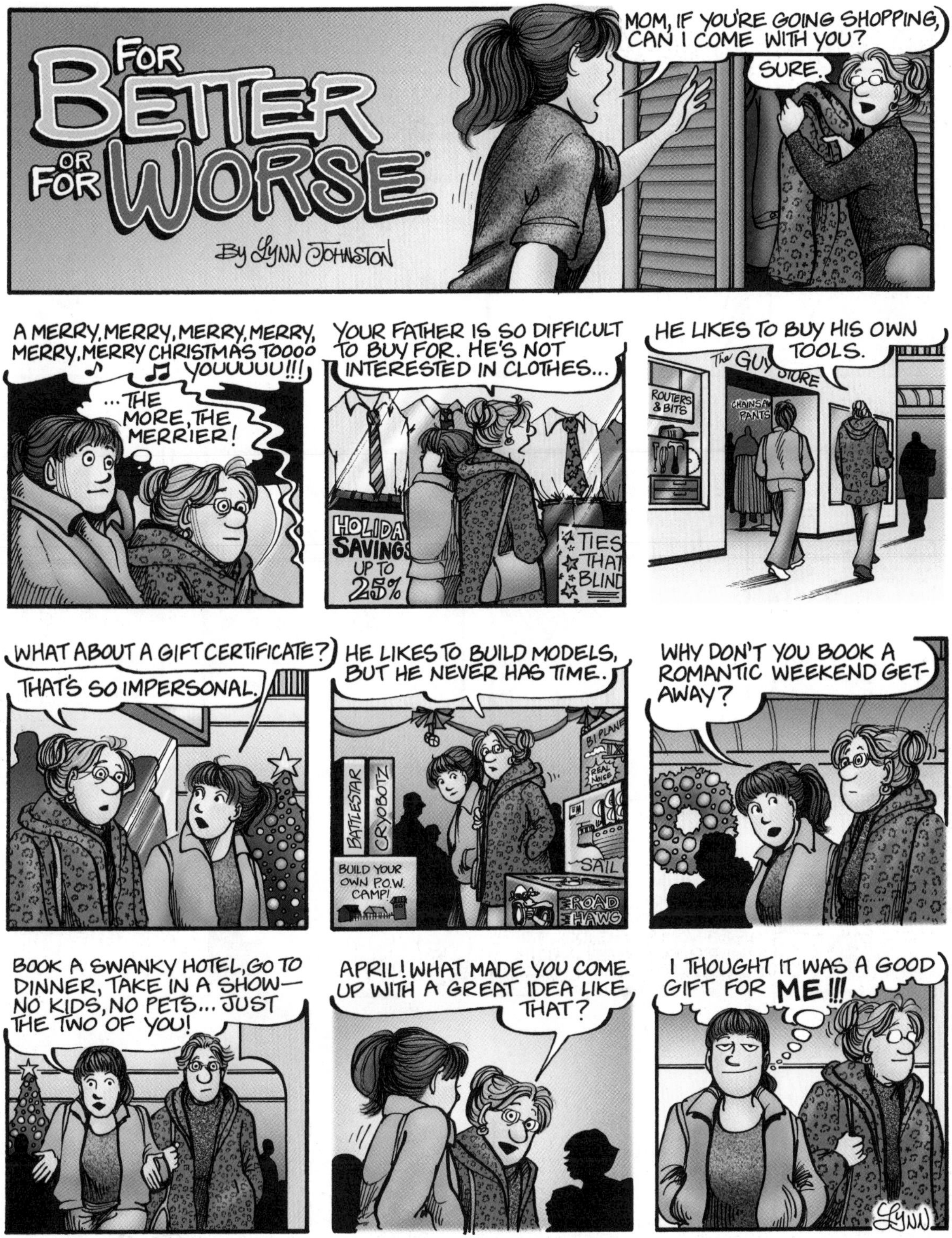
FOR BETTER OR FOR WORSE
BY LYNN JOHNSTON
MOM, IF YOU'RE GOING SHOPPING, CAN I COME WITH YOU?
SURE.
A MERRY, MERRY, MERRY, MERRY, MERRY, MERRY CHRISTMAS TOOOO YOUUUUU!!!
...THE MORE, THE MERRIER!
YOUR FATHER IS SO DIFFICULT TO BUY FOR. HE'S NOT INTERESTED IN CLOTHES...
HOLIDA SAVINGS UP TO 25%
TIES THAT BLIND
HE LIKES TO BUY HIS OWN TOOLS.
The GUY STORE
ROUTERS & BITS
WHAT ABOUT A GIFT CERTIFICATE?
THAT'S SO IMPERSONAL.
HE LIKES TO BUILD MODELS, BUT HE NEVER HAS TIME.
BATTLESTAR
CRYOBOTZ
BUILD YOUR OWN P.O.W. CAMP!
BI PLANE
REAL NOISE
SAIL
ROAD HAWG
WHY DON'T YOU BOOK A ROMANTIC WEEKEND GET-AWAY?
BOOK A SWANKY HOTEL, GO TO DINNER, TAKE IN A SHOW— NO KIDS, NO PETS... JUST THE TWO OF YOU!
APRIL! WHAT MADE YOU COME UP WITH A GREAT IDEA LIKE THAT?
I THOUGHT IT WAS A GOOD GIFT FOR ME!!!
LYNN

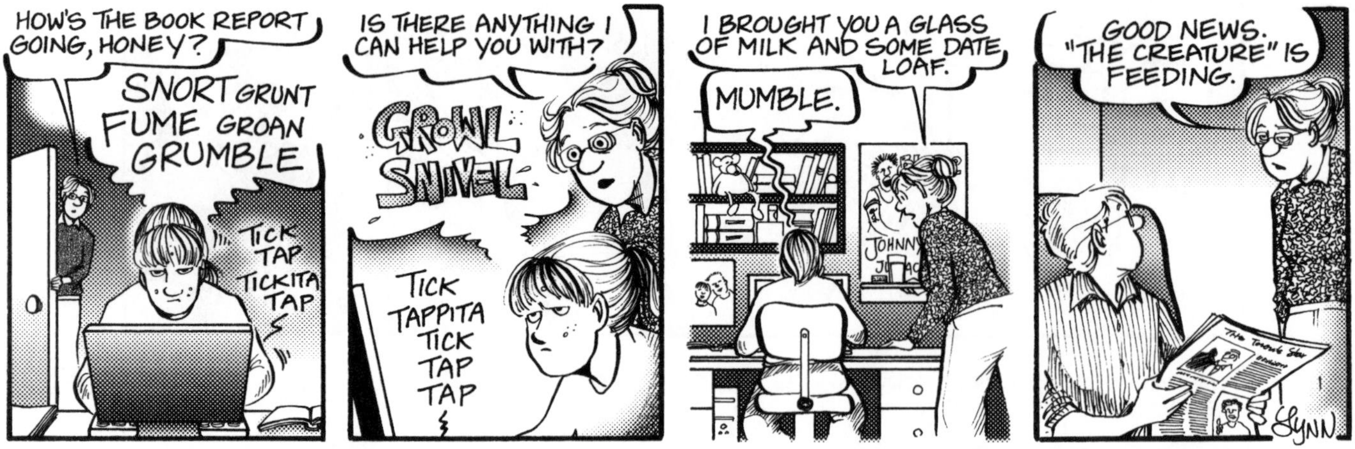
HOW'S THE BOOK REPORT GOING, HONEY?
SNORT GRUNT FUME GROAN GRUMBLE
TICK TAP TICKITA TAP
IS THERE ANYTHING I CAN HELP YOU WITH?
GROWL SNIVEL
TICK TAPPITA TICK TAP TAP
I BROUGHT YOU A GLASS OF MILK AND SOME DATE LOAF.
MUMBLE.
GOOD NEWS. "THE CREATURE" IS FEEDING.
LYNN

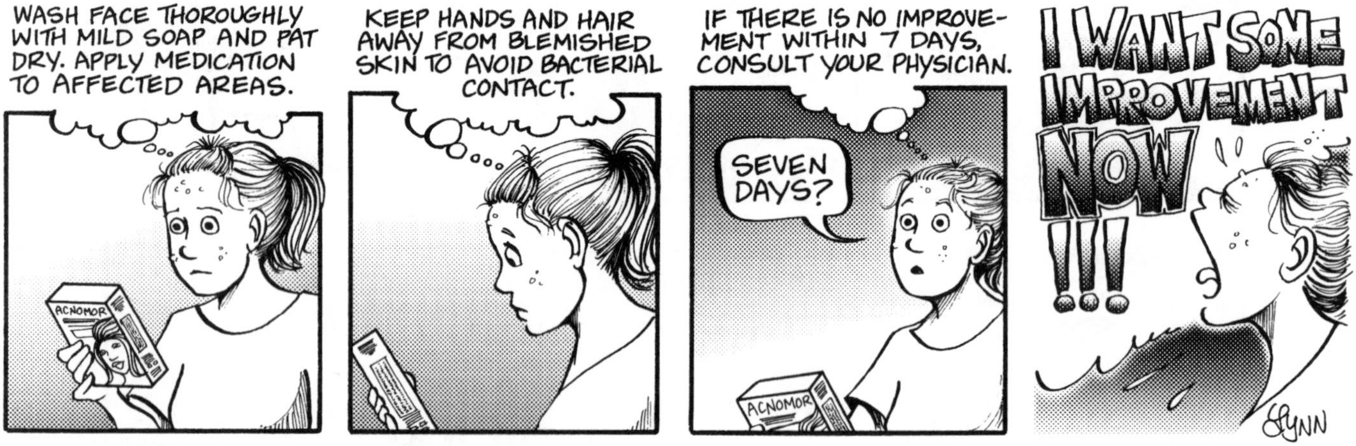
WASH FACE THOROUGHLY WITH MILD SOAP AND PAT DRY. APPLY MEDICATION TO AFFECTED AREAS.
ACNOMOR
KEEP HANDS AND HAIR AWAY FROM BLEMISHED SKIN TO AVOID BACTERIAL CONTACT.
IF THERE IS NO IMPROVEMENT WITHIN 7 DAYS, CONSULT YOUR PHYSICIAN.
SEVEN DAYS?
ACNOMOR
I WANT SOME IMPROVEMENT NOW!!!
LYNN

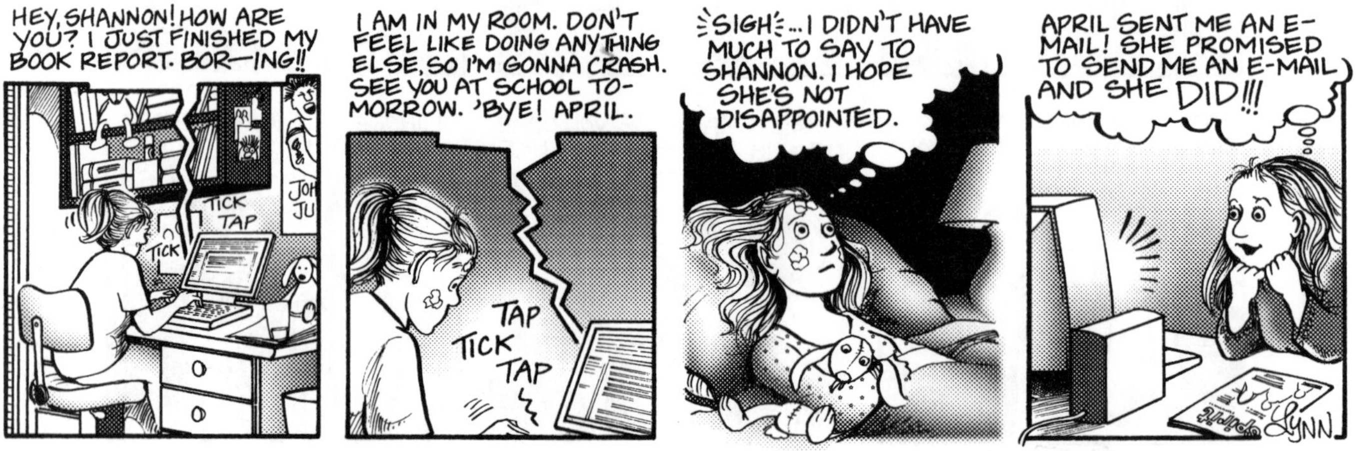
HEY, SHANNON! HOW ARE YOU? I JUST FINISHED MY BOOK REPORT. BOR—ING!!
TICK TAP
TICK
I AM IN MY ROOM. DON'T FEEL LIKE DOING ANYTHING ELSE, SO I'M GONNA CRASH. SEE YOU AT SCHOOL TOMORROW. 'BYE! APRIL.
TAP TICK TAP
SIGH ...I DIDN'T HAVE MUCH TO SAY TO SHANNON. I HOPE SHE'S NOT DISAPPOINTED.
APRIL SENT ME AN E-MAIL! SHE PROMISED TO SEND ME AN E-MAIL AND SHE DID!!!
LYNN

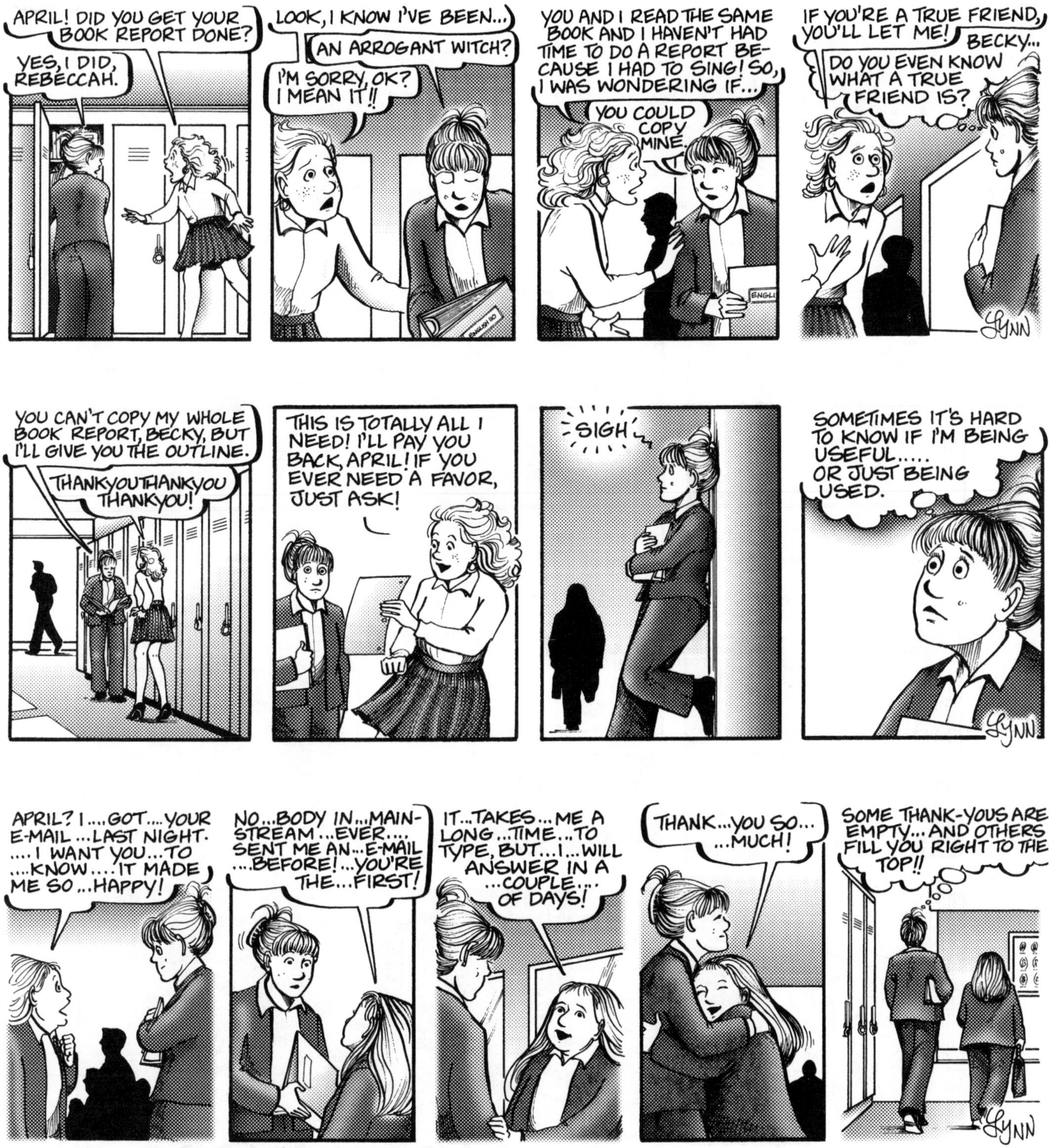
APRIL! DID YOU GET YOUR BOOK REPORT DONE?
YES, I DID, REBECCAH.
LOOK, I KNOW I'VE BEEN...
AN ARROGANT WITCH?
I'M SORRY, OK? I MEAN IT!!
YOU AND I READ THE SAME BOOK AND I HAVEN'T HAD TIME TO DO A REPORT BECAUSE I HAD TO SING! SO, I WAS WONDERING IF...
YOU COULD COPY MINE.
IF YOU'RE A TRUE FRIEND, YOU'LL LET ME!
BECKY...
DO YOU EVEN KNOW WHAT A TRUE FRIEND IS?
LYNN
YOU CAN'T COPY MY WHOLE BOOK REPORT, BECKY, BUT I'LL GIVE YOU THE OUTLINE.
THANKYOUTHANKYOU THANKYOU!
THIS IS TOTALLY ALL I NEED! I'LL PAY YOU BACK, APRIL! IF YOU EVER NEED A FAVOR, JUST ASK!
SIGH
SOMETIMES IT'S HARD TO KNOW IF I'M BEING USEFUL..... OR JUST BEING USED.
LYNN
APRIL? I....GOT....YOUR E-MAIL ...LAST NIGHT. ....I WANT YOU...TO ....KNOW....IT MADE ME SO...HAPPY!
NO...BODY IN...MAINSTREAM...EVER.... SENT ME AN...E-MAIL ....BEFORE!...YOU'RE THE...FIRST!
IT...TAKES...ME A LONG...TIME...TO TYPE, BUT...I...WILL ANSWER IN A ...COUPLE.... OF DAYS!
THANK...YOU SO... ...MUCH!
SOME THANK-YOUS ARE EMPTY... AND OTHERS FILL YOU RIGHT TO THE TOP!!
LYNN

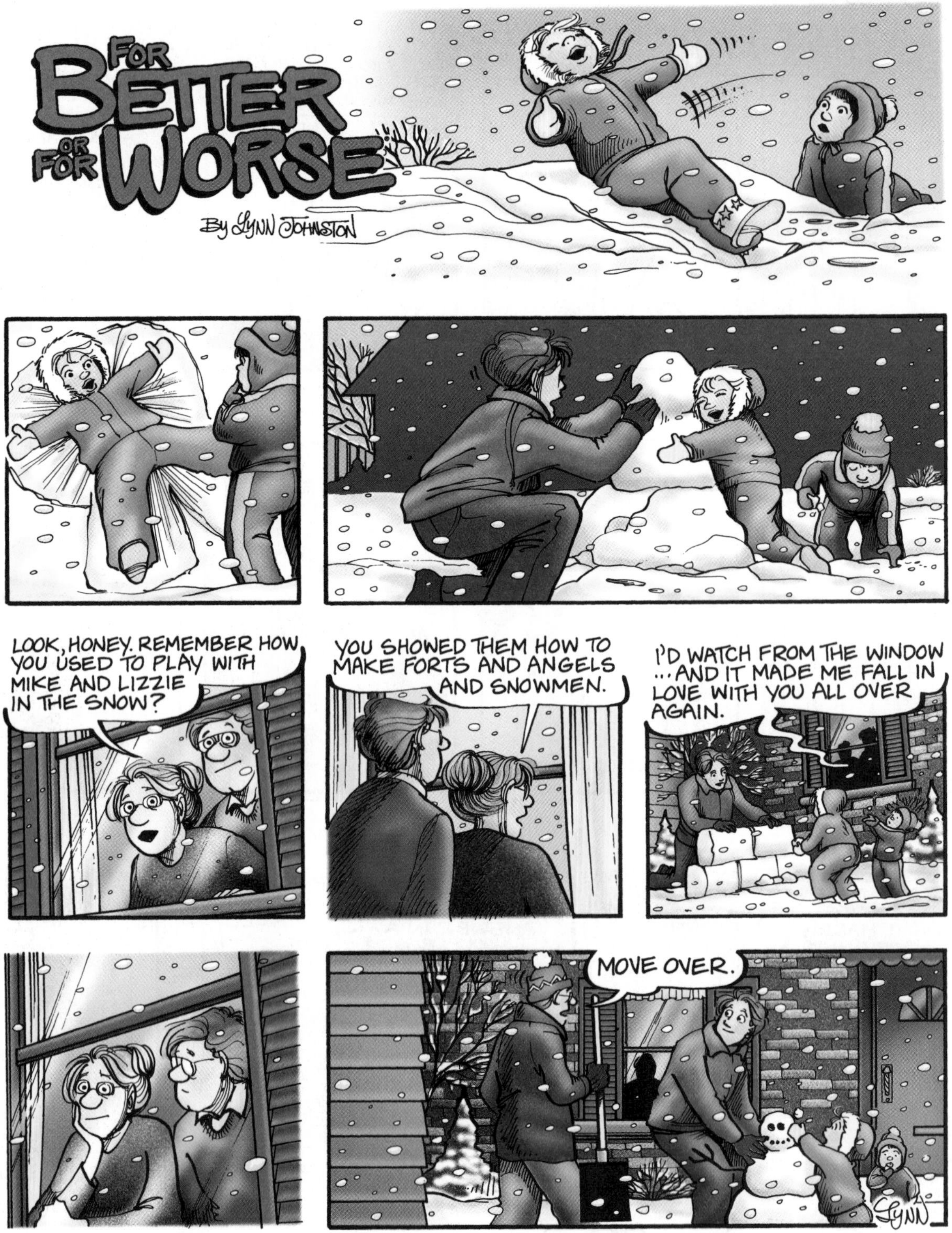
FOR BETTER OR FOR WORSE
BY LYNN JOHNSTON
LOOK, HONEY. REMEMBER HOW YOU USED TO PLAY WITH MIKE AND LIZZIE IN THE SNOW?
YOU SHOWED THEM HOW TO MAKE FORTS AND ANGELS AND SNOWMEN.
I'D WATCH FROM THE WINDOW ...AND IT MADE ME FALL IN LOVE WITH YOU ALL OVER AGAIN.
MOVE OVER.
LYNN

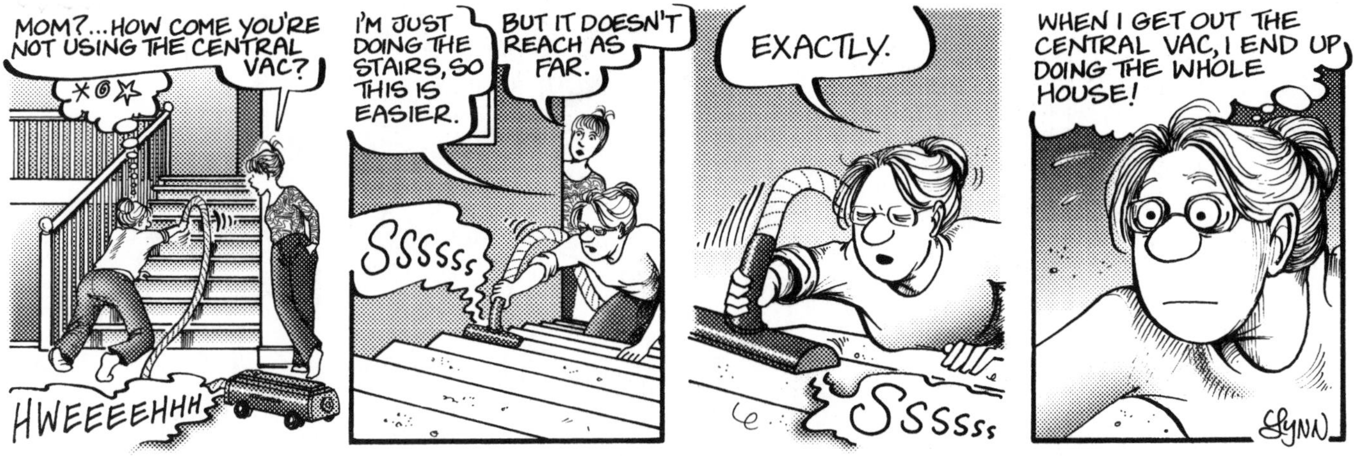
MOM?...HOW COME YOU'RE NOT USING THE CENTRAL VAC?
*@☆
HWEEEEHHH
I'M JUST DOING THE STAIRS, SO THIS IS EASIER.
BUT IT DOESN'T REACH AS FAR.
SSSSSS
EXACTLY.
SSSSSS
WHEN I GET OUT THE CENTRAL VAC, I END UP DOING THE WHOLE HOUSE!
LYNN

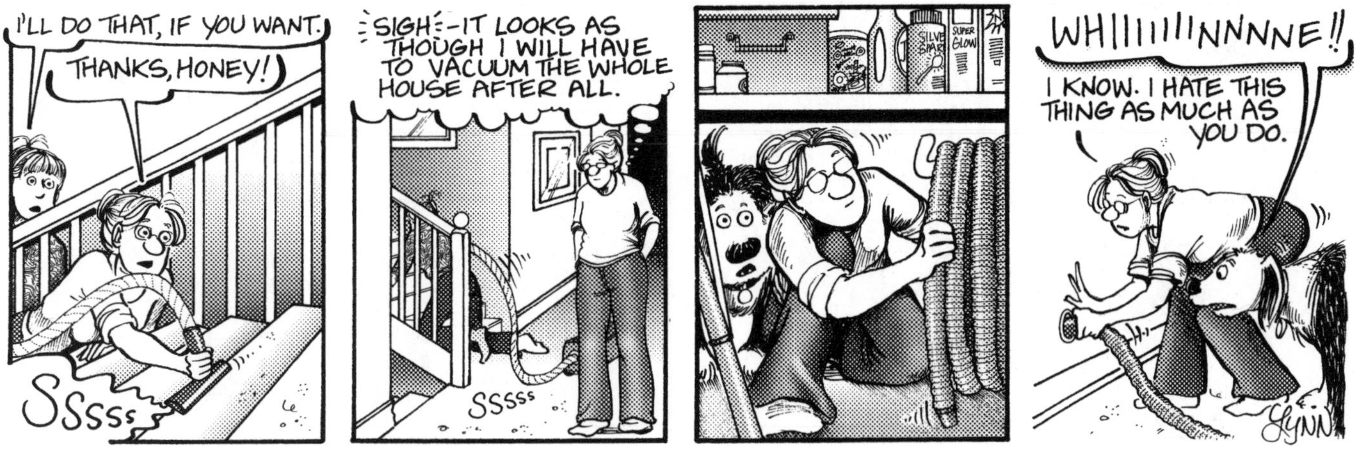
I'LL DO THAT, IF YOU WANT.
THANKS, HONEY!
SSSSS
SIGH -IT LOOKS AS THOUGH I WILL HAVE TO VACUUM THE WHOLE HOUSE AFTER ALL.
SSSSS
SUPER GLOW
WHIIIIIIINNNNE!!
I KNOW. I HATE THIS THING AS MUCH AS YOU DO.
LYNN

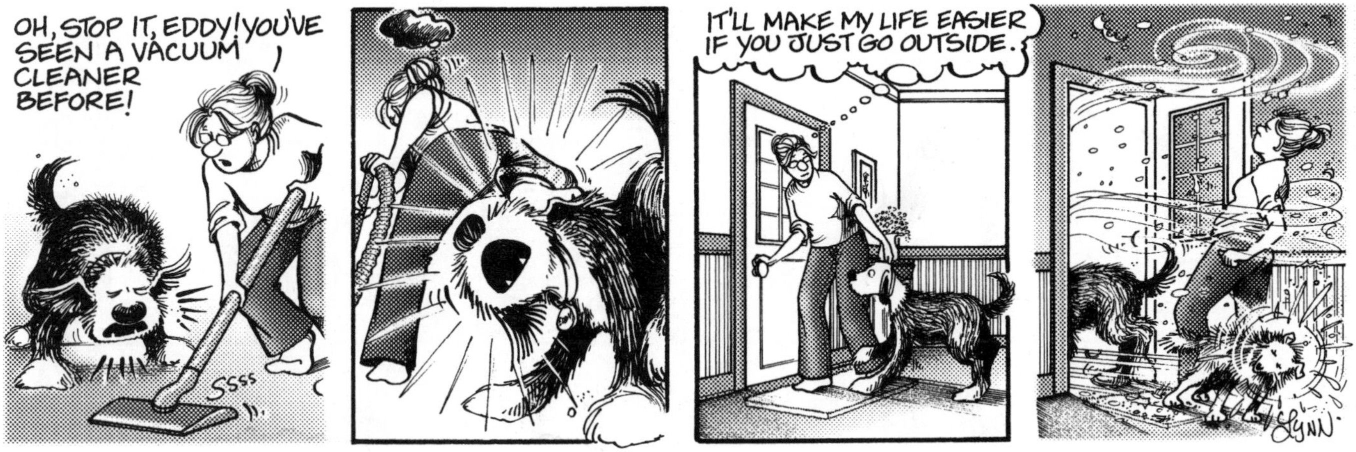
OH, STOP IT, EDDY! YOU'VE SEEN A VACUUM CLEANER BEFORE!
SSSS
IT'LL MAKE MY LIFE EASIER IF YOU JUST GO OUTSIDE.
LYNN

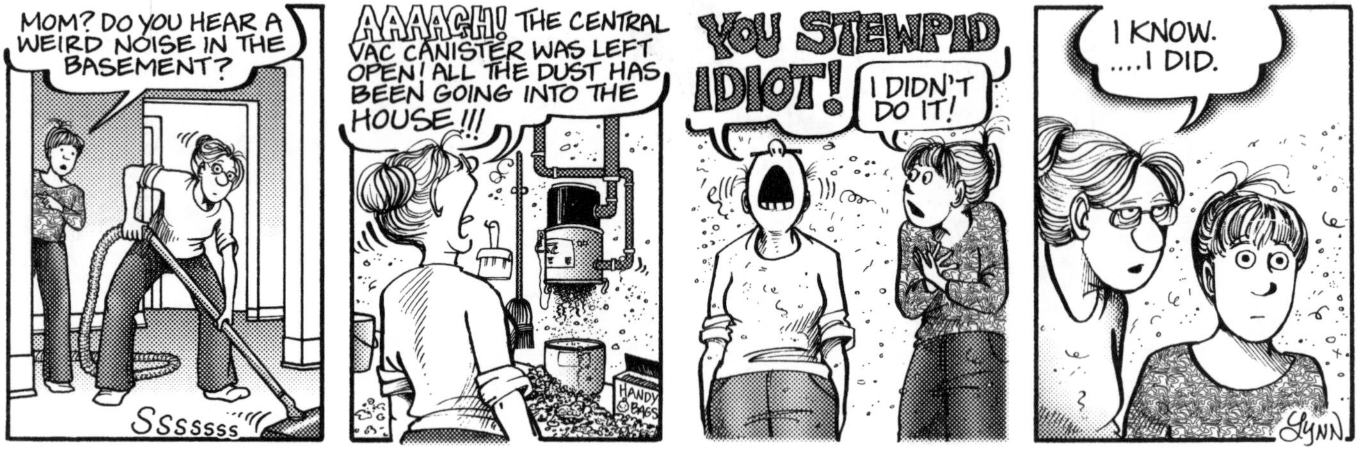
MOM? DO YOU HEAR A WEIRD NOISE IN THE BASEMENT?
SSSSSSS
AAAACH! THE CENTRAL VAC CANISTER WAS LEFT OPEN! ALL THE DUST HAS BEEN GOING INTO THE HOUSE!!!
HANDY BAGS
YOU STEWPID IDIOT!
I DIDN'T DO IT!
I KNOW. ....I DID.
LYNN

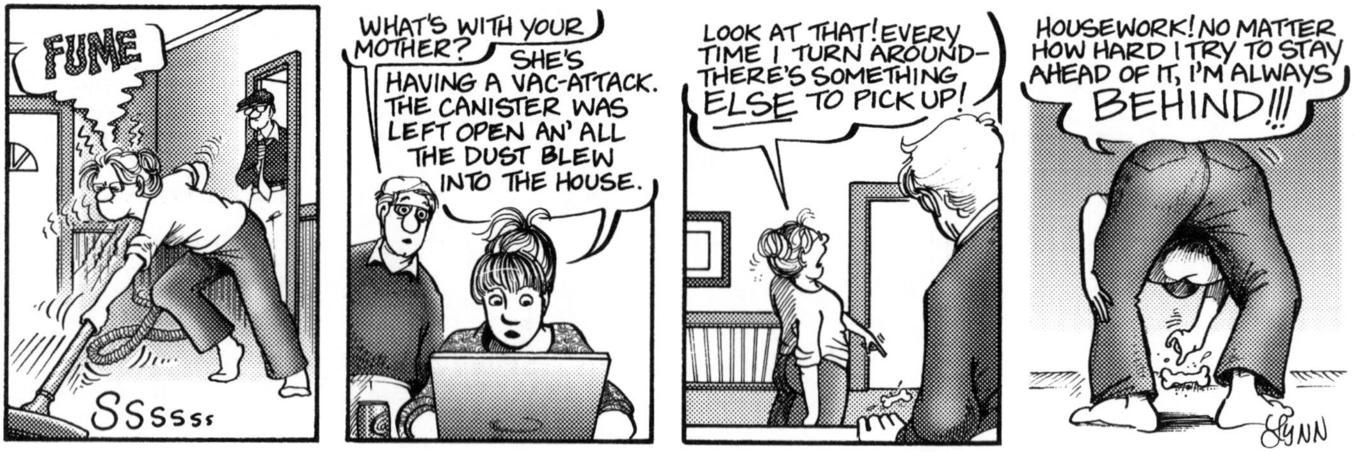
FUME
SSSSSS
WHAT'S WITH YOUR MOTHER?
SHE'S HAVING A VAC-ATTACK. THE CANISTER WAS LEFT OPEN AN' ALL THE DUST BLEW INTO THE HOUSE.
LOOK AT THAT! EVERY TIME I TURN AROUND- THERE'S SOMETHING ELSE TO PICK UP!
HOUSEWORK! NO MATTER HOW HARD I TRY TO STAY AHEAD OF IT, I'M ALWAYS BEHIND!!!
LYNN

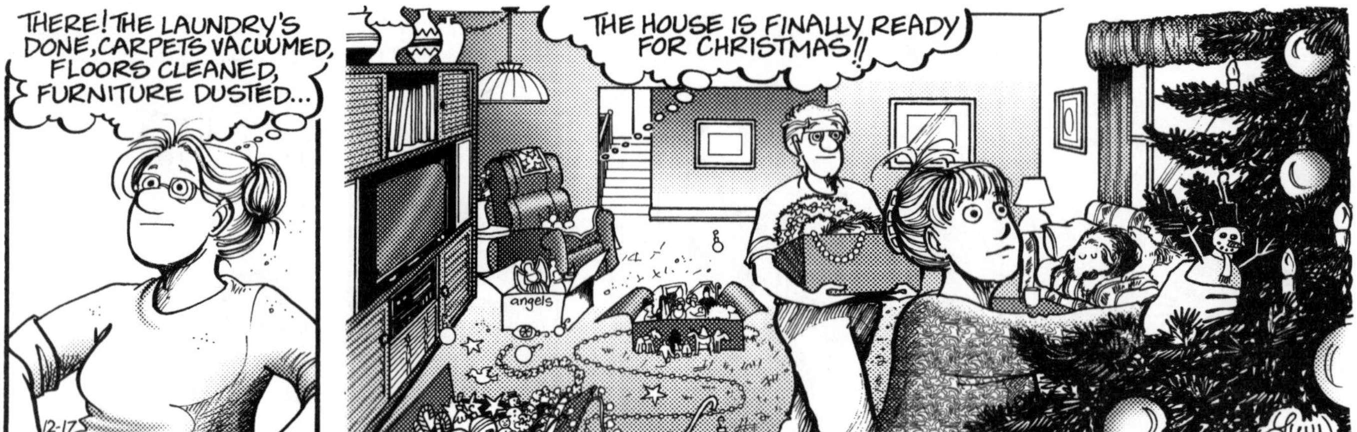
THERE! THE LAUNDRY'S DONE, CARPETS VACUUMED, FLOORS CLEANED, FURNITURE DUSTED...
12-17
THE HOUSE IS FINALLY READY FOR CHRISTMAS!!
angels
LYNN

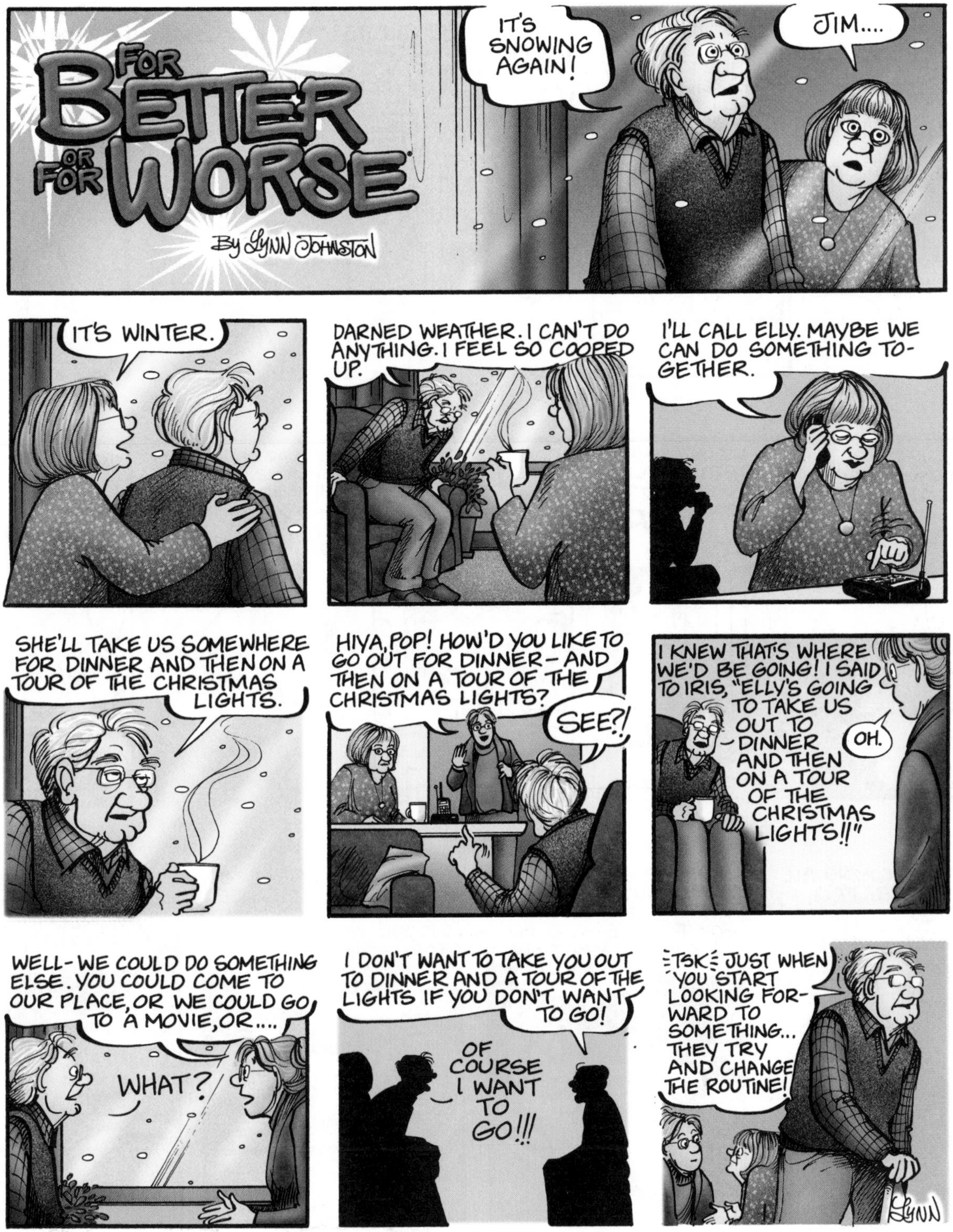
For Better or For Worse
By Lynn Johnston
IT'S SNOWING AGAIN!
JIM....
IT'S WINTER.
DARNED WEATHER. I CAN'T DO ANYTHING. I FEEL SO COOPED UP.
I'LL CALL ELLY. MAYBE WE CAN DO SOMETHING TOGETHER.
SHE'LL TAKE US SOMEWHERE FOR DINNER AND THEN ON A TOUR OF THE CHRISTMAS LIGHTS.
HIYA, POP! HOW'D YOU LIKE TO GO OUT FOR DINNER—AND THEN ON A TOUR OF THE CHRISTMAS LIGHTS?
SEE?!
I KNEW THAT'S WHERE WE'D BE GOING! I SAID TO IRIS, "ELLY'S GOING TO TAKE US OUT TO DINNER AND THEN ON A TOUR OF THE CHRISTMAS LIGHTS!!"
OH.
WELL- WE COULD DO SOMETHING ELSE. YOU COULD COME TO OUR PLACE, OR WE COULD GO TO A MOVIE, OR....
WHAT?
I DON'T WANT TO TAKE YOU OUT TO DINNER AND A TOUR OF THE LIGHTS IF YOU DON'T WANT TO GO!
OF COURSE I WANT TO GO!!!
TSK JUST WHEN YOU START LOOKING FORWARD TO SOMETHING... THEY TRY AND CHANGE THE ROUTINE!
LYNN

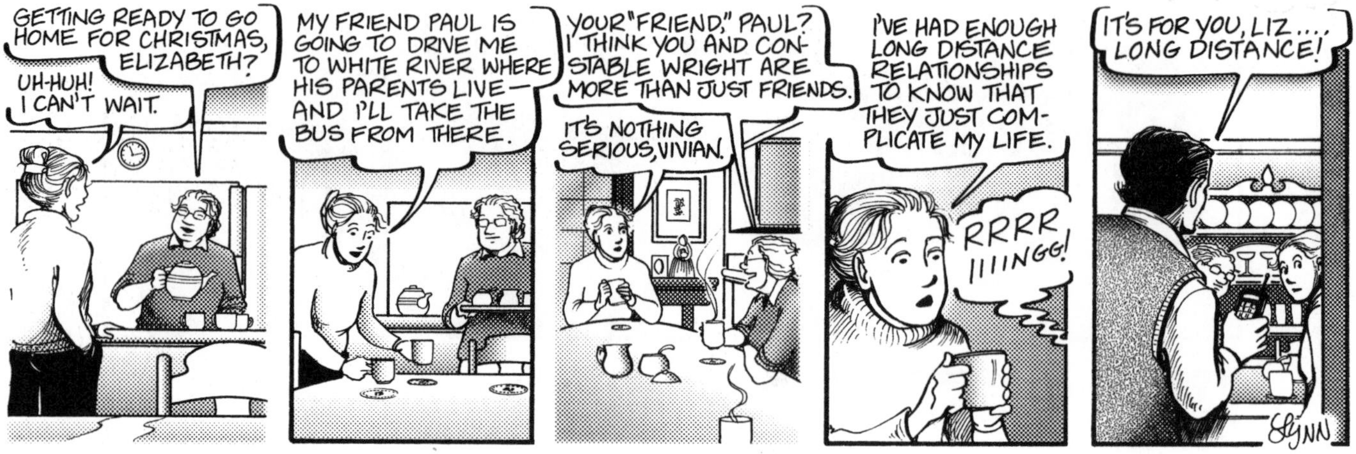
GETTING READY TO GO HOME FOR CHRISTMAS, ELIZABETH?
UH-HUH! I CAN'T WAIT.
MY FRIEND PAUL IS GOING TO DRIVE ME TO WHITE RIVER WHERE HIS PARENTS LIVE— AND I'LL TAKE THE BUS FROM THERE.
YOUR "FRIEND," PAUL? I THINK YOU AND CONSTABLE WRIGHT ARE MORE THAN JUST FRIENDS.
IT'S NOTHING SERIOUS, VIVIAN.
I'VE HAD ENOUGH LONG DISTANCE RELATIONSHIPS TO KNOW THAT THEY JUST COMPLICATE MY LIFE.
RRRR IIIINGG!
IT'S FOR YOU, LIZ...., LONG DISTANCE!
LYNN

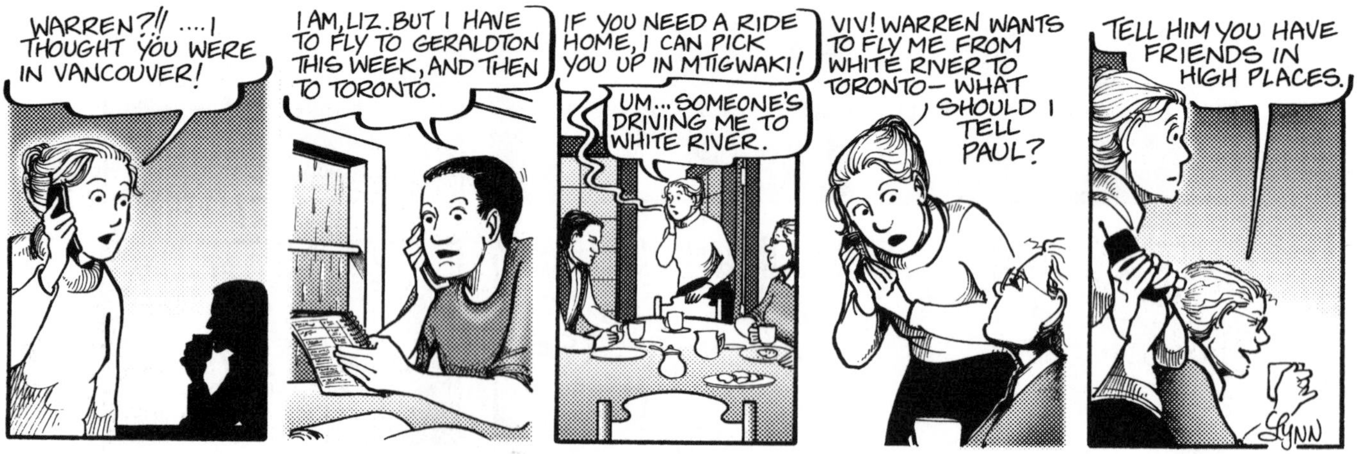
WARREN?!! ....I THOUGHT YOU WERE IN VANCOUVER!
I AM, LIZ. BUT I HAVE TO FLY TO GERALDTON THIS WEEK, AND THEN TO TORONTO.
IF YOU NEED A RIDE HOME, I CAN PICK YOU UP IN MTIGWAKI!
UM... SOMEONE'S DRIVING ME TO WHITE RIVER.
VIV! WARREN WANTS TO FLY ME FROM WHITE RIVER TO TORONTO— WHAT SHOULD I TELL PAUL?
TELL HIM YOU HAVE FRIENDS IN HIGH PLACES.
LYNN

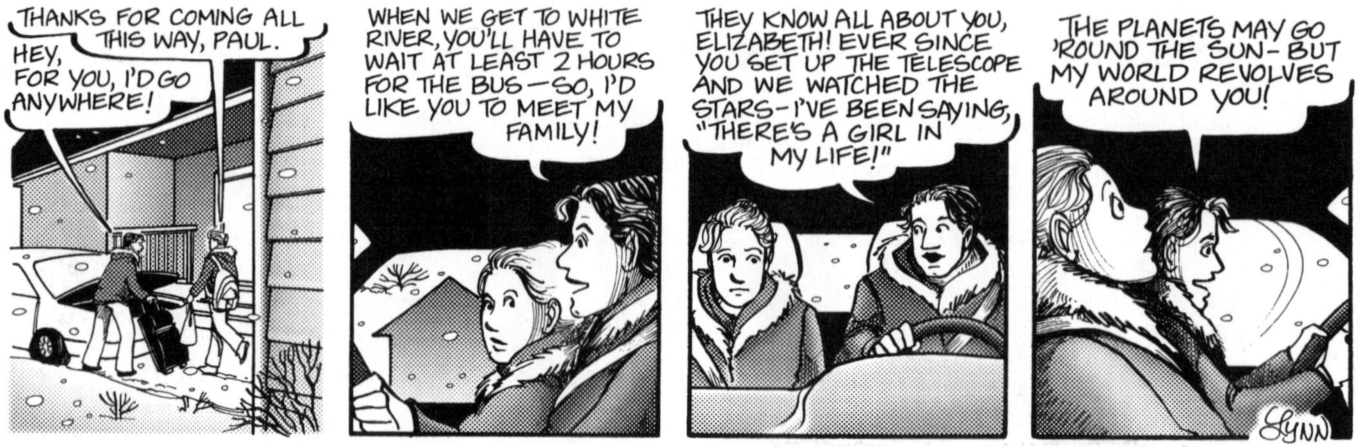
THANKS FOR COMING ALL THIS WAY, PAUL.
HEY, FOR YOU, I'D GO ANYWHERE!
WHEN WE GET TO WHITE RIVER, YOU'LL HAVE TO WAIT AT LEAST 2 HOURS FOR THE BUS—SO, I'D LIKE YOU TO MEET MY FAMILY!
THEY KNOW ALL ABOUT YOU, ELIZABETH! EVER SINCE YOU SET UP THE TELESCOPE AND WE WATCHED THE STARS- I'VE BEEN SAYING, "THERE'S A GIRL IN MY LIFE!"
THE PLANETS MAY GO 'ROUND THE SUN- BUT MY WORLD REVOLVES AROUND YOU!
LYNN

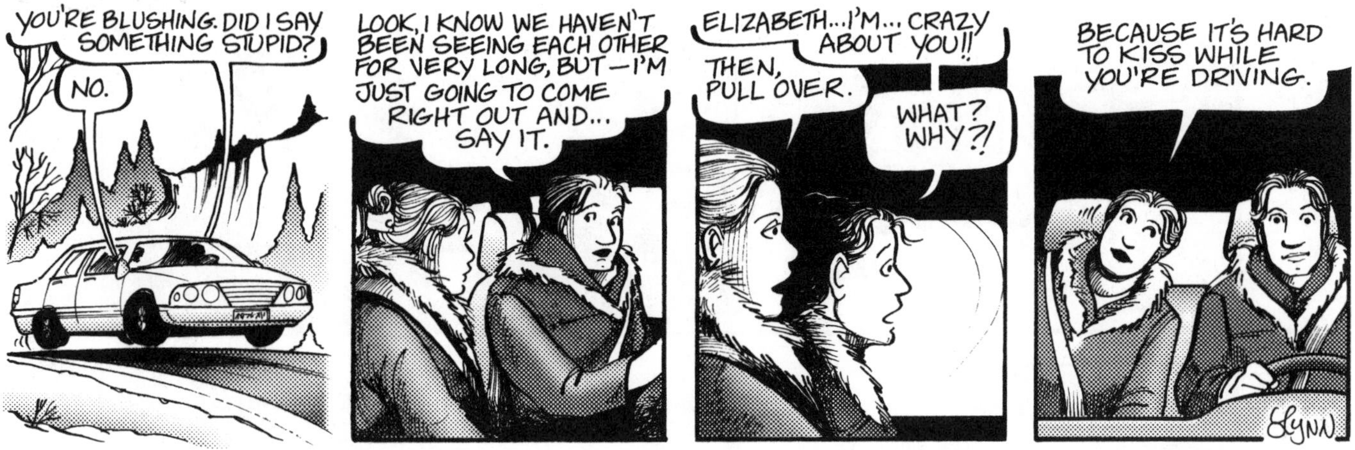
YOU'RE BLUSHING. DID I SAY SOMETHING STUPID?
NO.
LOOK, I KNOW WE HAVEN'T BEEN SEEING EACH OTHER FOR VERY LONG, BUT—I'M JUST GOING TO COME RIGHT OUT AND... SAY IT.
ELIZABETH...I'M... CRAZY ABOUT YOU!!
THEN, PULL OVER.
WHAT? WHY?!
BECAUSE IT'S HARD TO KISS WHILE YOU'RE DRIVING.

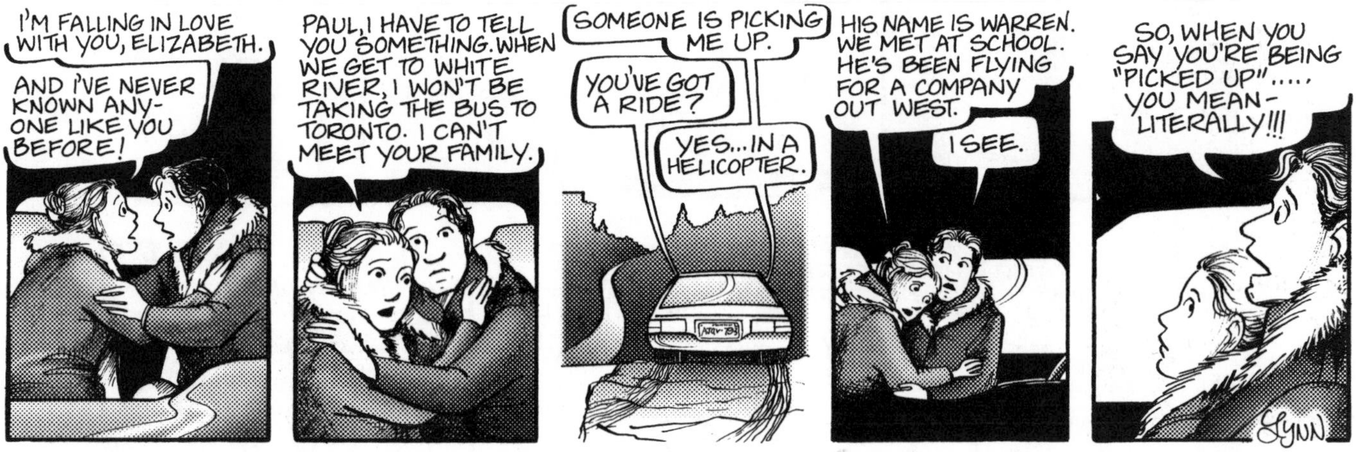
I'M FALLING IN LOVE WITH YOU, ELIZABETH.
AND I'VE NEVER KNOWN ANYONE LIKE YOU BEFORE!
PAUL, I HAVE TO TELL YOU SOMETHING. WHEN WE GET TO WHITE RIVER, I WON'T BE TAKING THE BUS TO TORONTO. I CAN'T MEET YOUR FAMILY.
SOMEONE IS PICKING ME UP.
YOU'VE GOT A RIDE?
YES...IN A HELICOPTER.
HIS NAME IS WARREN. WE MET AT SCHOOL. HE'S BEEN FLYING FOR A COMPANY OUT WEST.
I SEE.
SO, WHEN YOU SAY YOU'RE BEING "PICKED UP"..... YOU MEAN-LITERALLY!!!

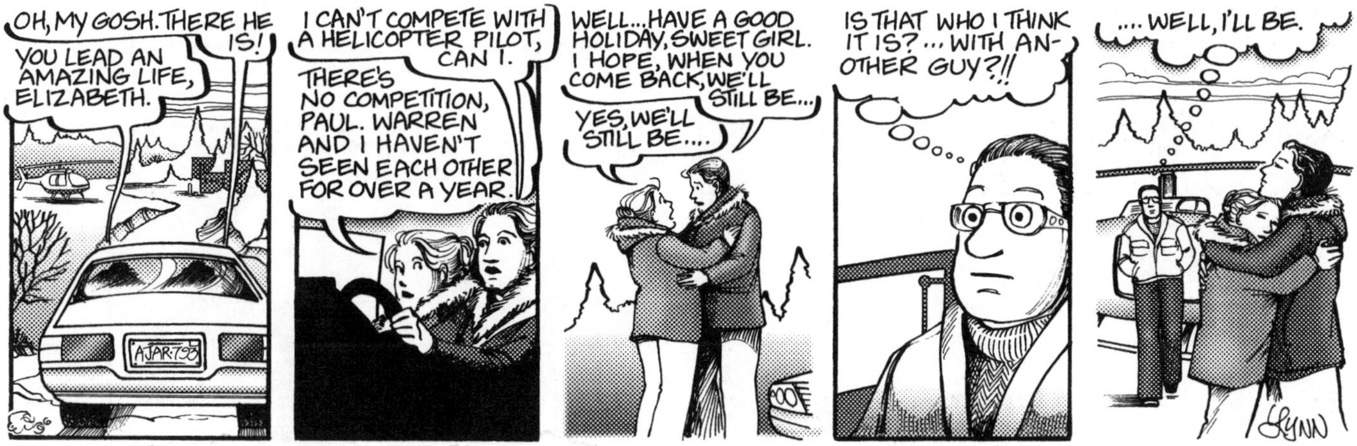
OH, MY GOSH. THERE HE IS!
YOU LEAD AN AMAZING LIFE, ELIZABETH.
I CAN'T COMPETE WITH A HELICOPTER PILOT, CAN I.
THERE'S NO COMPETITION, PAUL. WARREN AND I HAVEN'T SEEN EACH OTHER FOR OVER A YEAR.
WELL...HAVE A GOOD HOLIDAY, SWEET GIRL. I HOPE, WHEN YOU COME BACK, WE'LL STILL BE...
YES, WE'LL STILL BE....
IS THAT WHO I THINK IT IS?...WITH ANOTHER GUY?!!
....WELL, I'LL BE.

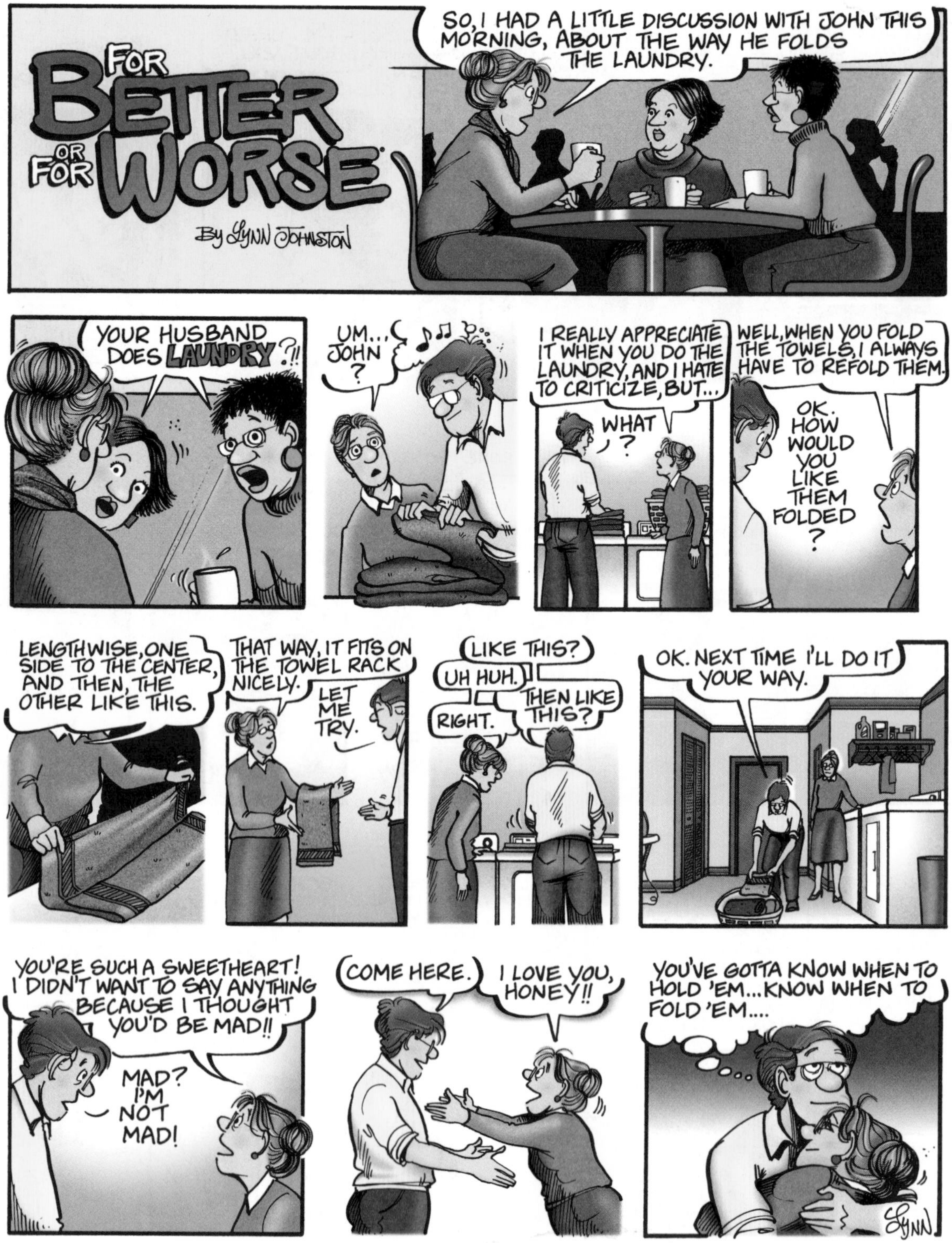
FOR BETTER OR FOR WORSE
BY LYNN JOHNSTON
SO, I HAD A LITTLE DISCUSSION WITH JOHN THIS MORNING, ABOUT THE WAY HE FOLDS THE LAUNDRY.
YOUR HUSBAND DOES LAUNDRY?!!
UM... JOHN?
I REALLY APPRECIATE IT WHEN YOU DO THE LAUNDRY, AND I HATE TO CRITICIZE, BUT...
WHAT?
WELL, WHEN YOU FOLD THE TOWELS, I ALWAYS HAVE TO REFOLD THEM.
OK. HOW WOULD YOU LIKE THEM FOLDED?
LENGTHWISE, ONE SIDE TO THE CENTER, AND THEN, THE OTHER LIKE THIS.
THAT WAY, IT FITS ON THE TOWEL RACK NICELY.
LET ME TRY.
LIKE THIS?
UH HUH.
THEN LIKE THIS?
RIGHT.
OK. NEXT TIME I'LL DO IT YOUR WAY.
YOU'RE SUCH A SWEETHEART! I DIDN'T WANT TO SAY ANYTHING BECAUSE I THOUGHT YOU'D BE MAD!!
MAD? I'M NOT MAD!
COME HERE.
I LOVE YOU, HONEY!!
YOU'VE GOTTA KNOW WHEN TO HOLD 'EM...KNOW WHEN TO FOLD 'EM....
LYNN

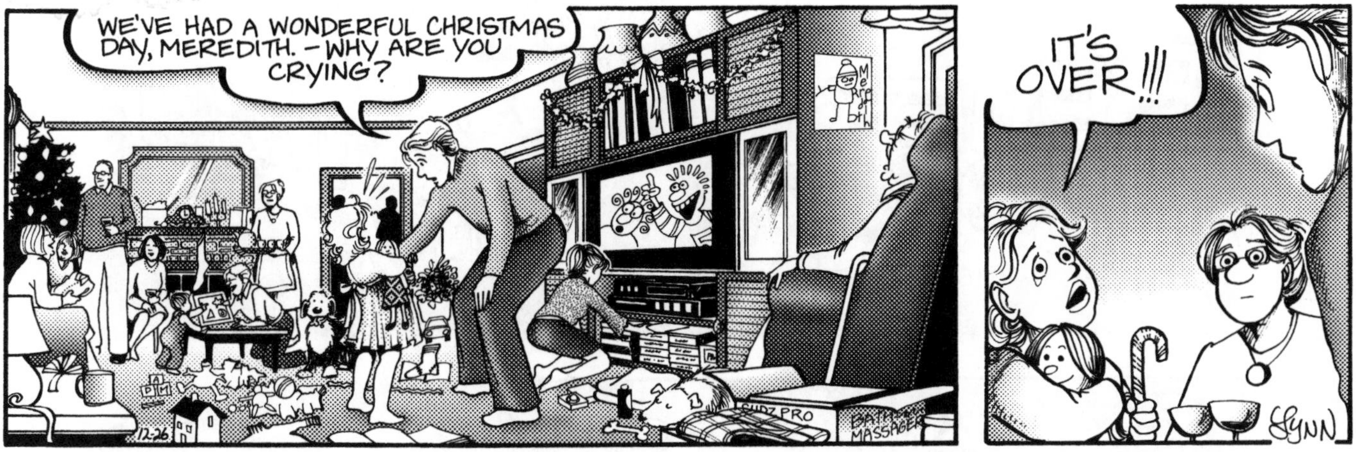
WE'VE HAD A WONDERFUL CHRISTMAS DAY, MEREDITH. – WHY ARE YOU CRYING?
IT'S OVER!!!
LYNN

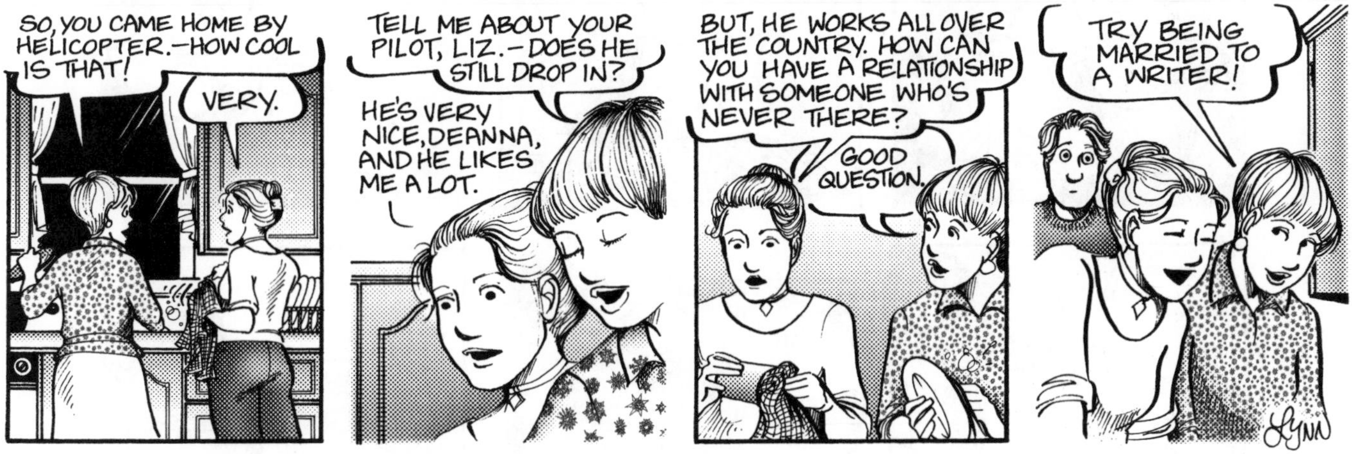
SO, YOU CAME HOME BY HELICOPTER. – HOW COOL IS THAT!
VERY.
TELL ME ABOUT YOUR PILOT, LIZ. – DOES HE STILL DROP IN?
HE'S VERY NICE, DEANNA, AND HE LIKES ME A LOT.
BUT, HE WORKS ALL OVER THE COUNTRY. HOW CAN YOU HAVE A RELATIONSHIP WITH SOMEONE WHO'S NEVER THERE?
GOOD QUESTION.
TRY BEING MARRIED TO A WRITER!
LYNN

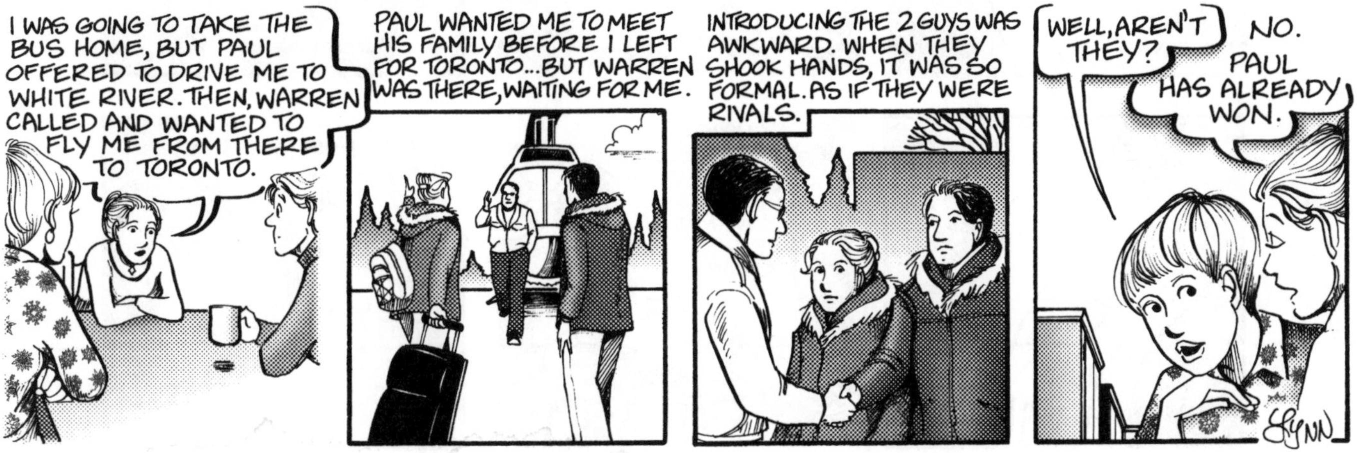
I WAS GOING TO TAKE THE BUS HOME, BUT PAUL OFFERED TO DRIVE ME TO WHITE RIVER. THEN, WARREN CALLED AND WANTED TO FLY ME FROM THERE TO TORONTO.
PAUL WANTED ME TO MEET HIS FAMILY BEFORE I LEFT FOR TORONTO... BUT WARREN WAS THERE, WAITING FOR ME.
INTRODUCING THE 2 GUYS WAS AWKWARD. WHEN THEY SHOOK HANDS, IT WAS SO FORMAL. AS IF THEY WERE RIVALS.
WELL, AREN'T THEY?
NO. PAUL HAS ALREADY WON.
LYNN

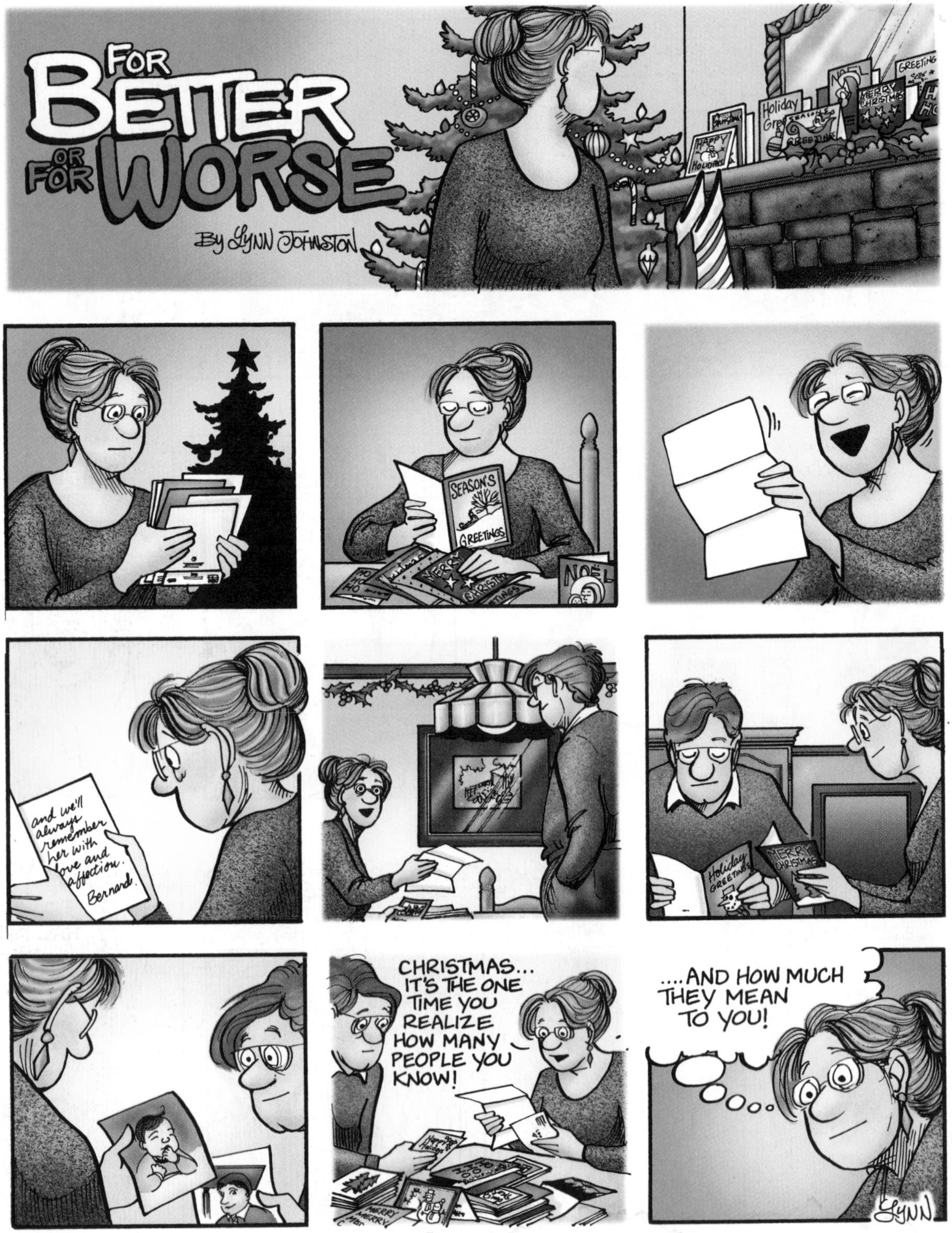
For Better or For Worse
By Lynn Johnston
SEASON'S GREETINGS
and we'll always remember her with love and affection.
Bernard.
CHRISTMAS... IT'S THE ONE TIME YOU REALIZE HOW MANY PEOPLE YOU KNOW!
....AND HOW MUCH THEY MEAN TO YOU!
Lynn

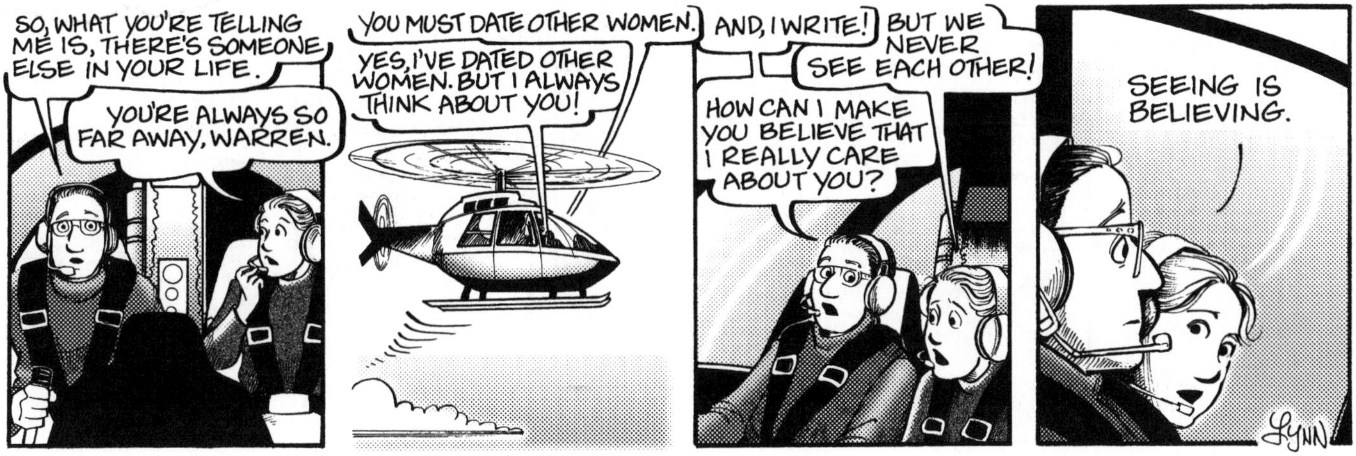
SO, WHAT YOU'RE TELLING ME IS, THERE'S SOMEONE ELSE IN YOUR LIFE.
YOU'RE ALWAYS SO FAR AWAY, WARREN.
YOU MUST DATE OTHER WOMEN.
YES, I'VE DATED OTHER WOMEN. BUT I ALWAYS THINK ABOUT YOU!
AND, I WRITE!
BUT WE NEVER SEE EACH OTHER!
HOW CAN I MAKE YOU BELIEVE THAT I REALLY CARE ABOUT YOU?
SEEING IS BELIEVING.
LYNN

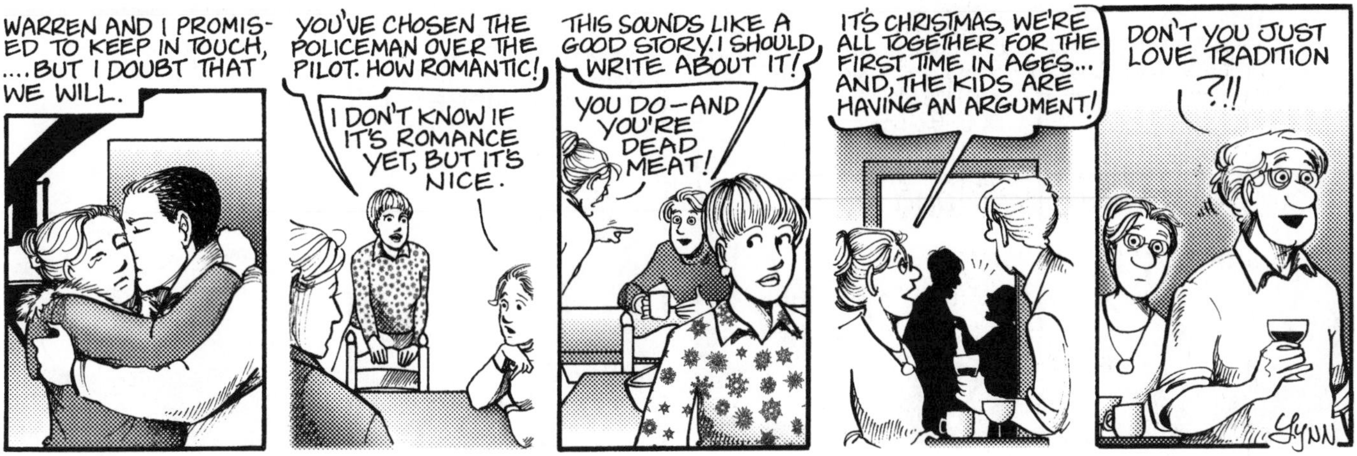
WARREN AND I PROMISED TO KEEP IN TOUCH, ...BUT I DOUBT THAT WE WILL.
YOU'VE CHOSEN THE POLICEMAN OVER THE PILOT. HOW ROMANTIC!
I DON'T KNOW IF IT'S ROMANCE YET, BUT IT'S NICE.
THIS SOUNDS LIKE A GOOD STORY. I SHOULD WRITE ABOUT IT!
YOU DO—AND YOU'RE DEAD MEAT!
IT'S CHRISTMAS, WE'RE ALL TOGETHER FOR THE FIRST TIME IN AGES... AND, THE KIDS ARE HAVING AN ARGUMENT!
DON'T YOU JUST LOVE TRADITION
?!!
LYNN

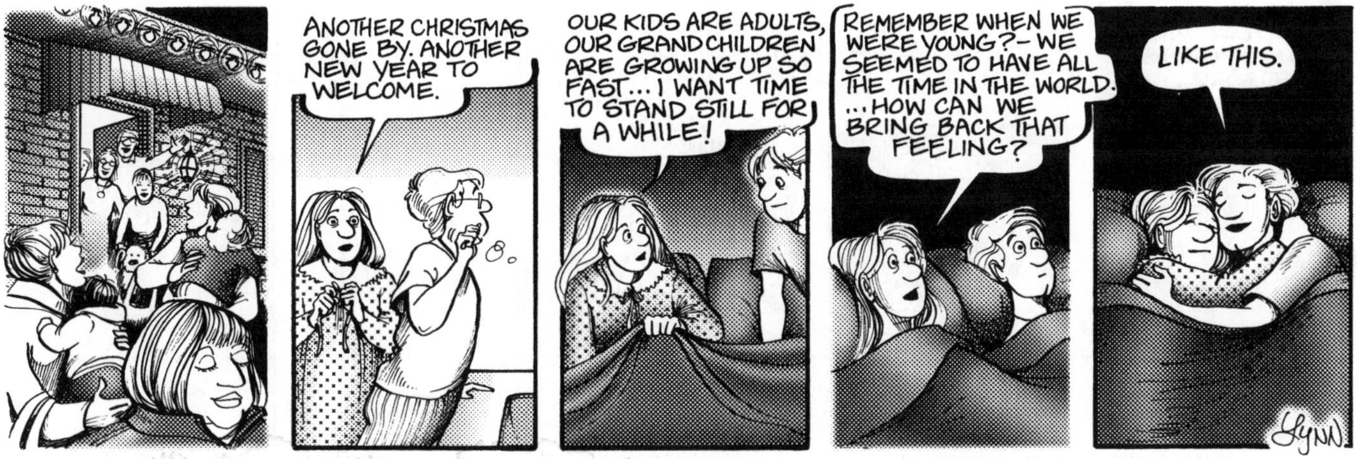
ANOTHER CHRISTMAS GONE BY. ANOTHER NEW YEAR TO WELCOME.
OUR KIDS ARE ADULTS, OUR GRANDCHILDREN ARE GROWING UP SO FAST... I WANT TIME TO STAND STILL FOR A WHILE!
REMEMBER WHEN WE WERE YOUNG?—WE SEEMED TO HAVE ALL THE TIME IN THE WORLD. ...HOW CAN WE BRING BACK THAT FEELING?
LIKE THIS.
LYNN

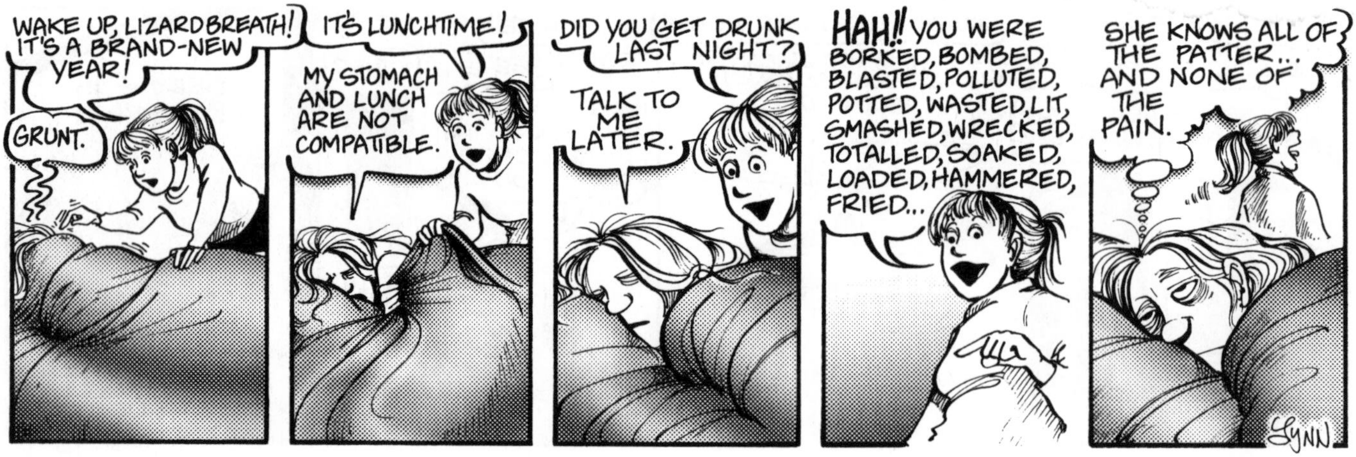
WAKE UP, LIZARDBREATH! IT'S A BRAND-NEW YEAR!
GRUNT.
IT'S LUNCHTIME!
MY STOMACH AND LUNCH ARE NOT COMPATIBLE.
DID YOU GET DRUNK LAST NIGHT?
TALK TO ME LATER.
HAH!! YOU WERE BORKED, BOMBED, BLASTED, POLLUTED, POTTED, WASTED, LIT, SMASHED, WRECKED, TOTALLED, SOAKED, LOADED, HAMMERED, FRIED...
SHE KNOWS ALL OF THE PATTER... AND NONE OF THE PAIN.
LYNN

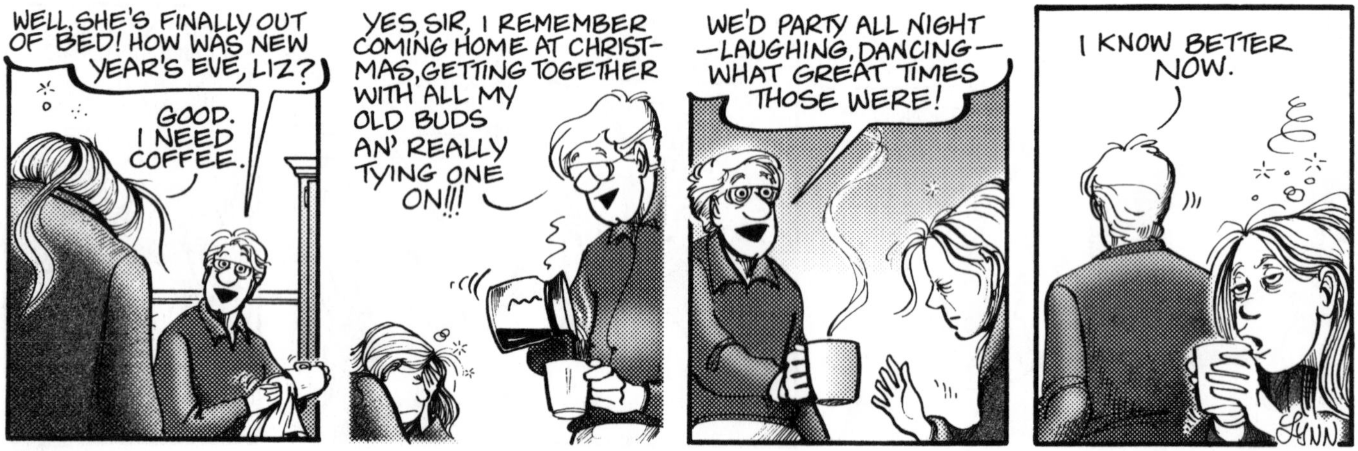
WELL, SHE'S FINALLY OUT OF BED! HOW WAS NEW YEAR'S EVE, LIZ?
GOOD. I NEED COFFEE.
YES, SIR, I REMEMBER COMING HOME AT CHRISTMAS, GETTING TOGETHER WITH ALL MY OLD BUDS AN' REALLY TYING ONE ON!!!
WE'D PARTY ALL NIGHT —LAUGHING, DANCING— WHAT GREAT TIMES THOSE WERE!
I KNOW BETTER NOW.
LYNN

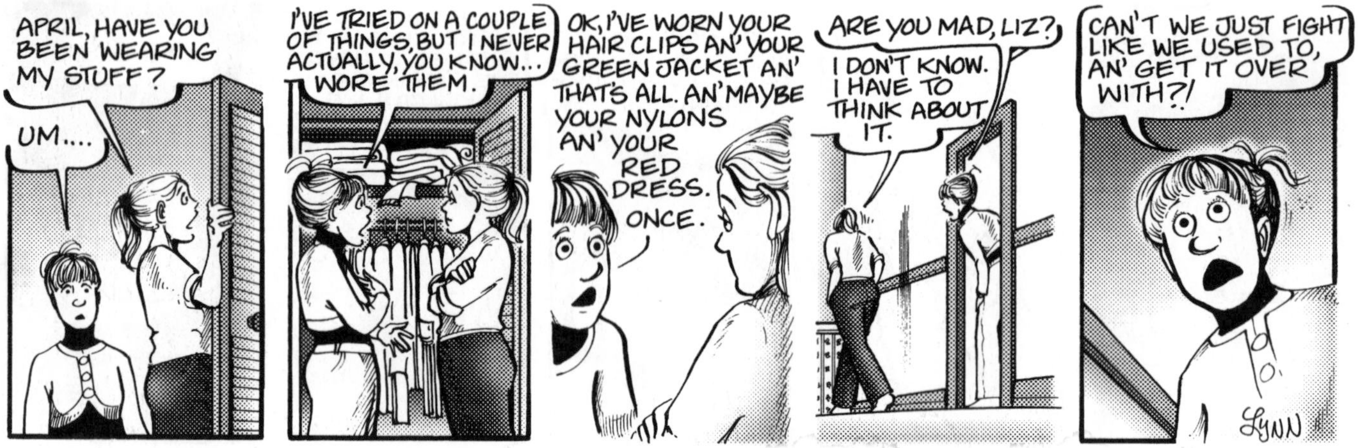
APRIL, HAVE YOU BEEN WEARING MY STUFF?
UM....
I'VE TRIED ON A COUPLE OF THINGS, BUT I NEVER ACTUALLY, YOU KNOW... WORE THEM.
OK, I'VE WORN YOUR HAIR CLIPS AN' YOUR GREEN JACKET AN' THAT'S ALL. AN' MAYBE YOUR NYLONS AN' YOUR RED DRESS.
ONCE.
ARE YOU MAD, LIZ?
I DON'T KNOW. I HAVE TO THINK ABOUT IT.
CAN'T WE JUST FIGHT LIKE WE USED TO, AN' GET IT OVER WITH?!
LYNN

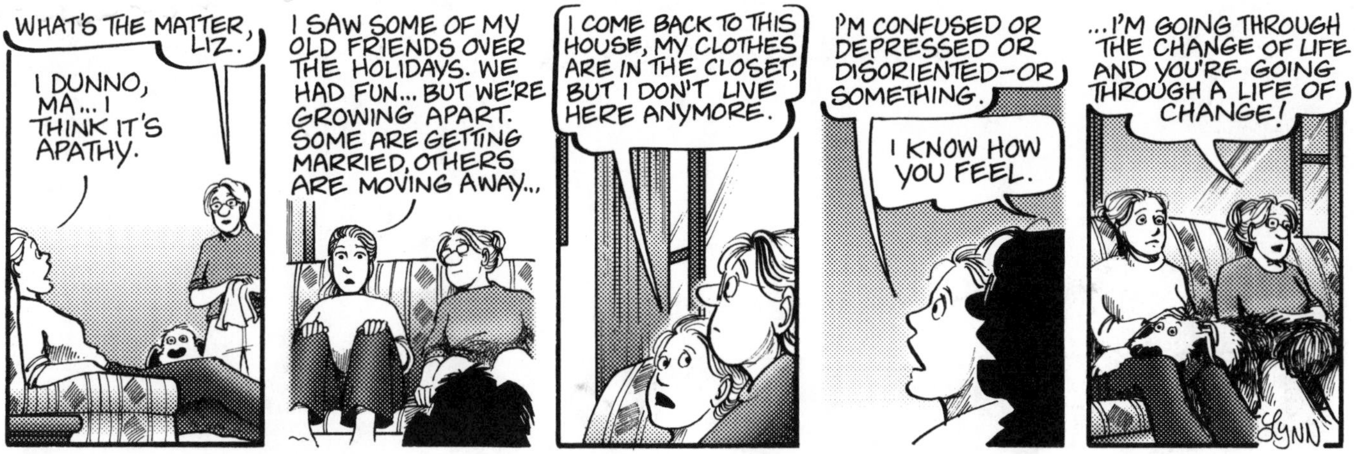
WHAT'S THE MATTER, LIZ?
I DUNNO, MA... I THINK IT'S APATHY.
I SAW SOME OF MY OLD FRIENDS OVER THE HOLIDAYS. WE HAD FUN... BUT WE'RE GROWING APART. SOME ARE GETTING MARRIED, OTHERS ARE MOVING AWAY...
I COME BACK TO THIS HOUSE, MY CLOTHES ARE IN THE CLOSET, BUT I DON'T LIVE HERE ANYMORE.
I'M CONFUSED OR DEPRESSED OR DISORIENTED—OR SOMETHING.
I KNOW HOW YOU FEEL.
...I'M GOING THROUGH THE CHANGE OF LIFE AND YOU'RE GOING THROUGH A LIFE OF CHANGE!
LYNN

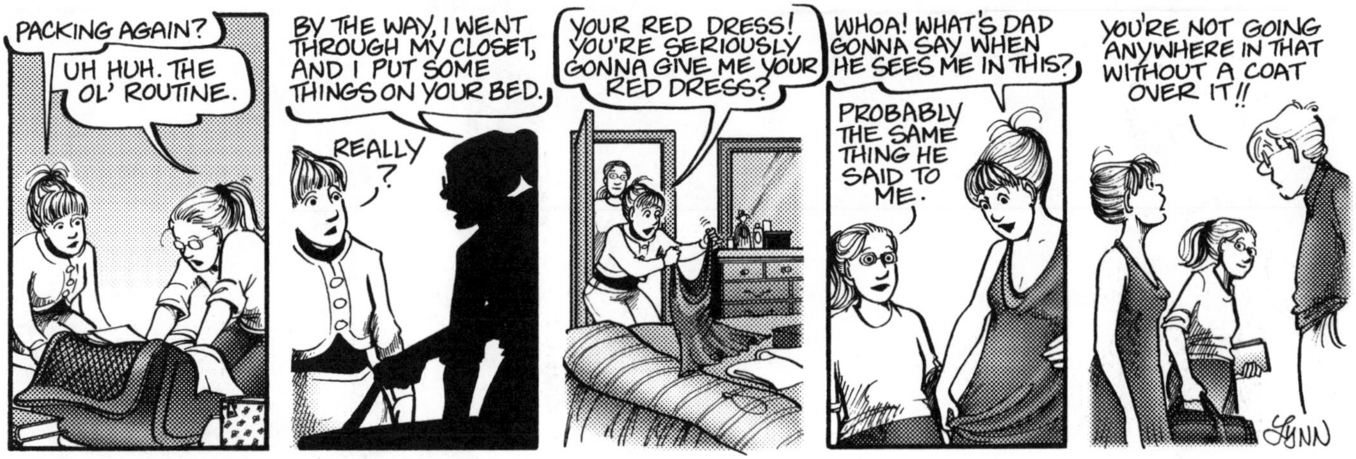
PACKING AGAIN?
UH HUH. THE OL' ROUTINE.
BY THE WAY, I WENT THROUGH MY CLOSET, AND I PUT SOME THINGS ON YOUR BED.
REALLY?
YOUR RED DRESS! YOU'RE SERIOUSLY GONNA GIVE ME YOUR RED DRESS?
WHOA! WHAT'S DAD GONNA SAY WHEN HE SEES ME IN THIS?
PROBABLY THE SAME THING HE SAID TO ME.
YOU'RE NOT GOING ANYWHERE IN THAT WITHOUT A COAT OVER IT!!
LYNN

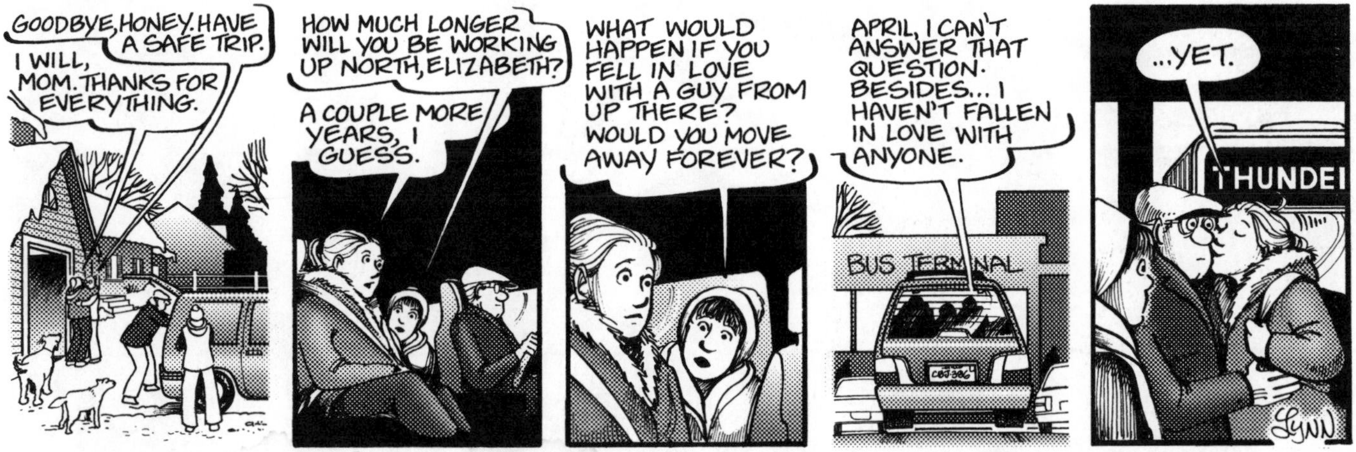
GOODBYE, HONEY. HAVE A SAFE TRIP.
I WILL, MOM. THANKS FOR EVERYTHING.
HOW MUCH LONGER WILL YOU BE WORKING UP NORTH, ELIZABETH?
A COUPLE MORE YEARS, I GUESS.
WHAT WOULD HAPPEN IF YOU FELL IN LOVE WITH A GUY FROM UP THERE? WOULD YOU MOVE AWAY FOREVER?
APRIL, I CAN'T ANSWER THAT QUESTION. BESIDES... I HAVEN'T FALLEN IN LOVE WITH ANYONE.
BUS TERMINAL
...YET.
THUNDEI
LYNN

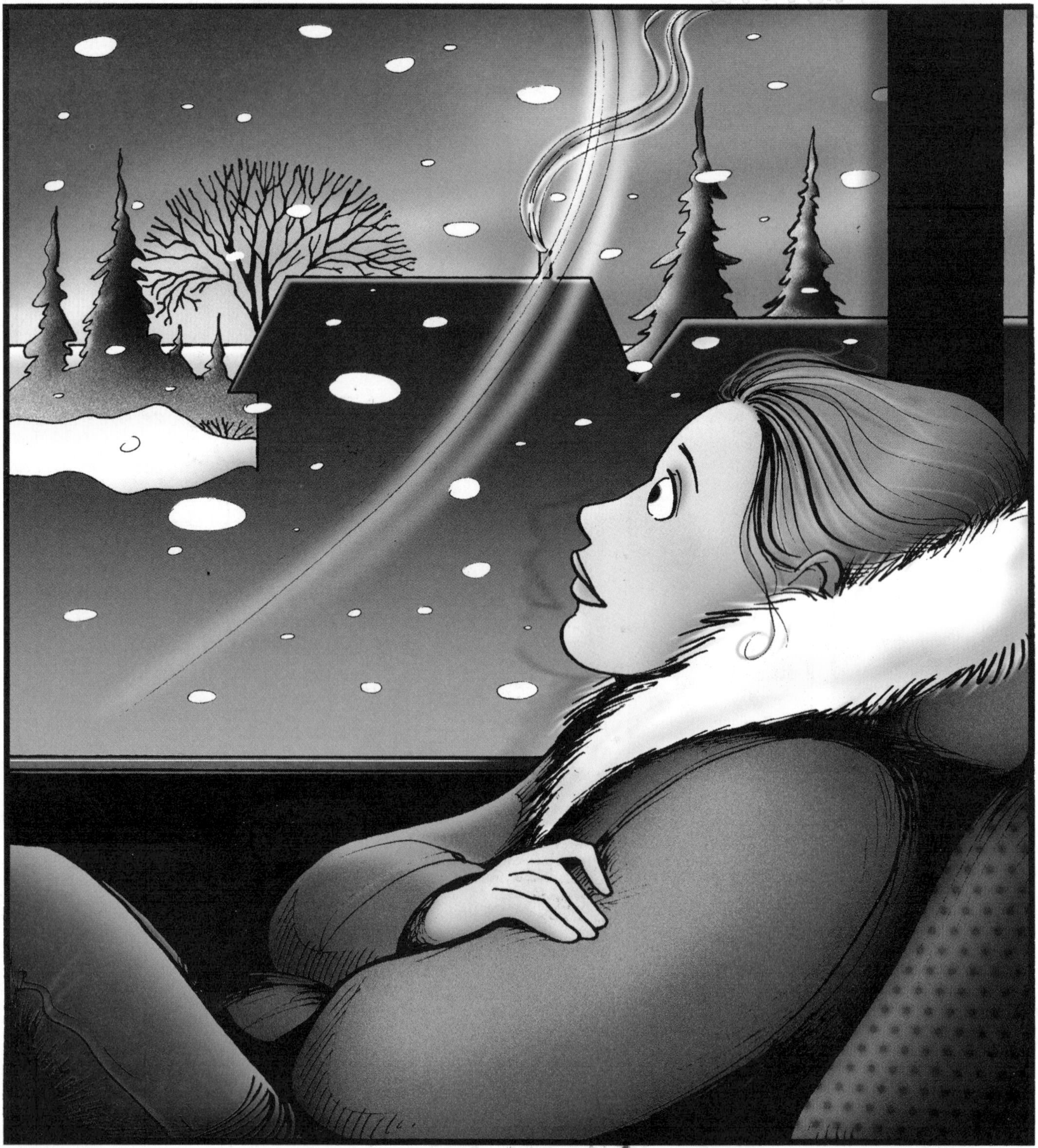